Lessons in Integration

Race, Ethnicity, and Politics
Luis Ricardo Fraga and Paula D. McClain, *Editors*

Lessons in Integration

*Realizing the Promise of Racial Diversity
in American Schools*

Edited by Erica Frankenberg and Gary Orfield

University of Virginia Press
Charlottesville and London

University of Virginia Press
© 2007 by the Rector and Visitors of the University of Virginia
All rights reserved
Printed in the United States of America on acid-free paper
First published 2007
First paperback edition published 2008
ISBN 978-0-8139-2631-5

9 8 7 6 5 4 3 2 1

The Library of Congress has cataloged the hardcover edition as follows:
Library of Congress Cataloging-in-Publication Data

Lessons in integration : realizing the promise of racial diversity in American
schools / edited by Erica Frankenberg and Gary Orfield.
    p. cm. — (Race, ethnicity, and politics)
  Includes bibliographical references and index.
  ISBN-13: 978-0-8139-2630-8 (alk. paper)
  1. School integration—United States. 2. Segregation in education—United
States. 3. Multicultural education—United States. 4. Educational equalization—
United States. I. Frankenberg, Erica. II. Orfield, Gary.
  LC214.2.L47 2007
  379.2′630973—dc22
                                                                    2006100759

Contents

Foreword   vii

Acknowledgments   ix

Prologue
Lessons Forgotten   1
Gary Orfield

Introduction
School Integration—The Time Is Now   7
Erica Frankenberg

The Benefits of Integration and Potential Harms of Segregation

Designing Schools That Use Student Diversity to Enhance Learning
of All Students   31
Willis D. Hawley

The Social Developmental Benefits of Intergroup Contact among
Children and Adolescents   57
Melanie Killen, David S. Crystal, and Martin Ruck

Can Reducing School Segregation Close the Achievement Gap?   74
Jaekyung Lee

New Dimensions of Integration
The Growth of Non-Black Minority Groups

Adolescent Immigrant Students in U.S. Schools
*Issues of Cultural Pluralism, Successful School Settings,
and Intergroup Relations*   101
M. Beatriz Arias, Christian Faltis, and James Cohen

"Desperate to Learn"
The Schooling Experience of Latinas in North Carolina   120
María Teresa Unger Palmer

Interracial Status as a Double-Edged Sword
The Educational Experiences of Interracial Children   145
Simon Cheng

Toward an Integrated Future of Schooling
Possible Solutions

Preparing Teachers for Multiracial and Historically
Underserved Schools   171
Christine E. Sleeter

Addressing Race and Racism in the Classroom   190
Julie Milligan Hughes and Rebecca S. Bigler

Classroom Integration and Accelerated Learning through
Detracking   207
Carol Corbett Burris and Kevin G. Welner

Fostering an Inclusive, Multiracial Democracy
*How Attorneys, Social Scientists, and Educators Made the Case
for School Integration in Lynn, Massachusetts*   228
Richard W. Cole

Future Directions

The Common Schools Democracy Requires
Expanding Membership through Inclusive Education   265
john a. powell and Rebecca High

Conclusion
*Challenges for This Generation: Integration and Social
Transformation*   291
Gary Orfield

Bibliography   297
Notes on Contributors   341
Index   347

Foreword

For over a decade *Teaching Tolerance* magazine has spotlighted teaching strategies and programs that promote educational equity and multicultural understanding. We have yet to run out of ideas—namely because educators are creative, spirited types who use their classrooms as laboratories to try out new lessons and approaches. Through the years we have learned that there is no dearth of seemingly good ideas.

There is, however, an absence of research that tells us what *really* works.

In this age of high-stakes testing, teachers have less flexibility and less time to experiment in their classrooms to find approaches that work best for a particular group of learners. And schools, under intense pressure from the No Child Left Behind Act, are less willing to put scarce resources into programs that sound good but have little empirical basis.

The field of education needs a new crop of research that aims squarely at advancing educational equity. What kinds of curricula are most likely to support learning across group lines? How can schools, which are becoming increasingly diverse, maximize positive interracial outcomes? Are some classroom strategies more effective than others in reducing prejudice and intergroup conflict? Are faulty assumptions impeding progress?

In the fall of 2004 the Southern Poverty Law Center in Montgomery, Alabama, partnered with the Civil Rights Project at Harvard University to sponsor a roundtable that brought leading researchers together to discuss such questions. This book is the fruit of our conversations.

The Center is honored to play a part in reinvigorating this line of educational research, and we hope that readers find practical wisdom and inspiration within these pages.

Jennifer Holladay
Director, Teaching Tolerance
Southern Poverty Law Center

Acknowledgments

In 2004, as our nation celebrated the fiftieth anniversary of the *Brown v. Board of Education* decision, the Civil Rights Project began to think about what our schools needed in order to achieve the promise of *Brown* in an increasingly diverse country. In collaboration with the Southern Poverty Law Center, we issued a call for papers to address how we could create positive interracial outcomes in our nation's schools. The origin of many of these chapters came from papers originally presented at a roundtable convened at Harvard Law School in November 2004. We are appreciative to the contributors to this book, who were responsive to our initial call for papers and to our editorial suggestions through subsequent revisions. The commitment of these scholars to doing careful research about such important issues offers us valuable information in a changing society.

This book, like many, is due to the collaboration of numerous people. We appreciate the assistance of the staff and graduate students working with the Civil Rights Project, including Jennifer Blatz, Mary Doyle, Lori Kelley, Nancy McArdle, Jerry Monde, Anna Rosefsky, Amanda Taylor, Christina Tobias-Nahi, Amanda Turner, and Christopher Tracey. Genevieve Siegel-Hawley, a graduate student working with the Civil Rights Project, offered helpful feedback to many authors and ably assisted the editors with a variety of editorial tasks, large and small. Cara Kissling helped edit a number of chapters, and her useful suggestions and meticulous attention to detail made the ideas clearer and consistent across chapters within this book. We thank Richard Holway and anonymous reviewers from the University of Virginia Press for insightful suggestions that greatly strengthened and clarified our ideas, making this a stronger volume in the process.

Lessons in Integration

Prologue
Lessons Forgotten

Gary Orfield

In an era of great hope for this country's racial transformation from the mid-1960s to the early 1970s, we committed ourselves to creating integrated schools. There was a brief period in our history in which there was serious policy and research attention on how to devise racially diverse schools to achieve integration and equal opportunity. Civil rights leaders and participants in the hundreds of demonstrations demanding integrated education knew the sorry history of "separate but equal" and fought for access to the opportunities concentrated in White schools.

The desegregation experience has often been described by critics as little more than a mechanistic transfer of students, but it was often much more than that. From thousands of desegregation plans implemented around the nation we learned about the ways to operate successful integrated schools and classrooms. Now, as we deal both with resegregation, where court orders are dropped, and with the emergence of racial diversity in thousands of other schools, not as the result of court orders but as the product of a great increase in the non-White population and of diversification of growing sectors of suburbia, that experience and the unfinished agenda of the civil rights era are relevant again. Too many hard-earned lessons have been forgotten.

Most of the public struggle for desegregation involved opening the doors of White schools to students who had been historically excluded— Black and, in some cases, Latino students who attended segregated schools that were commonly inferior on many dimensions.[1] There was a fierce, two-decade struggle after *Brown v. Board of Education of Topeka* to desegregate the South, followed, in the 1970s, by a brief and usually losing struggle to desegregate northern cities. The Supreme Court's 1974 decision in the metropolitan Detroit case of *Milliken v. Bradley* rejected the only remedy that could have produced substantial and lasting school desegregation in much of the North, and instead built a massive legal barrier between city school districts and the surrounding suburban districts, where most White children resided and where typically the best schools were located. President Richard Nixon, who ran on the "southern strategy" promising to roll back desegregation, had dismantled much of the civil rights machinery of the federal government by this time (Panetta & Gall, 1971).

Critics often describe this period as one of mandatory race mixing with no educational components. Many educational experts, civil rights advocates, and officials, however, understood early that more must be done. Simply letting some minority students into previously White schools operated by the same district officials was not likely to solve the problems of inequality. In fact, these officials often found new ways to discriminate within schools.

The deeper changes, in educational and social terms, involved going from the reality of desegregation—the fact that children of different racial and ethnic groups were now in the same school and faculties had been ordered to be desegregated—toward real integration, which required fair and equal treatment of each racial and ethnic group. Gordon Allport's classic book, *The Nature of Prejudice* (1954), published the year of the *Brown* decision, had concluded that creating desegregated settings could produce either positive or negative outcomes, which depended on how desegregation was done. The key, he said, was creating "equal status interaction" between the previously segregated groups. Allport wrote: "It required years of labor and billions of dollars to gain the secret of the atom. It will take a still greater investment to gain the secrets of man's irrational nature. It is easier, someone has said, to smash an atom than a prejudice" (as cited in Clark, 1979).

In the early days of desegregation there were too many reports of segregated classes, removal of minority teachers and principals, failure to integrate school activities, segregated classroom seating, discriminatory counseling, curricula that ignored minority history, and many other conditions that limited or prevented full access for minority students. Additionally, these conditions limited positive diversity experiences for White and minority students. Many educators, advocates, and researchers realized that factors influencing the nature of the transition from segregation to desegregation, and ultimately to integration, could shift the academic and social outcomes of students in these schools (Schofield, 1991). Most school staff members, who themselves attended segregated schools and were trained to work in one-race schools, did not have the knowledge and tools to address these issues.

Desegregation orders and plans by the late 1960s often went far beyond simply transferring students. The Supreme Court ended token desegregation that had been occurring through "freedom of choice" plans in 1968 and ordered "root and branch" desegregation to eliminate "dual school systems" organized on the basis of race (*Green v. County School Board of New Kent County,* 1968). To fulfill the constitutional requirement to create "unitary" school systems that were fully integrated, school desegregation plans had to include desegregation of teachers and students, and equalization of educational opportunities, facilities, and curriculum. The plans usually included strategies for informing the public of the plan, managing crises, retraining teachers and staff, developing new educational materials, and implementing policies for fair discipline and participation in student activities among the various groups of students.

Following the Supreme Court's decision in *Swann v. Charlotte-Mecklenburg Board of Education* (1971), there was massive controversy over court orders using tools such as busing to more thoroughly desegregate urban schools. Despite disagreements, both critics and supporters of desegregation recognized that help was needed in the suddenly integrated schools in hundreds of cities. Government responded, for a time. The Emergency School Aid Act was a bipartisan law initially intended to smooth the crises caused by sudden desegregation of urban school systems. In this act, negotiated between the Nixon White House and Senate liberals led by Senator Walter Mondale,[2] Congress enacted a policy of giving money to schools to support successful desegregation. Regardless of whether they supported desegregation plans, both sides could agree that if the plans must be implemented, schools required help to prevent dangerous cleavages in communities, such as those that did such severe damage to several cities, including Little Rock, Birmingham, and Boston, after racial violence flared. The programs funded under the desegregation assistance law did not provide money for busing itself, but they did provide hundreds of millions of dollars for helping the schools adapt.

The Emergency School Aid Act (G. Orfield, 1978, chap. 9) lasted from 1972 until 1981, when the Reagan administration ended it (G. Orfield and Eaton, 1996). While in operation, the law funded training, intervention programs, new curricula development, magnet schools for voluntary desegregation, and large-scale research on ways to improve race relations. Because courts were actively requiring desegregation, there was interest in obtaining help, and, as a result, school districts eagerly applied for these funds. The funding was so enthusiastically sought, in fact, that districts were often willing to do additional desegregation of students and teachers, not required by their own plan, to get it. Many magnet schools began and spread rapidly under this program, as school choice became a significant element in American education for the first time. The law required that magnets be desegregated—choice was designed to combine equity with educational options.

During the Carter administration, the law was rewritten to incorporate the lessons of the major evaluation studies, which showed that aid made a substantial difference for both achievement and race relations, and was needed for at least several years to facilitate successful change. At the same time, the National Institute of Education supported research on desegregated schools and developed a research agenda for the field. Research on the effects of the programs and changes funded by the desegregation assistance law produced important findings about the conditions under which race relations and educational achievement gains were most likely to occur in interracial schools. During the desegregation era the Black-White gap declined sharply. Major studies documented the benefits of certain classroom techniques in mixed-race classrooms. Teachers and administrators facing racial change were given a great deal of inservice preparation.[3]

During this same period, education schools across the country and their national accreditation agencies made significant efforts to require training of teachers in multicultural education. Sensing a large new market, publishers supported substantial revisions of texts that had an exclusively White perspective. Many districts commissioned new curriculum about local minority contributions. At the same time, the spread of bilingual education requirements and funding under the 1968 Bilingual Education Act, as well as the 1974 *Lau v. Nichols* Supreme Court decision about the rights of non-English-speaking students, brought into the schools an increasing number of Latino teachers and supported beginning education in a child's native language. Several desegregation orders, including those in school districts in Denver, Boston, and Texas, contained specific programs for language-minority students and their teachers.

The need for these efforts did not cease, but the support did. Training, school district programs, and research withered away. The Reagan administration in its first months opposed desegregation orders and eliminated the desegregation assistance program that had made desegregation plans work better; the research operation was shut down, and for the next quarter century there would be no significant federal funding for research or policy on effective race relations in diverse schools (G. Orfield & Eaton, 1996). The Reagan administration did, however, support research on "White flight," which it used to oppose desegregation in federal courts.

The country turned in a different direction when the standards movement emerged in the aftermath of the Reagan administration's *A Nation at Risk* report in 1983. The basic ideas of standards-based reform were that the social context of schools could be overlooked—both the problems of racial and economic inequality and the positive possibilities of racial diversity—and that standards, requirements, and sanctions would produce more equal outcomes in and of themselves or, if necessary, with the additional pressure of market competition from charter and private schools. Part of the basic analysis of the "excellence" movement was that schools had been diverted from traditional education responsibilities to counterproductive social reform efforts.

Virtually all states adopted this agenda, which was reinforced by the agreement between President George H. W. Bush and the nation's governors in 1989. At the Charlottesville Educational Summit, the National Governors Association's chair, Governor Bill Clinton of Arkansas, led the governors to agreement with the president on six national education goals to which the country should aspire by 2000, from school readiness to increasing high school graduation rates. Goal 3 (U.S. students should be first in the world in mathematics and science achievement) and goal 4 (all students should demonstrate achievement in core subjects) in particular spurred the bipartisan standards agenda (National Governors Association, 1989, 2000). The program to achieve the national goals became known as the America 2000 program, but it was not until the Goals 2000: Educate America Act passed in 1993 during Clinton's first presidential term that the six goals were adopted as part of federal education law. In addition, the 1994 reauthorization of the Elementary and Secondary Education Act (known as the Improving America's Schools Act, or IASA) further drove the standards movement, by requiring that all states adopt a system of standards, assessments, and accountability to measure student performance in order to qualify for Title I funding. The IASA also required states to disaggregate student performance data for schools' annual yearly progress by race, gender, and socioeconomic status, but sanctions were not seriously enforced. Ultimately, none of the goals for closing the racial gap were realized and the gaps widened in some dimensions.

The No Child Left Behind Act of 2001 (NCLB), however, imposed more demanding goals and deadlines on all American schools. NCLB had strong goals and sweeping sanctions for equalizing achievement among minority and White children, but had no requirement to equalize the very unequal schooling opportunities or take any action to end segregation of minority students in inferior schools and improve race relations. By insisting on equal outcomes from patently unequal schools highly segregated by race and poverty, the 2001 law's sanctions tended to strongly penalize minority schools and teachers (Sunderman, J. Kim, & G. Orfield, 2005).

The effects of segregated education cannot be cured by merely enacting strong demands for achievement gains and changing nothing else in schools that are usually unequal in every major dimension relating to student achievement, including the quality of teachers, curriculum offered, and the level of competition (peer group). In fact, enforcing rigid standards without equalizing opportunity can exacerbate the inequalities by stigmatizing minority schools as failures, narrowing their curriculum to endless testing drills, and leading strong, experienced teachers to transfer to less pressured situations. The massive publicity given to test scores may also help destabilize residentially integrated communities, as realtors use test scores to steer White buyers to outlying White communities. Thus, the ironic impact of ignoring the inequality of the segregated schools in the name of standards is to worsen them.

In the past quarter century of incredible demographic transformation of the American school-age population there has been virtually no investment in either determining the best policies for extraordinarily complex school communities or even in applying well-documented programs and policies that are likely to make things better. Federal funding of desegregation research and experiments ended in the early 1980s, and private foundations do not generally support research about these topics, which has drastically limited the development of new knowledge that could assist schools with the racial transformation. This myopia makes school communities less effective internally and much weaker as anchors for multiracial communities dealing with pressures of racial stratification, fear, and racial transformation. This book resumes the conversation, stopped a generation ago, to assist our schools and communities going through rapid racial changes with evidence on how to prepare children to be citizens in a diverse global environment.

Notes

1. The right for Latinos to desegregate was not acknowledged by the Supreme Court until 1973, after most active desegregation efforts had already ended. In striking contrast to the Johnson administration's role in the South, the Nixon administration did virtually nothing to enforce this policy.

2. Mondale, who became Jimmy Carter's vice president, chaired the Senate Select Committee on Equal Educational Opportunity, which compiled thirty volumes of congressional hearings on all aspects of desegregation and issued a comprehensive report in 1972 that included a chapter on conditions for successful integration (U.S. Senate, 1972, chapter 17).

3. Much of that research is summarized in Hawley et al., 1983.

Introduction
School Integration—The Time Is Now

Erica Frankenberg

Segregation is deepening in American schools as courts terminate desegregation plans, residential segregation spreads, the proportion of whites
in the population falls, and successful efforts to use choice for desegregation, such as magnet schools, are replaced by choice plans with no civil
rights requirements, including charter schools, which often increase segregation (G. Orfield & C. Lee, 2005; Frankenberg & C. Lee, 2003). This
book is based on strong evidence that desegregation is a positive educational and social force, that there were many successes as well as some
failures in the desegregation movement, and that students in segregated
schools, whether overwhelmingly minority or almost completely White,
are disadvantaged on some important educational and social dimensions
when compared to their peers in well-designed racially diverse schools.
Researchers have known that the largest payoffs, in terms of gains for
all groups of students and the community, come when educators actively
work to improve relationships with and treatment of all students within
interracial schools. As discussed in the prologue, because the federal government cut off significant research on these issues in 1981, it is not surprising that we have learned little since that time about these issues. In a
society with more than 40 percent non-White students and thousands of
suburban communities facing racial change, it is critical to learn the lessons of experience and to reexamine the research about the conditions
for positively operating racially diverse and inclusive schools. This book
reviews what we learned earlier and moves the discussion into a new generation.

The Twenty-first-Century Dimensions of Segregation

Far too often we celebrate the success of the civil rights movement in
schools that remain segregated. Segregated education is treated as some-

thing that was a terrible wrong that existed only in the past and can be conveniently overlooked in the present. For example, the fiftieth anniversary of the *Brown v. Board of Education* decision, in 2004, was widely celebrated at commemorative events at prominent law schools and at public schools and universities, community events across the United States, and in largely upbeat media coverage. The resounding message of these celebrations was that in *Brown,* one of the most important Supreme Court decisions in U.S. history, our society repudiated the country's racist history and reaffirmed our belief in the American Dream: that equal opportunity must be available to all, regardless of race. Listening to or reading such messages about *Brown,* it was easy to believe that we had "solved" the problem of racial inequality in the United States. Further, recent public opinion research continues to show that both Whites and non-Whites support, in general, the importance of having racially/ethnically diverse student bodies (e.g., Farkas, J. Johnson, Immerwahr, & McHugh, 1998; Reid, 2004; Pew Hispanic Center/Kaiser Family Foundation, 2004).

Demographic trends, however, belie a more complicated reality than these celebrations might suggest. Major shifts in U.S. population, of course, change the nature of the debates about the diversity of students in schools and colleges. Both the 2000 Census and subsequent Census reports show a burgeoning, diverse minority population. By 2000, racial and ethnic minorities comprised more than half of all residents in our nation's largest cities and were more than a quarter of all suburban residents, although minority suburbanization varied substantially among the largest metro areas (W. H. Frey, 2001; M. Orfield & Luce, 2005; U.S. Census Bureau, 2001a, 2001b, 2001c). Because of this growing diversity, White children were encountering by 2000 more non-Whites in their neighborhoods and schools than in 1990, but were still the most isolated children of any racial group (Logan et al., 2001; Frankenberg, C. Lee, & G. Orfield, 2003). White students, in fact, may be the least equipped to deal with this racial change in their schools and neighborhoods because of their continued isolation.

Nationally, public school enrollment at the beginning of the twenty-first century is also more racially diverse than ever before. White students comprise less than 60 percent of the nation's public school enrollment (compared with 80 percent of the enrollment during the civil rights era).[1] Latinos have overtaken Blacks as the largest minority group among public school students; in some areas of the country, Asians also comprise a substantial share of students. Before the middle of this century, fewer than half the students in the public schools will be White, a trend that has already occurred in the West and soon will in the South (G. Orfield &

C. Lee, 2005). Although far less than in earlier decades, in the fall of 2005 there were well over three hundred school districts still under federal desegregation court orders and many more under locally developed plans, which often lasted decades in many districts and were focused on preserving racially diverse schools. Other districts no longer under court order or that had never been sued were voluntarily maintaining racially desegregated schools through a variety of means, including magnet schools and voluntary transfer policies.

Racial and economic segregation of our K–12 schools continues to deepen in many areas, however. Black students are more segregated than they have been since the late 1960s, before many desegregation plans created widespread integration across the South. The segregation of Latino students continues to increase and is more severe than that of Blacks (G. Orfield & C. Lee, 2006). Many people still believe that school segregation is primarily a problem of the inner cities, and, indeed, many of our nation's central city school systems contain schools that are overwhelmingly racially isolated and severely challenged by the problems of concentrated poverty (G. Orfield & C. Lee, 2005). Yet minority population growth and increased migration of minorities to the suburbs are changing the complexion of large suburban districts that were almost entirely White during the civil rights era. Many suburban schools are experiencing racial diversity for the first time (see Frankenberg & C. Lee, 2002), and many other racially diverse schools still remain.

It is important to recognize the consequences if we re-create existing patterns of urban segregation in suburban areas that are undergoing racial transition. For example, when Blacks and Latinos live in the suburbs, they are more likely than their White suburban counterparts to live in areas with fewer public resources, such as high-quality public schools (M. Orfield & Luce, 2005; C. Lee, 2004). In order to prevent the resegregation of metropolitan areas, and encourage the formation and proliferation of durable, long-lasting schools that are desegregated, we need to contemplate future approaches to the creation of successful, integrated, equitable suburban and urban schools. It has been more than two decades since the demise of the last federal policy with an explicit focus on racial integration. Much of the research about intergroup relations—specifically, what conditions helped to ensure that interracial contact, when it occurred, did not exacerbate racial hostility or tension—is several decades old (see Schofield, 1991, 2001, for a review of this literature). The research in this book explores practices in schools and districts that are actively working to overcome between-school and within-school segregation and to capitalize on their diversity as essential to preparing children for the twenty-first century and the diverse global society in which they will live as adults.

This Book's Contribution

The Supreme Court in 2003, building on *Brown,* endorsed the importance of diversity in education, because, in part, "effective participation by members of all racial and ethnic groups in the civic life of our Nation is essential if the dream of one Nation, indivisible, is to be recognized" (*Grutter v. Bollinger,* 2003, p. 332). Specifically, they emphasized the importance of integrated education for the education of students of all races, for the training of leadership for institutions, and for the functioning of our democracy. Our public schools have historically been the means of preparing future citizens. Recent circuit court decisions upholding race-conscious integration plans voluntarily implemented by school districts have recognized a number of compelling interests K–12 public schools have in maintaining diversity to allow students to learn across racial lines and prepare students "for work and citizenship" (*Parents Involved in Community Schools v. Seattle School District No. 1,* 2005, p. 1175, quoting *Grutter;* see also *Comfort v. Lynn School Committee,* 2005; *McFarland v. Jefferson County Public Schools,* 2005). Affirming the Supreme Court's support of diversity in higher education and extending it to public schools, these courts have found that public schools may have an even more important role than higher education in helping students attain the educational and social benefits of diverse schools because of the universal nature of primary and secondary schools and the ability to educate students at an earlier age, where there may be stronger pedagogical benefits of diverse environments.[2]

The educational and social benefits of desegregation begin only when students from different racial and ethnic backgrounds are learning together, in classes with diverse populations. The design of student assignment plans such as those adopted voluntarily by school districts or creation of regional magnet schools, for example, is an essential first step to ensuring that schools are racially diverse. It is equally critical that schools and school systems change to accommodate a racially diverse student body. This includes developing strategies to maximize the educational benefits of this diversity—benefits documented by research a generation ago (G. Orfield, prologue, this volume) and recognized as compelling interests by courts—making sure that all students experience this racial diversity along multiple lines: academic, social, and developmental. This book provides a comprehensive set of essays that reflect on current research that has been conducted on this issue and that offer information that is relevant for today's educational climate and demographic realities. The research in this book demonstrating the value of racially diverse education should alleviate the concerns of parents or policymakers who frame educational choices as having to choose between school quality and school diversity. In fact, this research demonstrates that choosing racially diverse schools can provide educationally rich environments not available in homogeneous schools.

To address these compelling issues and to reengage a conversation largely silenced a generation ago about how to create racially diverse classrooms and how to achieve positive interracial outcomes in all classrooms, the Civil Rights Project at Harvard University partnered with the Southern Poverty Law Center to commission new research. Most of the essays in this book were originally commissioned for and presented at a roundtable convened in November 2004. This book offers important new evidence about the benefits of racially integrated schools and the dangers of segregated schools. It also suggests promising ways as to how we can achieve positive academic and social outcomes for students of all racial/ethnic backgrounds. Our authors approach these important issues from a variety of disciplines: education, law, psychology, and sociology. We know that schools and school systems are still organized inequitably in ways that relate to race and that outcomes and life opportunities for students are powerfully related to structural inequalities. The consequences of viewing schools and society through a color-blind perspective will perpetuate current educational inequities and limit opportunities for all students to learn and develop, particularly in a multicultural society, such as the United States.

Why Focus on Race?

In the Supreme Court's unanimous *Brown* decision, Chief Justice Earl Warren asked, "Does segregation of children in public schools solely on the basis of race, even though the physical facilities and other 'tangible' factors may be equal, deprive the children of the minority group of equal education opportunities?" He answered, "We believe that it does" (*Brown*, 1954, p. 493). Almost fifty years later, in her majority opinion in *Grutter v. Bollinger*, Justice Sandra Day O'Connor explained why the Court believed the University of Michigan Law School's use of race in admissions was constitutional. Echoing Warren's earlier statement, the perspective that minority applicants would bring to the law school environment was valued, she wrote, because of the "unique experience of being a racial minority in a society, like our own, in which race unfortunately still matters" (*Grutter,* 2003, p. 333). Twice, then, in the course of fifty years, the nation's highest court has affirmed the importance of race in our society and in our schools.

What *is* race? One hundred years ago race was still thought to be biological, and racial inequality was justified because of race's scientific nature. Race is now commonly thought of as a social construct, in that it is given meaning through social interactions. As a result, some argue that race is an illusion. Others argue that we live in a color-blind society—to make any race-based distinctions is to be racially discriminatory. While there is no longer a biological basis for racial distinctions, the effects of racial inequality and racism are marked and serious. Very real systems and structures in our society cause its formation and sustenance. In schools, especially, race continues to be reified and shapes students' experiences and their outcomes (Lewis, 2003).

Explicitly racist governmental policies or White ideology, which were targeted particularly toward African Americans, no longer exist in the United States in the same sense that they did in the first half of the twentieth century.[3] Does racism still exist, and, if so, what *is* racism? Psychologists have shown that implicit racism and biases remain quite pervasive (Dovidio & Gaertner, 1986). Some scholars suggest that Jim Crow racism has been replaced with laissez-faire racism, consisting of negative stereotyping, blaming minorities for their lower socioeconomic standing or educational attainment, and resisting affirmative government measures to improve racist conditions, to justify the inequalities that persist and defend White privilege (Bobo, Kluegel, & R. A. Smith, 1997; Bonilla-Silva, 2003). Bonilla-Silva has argued (2003) that Whites' color-blind ideology cloaks a laissez-faire racism, which allows them to justify the existing racial inequalities without seeming to be "racist" to themselves or to others. Winant (1998) has suggested that something can be labeled racist if it reproduces racially unequal structures, which means that, under this definition, color-blind ideology is racist because by casting a blind eye to the structures that reinforce racial inequality it serves to further perpetuate the racial hierarchy in our country. Laissez-faire racism and color-blind ideology help to explain how Americans can both purport to support in general the principle of integration but yet resist the actions that are needed in order to challenge systems of racial separation and inequality in our schools and society. Ironically, this form of racism may be even more impenetrable than more overt racism of the early to mid-twentieth century due to the rational-sounding, color-blind discourse.

The reality, however, is that although there is modest economic success for some members of the African American community, there are still high levels of residential segregation and economic inequality.[4] Hurricane Katrina, which struck Alabama, Louisiana, and Mississippi in August 2005, illuminated the stark racial and economic segregation and inequality in one of our largest metropolitan areas, New Orleans, and their very real life-and-death consequences. Viewing schools and their students through a color-blind prism, expecting all to perform equally, ignores the structural inequality that exists and the continuing significance of race. Just over fifty years have passed since the *Brown* decision officially declared racial segregation in schools to be illegal; even less time has been spent actually enforcing this decision in the South and across the nation. Certainly this is a small period of time in comparison with the centuries of discrimination against Blacks and other minority groups in our country. Further, schools are but one of many institutions in which change must occur to create a truly egalitarian society.

What Have We Learned about the Benefits of Racially Diverse Schools?

The *Brown* decision relied, in part, on social science evidence demonstrating that segregated minority schools were inherently unequal to those attended by White students (even when their resources were equal) because of the psychological harm suffered by Black children, which violated the constitutional rights of the Black children. The decision built on previous Court decisions that declared segregation in higher education to be illegal largely because of sociological evidence demonstrating how it limited Blacks' professional opportunities (*Sweatt v. Painter*, 1950; *McLaurin v. Oklahoma State Regents for Higher Education*, 1950).

The broad ideals of the *Brown* decision are still supported in principle, but there has been little attention on actually accomplishing true integration within our schools, but also within our communities in partnership with desegregating schools (e.g., housing policies). Most of the focus has been on the nuts and bolts of assigning students to schools or addressing resistance to such plans—although in many districts, creating racially diverse schools is still an important need. Less attention has been paid to defining school districts' and teachers' goals in creating inclusive communities in racially diverse schools and classrooms despite research on desegregation that consistently noted how and when desegregation occurred had implications for academic, developmental, and sociological outcomes (Schofield, 1995). In fact, structures resulting in within-school racial stratification were implemented in some schools as desegregation began to reduce racial mixing in classrooms (Mickelson, 2005).[5]

Since 1954, significant effort has been devoted to examining the academic effects of desegregation, although this was not an explicit focus of the *Brown* decision (e.g., Cook et al., 1984; Mahard & Crain, 1983; Weinberg, 1977). The focus of early social science research about the effects of desegregation was on the achievement of Blacks particularly, and Whites to a lesser extent (that is, whether desegregation reduced White students' achievement). The Coleman Report of the 1960s, using a large, national data set to evaluate different factors influencing student outcomes, suggested that the composition of a student's peers influenced his or her academic achievement, which supported those advocating for desegregation (J. S. Coleman et al., 1966). The Coleman Report was significant because it was the first such statistical examination of schools, and it had a major influence on how the nation and its policymakers viewed educational opportunity.

Most early studies showed positive, albeit modest, achievement gains for Blacks, and when integrated schools remained majority White, the achievement of White students, at worst, did not decline (Schofield, 1995). Ultimately, this narrowing of the discourse about the rationale for desegregation and the outcomes of education has led to White plaintiffs suing school systems to end desegregation plans, arguing that they suffer unconstitutional racial discrimination when their school districts make assignments that limit racial segregation of long-excluded minority groups (e.g., *Cappachione,* 1999; *Eisenberg,* 2000). Some White individuals also resist efforts to end tracking systems, which typically sort students within schools by race and social class.

Since the early days of desegregation research in the 1960s, there has been widespread agreement among researchers of different policy views that desegregation has no significant impact on the achievement of White students, as measured by test scores. This was the finding of James S. Coleman et al. (1966), of Nancy St. John in the first lengthy review of the research (1975), of Robert L. Crain and Rita Mahard (1978), of Meyer Weinberg (1970), of Janet Schofield (1995), and even in many writings of leading desegregation opponents, including David Armor (1995) and Christine Rossell (1990). In fact, the evidence was so clear that this issue was rarely raised in court battles by desegregation opponents, in spite of Whites' fears that White achievement would suffer. The basic reason for that finding may well be Coleman's conclusion (1966) that family background is far more influential in determining outcomes for middle-class students than school influences. Schools have larger effects on children from disadvantaged backgrounds, however. Subsequent research, especially at the higher education level, powerfully supports the idea that there can be strongly positive impacts on a variety of more complex intellectual and social skills for White students from the experience of integrated education (e.g., Gurin, Dey, Hurtado, & Gurin, 2002). The Civil Rights Project's surveys of White students in districts across the country show that students themselves perceive major benefits in being prepared to live and work in a diverse society (Kurlaender & Yun, 2001; Yun & Kurlaender, 2004). This does not mean, however, that there are not extreme conditions that could have harmful effects on any student's achievement, such as attending a very isolated, high poverty school without a critical mass of students from one's own group. Instead, within reasonable ranges the "risks" of a racially diverse school are not significant, and the potential gains—even for Whites—are considerable.

A wide, multidisciplinary range of evidence supporting the importance of a diverse student body in higher education was marshaled for the defense of the affirmative action policies of the University of Michigan, which were challenged in the late 1990s. The challenge reached the Supreme Court in 2003, which upheld Michigan's policy, citing diversity's educational benefits for all students (Whites as well as minorities), including cross-racial understanding; deeper, more complex class discussions; better workforce preparation; reduction of racial stereotypes; and preparation of a racially diverse, representative group of future leaders. University officials also cited research documenting the increasing segregation in K–12 education around the country, and particularly in Michigan, as rationale for the need to maintain racially conscious admissions policies. Although opinions differed as to how the university could attain a racially diverse student body, there was little public disagreement with its goal of diversity. Those who filed briefs in support of racial diversity included Fortune 500 companies and military leaders, as well as educational researchers, law professors, and college and graduate students from around the country. President George W. Bush even announced support for the idea of racial diversity in higher education, although his administration filed briefs before the Court opposing Michigan's policies (Bush, 2003).

We have learned a great deal about the benefits of racial integration in K–12 schools, as well as the continuing harms of racial segregation, and in contrast to earlier research, new research demonstrates benefits of integrated environments for White students as well as minority students. However, there is not the same public acclamation in support of racially integrated elementary and secondary schools as there is for integration in higher education, despite the fact that all children are required to attend

elementary and secondary schools. Research has found that racially integrated classrooms (not simply racially diverse schools) produce higher
academic achievement for minority students, higher aspirations for college or occupations, access to integrated social networks (which is important for knowledge about a variety of opportunities), more positive intergroup relations, and desire to live in and attend schools in racially diverse
environments for all students (Braddock & Dawkins, 1993; Kurlaender &
Yun, 2001; Schofield, 1989, 1995, 2001; W. G. Stephan & C. W. Stephan,
2001; Patchen, 1982). Further, research that diverse classrooms improve
the critical thinking of White and non-White students has been cited by
school districts as a reason for creating voluntary desegregation plans.[6]
Much of this research has been done in Black-White environments; less
is known about multiracial schools or for non-Black minority groups.
Racially segregated minority schools are likely to be schools with high
levels of concentrated poverty (G. Orfield & C. Lee, 2005) and tend to
have fewer educational resources, both tangible and intangible. Students
attending these schools are often at a disadvantage when seeking jobs or
college admission, even if they have been academically successful, because
of their schools' reputations and lack of networks. The disadvantage of
segregated White schools is of a different nature: the isolation of White
students prevents them from learning from others of different backgrounds or becoming comfortable living and working in racially diverse
settings (Frankenberg, C. Lee, & G. Orfield, 2003).

Willis D. Hawley is one of the leading voices in how to implement desegregation and realize the benefits that can occur in integrated schools.
His essay in this volume, "Designing Schools That Use Student Diversity
to Enhance Learning of All Students," synthesizes empirical evidence and
theory about creating learning environments that will be effective in educating a racially diverse group of students. He also discusses how racially
diverse schools benefit students (academically, socially, life chances) and
our society. Hawley suggests that, despite the demonstrated benefits of
racially diverse primary and secondary schools, policymakers have given
much less attention and support to the K–12 context relative to higher
education. His essay provides research-based ideas about how racially diverse schools can be structured to effectively achieve the benefits of desegregation.

The essay by Melanie Killen, David S. Crystal, and Martin Ruck, "The
Social Developmental Benefits of Intergroup Contact among Children
and Adolescents," focuses on developmental and social outcomes, specifically how students perceive and evaluate racial exclusion and discrimination. They find that students who report that they have more contact

with people of other racial groups demonstrate more tolerant and inclusive opinions than students who have less interracial contact. Their findings reaffirm Gordon Allport's contact theory (1954), one of the social science works cited in the *Brown* decision, specifying the conditions in which interracial contact would be most beneficial in overcoming racial prejudice and stereotypes. Significantly, Killen, Crystal, and Ruck found that these social benefits accrued only to students who actually encounter students of different races daily—and not to students who may be in racially diverse schools but who do not view their daily experiences as ones involving individuals from other racial and ethnic backgrounds. The implications of their study suggest that in order to attain the benefits of racially diverse schools, it is important that students perceive their school environment as racially and ethnically diverse. Further, the perspective held by Killen and her colleagues is unique in focusing on how racial and ethnic diversity in schools, as perceived from the students' perspective, contributes to the social developmental understanding about what makes racial and ethnic discrimination and exclusion wrong. Thus an outcome of racial diversity, when intergroup contact conditions are met, is the psychological knowledge that racial equality should be achieved, which, in turn, contributes to the existence of a supportive school environment.

When policymakers or educators mention "the achievement gap," they refer to the difference (or "gap") between the standardized test scores of White students and Black and/or Latino students.[7] This gap is of particular concern if such tests are required for graduation (as is increasingly the case) or entry to college, because the gap then measures limitations on the opportunities available to Blacks and Latinos. Closing the achievement gap has been the focus of many educational policies, including the recent No Child Left Behind Act of 2001 (NCLB), which sanctions schools for not making enough progress in closing the gap(s) regardless of the schools' degree of racial or poverty isolation, level of funding, or other school-level features that make it more difficult to provide a high-quality education.

Despite NCLB's narrow focus on closing achievement gaps, according to a recent study of Florida public schools, racial segregation predicts the percentage of students passing the state's mandatory promotion and graduation exams, even after accounting for other influential factors, such as teacher experience, class size, and per-pupil spending (Borman et al., 2004). After several decades of a narrowing of the Black-White achievement gap, progress reversed during the 1990s, a decade that also saw the growth of Black-White segregation between schools (Frankenberg, C. Lee, & G. Orfield, 2003, p. 10; see also generally Jencks & Phillips, 1998).

Within-school segregation is more difficult to measure, but one analysis suggested that it also rose toward the end of the 1990s (Clotfelter, 2004).

Jaekyung Lee explores the relationship between the achievement gap and segregation in his analysis reported in his essay, "Can Reducing School Segregation Close the Achievement Gap?" Lee's analysis of National Assessment of Educational Progress (NAEP) data challenges the notion that NCLB, which relies heavily on the pressure of sanctions to improve student achievement, will cause students in racially isolated minority schools to achieve at the same level of affluent, predominantly White schools. If Lee's conclusions are correct and increasing racial segregation (which has continued to accelerate after the time period Lee examined) parallels increasing achievement gaps, then new policies must include efforts to eliminate racial isolation, both between and within schools, if they are to be successful in closing the achievement gap.

How Does the Growth of Non-Black Minority Groups Affect Our Schools?

Today's public school composition is radically different from that at the time of *Brown,* when four out of every five children were White, or a generation ago when much of the prior research on desegregated schools occurred. The Immigration Act of 1965 forever changed the composition of the U.S. population and, therefore, the composition of the public schools. Passed a year after the Civil Rights Act of 1964, this act eliminated the prior requirement of immigration quotas based on national origin. The act's easing of immigration restrictions should not be considered a public embrace of foreign immigration. In this nation born of immigrants, people coming to America, documented or not, continue to face challenges in accessing many of the basic social services, including education. During the Clinton administration, welfare benefits were cut to all immigrants, even if here legally, unless they became citizens. Some states have also restricted admission to public universities and eligibility for financial aid to noncitizens. Other states have begun drastically limiting the amount of time, often only a year, immigrant students can spend in a bilingual education program before transitioning to English-only classes, regardless of whether they have mastered age- and subject-appropriate vocabulary. Additionally, immigrant families must often overcome language and cultural barriers to participating in their children's education.

One issue that affects all students, but has particular significance for immigrant students, is what happens when students' culture and the school's "mainstream" culture come into conflict. Language is the most noticed aspect of this conflict, but this can also include past schooling experiences or ethnic traditions. M. Beatriz Arias, Christian Faltis, and James Cohen explore how schools can foster positive outcomes for the diverse types of immigrant students in their essay, "Adolescent Immigrant Students in U.S. Schools: Issues of Cultural Pluralism, Successful School Settings, and Intergroup Relations." In particular, they argue that a school's philosophical stance in support of cultural pluralism, or the view that the school should foster each student's development without trying to subtract his or her identity as a member of an ethnic group, is crucial to helping immigrant students feel safe in their school environment and contributes to positive outcomes. Their argument flies in the face of the recent English-only initiatives or in states where bilingual teachers are in short supply. They reaffirm, however, Gordon Allport's argument that benefits flow from integrated settings when certain conditions are met, including that students interact as people with equal status (e.g., that each student's background is equally valued).

María Teresa Unger Palmer's case study of Latina immigrant students, "'Desperate to Learn': The Schooling Experience of Latinas in North Carolina," puts a face on the issues discussed in Arias, Faltis, and Cohen's essay and demonstrates the ways in which schools disempower this growing group of students. Through her role as a researcher and community advocate, Palmer documents the myriad ways that teachers and counselors—who purport to be acting in the best interests of the Latina students—alienate the Latina students and limit their postgraduation opportunities. In an increasingly multiracial world, Palmer's study is important in exploring the antagonism between Black and Latina students, who were often tracked together into lower-ability classes in this predominantly White, college preparatory high school.

Not until 1967, thirteen years after *Brown* declared racial distinctions in education to be illegal, did the Supreme Court extend this reasoning to statutes forbidding interracial marriage. In striking down the Virginia law banning such interracial unions, the Supreme Court determined that such laws were "designed to maintain White Supremacy" (*Loving v. Virginia,* 1967). Mixed-race children, of course, preceded this decision (e.g., children of White landowners and Black slaves), but until recently were considered Black (or of another minority group) under the "one-drop rule" classifying anyone as non-White if he or she, regardless of physical appearance, had any non-White ancestors. Our empirical knowledge, then, of this mixed-race population is recent, due to our prior racial classification systems.

Although data on race were first collected in the original U.S. Census, in 1790, the census of 2000 was the first time respondents were able to identify themselves as being of more than one race. Almost seven million Americans, or 2.4 percent of the total population according to the census, identified themselves as being two or more races.[8] Multiracial status was more commonly indicated among those younger than eighteen; 4 percent of young people identified themselves as belonging to more than one racial/ethnic group (U.S. Census Bureau, 2001a, 2001b, 2001c).

Simon Cheng's essay, "Interracial Status as a Double-Edged Sword: The Educational Experiences of Interracial Children," seeks to explore the particular issues educators must face with this increasing population of multiracial youths and their families. He examines how the child's multiracial status may affect the family's ability to support their child's education. His analysis carefully distinguishes biracial students with some White heritage (White biracial) from those of more than one non-White background (non-White biracial) and finds substantial differences between these two subsets of the multiracial population. Cheng finds that White biracial individuals, possibly because of their ability to identify both as White and minority, depending on the situation, are able to adapt better in schooling environments and have better outcomes than one-race minority or non-White biracial students. His essay underscores the importance of understanding the complexity of the biracial population and how these multiple racial identities may affect students' comfort in schools as well as important school outcomes.

What Are Possible Solutions in Our Multiracial Society?

A generation ago one of the foci of the desegregation assistance aid was on training teachers to be effective in desegregated schools, in recognition of the centrality of teachers to student outcomes and meaningful intergroup contact. In fact, all things being equal, the quality of teachers is the most important predictor of educational quality (Hanushek, Kain, & Rivkin, 1998; Sanders & Horn, 1998). This means, however, that the distribution of good teachers within schools, among schools, and among school districts matters a great deal. Black students are more likely to have novice teachers—who tend to be less effective on average than more experienced teachers—due to segregation within school districts that is caused by a variety of factors, including pressure from parents that influences how some teachers are assigned (Clotfelter, Ladd, & Vigdor, 2003). Experienced teachers are also likely to have more choice about where and whom they teach than do new teachers.

The teaching force today remains predominantly White, and most teachers are from backgrounds vastly different from the students they teach. Teachers are largely from middle-class backgrounds and native (and usually only) English speakers (Gomez, 1993). To the extent that these White teachers are typical of the White population, they themselves attended overwhelmingly isolated White schools as students and now live in predominantly White neighborhoods as adults.[9] For example, one survey of seventeen hundred early-career teachers found that most teachers in the more diverse schools reported that their own schooling experiences were less racially and economically diverse than the classrooms in which they were now teaching (Freeman, Brookhart, & Loadman, 1999).

Christine E. Sleeter, a prominent voice in the field of teacher education, reviews studies of how teacher education programs prepare educators for teaching in racially diverse schools and classrooms in "Preparing Teachers for Multiracial and Historically Underserved Schools." From her review she suggests ways in which teacher education programs can train teachers to help build upon the assets that students from racially and economically diverse backgrounds bring to the classroom. Essential elements include a significant cross-cultural immersion experience, excellent teaching models and mentors, and a longer amount of time in a classroom as a student teacher, with specific feedback on how to engage students from different backgrounds. Her essay also points to the need for developing or reinventing teacher education programs that will attract and train a more diverse teaching force, which may bring cultural and community knowledge that is less valued in more traditional higher-education institutions.

Julie Milligan Hughes and Rebecca S. Bigler draw on previous psychological developmental literature as well as their own studies to try to gain an understanding of how teachers might effectively address issues of race and racism in their classrooms. In their essay, "Addressing Race and Racism in the Classroom," they examine two issues that teachers must grapple with: should racial labels be used when discussing people, and how much should racism be explicitly discussed. They find that the psychological literature is mixed, that there are both negative and positive consequences that might arise from introducing racial labels to children and discussing racism. Hughes and Bigler found that using racial labels and addressing racism directly with young Black and White students generally had more positive (and fewer negative) outcomes than other methods of instruction. The issues this essay addresses are important for our society, for teachers, and also for parents to understand if we hope to lessen and eventually eliminate the formation and perpetuation of racial prejudice in future generations.

Of course, for teachers to be effective in racially diverse environments requires the creation of such schools. There are isolated examples in many school districts of creating positive interracial experiences, but replicating and extending these successes on a larger scale has proven to be more challenging. Although there is a strong focus on outcomes from standardized tests, there is less awareness of the specific policies and practices in schools and communities that encourage desirable academic or social results. The context of every school and district is slightly different, but lessons can be learned from what others are doing. Documenting successful examples of achieving positive interracial outcomes is a vital task so that we can better demonstrate the importance of integrated schools to students of all racial backgrounds and our country.

Carol Corbett Burris and Kevin G. Welner document one district's success in providing an excellent education for students from all backgrounds in their essay, "Classroom Integration and Accelerated Learning through Detracking." In an effort to ensure that all students, not just middle-class or White students, were gaining a diploma, this New York school district gradually eliminated classes in which low-achieving students were grouped in favor of heterogeneously grouped classes with an accelerated curriculum. Burris (who is the principal at this district's high school) and Welner's essay is important because the data provide extraordinary evidence of how schools can eradicate the structural barriers that often produce inequality for minority students and restructure themselves in a way that will help all students achieve. These authors also discuss the process of detracking and the political realities that administrators face in making such changes to established school norms. As they note, reforms such as this, which challenge the status quo or the privilege of certain groups, will never be universally embraced, but the school overcame most parents' concerns about the efficacy of tracking by combining detracking changes with improvements in curriculum and instruction and using data to demonstrate the effectiveness of these changes.[10] Theirs is a hopeful story of how one district has committed itself to improving the academic outcomes for White and minority students alike.

One of the realities that school systems must face in their efforts to achieve racial integration is that courts are increasingly suspicious of any use of race to assign students to schools despite the demonstrated benefits that come from integrated schools. Richard W. Cole, lead defense counsel in defending one district's voluntary racial desegregation plan, outlines what school districts—and their attorneys—must consider in designing district policy in his essay, "Fostering an Inclusive, Multiracial Democracy: How Attorneys, Social Scientists, and Educators Made the Case for School Integration in Lynn, Massachusetts." Lynn's vigorous defense of its racial integration plan has included extensive evaluation of how district-level and school-level policies and structures affect the education of students from all racial/ethnic groups. Cole took a unique approach when arguing this case by drawing on existing social psychological and developmental psychological findings demonstrating the educational, cognitive, and social advantages that result for all children when integration is achieved. Cole discusses extraordinary improvements due to actions large and small as a result of this integration plan, and his essay offers a practical example of how one district has sought to achieve many of the positive outcomes discussed in this book.

What Are the Costs to Society of Ignoring the Role of Race in Education?

The *Grutter* decision underscored the stake all Americans have in education as preparation for citizenship. Common schools were our nation's answer during the nineteenth century to preparing children to participate as democratic citizens. Although schools today have this as but one of many goals, public schools remain one of the few public institutions in which most people participate. As such, public elementary and secondary schools offer an important opportunity in a still-segregated society to encounter and learn from people of other racial/ethnic backgrounds. We must learn to structure our schools in ways that invite the participation of all as equals and offer the same opportunities to all regardless of race.

Despite the legal challenges that some school systems face to maintain voluntary integration plans, a wide range of public and academic support for integration exists. In Louisville, Kentucky, several business leaders testified in support of the school system's voluntary integration plan, echoing those of business leaders' briefs in the University of Michigan affirmative action cases. The CEO of a bank based in Louisville testified that there was "absolutely no question" that "receiving an educational background in a diverse, integrated environment . . . prepares students [both Black and White] for the ultimate work force [*sic*] that they will be joining" (Testimony of Malcolm Chancey Jr., 2003, p. 135). In addition to preparing workers to function in a diverse global economy, it is estimated that by 2020 there will be a shortage of white-collar workers due to retiring baby boomers (Carnevale & Deroschers, 2004). When schools push out students of color who are alienated from schools' dominant White culture or do not prepare them to meet increasingly stringent graduation requirements, our society's future pool of workers is diminished.

There are additional economic costs of racial discrimination to our society. Fifty percent of Black high school dropouts have been in jail at some point. This problem is particularly severe for Black males: more were in jails than in college in 2000 (Western, Schiraldi, & Ziedenberg, 2003). In addition to a diminished workforce, housing the prison population is an expensive burden for taxpayers. Another dimension of the costs to our society has been demonstrated by economic analyses indicating that racial discrimination lowers the United States' gross national product by 2 percent due to the racial differences in earnings (Updegrave, 1989). As non-White workers continue to become a larger part of the workforce, the impact of discrimination will likely only become larger. As reported in the Census of 2000, White annual median household income was over $44,000, as compared to $33,000 for Hispanics and only $29,000 for Blacks (U.S. Census Bureau, 2001c). Part of the income difference for Blacks is that there is a smaller pool of older, qualified workers to fill higher-paying managerial jobs due to historical racial discrimination in higher education. But as college education is more important for increasing African Americans' income than Whites', improving K–12 and higher educational outcomes for Black (and other minority) students is critical.

To improve educational outcomes for minority students means that we must continue to critically assess the effects that our educational structures have on opportunity for all students, of all races, in all schools. Current federal education policy was premised on President George W. Bush's 2000 campaign promise to "end the soft bigotry of low expectations" for minority students, but the reality shows that NCLB is actually making education in racially diverse and urban schools more difficult (Washington, 2004). Analysis of its implementation in California has shown that schools that are multiracial, or that have more subgroups, are more likely to be sanctioned under the act's policy of subgroup accountability (Kane, 2002; J. Kim & Sunderman, 2004b). This finding that NCLB has the effect of concentrating sanctions on diverse schools points to a flaw in the design of the current accountability system. Teachers in two urban districts surveyed about NCLB suggested that some of its key premises may be faulty. For example, they said that NCLB sanctions would likely cause teachers to transfer out of schools not making required progress, suggesting that the NCLB accountability system may make it more difficult to maintain a stable teaching force in urban schools already experiencing difficulty recruiting and retaining quality teachers (Sunderman, Tracey,

J. Kim, & G. Orfield, 2004). Additionally, in the predominantly urban areas studied by the Civil Rights Project, student participation is very low in choice and supplemental educational services, two programs meant to benefit students in underperforming schools (J. Kim & Sunderman, 2004a).

Policies that emphasize test-based accountability with high sanctions for schools not making appropriate progress are just one example of structures affecting education that appear to be race neutral but in practice have very real and serious racial (and educational) consequences. In their essay, "The Common Schools Democracy Requires: Expanding Membership through Inclusive Education," john a. powell and Rebecca High reflect on how education, as currently designed, is both influenced by and perpetuates the racial and economic stratification of our society. They analyze how public education has been limited by the focus on narrow testing programs evaluating students' attainment of basic skills. The authors suggest a reconceptualization of education needed to prepare students for a multiracial future and for America to truly achieve its ideal of an inclusive democracy.

The process of desegregating schools accomplished a great deal, particularly in the South, when the federal courts and enforcement agencies empowered by *Brown* and subsequent Supreme Court decisions (along with the Civil Rights Act of 1964) used political support and expertise to implement desegregation plans. These gains are being lost, rapidly, and yet this is only the first step of what must be done. According to the Reverend Martin Luther King Jr.,

> desegregation is eliminative and negative, for it simply removes these legal and social prohibitions. Integration is creative, and is therefore more profound and far-reaching than desegregation. Integration is the positive acceptance of desegregation and the welcomed participation of Negroes in the total range of human activities. Integration is genuine intergroup, interpersonal doing. Desegregation then, rightly is only a short-range goal. Integration is the ultimate goal of our national community. (King, 1991, p. 118)

Gary Orfield reflects on the lessons of this book in his conclusion, "Challenges for This Generation: Integration and Social Transformation." Building upon the older research a generation ago and the research reported here, Orfield offers an agenda for researchers, educators, and policymakers to meet the urgent need of our communities' and schools' growing racial diversity—and to finally achieve the ultimate goal of integration as Dr. King challenged us to do over four decades ago.

The *Grutter* decision expressed the Supreme Court's hope that race-based admissions for college won't be necessary in twenty-five years. That expectation would necessitate some real progress in K–12 education before then, as some affirmative action proponents have acknowledged.[11] Having racially integrated elementary schools, and knowing how to maximize the benefits of such a diverse school, could reduce the formation of racial stereotypes that higher education seeks to lessen. Integrated high schools, with students of all races having the same challenging curriculum and social networks for postgraduation opportunities, would lessen the need for racially conscious admissions or hiring policies. In metropolitan areas where there are no racially identifiable schools (schools with a student body that is disproportionately of one race), residential segregation is lower.[12] Thus, creating effective racially integrated schools could have very significant effects for our highly segregated society.

The authors contributing to this book offer us important new information about the social and academic benefits that result from racially integrated schools, and they provide timely and necessary solutions for how best to structure schools to accomplish these goals. To do nothing, or to continue a color-blind discourse favoring choice and high-stakes testing in our schools, without looking carefully at how these policies or the structures of schools and school systems affect all students, has the potential to be a grave disservice to these students, with serious costs to the larger society. To work to improve interracial outcomes is to strive toward creating a system that will benefit all. As the essays by these authors suggest, this is not a zero-sum game. When schools and districts thoughtfully examine their policies and redesign them to provide meaningful interracial experiences for their students, in which they interact across racial groups equally without privileging one group over another, everyone benefits. We have seen that individual students, even those with privileged racial status in our society, benefit from reforms targeted toward achieving positive interracial outcomes and experiences. Trying to achieve the integration and benefits discussed in this book should not be seen as a trade-off by any group; instead, it's a "trade-up" for all groups. The district strategies in the essays by Burris and Welner and by Cole were similar, in that integration was part of a larger plan presented to their communities as a means to improve educational quality and opportunities for all students. It is time for parents, politicians, and educators to commit themselves to helping all of our students "trade up." This book provides the theoretical, scientific, and educational bases for improving the quality of education in the United States for all children. The time is now.

Notes

1. This change in the percentage of White students is not because of white flight to private schools: the percentage of white students in private schools in the late 1990s was similar to that in the 1950s (Reardon & Yun, 2002).

2. On December 5, 2005, the Supreme Court declined to hear an appeal of the First Circuit's opinion upholding Lynn's voluntary integration plan. Two other voluntary integration cases are currently pending before the Supreme Court.

3. Although legal discrimination was most visible against African Americans—and violence quite apparent when these Jim Crow laws began to be dismantled—one must only think back to Japanese internment camps during World War II for one of many examples of discrimination toward those from other racial/ethnic backgrounds.

4. The same is true to a lesser extent for other minority groups, such as Latinos and Asians. Neither group, however, has experienced the extreme segregation that Blacks have (Massey & Denton, 1993), although issues such as citizenship or knowledge of English may impede the ability of members of these groups to experience integration and upward mobility.

5. This is not to say, however, that there wasn't attention in the research community about within-school integration efforts and how such efforts could improve student outcomes when schools were desegregated (e.g., Hawley et al., 1983; Chesler, Bryant, & Crowfoot, 1981).

6. For example, the Seattle district court, citing the testimony of Dr. William Trent on behalf of the Seattle school district, noted, "The research also shows that both white and minority students experienced improved critical thinking skills—the ability to both understand and challenge views which are different from their own—when they are educated in racially diverse schools" (*Parents Involved in Community Schools v. Seattle School District No. 1*, 2001, p. 1236).

7. Asian students actually score higher, on average, in most standardized testing than White students and have higher rates of college completion.

8. Although respondents were allowed to identify with as many races as they wished, the overwhelming majority (93.3 percent) of these respondents identified themselves as biracial (N. A. Jones & A. S. Smith, 2001).

9. A 1990 American Association of Colleges for Teacher Education (AACTE) study confirms that many White prospective teachers grew up in overwhelmingly White environments (Gomez, 1993).

10. They note that a few parents' concerns about detracking were an attempt to disguise their racial/class prejudices when moving to heterogeneously grouped classes.

11. See, for example, the remarks of Lee Bollinger, the president of Columbia University and a named defendant in the *Grutter* case (Bollinger, 2003).

12. Of course, in areas where residential segregation is lower and schools' enrollment is geographically based, it would seem that schools would also be less segregated (Pearce, 1980).

The Benefits of Integration
and Potential Harms of Segregation

Designing Schools That Use Student Diversity to Enhance Learning of All Students

Willis D. Hawley

The Challenge

It is easy to document that racial and ethnic discrimination and prejudice persist in the United States, despite progress made, and that such actions and dispositions undermine the lives of all Americans. While some will deny that there is a problem, when pressed, most people, especially people of color, will acknowledge that discrimination, indifference, tension, and misunderstanding often characterize relations among persons of different races and ethnicities (Goodheart, 2004).

In 2003 the U.S. Supreme Court heard from numerous business, civic, and military leaders regarding the importance of taking action to end racial and ethnic discrimination. In *Grutter v. Bollinger* (a challenge to affirmative action at the University of Michigan), testimony cited the importance of such action to the welfare of individuals of all races,[1] the viability of our political system and our economy, and to our national security. As Justice O'Connor asserted in the Court's support of affirmative action, these benefits "can only be developed through exposure to widely diverse people, cultures, ideas, and viewpoints" (*Grutter v. Bollinger*, p. 2340).

Despite the importance of enhancing students' opportunities to learn from and with persons of different races and ethnicities and the increasing racial isolation of many of our schools (Frankenberg, C. Lee, & G. Orfield, 2003), the ubiquitous public discourse about school improvement rarely mentions the desirability of fostering greater diversity in elementary and secondary schools and classrooms or of developing racially and ethnically diverse school programs that treat diversity as a learning opportunity. Indeed, diversity is often seen as an obstacle to be overcome.

Why is it that many of those in a position to pursue strategies that would increase intercultural knowledge, understanding, and competencies fail to do so? One answer to this question is that, despite evidence that racially and ethnically diverse schools can benefit all students, we do not know enough about programs and practices that result in benefits that clearly outweigh perceptions of the likelihood of political or educational costs involved in the pursuit of integration.

It follows that if policymakers, educators, and parents are to see a student's opportunity to learn with and from people of different races and ethnicities—what I will call a diverse learning opportunity (DLO)—as a valued resource for all students, two related conditions will have to be met: (1) It will have to be widely believed that schools that are genuinely integrated can (a) benefit students intellectually and enhance their future economic prospects and (b) contribute to the realization of valued social goals, such as the reduction of poverty and crime, in ways schools that are not racially and ethnically diverse cannot; and (2) Implementable strategies will have to be identified for designing DLOs in schools that predictably enhance the cognitive and social development of all students.

This essay focuses on the second of these conditions and seeks to identify school-level policies and practices that would make diverse schools and classrooms more effective than other schools. It is important to briefly discuss the first condition, because unless it is widely believed that DLOs have the potential to significantly benefit students and society, it is not likely that much attention will be given to the pursuit of policies and practices that foster their growth.

What Do We Know about the Value of Racially and Ethnically Integrated Schools?

Do DLOs Increase Students' Knowledge about, Positive Dispositions toward, and Capacity to Learn from and Interact Productively with Persons of Different Racial and Ethnic Backgrounds?

The answer to this question, generally speaking, is yes—if teachers and school administrators carefully and intelligently structure the students' interactions with others and lessons to be learned (Braddock, Crain, & McPartland, 1984; Hallinan & Teixeira, 1987; Schofield, 1982, 1989).[2] In other words, bringing students of different racial and ethnic backgrounds together in schools creates opportunities that then must be used wisely to achieve positive outcomes. The social learning that DLOs make possible is significantly enhanced when there is a comprehensive schoolwide commitment to eliminating prejudice and increasing intercultural competence. Collaborative activities (such as cooperative learning) aimed at achieving a shared goal are among the most effective ways of affecting attitudes and behavior when they attend to issues of status, cultural, and achievement differences among the students involved (E. B. Aronson et al., 1978; Hallinan & Teixeira, 1987; Slavin, 1979, 1985, 1990, 1995b; National Research Council, 1999; Allport, 1954).

Certain conditions substantially affect the impact of contact strategies. Interventions to improve students' "social cognition" appear to be effective if implemented well and take into account the developmental stages of the students involved. Social cognition includes the ability to differentiate personal characteristics in outgroups, the ability to accept and integrate multiple ways of organizing information about different people and social events, and understanding that personal characteristics of individuals are changeful and changeable. Efforts to combat prejudice by building information about and empathy for the victims of discrimination do not appear to be as effective as those that involve students in contact with students of other races and ethnicities or are experiential (e.g., involve role-playing) (Wood & Sonleitner, 1996).

It is possible to increase students' knowledge about and positive dispositions toward people different from themselves in racially and ethnically homogeneous schools and classrooms. This might be accomplished through appropriate curricula and in organizational environments in which those in positions of authority make clear that respecting and working with people of diverse races and ethnicities is socially expected and desirable (Killen, Lee-Kim, McGlothlin, & Stangor, 2002). However, there is reason to believe that such knowledge and dispositions learned in homogeneous settings are less well developed, less strongly believed, and more likely to dissipate when students are confronted with seemingly conflicting information and experiences. The development of intercultural competencies, such as the capability to work well with persons of different races, appears to require practice, and thus cannot be learned in homogeneous schools (Wells & Crain, 1994; Schofield & Sagar, 1977).

Stereotypes of persons of other races and ethnicities develop in early grades and are difficult to undo (Mahard & Crain, 1983). However, students can learn how to apply or not to apply the stereotypes they hold. Thus even persons who hold negative stereotypes of others may not act in discriminatory or other negative ways. Over time, positive interactions with others about whom one holds negative stereotypes can both undermine stereotypes and enhance dispositions and capabilities to behave as though the stereotype is not held (Schofield, 1995; Wood & Sonleitner,

1996; Jussim, L. M. Coleman, & Lerch, 1987; Salzer, 1998; Bransford & Schwartz, 1999).

Reasonably strong and extensive evidence exists on the efficacy of efforts to provide students with opportunities for productive interpersonal contact in DLOs. Relevant research appears well grounded in theory. Research on the effects of strategies involving the development of enhanced capacities for social cognition is less extensive but is reasonably convincing (Schofield, 1995). Research on antibias and antiracism curricula (see J. A. Banks & C. A. M. Banks, 1995; J. A. Banks et al., 2001; Nieto, 2001) suggests that these interventions can have modest, short-term effects, especially when they actively engage the learners. Research on the effects of curricular efforts that focus on increasing students' knowledge and understanding of the importance of unprejudiced behavior suggests that, by themselves, these strategies have small if any effects on behavioral change (e.g., the development of intercultural competence).

Do DLOs Foster Higher Academic Achievement and Cognitive Development?

With respect to academic achievement measured by conventional tests (that tend to focus on relatively simple skills and on knowledge acquisition), the available research suggests that:

- African American and Hispanic students learn somewhat more in schools that are majority White than in schools that are predominantly non-White (Borman et al., 2004; Kain & O'Brien, 2002; Schiff, Firestone, & J. Young, 1999). This appears to be particularly the case for higher-ability African American students (Hanushek, Kain, & Rivkin, 2004a).
- The positive effects of racially and ethnically heterogeneous schools and classrooms on the achievement of students of color are evidenced most often in tests of literacy and seldom in tests of mathematical competencies.
- The earlier that students experience DLOs, the greater the positive impact on achievement.
- The integration of schools that remain majority White appears to have little or no negative effect on White students' achievement. However, White students in predominantly non-White schools may achieve at lower levels than students from similar socioeconomic backgrounds who attend majority White schools (Bankston & C. Caldas, 2002).

- Students who perceive themselves as being discriminated against or as being stereotyped as less capable of achieving particular goals than others different from themselves will tend to underachieve in the pursuit of those goals (Steele, S. Spencer, & J. Aronson, 2002).

Most studies of the effects of DLOs on student achievement do not describe how variations in instructional strategies, learning resources, and organizational climates relate to differences in student performance. It may be that when DLOs are the result of court orders that seek to assure that students of color are provided more adequate learning opportunities and that teachers receive extra training, there are positive effects on student achievement, particularly for students of color. Furthermore, predominantly Black and Latino schools often have fewer well-qualified teachers, less rigorous curricula, more staff and student mobility, and are located in high-poverty communities that can undermine achievement (R. F. Ferguson & Mehta, 2004).

However, the strongest theoretical argument for the effects of DLOs on student achievement is that increasing racial and ethnic diversity can increase the average socioeconomic status (SES) of the classrooms in which students of color learn. There is substantial evidence that the higher the SES of a student's schoolmates and classmates, the higher the student's achievement (Hoxby, 2000; Kahlenberg, 2001; Ludwig, Ladd, & G. J. Duncan, 2001; Rumberger & Palardy, 2005). It is not just that peers influence what and how students learn; the more students of higher academic readiness in their classrooms, the more demanding teachers are likely to be and the greater the likelihood that the curriculum will be rigorous. Thus if academic achievement measured in conventional ways is the only objective, increasing the opportunities of low-income students to learn with and from students who are of higher SES would be more productive than focusing on the pursuit of racial and ethnic heterogeneity.

A reasonably strong case can be made that DLOs, when combined with appropriate instructional strategies, create exceptional opportunities for students to develop capabilities to solve complex problems and engage in critical thinking. This argument, derived from learning theory and studies of groups where there is diversity of ideas and ways of knowing, holds that students in diverse schools and classrooms can learn to take different perspectives, avoid making false assumptions, and examine meaning better than can students who learn in homogeneous settings (Bransford & Schwartz, 1999).

It seems likely that the development of student capabilities for problem solving and critical thinking is more likely in DLOs than in schools that are otherwise diverse. Race and ethnicity are probably more salient to most students than other types of social diversity (e.g., diverse religious or political views) since race/ethnicity is discernible and continues to determine opportunity in our society. Additionally, the application of capabilities for problem solving and critical thinking outside of school increasingly occurs in racially and ethnically diverse settings. We lack evidence, however, on the capabilities of students to engage in more complex cognitive tasks that compares racially and ethnically diverse learning environments with homogeneous schools and classrooms. Moreover, the validity of the case for the cognitive development benefits of DLOs depends on the implementation of instructional strategies few teachers employ, such as differentiated instruction and reciprocal teaching (see the second part of this essay for more about specific strategies).

Research on DLOs' effects on academic achievement focuses, with few exceptions, on Black-White comparisons. There are only a handful of studies that examine data from the 1990s forward (see Mickelson, 2005). For these reasons, and because many relevant variables that might account for variations in student learning are not specified in most studies, explaining the effects of DLOs on student academic achievement must rely more on theory than on convincing data.

Do DLOs Produce Positive Outcomes for Students Once They Leave School?

Students who experience DLOs are more likely than students who do not to go to integrated colleges, live in integrated neighborhoods, have friends of other races and ethnicities, and work in nontraditional occupations with higher status (Carlson & Lein, 1998; Sørensen & Hallinan, 1985; Hallinan & S. S. Smith, 1985; Hallinan & Teixeira, 1987; Wells & Crain, 1994; Dawkins, 1983). The more intense the positive intergroup contact a student experiences, the more likely he or she is to seek out intergroup relationships in later life. Students of color who attend predominantly Black schools may find that employers devalue their high school performance, and thus students are limited to lower-skill and lower-paid occupations than their actual abilities merit (Crain, 1984; Braddock, Crain, McPartland, & Dawkins, 1986). There is reason to believe that college students who participate in DLOs are more likely than other students to engage in civic activities that seek to serve others, although this finding may be correlational rather than causal (P. Gurin, 1999).

There are only a few studies that examine the long-term effects of DLOs on students (e.g., Braddock, Crain, & McPartland, 1984; Wells &

Crain, 1994). While the outcomes with which they are concerned differ, these studies all point in the same direction. However, most studies are based on data collected in the early 1980s and before. A recent study by Wells and her associates (in press) reminds us that many factors other than DLOs influence the race-relevant choices people make. These researchers interviewed almost 250 adults who graduated in 1980 from desegregated schools in communities where desegregation had a reputation for positive outcomes. Despite generally positive feelings about their experiences with people of other races, most of those interviewed reported, some wistfully, that they had chosen to live in neighborhoods and send their children to schools that were not racially and ethnically diverse. Few had close friends of another race (Wells, Holme, Revilla, & Atanda, in press).

Can DLOs Contribute to the Reduction of Crime and Poverty?

Direct evidence on this question is slim. To the extent that DLOs reduce racial isolation and prejudice and increase intercultural competence, they are likely to reduce interracial crime and antagonism (although intraracial violence is more common than interracial violence), increase employability, and enhance worker effectiveness in multiracial workplaces. To the extent that DLOs enhance academic achievement, cognitive capacity, and social competencies and reduce discrimination in employment, they will reduce poverty and this, in turn, will reduce crime. Indirect support for the relationship between DLOs and crime is found in a study showing that residential movement of low-income families from high- to low-poverty neighborhoods reduced teen involvement in violent criminal offending (Ludwig, Ladd, & Duncan, 2001).[3] R. F. Ferguson and Mehta conclude that integration is correlated with high school completion, college attendance, college completion, and lower rates of delinquency and teen childbearing (2004, p. 661).

The Design of Diverse Learning Opportunities in Schools and Classrooms

Much of the research on school desegregation/integration has focused on benefits for students of color, and most of this research has focused on African American students. In addition, much of the research used in debates about the net benefits of desegregation/integration makes use of survey research that tells us little about the experiences students have in schools that might explain differences in dispositions and achievement. Thus in order to develop a set of propositions that can guide the design of DLOs and the conditions that enhance their contributions to student learning, we need to draw heavily on a rather small number of studies that have examined what occurs in racially and ethnically diverse schools, research from nonschool settings, expert opinion, and theory.

It would be presumptuous to claim that the research is strong enough to meet the test I set out at the beginning of this essay—the specification of conditions in school that reliably predict positive outcomes that can be more powerfully achieved in schools that are racially and ethnically diverse than in schools that are not diverse. What follows is a start and will serve, at least, as an outline of future inquiry.

The research summaries in this essay's first section provide good reasons to believe that DLOs can offer all students significant learning opportunities they would not otherwise have. The creation of DLOs and the effective use of these opportunities require particular policies and practices that seek to attain four general goals:

1. Create and sustain racially and ethnically heterogeneous schools and classrooms;
2. Implement curricula and instructional strategies that address the challenges and utilize the opportunities presented by diverse learning environments;
3. Establish and nurture organizational capabilities and environments that promote the attainment of high academic standards and the development of positive dispositions and competences with respect to relations with diverse people;
4. Foster leadership that values and relentlessly pursues comprehensive strategies to maximize the unique learning opportunities possible in racially and ethnically diverse schools.

It is difficult to draw boundaries around the policies and practices to be discussed here. The literature on effective schools and instruction is enormous, and it is directly applicable to maximizing quality education in racially and ethnically diverse schools and classrooms. However, in order to place some limits on the concerns to be addressed below, I focus on those policies and practices that—in addition to the characteristics of good schools and quality teaching one would want to find in any effective school—are of particular importance in schools serving students from different racial and ethnic backgrounds.

This essay's first section separately discusses cognitive development and intercultural competence, but these two sets of outcomes are interdependent. Fortunately, the conditions in schools and classrooms needed to promote the attainment of these outcomes are, generally speaking, similar. While educators do face some dilemmas, in most cases, it is not necessary to choose between strategies that promote cross-cultural competence and those that foster student attainment of high academic standards and productive cognitive capabilities.

Creating and Sustaining Heterogeneous Schools and Classrooms

As educators and school boards consider how best to maximize the opportunities students of different races and ethnicities have to learn with and from one another, they must, of course, consider the changing interpretations of courts regarding the extent to which race can play a role in drawing student assignment plans and promoting student and parent choices about school enrollment. In this section of the essay, four considerations for maximizing and sustaining productively integrated schools are discussed:

- What is a productive mix of students of different races and ethnicities?
- At what grade level should integration begin?
- How can the diverse instructional needs of students be met without resegregating students within schools?
- Can extracurricular activities provide diverse learning opportunities?

Is There "Optimal Diversity"?

"Heterogeneity" and "diversity" are imprecise terms. There is no research that would allow us to specify what the ideal racial and ethnic mix of a school or classroom might be, especially where there are students of many racial and ethnic backgrounds who might attend that school. In the previous discussion about the effects of school integration on academic achievement, it was noted that Black, White, and Latino students typically achieve at somewhat higher levels in majority White schools. S. Brown (1999) found, analyzing national data, that the "ideal" racial mix for all students was 61–90 percent White and Asian American and 10–39 percent Black and Hispanic in schools with the highest average achievement. In a survey conducted in the early 1980s, when the primary issue on the desegregation agenda was eliminating the racial isolation of Blacks, many experts believed that there should be critical mass of no fewer than 14 percent to 20 percent of non-White students in a school being desegregated (Hawley et al., 1983). The primary consideration that motivated this estimate was the belief that when the number of "minority" students is small, especially if minority students might have special needs compared to the dominant racial group, the difficulties of avoiding resegregation within the school and of meeting the needs of minority students will be great. Moreover, it was believed that students in such circumstances are likely to feel isolated and powerless (Hawley et al., 1983).

Summarizing several studies, Cushner (2004) concluded that in schools where most students come from two racial or ethnic groups, racial tensions increase as the size of a minority group becomes large enough to threaten the dominance of the majority group. Similarly, Moody (2001) found that cross-race friendships are lowest when there are two racial groups of approximate size and reasoned that this is because issues of dominance encourage group cohesiveness and self-segregation. We do not know much about intergroup dynamics of multiracial schools where there is not a clearly dominant racial or ethnic group. Moody (2001) found that cross-race friendships are more likely in multiracial situations where no group is dominant. In multiracial settings, Moody found that both Blacks and Whites are more likely to have friends who are Hispanic than to have friends who are White and Black, respectively.

Race, ethnic, and language differences are not, of course, the only sources of diversity that affect race and ethnic relations. Gender affects relationships, as does the SES of different student groups. For example, the more highly correlated are race and SES, and the greater the differences in SES of different races, the more friendship segregation (Moody, 2001).

There is some reason to believe that the closer most classrooms in a school are to the racial and ethnic mix of students in the entire school, the more positive the intergroup relationships (Hallinan & Teixeira, 1987; S. Koslin, B. Koslin, & Pargament, 1972), perhaps because this would indicate the absence of sorting mechanisms (such as tracking or pullout programs).

While the proportions of students from different races or ethnic groups affect the prospects of achieving the potential benefits of DLOs, this may be less important than the history of diverse groups and their relationships in surrounding communities, geography, and the experiences and competencies of school staff to provide relevant learning opportunities (Dovidio et al., 2004). The goal is not to achieve "racial balance"—the equal distribution of students of different races and ethnicities across schools and classrooms—but to create diverse and effective learning opportunities for as many students as possible.

Beginning in Early Grades

It may be easier to achieve positive benefits in racially and ethnically diverse schools in earlier grades, when cross-cultural competencies are being developed and when achievement differences within student cohorts are relatively small (Cook, 1984; Crain, 1984; Mahard & Crain, 1983; St. John, 1975). Moreover, primary and elementary schools tend to be smaller, have smaller classes, have greater parent engagement, and provide curricula that allow students and teachers to develop more knowledge about one another. As students grow older, they increasingly choose to be with peers most like themselves (Brawarsky, 1996). In short, elementary schools, for various reasons, are the best place to create viable learning communities in diverse schools and to achieve the benefits therefrom. The lessons learned in lower grades, though, can be unlearned and usually need to be reinforced as students proceed through their stages of cognitive and social development.

Ensuring Diversity within Schools

There is considerable evidence that even when school populations are diverse, students within the school, and within classrooms, are often resegregated (Heck, Price, & S. L. Thomas, 2004; Mickelson, 2001; Oakes, 2005). Clearly, schools that adopt practices that result in the racial and ethnic resegregation of students reduce or largely eliminate the potential benefits of diverse learning opportunities. Racial and ethnic resegregation is never an explicit policy. However, because African American, Latino, and Native Alaskan and American Indian students, as well as some Asian students, are disproportionately low income and often score lower on tests of achievement than other students, policies and practices that are intended to focus resources on students with special needs often separate many students of color from their White peers in school. Moreover, there is evidence that non-White students are more likely to be placed in remedial classes than White students of similar tested ability (see Mickelson, 2001). The resegregation of students within schools is the product of four types of strategies: tracking, instructional (that is, "ability") grouping, pullout programs for students with special needs, and differential teaching practices that minimize cognitive demand on low-achieving students. While the distinction may break down in some cases where ability grouping and special programs lead to formal and informal tracking, it seems useful to examine these practices separately.

Tracking. Tracking groups students for instruction based on prior measures of their academic achievement and keeps students in the same groups over time and across subjects. (For an extensive review of the research on tracking, see Burris & Welner, this volume.) Tracking can be the result of formal school policies or, more often, is the consequence of actions by teachers and counselors, or decisions by students and their parents (Heck, Price, & S. L. Thomas, 2004; Yonezawa, Wells, & Serna, 2002; S. Lucas, 1999). For example, students who are struggling in school often select less demanding classes (R. F. Ferguson & Mehta, 2004, p. 663), and this self-tracking is acceded to, and often supported, by teachers and counselors. Two arguments that support tracking are: (1) it allows teachers to focus content on students' level of achievement; and (2) teachers who are unable to effectively teach in heterogeneous settings will better serve students they do teach when the students are in homogeneous groups.

There is some research that supports tracking, challenging the long-held consensus among researchers that the potential benefits of tracking are outweighed by the likely costs to most students (Figlio & M. Page, 2000; Loveless, 1998). Kulik (1992) concludes that when students in different tracks are taught with the same proficiency and matched with appropriate curricula, students at all levels of achievement benefit. The preponderance of research, however, suggests that tracking has negative consequences for lower-achieving students. For example, researchers have shown that (1) the performance level of a student's peers significantly affects student performance, especially for lower-achieving students and older students (Betts, Zau, & Rice, 2003; Hoxby, 2000); (2) students in lower-ability groups tend to be taught by less experienced and less qualified teachers (Oakes, Wells, M. Jones, & Datnow, 1997) and otherwise receive routinely inferior instruction (R. F. Ferguson & Mehta, 2004); (3) learning opportunities for students in lower-achieving groups are often "dumbed down" and do not provide the level of learning needed to be successful in college or in the workplace (Burris, Heubert, & Levin, 2004; Gamoran, Nystrand, Berends, & LaPore, 1995); and (4) students of color are more likely to be assigned to less demanding courses than their ability warrants (Mickelson, 2001).

The national Center on English Learning and Achievement (CELA) has succinctly summarized a common consequence of tracking:

> Because track assignments are usually determined by students' prior achievement and since prior achievement is usually associated with SES, students of higher SES are usually over-represented in the higher tracks, and students of lower SES in the lower tracks. And since instruction differs between the tracks in ways that privilege higher track students, the overall effect is to

widen the achievement gap between high and low performing students over time. (CELA, 2003, p. 3)

Two relatively recent reports by panels of prominent scholars conclude that tracking undermines the quality of education received by children in the lower tracks and does not help many other students (Heubert & Hauser, 1999; National Academy of Education, 1999). Hanushek and Wobmann (2005) studied international assessments of student performance and conclude that early tracking increases educational inequality and reduces mean achievement. Thus, while recognizing that students have different capabilities that need to be addressed, including students with exceptionally high academic achievement or truly unique abilities, it seems safe to say that tracking is a practice that usually does not benefit most students. There is research, however, that suggests that tracking benefits the highest-achieving students when the measure is performance on standardized tests (Heck, Price, & S. L. Thomas, 2004). It may be that higher-achieving students can achieve at least as well in heterogeneous classrooms as in tracked classes, but this probably requires that teachers employ a repertoire of instructional strategies that is not commonly in evidence. I return to these professional capabilities below.

Needs-based instructional grouping. Needs-based instruction groups students on the basis of past academic performance; it is commonly called ability grouping. The distinction between ability grouping and tracking I make here is the extent to which students learn in classes with students of similar prior achievement. Teachers overwhelmingly favor ability grouping that minimizes differences among students' current achievement levels (Wadsworth, 2004).

Ability grouping often turns into tracking, and some critics of tracking equate it with ability grouping. Because there is considerable agreement about the need for grouping students who face similar learning challenges for specific purposes and times, most often in literacy and mathematics, it is useful to define what is being discussed here as flexible needs-based instructional grouping. There are two main issues fueling considerable debate about how flexible needs-based grouping should be implemented: (1) how heterogeneous groups should be; and (2) if groups are homogeneous, how much time students should spend in such homogeneous groups. These issues apply when assigning students to classes, across classes, and within classrooms.

There are complex considerations related to needs-based grouping that should be addressed in order to maximize the learning of students. These include:

1. The students and faculty involved, the subject matter, and the resources—both human and material—to which schools have access affect the efficacy of any educational strategy, and this is surely the case with respect to needs-based grouping.
2. Outcomes other than scores on academic tests, which capture a small range of student learning, should be taken into account when evaluating the potential effects of an educational practice such as instructional grouping. Such other outcomes include student participation in high-demand curricula, attendance, and persistence in school.
3. Students learn many things in schools that aren't well assessed, if they are assessed at all. One of the most important of these may be the capability to learn with and from others, especially others who have different dispositions and experiences. In many cases groups and classes that are homogeneous in terms of academic performance may also be relatively homogeneous with respect to race and ethnicity. Students learning in racially and ethnically homogeneous groups will have less opportunity than other students to develop the knowledge and skills they will need to be successful in multicultural communities and workplaces (J. A. Banks et al., 2001; Hawley, 2003; Hawley et al., 1995; Laosa, 2002).

Students differ in their readiness to pursue particular learning objectives. Needs-based grouping based on prior achievement tests is a much used and sometimes necessary instructional strategy. Because needs-based grouping takes many forms and has many purposes, it is not possible to say that needs-based grouping does or does not work. Tests of the efficacy of grouping in promoting academically productive interracial and interethnic contact in diverse schools include:

1. Do such practices result in sorting students by race and ethnicity?
2. How specific and well defined are the learning needs being addressed?
3. How much of the school day do students find themselves learning with the same group?
4. Do the student groupings remain stable over time and from class to class?

Schools that fail these tests are, in effect, tracking students, and the justification for sorting students in order to accelerate their learning and the consequences are likely to be negative. Whatever decisions are made about instructional grouping within or across classes, educators and parents should, for each student, continually ask whether there is solid evidence that the practices being implemented benefit the students involved.

While the consensus among researchers supports flexible and varied approaches to needs-based instructional grouping, the fact that students influence the performance of their peers poses a dilemma for educators—and parents. Homogeneous grouping would seem to be in the interests of the most academically able students, at least with respect to academic performance, and to have negative consequences for lower-achieving students (Heck, Price, & S. L. Thomas, 2004). One way in which educators may address this dilemma is to engage in strategies such as differentiated instruction and make efforts to challenge all students to excel (Slavin, 1995b; Tomlinson, 2003; Burris & Welner, this volume). As noted earlier, not every teacher is prepared to implement a broad instructional repertoire.

Pullout programs. Like needs-based grouping, pullout programs come in many forms. For purposes here they are programs that take students out of their regular classroom for certain subjects, such as reading. In general, the available evidence is negative regarding pullout programs that have remedial purpose. The same tests that apply to needs-based grouping can be applied to these programs. Programs to meet the needs of English-language learners represent a particular challenge (Laosa, 2002). This may be especially true when employing bilingual education, which recent reviews of research suggest is the most effective approach to English-language learning (Slavin & Chueng, 2004; Rolstad, Mahoney & Glass, 2005).

Low-level instruction for low-achieving students. Most studies of tracking and ability grouping focus on students' experiences within academically homogeneous groups, but even within classes that are not formally grouped by ability, students may systematically receive different levels of instruction; low-achieving students predictably receive less sophisticated instruction and are expected to achieve at lower levels (Good, 1987). This not only affects achievement but it almost certainly discourages social interaction among students who have received different treatment from teachers.

Extracurricular Activities

Learning opportunities in schools include those provided by extracurricular activities—sports, clubs, band, etc. These opportunities may be more racially and ethnically heterogeneous than classrooms and be structured in ways that facilitate intergroup relationships (Brawarsky, 1996; Slavin, 1995b; Slavin & Madden, 1979). Care should be taken in structuring these activities so that they foster participation, collaboration, and teamwork among students from different racial and ethnic backgrounds (E. G. Cohen, 2004; Hawley et al., 1983, 1995).

Instructional Strategies and Curricula

The quality of teaching that students experience is the single most important determinant of the quality of education students receive (Darling-Hammond, 2000; Rice, 2003). Quality teaching in diverse classrooms would, among other things: clearly reflect high expectations for all students; embody academic rigor in a curriculum that involves students in authentic problem solving; draw out and work with the understandings and experiences that students bring to the classroom; engage some subject matter in depth, providing many examples of the same concept being applied and providing a strong base of factual knowledge; explicitly develop students' metacognitive skills; and develop language and literacy skills across the curriculum (P. A. Alexander & K. Murphy, 1998; Bransford, A. L. Brown, & Cocking, 2000; CREDE, 2002; Resnick, Levine, & Teasley, 1991).

Moreover, in order to take full advantage of the learning opportunities provided by diversity, instruction would need to involve students of different races and ethnicities in collaborative activities, paying attention to the importance of the difficult task of having each student make positive contributions to the learning of other students (E. G. Cohen, 1994, 2004).

There are a number of specific approaches to instruction that have been found to be successful in facilitating learning in diverse classrooms. These include cooperative learning, complex instruction, reciprocal teaching, peer tutoring, and differentiated instruction.[4]

These instructional strategies for effectively teaching students with different levels of achievement require high levels of teacher expertise and extensive opportunities for teacher learning. In a school with students of different races and ethnicities, teacher effectiveness will be enhanced by the teacher's deep understanding of students' backgrounds and the ability to use that knowledge to draw students into active learning and complex thinking (P. A. Alexander & K. Murphy, 1998; Hatano & Miyake, 1991; Ladson-Billings, 1995; Moll, Amanti, Neff, & Gonzalez, 1994). This involves more than knowing the general characteristics of students from different cultures. Indeed, the overgeneralization of cultural traits can lead to stereotyping of students and ineffective teaching (Hawley et al., 1995).

Many studies show the positive effects on social cognition of assigning students to interracial groups for instructional purposes (E. B. Aronson et al., 1978; Sørensen & Hallinan, 1985; Hallinan & Teixeira, 1987; Slavin, 1979, 1990, 1995a). Creating opportunities for individuals from different backgrounds to work together toward shared goals has been shown to produce positive outcomes, including increased cross-race friendships, more positive cross-race attitudes, and reduction of inter-ethnic conflict (Slavin, 1990). To maximize effectiveness groups must be structured so that shared goals could not be obtainable otherwise, all group members can make valuable contributions, and activities must be cooperative rather than competitive (E. G. Cohen, 1994, 2004; Pettigrew & Tropp, 2000), themes grounded in the seminal work of Gordon Allport (1954). As with any teaching strategy, the expertise of teachers and the appropriateness to particular contexts determine how well instructional techniques maximize the benefits of DLOs to facilitate student learning. If these strategies do not engage students in learning activities that embody most of the characteristics of effective instruction for diverse classrooms identified above, they are not likely to be very productive.

What students are taught is obviously important. Thousands of books and articles describe what a curriculum for a multicultural society should contain. Central themes of this curriculum work include the fair and accurate representation of the voices of different races and ethnic groups and the roles they have played in this and other societies, candid accounts of the history of discrimination experienced by different groups, and affirmation of the normative bases of tolerance (J. A. Banks & McGee-Banks, 2004; Nieto, 2001). Reviews of research on the efficacy of multicultural curricula indicate that they have mildly positive effects on attitudes and behavior, although assessments of behavioral change are often based on self-reports (C. W. Stephan, Renfro, & W. Stephan, 2004; W. G. Stephan & C. W. Stephan, 2004). What is quite clear is that students can be taught what they should do in their relationships with others. This is important, because if students can be helped to understand when their behavior is in conflict with widely held beliefs in a school or community—particularly when these beliefs are manifest in the behavior of student leaders, teachers, and administrators—the likelihood of positive behavioral change is high (Dovidio et al., 2004).

In addition to proposals for embedding multicultural values and content in the overall curriculum, there are hundreds of programs aimed specifically at improving intergroup relations, reducing prejudice, and resolving conflict among students. Most of these programs have not been rigorously evaluated, and only a handful specifically deal with the improvement of academic achievement. In addition to studies of cooperative learning (Cooper & Slavin, 2004), a notable exception to this observation is the AVID (Advancement Via Individual Determination) program (Mehan & Hubbard, 1999). The characteristics of effective race relations programs for schools have been identified by a panel convened for this purpose with the support of the Carnegie Corporation (Hawley et al., 1995), but these principles for program design are grounded on inferences derived from research rather than definitive evidence. In general, such programs do not focus on skill development, but those that provide for intergroup interactions, experiential learning, and intercultural competence are more effective than those that rely primarily on increasing information, empathy, and awareness. (For recent critical but sympathetic reviews of race relations programs for schools, see Aboud & Levy, 2000; Dovidio et al., 2004; C. W. Stephan, Renfro & W. Stephan, 2004; W. G. Stephan & C. W. Stephan 2004.)

It is important that schools seeking to achieve the benefits of diversity recognize that mixing students and teachers of different racial and ethnic backgrounds, in itself, provides no assurance of positive outcomes (Moody, 2001). In schools experiencing increased diversity, teachers and students may bring with them racial and ethnic prejudice and histories of discrimination that influence whether students benefit from DLOs. Thus it is important that well-conceived programs build understanding and intercultural competence and awareness, as well as anticipate and resolve conflict (P. T. Coleman & Deutsch, 1995). Moreover, as Dovidio and his colleagues (2004) assert, it is not sufficient to have a good program; programs must be targeted on the achievement of specific objectives that are related to the situation in each school and classroom.

Organizational Contexts That Support Learning among Diverse Students

Student learning in schools is shaped not only by what happens in particular classrooms but by the overall experiences that students have as they witness and engage in interactions with peers, teachers, school administrators, and staff throughout their school. School context or climate is not just the backdrop for student learning; it is both a source of, and a constraint on, learning in itself and a major influence on what happens in classrooms.

Research on the effectiveness of various interventions to improve intergroup attitudes, understanding, and behavior indicates that their effectiveness depends heavily on the overall organizational context in which these efforts are made (Dovidio et al., 2004; C. W. Stephan, Renfro, & W. Stephan, 2004). There is also significant research demonstrating that the organizational characteristics of schools influence students' academic achievement (Leithwood, Jantzi, & Steinbach, 1998; Smylie & Hart,

1999). Of particular interest to this report is the summary of research by the National Center on School Restructuring that focused on the characteristics of schools that promoted higher-order learning of all children (Newmann & Wehlage, 1995). These characteristics include:

- A shared vision of high standards for all students that includes learning to apply knowledge, disciplined inquiry, and relevance to the world beyond the school;
- Authentic pedagogy that requires students to think and develop in-depth understanding.
- A commitment among teachers and administrators to shared responsibility for student learning and to collaborative professional learning and action needed to promote student learning of high intellectual quality;
- Support from district offices, independent school improvement projects, parents, and the community.

There is no reason to believe that the conditions that support higher-order learning generally are different for schools with diverse learning opportunities.

Although there is no shortage of proposals specifying school characteristics that are especially important for schools serving diverse populations, most of these focus on equitable and just treatment and academic achievement and give little attention to the development of intercultural competence in racially and ethnically diverse schools. Two panels of scholars convened by the Common Destiny Alliance (J. A. Banks et al., 2001; Hawley et al., 1995) have reviewed relevant research and identified the following organizational conditions in schools as being particularly important for student learning in racially and ethnically diverse schools (cf. also Cushner, 2004):

- Policies and processes for fairly adjudicating school rules, perceived inequity and discrimination, and interpersonal conflicts.
- Instructional practices and curricula that promote positive interactions among students of different races and ethnicities in the context of cooperative, equal-status activities.
- A diverse school staff that continually reinforces, by word and deed, the importance to individuals, the school, and the society of intercultural collaboration.
- Schoolwide activities that examine similarities and differences across and within racial and ethnic groups, including differences related to

social class, gender, and language. Such activities should recognize the value of bicultural and multicultural identities of individuals in the school.

- Active engagement of families and community organizations with respect to issues and opportunities confronting the school.
- Continuing professional development driven by continuing efforts to discover whether the school's goals for all students are being met.

Moreover, understanding students' predispositions and ways of knowing and their personal histories requires knowledge of different cultures and strong analytical abilities. Certain practices in schools can help teachers know their students well. Such practices include "looping," so that teachers follow students from one grade to another; smaller schools; schools within schools; and "blocking" of subjects. These arrangements not only create opportunities for teachers to build their understanding of students but they give students opportunities to know one another better.

Continuing professional development is important to teacher effectiveness in all schools, but it is particularly important in schools with high levels of student diversity. The reasons for this are that diversity presents teachers with particular challenges, and, as noted earlier, effective teaching requires the mastery of a broad range of instructional strategies and knowledge that teachers share with one another. What is needed here is more than a heavier dose of college courses and workshops (Knapp, McCaffrey, & J. Swanson, 2003; Valli & Hawley, 2002). Professional learning should be linked to program coherence and to meeting specific challenges that are identified by the continuous analysis of student performance with particular concern for differences in learning and behavior among students of different races and ethnicities. Significant professional interaction among teachers facilitates the sharing of knowledge about how best to meet students' needs.

School conditions like these, taken together, create and sustain the culture of the school—the shared expectations and values that shape the behavior of students and school personnel.

Fostering Effective School Leadership

Those who observe diverse schools that effectively nurture the development of all students commonly emphasize the importance of effective leadership, especially the actions of school principals. Almost all of the organizational conditions that foster DLOs (discussed earlier) provide an agenda for action by school leaders.

Principals need to examine their own beliefs and understandings related to racial differences and consider how best to enhance the capabilities of staff and students. (See Weissglass, 2003, for a list of questions leaders can ask themselves.) They need to know, for example, that biological differences among people of different races are virtually nonexistent; changes in behavior may lead to changes in attitudes more effectively than changes in attitude lead to more appropriate behavior; even people of good will may harbor subtle prejudices or lack the skills to interact productively with people whose ethnicity or skin color is different from their own; and efforts to improve race by changing textbooks or other learning materials or sensitizing students to the strengths and unique characteristics of different cultures are not likely, by themselves, to be very effective (Aboud & Levy, 2000; National Research Council, 2004).

School leaders must be aware of what McKenzie and Scheurich (2003) call "equity traps." Equity traps include the desire among educators to believe that discrimination is a thing of the past and the related belief that interactions with and among students should be color-blind. Such beliefs undermine educators' abilities to diagnose existing and potential sources of student misbehavior, disengagement, and underperformance. Another form of equity trap is well-intentioned stereotyping (never called that, of course) that is sometimes employed to deal with the complexity of racial and ethnic differences while being "culturally responsive" to students. Even some advocates for cultural sensitivity inadvertently overgeneralize about the dispositions and needs of people of color (e.g., "When teaching Latino students, pay attention to . . ."). Further defining the achievement gap in racial and ethnic terms reinforces negative stereotypes while masking the more powerful impact of poverty on achievement and the substantial variations in achievement within Black, Hispanic, and other minority groups of students. For example, pointing to Asian Americans as "the model minority" diminishes attention to the learning needs of many Asian American students who are not doing well in schools (Coalition for Asian American Children and Families, 2004).

Dealing with race relations in schools is hard work and can, initially, raise issues that are stressful and even produce conflict. In the absence of severe cases of interracial conflict, some educators would like to believe that "race is not an issue here." For example, students are twice as likely to say that conflict and tensions exist among students of different races than are teachers (Reid, 2004). However, school principals and teacher leaders can foster conditions in schools and can act in ways that simultaneously improve intergroup relations, hold student diversity as an opportunity for learning, reduce problem behavior, and improve academic performance (J. A. Banks et al., 2001; Hawley et al., 1995; Henze, 2000; Lindsey, Robins, & Terrell, 2003; Schofield, 2004; Weissglass, 2003). Intergroup relations can be improved in the following ways:

- Articulating relevant values and goals and modeling appropriate behaviors.
- Facilitating teacher and student learning in a way that enhances intercultural proficiency (e.g., by understanding the nature and consequences of stereotyping and developing the social skills that are particularly important in intergroup interactions).
- Organizing instruction that maximizes the opportunities of students of all races and ethnicities to learn with and from one another (such as cooperative learning, differentiated instruction, peer tutoring, reciprocal teaching, complex instruction, and flexible ability grouping).
- Monitoring information about student achievement, student discipline, and the composition of both informal and formal learning settings, including extracurricular activities, in order to identify programs and practices that might need improvement in order to maximize the benefits of student diversity.
- While respecting and nurturing students' cultural identities (which students, not others, define), focusing on shared values (e.g., justice and equality), and creating or drawing attention to groups and activities that cut across race and ethnic "lines."
- Making efforts to improve race and ethnic relations integral to the overall mission of the school to enhance student learning. Issues and opportunities related to race and ethnic differences and similarities cannot be effectively dealt with if they are compartmentalized in the curriculum or in particular student groups.
- Addressing issues of intergroup conflict immediately and openly and, in general, promoting discussions of potentially conflictual issues (such as the meaning of self-segregation by racial and ethnic groups).
- Continually sensitizing the school community to the importance of positive intergroup interactions by drawing attention to such issues and rewarding positive practices and discouraging negative ones.

Conclusion

Research Priorities

There appears to be growing agreement among researchers that the opportunity to learn with and from people from different racial and ethnic backgrounds can, under the right conditions, enhance students' academic achievement and cognitive development, increase cross-cultural competence, and promote positive dispositions and behaviors that will have economic and social consequences for individuals and communities. This belief is built upon theories grounded in a large number of studies of learning and group behavior in different contexts. However, research that directly links learning in diverse schools to both intercultural competence and academic achievement—both long-term and short-term—is not extensive, and much of this research was conducted many years ago and deals largely with Black-White relationships. Furthermore, aside from the studies of various forms of cooperative learning, the available research seldom says much about the efficacy of different instructional strategies for bringing about positive outcomes in diverse schools.

If new research is to affect policy and practice in significant ways it will have to be methodologically rigorous and address the following concerns, among others: (1) What are the costs and benefits to students and to society of creating more schools that maximize DLOs? (2) What are the conditions in schools and communities that affect the nature and extent of the consequences of DLOs? (3) What is the relative effectiveness of maximizing DLOs as compared to other strategies for attaining similar outcomes in homogeneous schools and classrooms?

It is important to document the benefits of DLOs. It is also important to know the costs of discrimination and underachievement to the victims of discrimination. Despite obvious progress in reducing prejudice and discrimination—a reality that leads many to argue for other priorities—discrimination and its consequences remain pervasive. The wage gap between racial and ethnic groups is large, persistent, and not diminishing (D. Reed & J. Cheng, 2003), and the large differences in the academic performance of Whites on the one hand and Latinos, American Indians, and African Americans on the other are well known. But the extent to which prejudicial stereotyping and discrimination account for these inequalities needs to be documented and publicly understood.

The Importance of Diverse Learning Opportunities

Prejudicial dispositions and the absence of intercultural competence reinforce one another. The beliefs and actions that are the product of these personal characteristics directly or indirectly affect almost everyone in the United States.

Racial and ethnic discrimination and the related characterizations of others' inadequacy lead to a number of negative consequences for the victims. These often include low academic achievement, diminished self-confidence, disengagement from school, unemployment or underemployment, and alienation from so-called mainstream society. These outcomes, and others, deny opportunities to learn, undermine motivation to achieve in school and at work, and result in low income. Low achievement and underdeveloped intellectual capabilities of the victims of prejudice and discrimination, in turn, feed racial and ethnic stereotypes.

Those who stereotype others and engage in discriminatory behavior reduce their own opportunities to learn. First, they avoid DLOs (in schools and elsewhere) and deny themselves the potential benefits thereof. Second, when they do interact with persons of different racial and ethnic backgrounds than their own, they do not know how to make effective use of those opportunities. Third, when persons who are the traditional victims of prejudice and discrimination perceive the absence of intercultural competence, they withhold the exchanges that would enrich the learning of everyone involved. When persons who are the usual victims of racial and ethnic discrimination act to protect themselves from those who would discriminate against them, this defensive behavior is often interpreted as justification for avoiding intercultural contact (Cross, 1995).

Given the increasing ethnic and racial diversity of the nation and ever-expanding globalization, the incentives have increased for becoming more competent in collaborative problem solving that involves people of different racial and ethnic backgrounds. Likewise, reducing the social and psychological barriers that limit opportunities for persons of color is both a moral and a social imperative in which everyone has a stake. Given these realities, and the increasing racial segregation of our schools, it is striking that strategies to promote the incidence of diverse learning opportunities receive so little attention by policymakers, educators, and the rest of us. The contemporary professional literature and public discourse on school improvement is markedly absent of commentary on the potential benefits of DLOs, much less strategies to secure and make good use of them.

Significantly increasing the number of students who can benefit from DLOs will be hard and steady work for everyone involved and, in many contexts, will appear to conflict with other needs and values. However, if we do not actively seek to use education as a way to improve racial and ethnic relations and intercultural competencies, we will, indeed, be a nation at risk. Our willingness to pursue this challenge will depend on how we assess the costs and benefits of meeting it. Research on the benefits of DLOs, testimonials from those who experience DLOs, and endorsements of policies that support DLOs by business, civic, and religious leaders will motivate parents, educators, policymakers, and judges to take needed action.

Notes

My thanks for Jomills Braddock, Melanie Killen, Jeffrey Milem, Gary Orfield, and Janet Schofield, who most generously shared their ideas about this essay with me.

1. Social and behavioral scientists agree that the concept of race has little biological base and is, instead, "a social construct" (National Research Council, 2004). Nonetheless, "race" is used widely to describe differences in skin color and, sometimes, ethnicity. There does not appear to be another term that can readily substitute for most people's understanding, however vague, of what "race" means.

2. The conclusions in the first section of this essay are based on syntheses of research by the author and others. See Aboud & Levy, 2000; Braddock & Eitle, 2004; Bransford, A. L. Brown, & Cocking, 2000; Hawley, 2003, 1992; Pettigrew, 2003; Schofield, 2004; W. G. Stephan & C. W. Stephan, 2004; C. W. Stephan, Renfro, & W. Stephan, 2004. I cite some research not included in these reviews but otherwise do not reference particular studies.

3. Ludwig, Ladd, & Duncan (2001) caution that teens who moved to integrated schools and neighborhoods as a result of housing vouchers, while they benefited in some ways, were more likely than their segregated peers to be retained and disciplined and were more likely to drop out of school. Whether this is because they were unprepared for the more rigorous schools to which they moved or because the schools were not responsive to their needs cannot be determined from the available evidence.

4. Four of the strategies listed here are effective in racially and ethnically homogeneous classrooms, but they offer particular opportunities to foster both high academic achievement and the development of intercultural competence and understanding in diverse learning environments. Cooperative learning takes many forms, and its efficacy, when effectively implemented, is well documented (Cooper & Slavin, 2004). Peer tutoring can also take many forms but involves structured and teacher-supervised interactions among students focused on particular learning objectives. The What Works Clearinghouse (2006) has recently reviewed numerous studies and concluded that peer tutoring is usually effective. In its endorsement, a National Research Council panel describes reciprocal teaching as providing "guided practice in the use of four strategies (predicting, question generating, summarizing, and clarifying) that are designed to enhance children's ability to construct the meaning of text" (Snow, Burns, & Griffin, 1998, p. 221). "Differentiated instruction" is a more generic term that could encompass each of the three strategies just discussed. According to the Educational Research Service (2003), "It [differentiated instruction] promotes a challenging curriculum for all students but varies the level of teacher support, task complexity, pacing and avenues for learning based on each student's readiness, interest and learning profile" (p. 1; see also Tomlinson, 2003). Complex instruction was developed by Elizabeth Cohen and her

colleagues to deal with the likelihood that racially and ethnically heterogeneous groups will involve students with different levels of achievement and different habits of interaction in groups (E. G. Cohen, 2004). It involves the teacher presenting students with complex tasks that will draw on the multiple abilities of the different students in the learning group. Teachers foster interaction and problem solving while giving students considerable autonomy.

The Social Developmental Benefits of Intergroup Contact among Children and Adolescents

Melanie Killen, David S. Crystal, and Martin Ruck

What are the social developmental benefits of intergroup contact for children and adolescents attending ethnically heterogeneous and homogeneous schools? We are developmental psychologists who have been investigating how children's and adolescents' evaluations of racial exclusion and their perceptions of racial discrimination are influenced by their social experiences, which include interactions with members of other racial and ethnic groups and school environments (referred to as "intergroup contact"). Our research findings indicate that there are compelling short- and long-term educational benefits that result from interactions with others who are from different racial and ethnic backgrounds. When particular conditions are met, learning in a racially diverse, integrated educational environment will have significant social and social-cognitive benefits for all students, and particularly so at the younger ages.

In general, we theorize that being educated in heterogeneous school environments enables children and adolescents to become more sensitive to and better able to recognize and understand the effects of exclusion and discrimination on others. This is because social cognition and analytic skills facilitate young people's capacities to make judgments and decisions about fairness, rights, and justice and to avoid acting on stereotypes. Further, these abilities enable students to learn to appreciate and respect racial differences, overcome racial stereotypes, avoid scapegoating, prevent racial hatreds and fears, and develop positive racial attitudes.

How are these connections made, and what is the empirical evidence to support these claims? This essay draws on existing empirical findings from three distinct, but overlapping, areas of investigation: the school desegregation literature (Kurlaender & Yun, 2001; G. Orfield, 2001; W. G. Stephan, 2002); the social psychology literature on prejudice, racism, and intergroup contact (Dovidio & Gaertner, 1986; Gaertner & Dovidio, 1986); and the social developmental psychology literature on social reasoning about exclusion, perceptions of discrimination, and attitudes about social experience (Killen, Lee-Kim, McGlothlin, & Stangor, 2002). It is our position that through children's development they become able to apply social judgments to decisions that arise in their everyday social interactions with peers (Killen & Hart, 1995; Killen & Nucci, 1995) and that these types of peer experiences become the foundation of their social knowledge and social cognition. Experiences with children from different ethnic and racial backgrounds are an important part of this foundation.

In this essay we report findings using multiple measures to assess children's and adolescents' racial attitudes. Further, we include data collected from students attending racially homogeneous and heterogeneous public schools in the Maryland and Virginia suburbs of Washington, D.C. These schools were middle income and reflected a range of homogeneous (European American) and heterogeneous (European American, African American, Latin American, and Asian American) ethnic backgrounds. Our measures included students' perceptions of the school environment, their self-reported intergroup contact, and their perceptions and judgments about social exclusion in peer contexts.

From our viewpoint it is important that children's critical thinking and social reasoning skills about the importance of racial and ethnic diversity and tolerance be encouraged to develop prior to adolescence. By middle school, cliques are often based on racial and ethnic identity, and group identity has an increasingly important effect on attitudes and behavior. Thus if we are to reduce racial, ethnic, and gender stereotyping in our culture, it has to happen in childhood, before discriminatory attitudes are firmly entrenched in an individual's social knowledge and concepts (Aboud & Levy, 2000). Social psychological research has shown that stereotypes are hard to change in adulthood (Macrae, Stangor, & Hewstone, 1996). Even an explicit desire to change one's own stereotypes is quite difficult due to the years of formulating such attitudes (Stangor & Schaller, 1996). In adulthood, stereotypes become implicit and subconscious such that even individuals who hold egalitarian principles demonstrate implicit biases developed over years of reinforcement from a society in which stereotypical representations of individuals based on group membership are still apparent and salient (Dovidio & Gaertner, 1986; Gaertner & Dovidio, 1986).

School Desegregation Findings

The 1954 *Brown v. Board of Education* ruling began the process of dismantling state-imposed school segregation in the United States. One important basis of the decision was that school segregation resulted in prejudicial attitudes in European American students and low self-esteem in African American students (W. G. Stephan, 2002). Thus the psychological evidence was key to understanding what made segregation wrong and therefore illegal. In the years that followed, researchers examined the short- and long-term benefits on intergroup relationships of attending desegregated schools, looking for the positive psychological benefits of undoing segregated school environments (for a review, see W. G. Stephan, 2002). Typically, psychologically oriented studies conducted in the 1970s and 1980s compared European American attitudes toward African Americans (positive or negative) as a function of attending a desegregated or segregated school. As Stephan (2002) describes, however, the findings on the short-term benefits were mixed, with more positive findings for the long-term benefits. He pointed to a number of limitations with the short-term studies, though, which included a lack of differentiation for the age of the children studied, confounds between race and socioeconomic status (SES), and, importantly, the fact that of the conditions that are necessary for intergroup contact to reduce prejudice, few were in place.

In his review of the literature, Stephan pointed out that the initial mixed findings were not surprising given intergroup contact theory. Allport's (1954) classic intergroup contact theory stated that four optimal conditions must be met for contact to reduce prejudice: (1) equal status among individuals, (2) common goals, (3) intergroup cooperation, and (4) support of authorities, law, or custom. "Equal status" refers to equal group status within the situation. "Common goals" refers to the notion that different groups need a common goal to achieve reduced prejudice, such as found in interracial sports teams, in which the goal of winning serves to reduce racial prejudice within the group. "Intergroup cooperation" has to do with an emphasis on cooperation, not competition. "Support of authorities, law, or custom" suggests—at least in the context of schools—that powerful figures such as administrators and teachers agree with the goals of integration and lend their moral and practical authority to the effort to reduce prejudice. Yet few mandatory desegregated school systems met these criteria, and few studies examined the extent to which these conditions were met in the schools. For example, many of the principals, teachers, and parents in the school districts studied were not supportive of the goals of desegregation, and this undermined the chances for positive benefits of intergroup contact (W. G. Stephan, 2002). Stephan noted that the long-term positive benefits were stronger and more extensive than the short-term benefits, such as improved academic achievement and aspirations. Students who attended desegregated schools were more likely than students in segregated schools to be comfortable in a diverse workforce, have friends from different ethnic backgrounds in adulthood, and marry someone of another race or ethnicity (see Braddock & McPartland, 1989).

From our viewpoint a major limitation of the school desegregation studies, and particularly the studies on short-term effects of desegregated experiences, resulted from how racial and intergroup attitudes were measured. In most of the school desegregation studies, assessments of racial attitudes were very broad and not developmentally appropriate or sensitive. For example, in many studies, assessments were based on the Preschool Racial Attitudes Measure (J. E. Williams et al., 1975). In the Preschool Racial Attitudes Measure, children are asked to assign traits (good, bad) to pictures representing White and Black children, which has the problematic confound of ingroup bias and outgroup negativity. Ingroup bias (assigning positive traits to one's own group) is not the same as outgroup negativity (disliking someone of the outgroup, that is, people of different ethnic and racial backgrounds). A number of recent reviews of research on racial attitudes have said that these types of measures conflate ingroup bias and outgroup negativity. This is because when asked to assign a negative trait to someone who either (a) looks like you or (b) does not look like you, most individuals will assign the trait to the outgroup, mostly to avoid associating the negative trait with the self, regardless of positive or negative feelings about an outgroup member (see Rutland, 2004). Thus ingroup bias and outgroup negativity are not equivalent. Yet many of the early assessments of racial attitudes employed techniques with this type of limitation (among others), which cast doubt on the interpretations of the findings.

More recently, methodologies have evolved to more closely assess how racial attitudes function in children's everyday social exchanges, which has revealed the multiple aspects of racial attitudes (Killen, Lee-Kim, McGlothlin, & Stangor, 2002; Killen, Margie, & Sinno, 2006; Levy, 1999; Rutland, 2004; McGlothlin & Killen, 2006). These assessments tap the range and complexity of racial judgments and provide for more comprehensive portrayals of how children view the concept of race. Thus these assessments more closely match the actual intergroup contexts that children encounter and avoid the methodological weaknesses of trait-assignment measures. Yet these measures have not been examined in relation to students' intergroup contact experiences, particularly experiences with members of outgroups. Further, along with direct assessments of children's judgments and social reasoning, indirect measures have been constructed to assess the ways in which children's implicit biases are revealed (Baron & Banaji, 2005; Margie, Killen, Sinno, & McGlothlin,

2005; McGlothlin, Killen, & Edmonds, 2005; Rutland, 2004). Thus to fully assess the impact of attending integrated school environments, it is essential that the evaluative measurements analyze children's perceptions of intergroup contact and how children make social judgments involving others who are different from them.

Another important issue from our viewpoint is that little of the school desegregation psychological research has examined age-related differences in children's thinking. Yet there are striking changes that take place from six to eighteen years of age regarding social understanding about race and ethnicity. To capture developmental differences in race-related social cognitions requires assessments of individual children's perceptions of intergroup contact and discrimination at different age periods, from childhood through adolescence. It is also important to consider how individual children perceive the social context and social interactions within a desegregated or segregated school.

Gary Orfield, accompanied by his research team at The Civil Rights Project at Harvard University, is one of the leaders of research on how to assess the variability of school environments (Kurlaender & Yun, 2001; G. Orfield, 2001; Yun & Kurlaender, 2004). The Civil Rights Project team has surveyed adolescents in a wide range of high schools to assess students' perceptions of how much diversity their schools encourage and sanction, as well as their perceptions of their comfort level in working with others from different racial backgrounds. The team's findings indicate that students in desegregated schools have more positive attitudes toward members of other racial groups than do children attending homogeneous schools (see Kurlaender & Yun, 2001, for recent findings). This research has also revealed that over the past fifteen years, U.S. schools have become increasingly segregated, which effectively diminishes students' opportunities for cross-race friendships and experiences in diverse learning environments. Clearly, children's and adolescents' experiences with diversity and intergroup contact have different outcomes at different points in their development, and this must be taken into account when assessing the impact of desegregation on attitudes about race and ethnicity. The Civil Rights Project research has generated extensive measures about intergroup contact that enable developmental researchers to more closely examine how social experience influences children's social development.

Social Psychological Concepts

Social psychology research has provided a plethora of information on intergroup relationships, stereotypes, prejudice, social identity, and

ingroup/outgroup perceptions. This work has demonstrated that social beliefs (stereotypes) influence attitudes and intergroup relationships (Dovidio & Gaertner, 1986; Gaertner & Dovidio, 1986; Hamilton & Sherman, 1994; Fiske, 1998; Leyens, Yzerbyt, & Schadron, 1994;
Mackie, Hamilton, Susskind, & Rosselli, 1996; Macrae, Stangor, &
Hewstone, 1996; Abrams, Hogg, & Marques, 2005). Stereotypes are defined as overgeneralizations about social groups that take the form of
attributions or beliefs about individuals, and that do not take into account individual variation within the group (see Mackie, Stangor, &
Hewstone, 1996; Stangor & Schaller, 1996). These beliefs reflect cognitive structures that contain an individual's perception of knowledge,
beliefs, and expectations about social groups (see Macrae, Stangor, &
Hewstone, 1996). Recently social psychologists have also studied the
mechanisms and strategies that contribute to the reduction of prejudice
and discrimination (see Oskamp, 2000). These studies have revealed that
while changing prejudiced attitudes is very difficult (Devine, Plant, &
Boswell, 2000; Hamilton & Sherman, 1994), progress can be demonstrated in certain conditions involving intergroup contact (Pettigrew &
Tropp, 2000), heightened interdependence among members of different
groups (Fiske, 2000), and the experience of multiple (bicultural) identities (M. B. Brewer, 2000). These models and findings provide a basis for
investigating social reasoning about intergroup relationships in childhood and adolescence. Given our space constraints, we will concentrate
on findings from the intergroup contact hypothesis, which has generated
several decades of research.

Allport's (1954) theory on intergroup contact has been validated in a
number of recent meta-analyses indicating that intergroup contact reduces prejudice (Aboud & Amato, 2001; Pettigrew & Tropp, 2000). Pettigrew and Tropp's (2000) meta-analysis of intergroup contact revealed
that cross-race friendship is one of the best predictors of prejudice reduction. To some extent intergroup conditions can be interpreted as involving both peer (common goals, equal status) and authority (authority
sanctioning) dimensions. Overall, few studies on the contact hypothesis
have focused on school-age children. Yet intergroup contact is an important qualitative measure of children's experiences, and it provides a way
of examining what it is about heterogeneous and homogeneous school
environments that may be beneficial for promoting positive racial attitudes. Children who attend heterogeneous schools may, in fact, have little
intergroup contact due to intraschool tracking, where students are placed
in groups or classes of matched ability. Not surprisingly, school tracking
perpetuates existing racial and social class differences. Conversely, chil-

dren who attend homogeneous schools may have a moderate amount of intergroup contact outside of the school context. While these are hypothetical cases, the point remains that measuring students' perceptions of intergroup contact provides a more detailed examination of the nature and quality of the social experiences that may lead to positive intergroup attitudes than would a more global focus on homogeneous or heterogeneous school environments.

We now turn to the developmental literature that has provided the theoretical framework for our approach to social reasoning and stereotyping in childhood and adolescence.

Developmental Research on Intergroup Bias and Social Knowledge

Children's Stereotype Knowledge

A fair amount of research has been conducted on children's stereotypical thinking. Research on children's stereotyped knowledge indicates that children begin recognizing and thinking about stereotypical expectations as early as the preschool years (Aboud, 1992; Bigler & Liben, 1992; D. Ruble & C. Martin, 1998). This includes children in North America (D. Ruble & C. Martin, 1998), Europe (see M. Bennett, Barrett, Lyons, & Sani, 1998; Cairns, 1989), and the Middle East (see Bar-Tal, 1996; C. Cole et al., 2003). Most of this evidence is based on either information processing models (C. L. Martin & Halverson, 1981; Stangor & D. N. Ruble, 1989), which examine how children process information before making a decision; cognitive-developmental approaches (Aboud, 1988, 1992; Bigler & Liben, 1992; Liben & Bigler, 2002), which examine stage-related aspects of development; or developmental social-cognitive models (D. B. Carter & Patterson, 1982; Killen & Stangor, 2001; Stoddart & Turiel, 1985), which focus on the forms of social and moral reasoning categories that are applied by individuals to their evaluations of stereotyping. While all three models have generated much research, we will focus on research from developmental social cognition, which has guided our work on children's and adolescents' evaluations of racial exclusion.

Racial stereotypes and stereotypes about members of other cultures emerge during the preschool and elementary school years (Aboud, 1992; Bar-Tal, 1996; Fisher, Jackson, & Villarruel, 1998); some measures indicate preschool awareness, whereas other indices suggest that this knowledge emerges later. Many studies have demonstrated that stereotypes influence children's memory and other social-cognitive abilities (e.g., D. B.

Carter & Patterson, 1982; Kuhn, Nash, & Brucken, 1978; Liben & Signo-rella, 1993; C. L. Martin & Halverson, 1981). Specifically, these studies have found that children have a better memory for information that is consistent with their stereotypes than for information that is inconsistent with stereotypes. This has been shown with studies of preschoolers, for example, in which children exhibited poorer memory for information that was inconsistent with racial stereotypes (Bigler & Liben, 1993). In the area of children's prejudice, Aboud's (1988, 1992) work suggests that cognitive limitations of young children make them more likely than older children to judge different races in a biased way. More recently, research-ers have examined other indices of prejudice, ones that focus more specif-ically on intergroup processes, such as perceptions of within-group vari-ability (e.g., differences among African Americans) and between-group variability (e.g., differences between African Americans and European Americans) (Bigler, L. S. Jones, & Lobliner, 1997). In general, researchers have argued that intergroup processes, such as ingroup/outgroup biases, are important components of prejudice and stereotyping (Bigler, L. S. Jones, & Lobliner, 1997; Powlishta, 1995).

Thus there is sufficient evidence to indicate that children have stereo-types about others based on race. Yet little is known about whether chil-dren use their stereotypical knowledge to make decisions about others in morally relevant situations. For example, do children use stereotypical knowledge to deprive others of resources or to exclude someone from a group activity? The few studies conducted on this question have shown that in straightforward situations, children and adolescents do not use stereotypical knowledge; yet in complex or ambiguous situations, stereo-types seem to influence decisions involving fairness and rights (Killen & Stangor, 2001). This distinction supports findings with adults by Dovidio and his colleagues (Gaertner & Dovidio, 1986).

Children's Social and Moral Knowledge

At the same time that children are acquiring stereotypes about others, children are also developing concepts about fairness, equality, and rights. Research using a social-cognitive domain model, which proposes that in-dividuals apply different types of reasoning across a range of situations, has found that children differentiate rules involving fairness and equality from rules about social conventions, regulations, and rituals (see Killen, 1991; Smetana, 1995; Tisak, 1995; Turiel, 1983, 1998; Turiel, Killen, & Helwig, 1987, for reviews). This work has been based, for the most part, on prototypic acts, such as straightforward moral transgressions (e.g., un-provoked harm and the denial of resources) and straightforward social-conventional transgressions (e.g., wearing inappropriate dress, driving on the wrong side of the road). Researchers have also examined how individuals evaluate complex and multifaceted phenomena, such as rights, drug use, and tolerance for others (see Ruck, Abramovitch, & Keating, 1998; Turiel, Hildebrandt, & Wainryb, 1985). These studies have shown that individuals use multiple forms of reasoning to evaluate complex phenomena. Based on this work we have proposed that exclusion is a multifaceted phenomenon, one that invokes moral, social-conventional, and psychological reasoning (see Killen & Stangor, 2001). Moreover, social psychologists studying exclusion in adult populations have documented the severe moral consequences of exclusion (e.g., genocide) when conducted on a wide scale (see Opotow, 1990).

Very few studies have used the social-cognitive domain model to examine how knowledge about intergroup relationships affects children's social and moral reasoning. Until recently it has not been known how children evaluate morally relevant decisions (e.g., deciding whether to exclude an individual) among children who belong to different social groups, such as those based on race and ethnicity (see Killen, Lee-Kim, McGlothlin, & Stangor, 2002).

Judgments about Exclusion

One of the findings from a prior study on evaluations of exclusion from social groups (Killen, Lee-Kim, McGlothlin, & Stangor, 2002) was that children and adolescents more readily justified gender exclusion (e.g., a boy not wanting to be friends with a child who is a girl) than racial exclusion (e.g., a boy not wanting to be friends with a child who is Black). The vast majority of children studied viewed racial exclusion as wrong and based their judgment on moral reasons (such as unfairness). Our scenarios were quite direct and did not require participants to consider competing elements of information in addition to the race/ethnicity of the target. Thus in our previous work the situations' unambiguous nature involving racial exclusion (e.g., a Black child is excluded from attending school, excluded as a potential friend, excluded from joining a club) generated a "ceiling effect," whereby the clear majority of participants judged such exclusion to be wrong. Our new line of work examines social reasoning in regard to more complex situations of race-based exclusion and systematically assesses students' perceptions of intergroup contact and social experience.

Social Reasoning and Intergroup Contact

On the basis of our previous findings, we are conducting a new set of studies to use more indirect methods to assess racial exclusion. One way that our protocol is more indirect is that, in addition to assessing students' evaluations of exclusion, we also measure when and whether children and adolescents focus on race-based—in contrast to non-race-based—reasons for exclusion (both are provided in the scenarios). In addition, we assess participants' evaluations of group functioning and their views regarding the obligations of bystanders to do something about racial exclusion. These changes were made based on current social psychological research, which has shown that while explicit racial prejudice has dramatically decreased in the past fifty years, implicit racial biases remain quite prevalent (Dovidio, Kawakami, & Beach, 2001; Gaertner & Dovidio, 1986). We were particularly interested in documenting age-related differences regarding our assessments of racial exclusion, in addition to how the ethnicity of the participant influences evaluations of, and social reasoning about, exclusion.

The Current Project

In our currently funded National Institute of Child Health and Human Development (NICHD) project, we are investigating children's and adolescents' evaluations of racial exclusion for three contexts: friendship, sleepover, and a school dance. We interviewed students in two types of school systems: racially/ethnically heterogeneous and racially/ethnically homogeneous. We interviewed students at three grade levels (fourth, seventh, and tenth) and assessed the links between intergroup contact and judgments about exclusion.

This investigation examines individual children's social judgments, perceptions, and experiences. This was not the case with the school desegregation analyses, which formed the basis for most of the prior research on the intergroup contact hypothesis in children (see Pettigrew, 1998; W. G. Stephan, 2002). Further, we have charted the developmental course of the connection between social judgments and intergroup contact by including children and adolescents in our project. Students participated in thirty-minute, one-on-one interviews with a trained interviewer and then filled out a survey on their attitudes and judgments about intergroup relationships.

Participants were 685 children and adolescents in fourth, seventh, and tenth grades, attending thirteen public schools in the Maryland and Virginia suburbs of Washington, D.C. In one school district (School District A; 343 students interviewed), students were enrolled in homogeneously European American schools; in the second school district (School District B; 342 students interviewed), students were enrolled in racially/ethnically heterogeneous schools. For the sample from School District A, the ethnic breakdown overall was 75 percent majority group members (that is, European American) and 25 percent minority group members (11 percent Asian American, 3 percent African American, 3 percent Latino/Latina, 8 percent other). In School District B, 46 percent of the sample was European American and 54 percent minority (25 percent African American, 13 percent Asian American, 8 percent Latino/Latina, 8 percent other). The sample was relatively evenly divided by gender for each ethnic group. Students in both districts were from middle-income to middle-low-income backgrounds as assessed by school records.

Comparisons between Heterogeneous and Homogeneous Schools

Attitudes about Diversity

We first looked at whether there were differences between students in heterogeneous and homogeneous schools on twelve items taken from the Diversity Assessment Questionnaire (DAQ) (Kurlaender & Yun, 2001), as listed in the appendix. These questions included inquiries about whether teachers fostered inclusion (e.g., "My teacher encourages me to work with students of other racial/ethnic backgrounds"), whether students had friends and neighbors from different ethnic and racial backgrounds (e.g., "Outside of school do you have friends who are from a different racial/ ethnic group than you?"), and students' general comfort level interacting with students from other racial and ethnic groups (that is, intergroup relations) (e.g., "How comfortable would you be working with students from different racial/ethnic backgrounds on group projects?"). Answers from students in Districts A and B were significantly different on eleven of the twelve DAQ items: for all eleven items, students in heterogeneous schools had significantly more positive attitudes toward racial and ethnic diversity than their counterparts in homogeneous schools. These aspects of diversity included, but were not limited to, racial/ethnic composition of the schools, classroom discussions of racial issues, other-race friends at school, and interracial dating among schoolmates.

Intergroup Contact

Next we conducted analyses to determine which factors on the DAQ were highly correlated and would provide an intergroup contact score for our analyses. The frequencies and percentages for intergroup contact scores are depicted in table 1.

The intergroup contact score was based on six DAQ items that were identified as grouping together using statistical procedures (specifically, factor analysis analytic techniques). These six items were as follows: (1) How many students in your school are from racial or ethnic groups different from your own? (2) How often do you work on school projects and/or study with students from other racial or ethnic groups? (3) At school how many friends do you have who are from a different racial or ethnic group than you? (4) Outside of school how many friends do you have who are from a different racial or ethnic group than you? (5) In the neighborhood where you live do you have neighbors from other racial or ethnic backgrounds? (6) How many of your friends from your neighborhood are from a different racial or ethnic group than you? Using a four-point rating scale—responses ranged from one ("none") to four ("many")—we then created a "high" versus "low" intergroup contact variable. This variable served as our chief independent predictor to determine whether students' moral and social reasoning about racial exclusion was influenced by their intergroup contact.

Social Reasoning about Exclusion

Interviewers read three stories, each representing a different context in which racial exclusion might have occurred (for each story there were multiple potential reasons for exclusion, including race, because the main protagonists were of different ethnic backgrounds, and other differences, such as a lack of shared sports interest). The contexts were: friendship (personal choice about cross-race friendship with no explicit external pressure); sleepover (having a cross-race friend in the home with negative external pressure from parental authority); and a school dance (cross-race dating in high school with external pressure from peer group). After each story, participants were asked to evaluate the situations.

We will describe a few brief findings to provide an overall view of our developmental approach (for details, see Crystal, under review; Killen et al., in press). We found that moral reasoning was used primarily when evaluating straightforward race-based exclusion ("It's bad to exclude someone because all races are equal"; "It's bad to exclude based on someone's skin color"). Also in line with hypotheses, when evaluating

Table 1. Frequencies and percentages for intergroup contact score by site and grade

Site by intergroup contact	Grade			Total
	4th	7th	10th	
Homogeneous				
Low	81	72	59	212
	23.7%	21.1%	17.3%	62.1%
High	10	66	54	130
	2.9%	19.3%	15.8%	38.0%
Total	91	138	113	342
Heterogeneous				
Low	27	47	27	101
	7.9%	13.7%	7.9%	29.5%
High	46	95	100	241
	13.5%	27.8%	29.2%	70.5%
Total	73	142	127	342

more complex situations of exclusion, such as that based on competing interests or group functioning, students used a combination of different kinds of social reasoning, specifically both moral and social-conventional reasons (e.g., "If his other friends don't like him then they won't get along and it won't be any fun"). As predicted, older students were more likely to use moral reasoning in regard to straightforward race-based exclusion, and less likely to use moral reasoning in explaining exclusion based on competing interests. Further, students with high intergroup contact were more likely than those with low intergroup contact to use moral reasoning in regard to race-based exclusion, but these results were qualified by grade level and majority/minority status. Grade level and intergroup contact were the most consistent predictors of social reasoning in the friendship context.

When we examined students' evaluations of the parental context (sleepover), students overwhelmingly used moral reasoning when responding to straightforward race-based exclusion in a situation in which parental discomfort was made salient, and employed more complex reasoning in the questions on nonracial factors and group functioning than in that on race-based exclusion. As for age-related findings, more seventh and tenth graders than fourth graders used moral reasoning in evaluating straightforward race-based exclusion. Also in line with expectations, more students with high intergroup contact used moral reasoning in regard to explanations of group functioning-based exclusion than did their low-contact peers. Again, grade was the most consistent predictor of social reasoning in the parent context.

Finally, analyses of students' responses to the dance scenario revealed that although students used both moral and social-conventional reasoning in answering the question on race-based exclusion, in accord with predictions, the vast majority of students reasoned in moral terms. Students employed both moral and social-conventional reasoning in responding to the more complex exclusion situations based on competing considerations and group functioning ("If your friends aren't going to like what you do then you have to listen to them"). Also in accord with predictions, seventh graders with high intergroup contact were more likely than their younger counterparts to use moral reasoning in the straightforward race-based exclusion question, and seventh-grade majority students were more likely than their younger peers to use moral reasoning in answering the group functioning question. Contrary to expectations, however, seventh graders with high intergroup contact were more likely than their fourth-grade counterparts to reason in moral terms when considering nonracial social factors such as school rivalry. Grade and intergroup contact were the most common predictors of students' social reasoning in the dance context (see Crystal, under review; Killen, Crystal, & Ruck, 2006).

Our findings for the role of intergroup contact indicated that the vast majority of students used moral reasoning in their explanations of the wrongfulness of race-based exclusion in the friendship context (e.g., "It's not fair to use race as a reason not to be friends with someone; it's kind of like being prejudiced"). Our close examination of the data indicated that students with high intergroup contact used more reasoning focusing on fairness and equality (that is, moral reasoning) than did students with low intergroup contact. For the sleepover context the vast majority of students also employed moral reasoning in evaluating straightforward race-based exclusion, and there were no significant relationships to intergroup contact. For the dating context, however, students used both moral ("It wouldn't be right; it's like discrimination") and social-conventional ("Sometimes you should do what your friends say or you won't have any more friends") reasoning in their explanations. In this context, intergroup contact was significantly related to the use of moral reasoning. Students with high intergroup contact used more moral reasoning than students with low intergroup contact. Thus students with high intergroup contact were more likely to view a decision not to date someone because of their race as wrong from a moral viewpoint (e.g., unfair and discriminatory), whereas students with low intergroup contact were more likely to view this same type of decision from a social-conventional viewpoint where the goal is to maintain the interests of the group (e.g., "It's okay not to bring her [Black girlfriend] to the dance if her friends are going to feel uncomfortable").

Finally, we found that students with high intergroup contact were more likely to say that something proactive should be done about racial exclusion than were students with low intergroup contact. When students were asked whether an observer should do something about the racial exclusion, students with high intergroup contact were more likely than students with low intergroup contact to say that the observer should talk to the person doing the excluding. This indicates a more activist attitude toward changing race-based exclusion among students with high intergroup contact.

These patterns of findings were complex and depended on the question and category of response under consideration. One measure of racial bias is not enough to provide a comprehensive picture of racial attitudes. Racial attitudes are changing throughout childhood and adolescence (and adulthood) and vary depending on the context, and importantly, for the purposes of this essay, on social experience, that is, intergroup contact.

Conclusions

Overall, these findings provide new and striking evidence about the ways in which school social environments influence children's and adolescents' social cognition and social reasoning about race. It is important to clarify that the vast majority of all students, from both heterogeneous and homogeneous school environments, evaluated racial exclusion as wrong, and many students in both types of schools spoke eloquently about the wrongfulness of racial exclusion. What varied were subtle and nuanced differences regarding interpretations of motives, intentions, and relationships among members of different groups. Nonetheless, we found clear differences between how students in homogeneous school environments evaluated racial exclusion in multiple contexts from students in heterogeneous school environments, and specifically, as a function of their perceptions of intergroup contact. There is much more to discover about young people's thinking about racial exclusion in both types of school environments, and extensive data have yet to be analyzed and interpreted. We are in the process of analyzing the data and relating a number of our findings to multiple measures that include perceptions of societal discrimination, personal discrimination, and intergroup contact in the students' classrooms and neighborhoods (see Crystal, under review; Killen et al., in press).

It would be fruitful to conduct direct comparisons between our findings with intergroup contact and adolescents' evaluations of racial exclusion with recent findings on school racial composition and long-term goals (Yun & Kurlaender, 2004). For example, Yun and Kurlaender (2004) surveyed more than fifteen thousand high school students from three urban school districts and found that school racial composition was related to different levels of educational aspirations. Further, integrating research on school composition with developmental analyses of social and moral evaluations of intergroup interactions would be beneficial.

We propose that research that takes a developmental approach, informed by the key constructs identified by social psychologists, will provide essential information necessary for understanding the complex ways in which social experience and school environments contribute to children's social and moral development. A key condition of successful intergroup contact is cross-race friendships (see Pettigrew & Tropp, 2000). Peer relationships are powerful predictors of healthy social adjustment and development; furthering the goals of an integrated society lies with promoting positive intergroup friendships. School environments that (1) fulfill the conditions articulated by Allport's (1954) intergroup contact theory, (2) provide a diverse learning environment for students, (3) implement curriculum designed to teach students about the diverse histories of various racial and ethnic groups, and (4) promote the achievements and accomplishments of groups from all realms of society serve as important venues for facilitating children's and adolescents' understandings of justice, fairness, and rights, which ultimately enables us to move toward the goals of a more just and civil society.

Appendix: Items from the Diversity Assessment Questionnaire (DAQ) (Adapted from Kurlaender & Yun, 2001)

1. How many students in your school are from racial or ethnic groups that are different from your own?
2. During classroom discussions, how often are racial issues discussed and explored?
3. To what extent do you believe that these discussions have changed your understanding of different points of view?
4. How often do your teachers encourage you to work with students of other racial/ethnic backgrounds?
5. How comfortable would you be working with students from different racial or ethnic backgrounds on group or class projects?

6. How often do you work on school projects and/or study with students from other racial or ethnic groups?

7. At school how many friends do you have who are from a different racial or ethnic group than you?

8. Outside of school how many friends do you have who are from a different racial or ethnic group than you?

9. In the neighborhood where you live do you have neighbors from other racial or ethnic backgrounds?

10. How many of your friends from your neighborhood are from a different racial or ethnic group than you?

11. How many people your age from your school date someone from a different racial/ethnic group?

12. How many people your age from your neighborhood date someone from a different racial/ethnic group?

Note

The research described in this essay was supported by a grant from the National Institute of Child Health and Human Development (#R01HD04121). We thank the research team at the University of Maryland (Marguerite Adams, Holly Bozeman, Alaina Brenick, Michael J. Collins, Christina Edmonds, Julia Hadricky, Alexandra Henning, Megan Clark Kelly, Nancy Geyelin Margie, Heidi McGlothlin, Alexander O'Connor, Christine Pitocchelli, and Stefanie Sinno) and the research team at Georgetown University (Anne Blossom, Lindsey Gansen, Nancy Gibbs, Elizabeth Kravec, Dayna McGill, Meredith Mellody, and Mia Shorteno-Fraser) for assistance with the research described in this essay. We are grateful for the insightful feedback from Erica Frankenberg and Gary Orfield on earlier versions of this manuscript and for inviting us to participate in the Civil Rights Project roundtable.

Can Reducing School Segregation Close the Achievement Gap?

Jaekyung Lee

One of the often debated arguments regarding desegregated schools has been how racially diverse schools affect student achievement (see Hawley, in this volume). There has been much less attention paid to how segregation within schools might also affect student achievement (see Mickelson, 2005). At a time when school resegregation threatens to reduce the number of racially diverse schools, demonstrating the academic benefits—as well as other benefits—that accrue to students in racially heterogeneous schools and classrooms is a likely prerequisite to devising policies to stem this resegregating trend. Thus, at a time when many educational policies are focused on trying to narrow the racial achievement gap, it is worth analyzing the relationship between school and classroom racial composition and the achievement gap.

Racial desegregation and equalization efforts since *Brown v. Board of Education of Topeka* (1954) can be grouped into three general categories (W. F. Tate, Ladson-Billings, & Grant, 1996; Weiler, 1998). The first efforts were to eliminate physical segregation of Blacks and Whites between schools; these have seen some success, particularly in the South, where school systems were required to eliminate the vestiges of prior legal segregation. However, there have been recent setbacks in that progress, along with increasing resegregation (Boger & G. Orfield, 2005; Frankenberg, C. Lee, & G. Orfield, 2003; G. Orfield & Yun, 1999). The second category of efforts, the elimination of inequities within schools, has been slow to occur. In mixed-race schools, students of color are often placed on lower academic tracks than White students, and are disproportionately more likely than Whites to be suspended from school and placed in special (remedial or compensatory) classrooms (K. J. Meier, Stewart, & England, 1989; Oakes, 1990, 2005).

The third category of racial desegregation and equalization efforts—the goal of achieving equal learning outcomes for all students across racial and ethnic backgrounds—has had mixed results. Black and Hispanic students scored below basic achievement levels in the National Assessment of Educational Progress (NAEP)[1] mathematics test at two to three times higher rates than their White peers in 2000.[2] The differences in the levels of Black and Hispanic students' achievement in comparison to the higher achievement of Whites and Asians, commonly referred to as "the achievement gap," did decrease substantially in the 1970s and 1980s (Jencks & M. Phillips, 1998). During the 1990s, however, there were significant setbacks, as the narrowing of the racial gaps slowed or even reversed (J. Lee, 2002; J. Lee, 2004). Closing this persistent, well-documented racial achievement gap is a major focus of the most recent federal education initiative, the No Child Left Behind Act of 2001 (NCLB). The new NAEP reports (Perie, Grigg, & Donahue, 2005; Perie, Grigg, & Dion, 2005) reveal that the White-Black and White-Hispanic gaps among fourth and eighth graders did not narrow significantly between 2002 and 2005 in reading, and between 2003 and 2005 in math, and that despite the implementation of NCLB, racial achievement gaps in U.S. public schools persist.

Foundations of the Study

This essay examines the links between racial segregation and achievement gaps at the statewide level by comparing within-school and between-school variations in NAEP data on mathematics achievement (see J. Lee, 1998) of Whites, Blacks, and Hispanics. Few studies have examined the relationship between racial segregation and the achievement gap at the state level. Racial achievement gaps vary significantly among states, however (J. Lee, 1998; Wong & J. Lee, 1998). These variations can be attributed to the effects of particular court decisions, a given state's reliance on small township-level school districts as opposed to countywide school districts, or patterns of demographic change and immigration (G. Orfield, 1996). Sullivan and Crain (cited in Kunen, 1996) found that the Black-White reading gap was narrowest in states in which Blacks were least segregated from Whites (West Virginia and Iowa) and largest in states where Blacks were most isolated (New York and Michigan). While Kahlenberg (2001) cited this finding as circumstantial evidence for supporting racial desegregation, it must be noted that the study was restricted to the relationship between Black-White segregation and fourth-grade reading test score gaps in a single year.

School segregation for Blacks has paralleled that of the Black-White achievement gap. It is argued that the earlier progress in desegregation contributed to narrowing the Black-White achievement gaps: Black reading and mathematics achievement gains in the 1970s and 1980s were largest in the Southeast, where desegregation occurred most (Grissmer, Flanagan, & Willamson, 1998). Similarly, the widening of the Black-White achievement gap that began in the 1990s might be related to the national setback in desegregation during that period (Kahlenberg, 2001; J. Lee, 2002). A large number of court-ordered desegregation plans were ended then, which likely influenced this trend (see Frankenberg, C. Lee, & G. Orfield, 2003). School segregation trends for Hispanics differ from those for Blacks, perhaps because the Supreme Court extended to Hispanics the right to desegregate in 1973, after the largest gains in desegregation for Blacks had been achieved (Laosa, 2001). Hispanic segregation has grown steadily over the past three decades, and although the Hispanic-White achievement gap narrowed somewhat in the 1970s and 1980s, progress stalled in the 1990s (J. Lee, 2002).

If this trend toward increasing racial segregation means that educational opportunities for Black and Hispanic students are decreasing and achievement gaps widening, there would be policy implications in regard to segregation both between and within schools. For example, during the 1980s and 1990s there was some movement away from the assignment of students by school administrators toward school choice plans, in which students and parents determine, to varying degrees, which schools students will attend (Kahlenberg, 2001). Within schools, particularly in high schools, efforts to eliminate the practice of tracking (also known as ability grouping) have been uneven and limited in scope; curriculum differentiation persists, with fewer opportunities for minority students to take higher-level courses such as honors and Advanced Placement (AP) (Mickelson, 2001; Oakes & Wells, 1999; see Burris & Welner, in this volume). If these policies contribute to achievement gaps that run counter to current federal educational mandates (the NCLB Act of 2001), they would need to be addressed on that basis, even aside from school desegregation's contributions to other larger social goals.

Previous studies have not fully differentiated within-school segregation from between-school segregation, nor have they examined segregation patterns in relation to achievement gap patterns. To address these concerns, this study posed three research questions: (1) What is the nature and extent of interstate variation in within-school and between-school racial segregation and the achievement gaps? (2) What progress have states made in reducing racial segregation and narrowing achievement gaps during the 1990s? (3) What is the relationship between both between-school and within-school racial segregation patterns and racial achievement gaps across states?

Analytical Framework

Although the literature is not conclusive as to the effects of desegregation on achievement, it does suggest a connection between racial composition of schools and educational opportunities, which are themselves linked with higher achievement (G. Orfield & C. Lee, 2005). Schools with large minority populations are more likely to be high-poverty schools, and, in comparison to schools with majority White populations, they tend to suffer from low parental involvement, lack of resources, less challenging curricula, less experienced and credentialed teachers, and higher teacher turnover (G. Orfield & Eaton, 1996; Schofield, 2001). A recent study of all Florida schools found that fewer students passed the state-mandated achievement test (the FCAT) in schools that were racially segregated Black schools, even after testing for other factors such as class size or per-pupil funding (Borman et al., 2004). By contrast, desegregation ensures that minority students attend schools with better educational opportunities and higher-achieving peer groups (Wells & Crain, 1994), at least in schools that are structured to facilitate their access to these educational assets.

The 1988 National Educational Longitudinal Study survey found that low-income and minority eighth graders were twice as likely as White and upper-income eighth graders to be placed in remedial math classes (Kahlenberg, 2001). Mickelson (2005), moreover, found in her study in Charlotte-Mecklenburg schools that, of students scoring in the top decile on achievement tests, three times as many Black students were enrolled in regular (lower-track) English than Whites of similar ability. Nevertheless, questions remain as to whether within-school racial segregation is the cause or outcome of the racial achievement gap, or both, and thus a self-perpetuating cycle; the research evidence is mixed (R. F. Ferguson, 1998; see also Burris & Welner, in this volume). But although some argue that most tracking is self-tracking and that academic segregation simply reflects the racial achievement gap (e.g., Thernstrom & Thernstrom, 2003), the practice of ability grouping has specific negative consequences for lower-tracked students in terms of distribution of teachers, curriculum differentiation, race and class stratification, and student outcomes (Oakes, 1990).

Data and Methods

The NAEP state eighth-grade math assessment and survey served as the primary data sources in this study. I used the 1992 and 1996 results for eighth-grade students attending public schools in the thirty-five states that participated in both assessments. For the analysis of racial segregation, I focused on White, Black, and Hispanic students. The samples each contained over thirty thousand eighth-grade students in over one thousand schools in 1992 and 1996; the racial composition was 64 percent White (65 percent in 1992), 22 percent Black, and 14 percent Hispanic (13 percent in 1992). The following discussion of definitions and measures, framed in terms of Black and White students, also applies for comparisons between Hispanic and White students.

For the purposes of this essay I refer to the segregation of White and Black students among different schools in the same state as between-school Black-White segregation, which is a measure of the extent to which the percentages of Black and White students in each school match the corresponding statewide percentages. Within-school Black-White segregation is the segregation of White and Black students among different types of mathematics classes within the same school, and measures the extent to which the proportions of Black and White students in each classroom reflect the school's racial composition.

Racial segregation within and between schools was measured by the dissimilarity index (see O. D. Duncan & B. Duncan, 1955). The dissimilarity, or displacement, index (D) was used as an indicator of racial imbalance, showing the proportion of non-White students (Blacks or Hispanics in this study) who would have to change their classrooms or schools to match the minority percentage in the school or state, respectively (see appendix A). It should be noted that this measurement of disparities among schools' racial composition at the state level is less common than calculating racial disparities at the district level. The between-school segregation measure was calculated using NAEP student survey information on race/ethnicity along with school and state student information. The within-school segregation measure utilized information from the NAEP student survey about the type of mathematics course (that is, no math, regular math class, pre-algebra class, and algebra class) in which each eighth-grade student was enrolled.

The between-school Black-White achievement gap was defined as the difference in the average mathematics achievement test scores of predominantly White and predominantly Black schools in the same state. The within-school Black-White achievement gap was defined as the difference between overall test score averages of White and Black students attending the same school. This measured the extent to which Black students' average achievement fell behind that of their White peers in each school.

The achievement data collected through the NAEP state assessment are hierarchical in nature, meaning that students are nested within schools, which in turn are nested within states. Using hierarchical linear models (HLMs), both within-school and between-school racial achievement gaps were estimated for each state and the change in each achievement gap, by state, from 1992 to 1996 (see appendix B, for methodology).[3] For each state, within-school and between-school racial achievement gaps were related to the corresponding measures of racial segregation for 1992 and 1996.

There are limitations to the drawing of causal inferences about the relationship between racial segregation and the achievement gaps found in this study. For example, students were not randomly assigned to schools of varying racial compositions; rather, their parents, or the students themselves, may have chosen schools based on their preferences of racial composition and achievement outcomes. Because of this element of self-selection, one cannot ascertain cause and effect. Racial segregation may be associated with the achievement gap because increased racial segregation deepens the inequalities of educational opportunities, as happens when predominantly minority schools lack challenging coursework for their students. The achievement gap itself may result in racial segregation when a school relies only on prior student achievement for class placement. At the same time, large achievement gaps among racial groups can be used to justify tracking, thereby causing further segregation within schools. For these and other reasons—although the formation of the gap in separate and unequal schools need hardly be debated—it is not possible using data from one point in time to determine whether ongoing segregation causes the achievement gap or is a result of it.

Given this problem, the study's design used two measures of segregation and achievement gaps at the state level. With correlational analysis of segregation and achievement measures from the two successive waves of NAEP (1992 and 1996), three types of effects were examined: stability, synchronous correlations, and cross-lagged correlations.[4] Of particular interest was comparison of the cross-lagged correlations between racial segregation and the racial achievement gap because this comparison helps determine which is more likely to be the cause. If the correlation between segregation in 1992 and the corresponding achievement gap in 1996 is stronger than the correlation between segregation in 1996 and at the corresponding achievement gap in 1992, then segregation is more likely to be the cause of the achievement gap. However, it needs to be noted that this cross-lagged panel correlation analysis has drawbacks that limit inferences about the causal direction between two variables (see D. T. Campbell & Kenny, 1999; D. T. Campbell & Stanley, 1963; Finkel, 1995).

This analysis assumes a steady or linear relationship between the variables, at the state level, meaning that a change in one variable will be associated with a certain change in the other, regardless of the values of either variable. However, prior research suggests that there may be a tipping point, or a threshold, at which the cumulative impact of racial isolation and concentrated poverty on minority achievement becomes much worse (Kahlenberg, 2001; Lippman, Burns, & McArthur, 1996; W. J. Wilson, 1987).[5] Second, this cross-lagged correlation analysis linking the 1992 and 1996 measures of racial segregation and the racial achievement gap assumes that it would take a few years for segregation to have a statewide impact on the achievement gap and vice versa. Although this assumption cannot be tested in this study, the short-term versus long-term effects of racial segregation need future investigation. Further study is also needed to understand the effect of the segregation that has accelerated since 1996.

Results

How Much Do Racial Segregation and Achievement Gaps Vary among States?

Figure 1 shows the extent to which Black and Hispanic students are segregated from White students in 1992 and 1996 at both the between-school and within-school (classroom) levels across the states included in the study. By and large, both Black and Hispanic students were highly segregated between and within schools. Across the states, the average dissimilarity (D) for between-school Black-White segregation was 64 percent in 1992, while the corresponding D for within-school Black-White segregation was 38 percent. This means that almost two-thirds of all Black students, for example, would need to switch schools for Black and White students to be evenly distributed within each state. Both of these measures had increased by 1996, especially within-school segregation (43 percent). Similarly, Hispanic-White segregation was higher at the between-school than the within-school level: the average D in 1992 for between-school segregation was 51 percent, while the corresponding D for within-school segregation was 40 percent. Both Hispanic-White segregation measures increased by 1996. These data, in many regards, are similar to trends of other segregation measures computed using enrollment data from virtually all public schools showing increasing between-school segregation during—and after—the 1992–96 period in this study (e.g., Frankenberg, C. Lee, & G. Orfield, 2003).

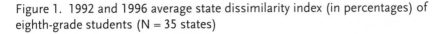

Figure 1. 1992 and 1996 average state dissimilarity index (in percentages) of eighth-grade students (N = 35 states)

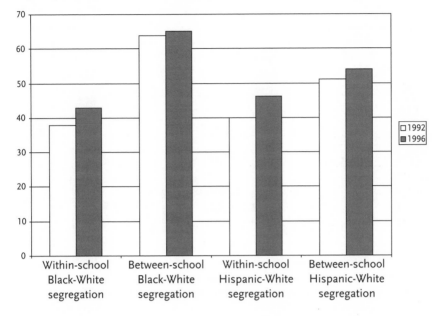

These data indicate that more than half of students in each of these minority groups would have had to change schools if they were to be evenly distributed across the schools of their states.[6] About 40 percent of students in these minority groups would have had to change their math classes to accomplish a racial balance that matched their schools' racial compositions. On average, Hispanic between-school segregation was lower than Black between-school segregation, but within-school segregation for Hispanics was similar to within-school segregation for Blacks (and, in fact, within-school segregation for Hispanics surpassed that of Blacks in 1996).

Figure 2 shows the collective patterns of the thirty-five states' Black-White achievement gap and Hispanic-White achievement gap. The Black-White and Hispanic-White gaps were substantial between and within schools. Black students, on average, scored 27 points lower than White students attending the same school.[7] At the same time, all-White schools (100 percent White), on average, scored about 50 points higher than all-Black schools (100 percent Black). Similar patterns were found for the Hispanic-White gap, although it was slightly smaller than the Black-White gap. For both Blacks and Hispanics, the magnitude of the between-school math achievement gap was almost two times larger than that of the

Figure 2. 1992 and 1996 NAEP eighth-grade mathematics average state test score gaps (N = 35 states)

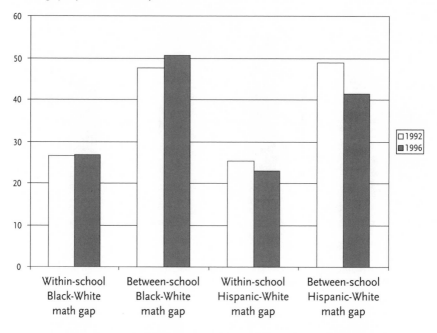

within-school gap. This relatively larger between-school racial achievement gap may reflect a racial/social compositional effect (e.g., concentration of disadvantaged minority students in inner-city schools) and a peer group effect (e.g., lack of exposure to academically motivated, high-achieving classmates) on a student's academic achievement.

These aggregate patterns notwithstanding, there were substantial variations among states in the degree of racial segregation and in the size of the achievement gap. In 1992, between-school Black-White segregation ranged from 19 percent to 89 percent among the thirty-five states studied, while within-school Black-White segregation ranged from 21 percent to 67 percent (see appendix C). For example, Connecticut had extremely high measures of between-school Black-White segregation in 1992 and 1996, 71 percent and 74 percent, respectively. Connecticut also had high within-school segregation—at least 50 percent in 1992 and 1996. In contrast, Louisiana was moderately segregated for Blacks during this period between schools (52 percent in 1992, 51 percent in 1996), but its within-school segregation was remarkably lower—just 21 percent in 1992. Nationally, between-school Hispanic-White segregation did not vary as widely as Black-White segregation, ranging from 25 percent to 69 percent. Similarly, within-school Hispanic-White segregation ranged from

27 percent to 56 percent, smaller variation than Black-White segregation (see appendix D).

Overall, between-school racial achievement gaps were larger and more varied than within-school achievement gaps. During the same time period, statewide between-school Black-White achievement gaps ranged from 32 to 58 points, while within-school Black-White gaps ranged from 22 to 33. Contrasting the segregation trends, there was greater variation in Hispanic-White achievement gaps by state. This cohort's between-school average math gap ranged from 25 to 76 points; within-schools, the range was from 17 to 37 points.

Did Segregation and Achievement Gaps Change during the 1990s?

Black segregation changed very little during the four-year period from 1992 to 1996 (see figure 1). Between-school segregation increased by 1 percentage point overall, while within-school segregation increased by 5 percentage points. In other words, the proportion of Black eighth graders who had been segregated from their White peers for different levels of math classes within the same school increased 5 percent in only four years when averaged across the thirty-five states studied. Hispanic segregation also increased slightly between 1992 and 1996—by 3 percentage points between schools, and by 6 percentage points within them.

These increasing levels of segregation of Hispanic students occurred across more states than did that of Black students during the 1992–96 period. At the individual state level, there were no states in which Black between-school segregation changed significantly (more than 10 percentage points), although seven states experienced significant changes in the segregation of Black students within schools (six increased, one declined) (see appendix C). Five states, however, recorded significant increases in Hispanic segregation at the between-school level, and seven states did so within schools. Of particular concern is the fact that there were no states in which there were significant decreases in Hispanic segregation (see appendix D).[8] Further, since several Supreme Court decisions in the 1990s made it easier for school systems to end their school desegregation plans, between-school segregation, at least, continued to increase after 1996.[9]

Figure 2 also shows that racial achievement gaps changed very little between 1992 and 1996. The between-school math gap for Blacks increased by 3 points, while the within-school gap remained the same. The between-school math gap for Hispanics dropped by 7 points, and the gap within schools by 2. Both Black-White and Hispanic-White math achievement gaps remained large, however, during the period, and there were no

Figure 3. Relationships over time of Black-White segregation and mathematics achievement gaps (N = 35 states)

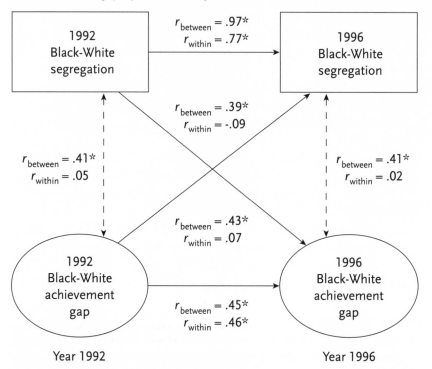

Note: $r_{between}$ = correlation for between-school segregation/gap measures; r_{within} = correlation for within-school segregation/gap measures.
*p < .05

states in which the achievement gaps declined significantly (more than 10 points).

The stability of segregation and achievement gaps for Black and Hispanic students during this period is shown with horizontal solid-line arrows in figures 3 and 4. Between-school Black-White segregation in 1992 was almost perfectly related to segregation in 1996 ($r = .97$), indicating a high level of stability over time and across the thirty-five states studied. Within-school segregation was not as strongly related, but was also very high ($r = .77$) for Blacks and Whites. A similar pattern of strong, positive relationships between 1992 and 1996 measures of segregation was seen with Hispanic-White segregation, although on both dimensions, it was not quite as strong as Black-White segregation ($r = .80$ for between-school segregation, $r = .76$ for within-school segregation). Thus states changed neither within-school nor between-school segregation systematically.

There are relatively moderate correlations between matched 1992 and

Figure 4. Relationships over time of Hispanic-White segregation and math achievement gaps (N = 35 states)

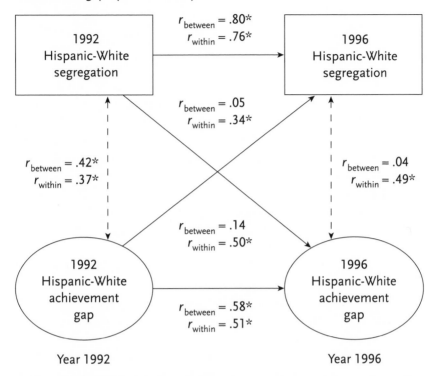

Note: $r_{between}$ = correlation for between-school segregation/gap measures; r_{within} = correlation for within-school segregation/gap measures.
*$p < .05$

1996 math gap measures (see figures 3 and 4 for the Black-White gap and Hispanic-White gap correlations, respectively), with a somewhat stronger relationship for the Hispanic-White measures, both within and between schools, than for the Black-White measures. Taken together, the lower correlations suggest that the racial achievement gaps did not change much over this time period, although they could be more malleable than segregation.[10]

How Are Racial Segregation Patterns Associated with the Achievement Gaps?

The correlation analysis suggests that systematic relationships exist between racial segregation and the mathematics achievement gap at the state level. First, the correlations between measures from the same years, that is, synchronous correlations (shown by vertical broken arrows in figures 3 and 4), show moderately positive relationships. This means that states with a higher degree of between-school Black segregation have a significantly larger between-school achievement gap ($r = .41$ in 1992 and 1996). In contrast, the within-school Black-White achievement gap is not significantly related to the within-school Black-White segregation ($r = .05$ in 1992; $r = .02$ in 1996). States with a higher degree of within-school Black segregation do not necessarily have a larger within-school achievement gap. The between-school Hispanic-White segregation is positively associated with the between-school Hispanic-White achievement gap ($r = .42$ in 1992), indicating that higher segregation is associated with larger gaps. Likewise, the within-school Hispanic-White achievement gap is positively related to within-school segregation ($r = .37$ in 1992; $r = .49$ in 1996). This statistically significant correlation for Hispanics contrasts with the finding for Blacks, and explanation of the discrepancy requires further investigation.

Additionally, the correlations among measures from different years, that is, cross-lagged correlations (shown by diagonal arrows in figures 3 and 4), suggest that the relationship between segregation and the achievement gap can be reciprocal.[11] Although the correlations between 1992 segregation and 1996 achievement gap measures tend to be slightly lower than the correlations between 1992 achievement gap and 1996 segregation measures, the differences are not statistically significant. For example, the correlation between 1992 between-school segregation and 1996 between-school achievement gap measures for Blacks is moderate ($r = .39$), and the correlation between 1992 achievement gap and 1996 segregation measures for Blacks is also moderate ($r = .43$). This indicates that the achievement gap may lead to racial segregation as much as segregation can lead to the achievement gap. It is also plausible that both variables share some common causes (e.g., socioeconomic inequalities). Further research is needed to examine extraneous variables that may confound the relationship between segregation and the achievement gap.

Summary and Conclusion

Findings

This study revealed substantial interstate variations in the degree of segregation and the size of achievement gaps among the three racial groups studied, both within and between schools. Although the phenomena of between- and within-school racial segregation and achievement gaps may share some common causes, states tend to differ along the two dimensions. Between-school segregation tends to be more severe than within-school segregation, and the between-school achievement gap tends to be twice as large as the average gap within schools. This suggests that states need to put more systemic policy efforts into reducing racial segregation, equalizing resources, and closing achievement gaps between schools. In places where there are legal constraints on efforts to address between-school segregation, educators may still make progress by reducing within-school segregation as a means of closing achievement gaps.

Second, the analysis suggests that none of the thirty-five states significantly reduced racial segregation and achievement gaps during this time. State patterns of racial segregation remained largely unchanged, while patterns of racial achievement gaps did not change much. It seems more difficult to change segregation than achievement gaps at the state level, at least in these four years.

Third, there is generally a modest, positive correlation between racial segregation and achievement gaps at the state level. The between-school Black-White gap is significantly associated with between-school segregation, and the within-school Hispanic-White gap is significantly associated with within-school segregation. Cross-lagged correlation analysis also suggests that the relationship between racial segregation and achievement gaps could be reciprocal, meaning that aside from the benefits that come from decreasing both within-school and between-school racial segregation (see Hawley, in this volume), these policy efforts may also contribute to reducing achievement gaps. Likewise, narrowing the racial achievement gaps themselves may facilitate racial integration between and within schools. The data in this essay indicate, however, that during the mid-1990s many states made no impact on large racial achievement gaps and segregation of their students.

Limitations

Available data limit the extent of the analysis in this study, particularly in terms of causal inferences and policy recommendations. NAEP state assessments do not collect data at the high school level; thus this study includes only eighth-grade results on segregation and achievement gaps. Cross-state comparisons of high school level results may differ.[12] High school is, moreover, a crucial educational level to investigate, particularly because of the effects of further curriculum differentiation and racial stratification on within-school racial segregation patterns. Additionally, long-term effects of segregation on achievement gaps may be different from short-term effects. This study focused on changes over a four-year period, a relatively short time frame for analyzing, particularly at the state level, policies addressing long-standing racial segregation and achievement gaps. Careful and ongoing data collection is needed to more fully illuminate both problems and policy solutions.

Another limitation of the study is that the focus on state comparisons may obscure substantial variations in within-school segregation patterns among schools or even within districts. The Common Core of Data (CCD), a national education database often used for school segregation studies, records only between-school racial segregation, not within-school segregation. Although the use of national assessment/survey databases, including NAEP, can help examine the relationship between segregation and the achievement gap, they also were not properly designed for addressing the within-school segregation issue. Thus we have no clear idea of the extent to which within-school segregation exists across the country or how these trends might change over time. Future NAEP assessments should consider sampling data at the classroom level, which would enable more reliable investigation of minority students' placement in lower-level tracks or courses and the relationship of such placements to within-school achievement gaps.[13]

A final, and significant, limitation to this study is that it did not consider economic differences among racial groups. Because we know that there is a high correlation of racially segregated minority schools and schools with concentrated poverty (Frankenberg, C. Lee, & G. Orfield, 2003; G. Orfield & C. Lee, 2005), and because it is almost impossible to disentangle the problems of race and poverty in contemporary American education, we should always consider both factors and their joint effects on the achievement gap. Past NAEP data do not include information on students' family income and poverty level,[14] and it is unknown whether and how the observed trends of racial segregation and achievement may change in relation to poverty levels.[15]

Recommendations

This research has charted the multilevel, organizational nature of the achievement gap among racial groups both within and between schools. This raises questions about policy factors that can affect the achievement gaps among racial groups and what tools policymakers currently have to address these problems. Current educational policies that focus on high-stakes testing and school accountability can be seen as a move toward emphasizing academic achievement for low-income minority students in low-achieving schools. Some have suggested that high-stakes testing may provide a powerful legal basis for racial and socioeconomic integration if segregated schools effectively deny students an opportunity to learn and pass statewide tests (Kahlenberg, 2001).[16] Accountability policies up to this point, however, have failed to address the existing racial and social inequities in learning opportunities and outcomes within and between schools (Borman et al., 2004; J. Lee & Wong, 2004).

Improving classroom learning opportunities within schools is critical but cannot fully compensate for racial inequity due to racial isolation in metropolitan areas. In contrast to suburban schools, inner-city schools with high concentrations of minority students are constrained by poor learning environments overall, such as problems with safety and orderliness, absenteeism and truancy, fewer certified teachers, less challenging curriculum, and class disruptions (Kozol, 1991, 2005; Lippman, Burns, & McArthur, 1996). These constraints undermine the learning opportunities that minority students may gain from new accountability practices. In light of the challenges of poor classroom environment and social stratification, policymakers need to coordinate education and social policy more effectively in order to reduce underlying structural problems of racial isolation, between-school disparities in educational opportunities, and concentrated poverty that cross the boundaries of urban and suburban school systems.

At the same time, school administrators and teachers should strive to provide more racially integrated learning opportunities within schools. Racial reciprocity may be enhanced through detracking, cooperative learning, and peer tutoring, particularly when schools help the lower-achieving students benefit from learning with their higher-achieving peers by creating racially integrated classrooms (J. Lee, 2004; see Hawley, in this volume).[17] Reducing racial segregation and closing achievement gaps should be pursued together; making progress on one goal can advance the other, and simultaneous policy efforts would be the best path toward greater racial equity.

Appendix A: Description of Within-School versus Between-School Segregation Measures

The dissimilarity index of between-school segregation for each state is obtained by dividing the sum of absolute value of the difference between White ratio and minority (Black or Hispanic) ratio across all schools in the state's NAEP sample by 2. White or minority ratio is the number of White or minority students in each school over the number of their corresponding target population statewide. D lies between 0 and 1 (or 0 and 100 percent). It measures how much racial composition of individual schools in each state deviates from their statewide racial composition. Therefore, the between-school segregation measure takes into account both interdistrict and intradistrict racial segregation across the state.

Within-school racial segregation is measured by applying the same dissimilarity index to racial distributions of students among varying levels of eighth-grade math classes within each school in the NAEP sample. It measures how much the racial composition of individual classrooms in each school deviates from their school-wide racial composition. Because the eighth-grade students in NAEP were randomly sampled in each state from schools but not from classes, this comparison of racial distributions among different classes can be biased, and thus the within-school segregation index must be interpreted with caution. Despite the sampling errors of within-school racial segregation, it needs to be noted that the primary unit of analysis is the state, so that individual schools' estimates are aggregated up to the state level for cross-state comparison. Assuming the errors are randomly distributed across schools, they may balance out each other, increasing the validity of the statewide within-school segregation index.

Appendix B: HLM Specifications for the Analysis of Racial Achievement Gaps

The relationship between individual students' racial/ethnic characteristics and mathematics achievement outcomes comprise the level 1 model; the variation among schools within a state is captured in the level 2 model; and the variation among states is represented in the level 3 model. Both level 1 and level 2 predictors are group-mean centered so that the level 2 and level 3 intercepts can be interpreted as the average mathematics achievement in each school and state. The data are also weighted at the student and school levels, and the weights at each level are normalized. NAEP used item response theory (IRT) to estimate proficiency scores in mathematics for each individual student. There are five plausible values for each sampled student resulting from five random draws from the conditional distribution of proficiency scores for each student. The parameter estimates from the HLM analyses are based on the average parameter estimates from separate HLM analyses of the five plausible values.

Level 1 Model (Student Level)

$Yijk = p_{0jk} + p_{1jk} (\text{Black})_{ijk} + p_{2jk} (\text{Hispanic})_{ijk} + e_{ijk}$

   $Yijk$ is the mathematics achievement of student i in school j, and state k;

   p_{0jk} is the intercept for school j in state k;

   $(\text{Black})_{ijk}$ is a dummy variable for Black students: 1 for Black and 0 for others.

   $(\text{Hispanic})_{ijk}$ is a dummy variable for Hispanic students: 1 for Hispanics and 0 for others.

   e_{ijk} is a level 1 random effect that represents the deviation of the student$_{ijk}$ score from the predicted score based on student-level model.

Level 2 Model (School Level)

$p_{0jk} = b_{00k} + b_{01k} \text{ (percent Black)}_{jk} + b_{02k} \text{ (percent Hispanic)}_{jk} + r_{0jk}$

p_{0jk} represents school-level mean mathematics achievement.

(percent Black)$_{jk}$ is the average of (Black) variable, that is, the proportion of Black students in each school jk.

(percent Hispanic)$_{jk}$ is the average of (Hispanic) variable, that is, the proportion of Hispanic students in each school jk.

$p_{1jk} = b_{10k} + r_{1jk}$

p_{1jk} represents the within-school mathematics achievement gap between Black and White students in school j and state k.

$p_{2jk} = b_{20k} + r_{2jk}$

p_{2jk} represents the within-school mathematics achievement gap between Hispanic and White students in school j and state k.

Level 3 Model (State Level)

$b_{00k} = g_{000} + u_{00k}$

b_{00k} represents the state average mathematics achievement.

$b_{01k} = g_{010} + u_{01k}$

b_{01k} represents the between-school mathematics achievement gap between Black and White students in state k.

$b_{02k} = g_{020} + u_{02k}$

b_{02k} represents the between-school mathematics achievement gap between Hispanic and White students in state k.

$b_{10k} = g_{100} + u_{10k}$

b_{10k} represents the pooled within-school mathematics achievement gap between Black and White students in state k.

$b_{20k} = g_{200} + u_{20k}$

b_{20k} represents the pooled within-school mathematics achievement gap between Hispanic and White students in state k.

Appendix C

State-by-state dissimilarity measures of Black-White eighth graders' segregation
between and within schools (N = 35 states)

State	1992		1996		Change	
	Between-school	Within-school	Between-school	Within-school	Between-school	Within-school
Alabama	0.58	0.29	0.62	0.39	0.04	0.10
Arizona*	0.54	0.51	0.61	0.48	0.07	−0.03
Arkansas	0.63	0.28	0.64	0.36	0.02	0.09
California	0.69	0.45	0.63	0.47	−0.05	0.02
Colorado	0.75	0.46	0.76	0.47	0.01	0.01
Connecticut	0.71	0.50	0.74	0.53	0.03	0.03
Delaware	0.19	0.25	0.20	0.32	0.01	0.07
Florida	0.49	0.35	0.56	0.44	0.07	0.09
Georgia	0.55	0.32	0.60	0.41	0.04	0.09
Hawaii*	0.45	0.47	0.47	0.44	0.02	−0.03
Indiana	0.75	0.28	0.73	0.36	−0.02	0.09
Iowa*	0.74	0.37	0.71	0.47	−0.03	0.09
Kentucky	0.60	0.34	0.64	0.36	0.04	0.02
Louisiana	0.52	0.21	0.51	0.27	−0.01	0.06
Maine*	0.87	0.41	0.91	0.57	0.04	0.16
Maryland	0.63	0.44	0.67	0.46	0.04	0.02
Massachusetts	0.69	0.52	0.68	0.52	−0.01	0.01
Michigan	0.84	0.31	0.83	0.42	−0.01	0.11
Minnesota	0.73	0.50	0.73	0.51	0.00	0.01
Mississippi	0.56	0.27	0.54	0.38	−0.02	0.11
Missouri	0.69	0.35	0.70	0.33	0.01	−0.02
Nebraska	0.80	0.34	0.77	0.41	−0.03	0.08
New Mexico*	0.61	0.48	0.68	0.45	0.07	−0.03
New York	0.80	0.37	0.76	0.43	−0.04	0.06
North Carolina	0.46	0.32	0.46	0.37	0.00	0.05
North Dakota*	0.78	0.33	0.77	0.46	−0.02	0.13
Rhode Island	0.61	0.42	0.60	0.43	−0.01	0.01
South Carolina	0.43	0.33	0.40	0.31	−0.03	−0.02

(continued)

Appendix C *(continued)*

	1992		1996		Change	
State	Between-school	Within-school	Between-school	Within-school	Between-school	Within-school
Tennessee	0.65	0.25	0.71	0.40	0.06	0.15
Texas	0.55	0.38	0.62	0.49	0.07	0.10
Utah*	0.89	0.67	0.87	0.54	−0.02	−0.13
Virginia	0.50	0.32	0.53	0.38	0.02	0.06
West Virginia*	0.69	0.40	0.70	0.55	0.01	0.15
Wisconsin	0.81	0.36	0.78	0.42	−0.03	0.05
Wyoming*	0.64	0.51	0.71	0.51	0.07	0.00
Mean	0.64	0.38	0.65	0.43	0.01	0.05
Standard deviation	0.15	0.10	0.14	0.17	0.04	0.06

Note: The measures of change may differ slightly because of rounding. Asterisk (*) indicates that the state has less than 5 percent of Black students in its total public school enrollment, which means the segregation measures should be interpreted with caution.

Appendix D

State-by-state measures of Hispanic-White eighth graders' segregation between and within schools (N = 35 states)

	1992		1996		Change	
State	Between-school	Within-school	Between-school	Within-school	Between-school	Within-school
Alabama*	0.62	0.40	0.54	0.53	−0.08	0.13
Arizona	0.48	0.34	0.52	0.39	0.04	0.05
Arkansas*	0.49	0.41	0.55	0.47	0.06	0.06
California	0.53	0.38	0.53	0.39	0.00	0.01
Colorado	0.44	0.37	0.49	0.42	0.05	0.05
Connecticut	0.67	0.43	0.65	0.50	−0.01	0.07
Delaware*	0.25	0.44	0.30	0.43	0.05	−0.01
Florida	0.59	0.38	0.66	0.51	0.08	0.13
Georgia*	0.57	0.55	0.56	0.59	−0.01	0.04
Hawaii*	0.34	0.36	0.35	0.37	0.01	0.01
Indiana*	0.50	0.36	0.48	0.48	−0.02	0.12

(continued)

94   Jaekyung Lee

Appendix D *(continued)*

State	1992 Between-school	1992 Within-school	1996 Between-school	1996 Within-school	Change Between-school	Change Within-school
Iowa*	0.43	0.39	0.62	0.42	0.18	0.03
Kentucky*	0.52	0.43	0.59	0.48	0.07	0.05
Louisiana*	0.63	0.29	0.53	0.41	−0.09	0.12
Maine*	0.42	0.46	0.60	0.53	0.18	0.07
Maryland*	0.51	0.56	0.58	0.57	0.06	0.01
Massachusetts	0.64	0.48	0.69	0.47	0.04	0.00
Michigan*	0.55	0.38	0.49	0.47	−0.05	0.10
Minnesota*	0.40	0.42	0.51	0.48	0.11	0.06
Mississippi*	0.65	0.34	0.62	0.53	−0.04	0.20
Missouri*	0.49	0.43	0.61	0.45	0.12	0.02
Nebraska	0.48	0.30	0.51	0.39	0.02	0.09
New Mexico*	0.38	0.28	0.47	0.35	0.09	0.06
New York	0.69	0.34	0.69	0.38	0.00	0.03
North Carolina	0.56	0.52	0.54	0.51	−0.02	−0.01
North Dakota*	0.50	0.27	0.47	0.32	−0.04	0.05
Rhode Island	0.63	0.44	0.67	0.47	0.04	0.03
South Carolina	0.48	0.46	0.45	0.48	−0.03	0.02
Tennessee	0.53	0.34	0.65	0.40	0.12	0.06
Texas	0.60	0.35	0.63	0.41	0.03	0.06
Utah*	0.38	0.51	0.40	0.47	0.02	−0.05
Virginia	0.49	0.47	0.50	0.56	0.01	0.08
West Virginia*	0.59	0.49	0.60	0.61	0.01	0.12
Wisconsin	0.56	0.36	0.56	0.41	0.00	0.05
Wyoming*	0.31	0.29	0.30	0.42	−0.01	0.13
Mean	0.51	0.40	0.54	0.46	0.03	0.06
Standard deviation	0.10	0.08	0.10	0.07	0.06	0.05

Note: The measures of change may differ slightly because of rounding. Asterisk (*) indicates that the state has less than 5 percent of Hispanic students in its total public school enrollment, which means the segregation measures should be interpreted with caution.

Notes

1. NAEP is the only nationally representative, continuous assessment, administered periodically to fourth, eighth, and twelfth graders by the U.S. Department of Education since 1969 in a variety of academic subjects.

2. "Basic" denotes partial mastery of prerequisite knowledge and skills for proficient work at each grade and thus may be regarded as the minimally adequate level of achievement on the NAEP. Percentages of students below the basic achievement levels in the 2000 NAEP mathematics test varied much by race/ethnicity: 22 percent for Whites versus 62 percent for Blacks and 53 percent for Hispanics in grade 4; 23 percent for Whites versus 68 percent for Blacks and 59 percent for Hispanics in grade 8; 26 percent for Whites versus 69 percent for Blacks and 56 percent for Hispanics in grade 12.

3. HLM is a form of multilevel regression modeling designed to handle hierarchical and clustered data. Such data involve group effects on individuals that may be assessed invalidly by traditional statistical techniques. Due to grouping (students nested in schools), observations within a group are often more similar than would be predicted on a pooled-data basis, and hence the assumption of independence of observations is violated. Multilevel modeling is also helpful when data are sparse. For instance, in this study, there may be too few minority students in some schools to enable valid statistical inferences on the racial achievement gap, using traditional regression models. Multilevel models can use not only the individual data in those racially segregated schools but also information in the pooled data for all schools, including schools that are racially mixed. Therefore, the pooling involved in multilevel models affords a "borrowing of strength" that supports statistical inference in a situation where no inference would be possible using traditional methods (Raudenbush & Bryk, 2002). Particularly, the use of HLMs on NAEP data addresses the problem of sampling error resulting from the multistage sampling in NAEP and the measurement error resulting from the multiple imputation of NAEP scores (see Arnold, 1993; Raudenbush, Bryk, Cheong, & Congdon, 2002).

4. Correlation measures the strength and direction of relationship between two variables, possibly ranging from -1 to $+1$. Positive values suggest that an increase in one variable is associated with an increase in the other. Negative correlation values suggest inverse relationships between the two variables. Whether positive or negative, the greater absolute values of correlations imply the stronger relationships. In this study using a cross-lagged panel design, three types of correlations were examined. First, "stability effects" were examined through the correlations of the same variables over time (e.g., correlation between 1992 and 1996 segregation measures) to see if the racial segregation changed across the states. Second, "synchronous effects" were examined through the correlations between segregation and gap variables in the same year (e.g., correlation between 1996 segregation and achievement gap) to see if racial segregation is associated with the achievement gap. Finally, "cross-lagged effects" were examined through the correlations

between segregation and gap variables across years (e.g., correlation between 1992 segregation and 1996 achievement gap).

5. The assumptions discussed are implicit in this cross-lagged panel correlation analysis, and possible violations of these threaten the validity of the interpretation of the results. Further, if the tipping point effect operates at the state level as well, the correlation will not capture this nonlinear relationship.

6. It is conceivable that it is geographically impossible to transport students across a state in order to completely balance them, as a D of 0 would imply. For these reasons, dissimilarity is usually calculated at the district level. D here, however, allows us to monitor the evenness of the distribution of students in schools even if achieving no segregation, as measured at the state level, might be difficult. Nevertheless, the trends reported in this essay are similar, in general, to other measurements using comprehensive enrollment data (G. Orfield & C. Lee, 2005; Clotfelter, 2004).

7. This within-school Black-White gap amounts to about two standard deviations of the NAEP test scores.

8. Although four years is a short time period to see such a significant decrease, it was more than enough time to allow for significant increases in a number of different states. Further analyses should determine how these trends change over a longer period of time.

9. For one examination of the growth from 1994 to 2001 of between-school and within-school segregation across North Carolina, see Clotfelter, 2004.

10. The relatively weaker correlations between 1992 and 1996 gap measures may be partly due to the measurement errors. This is demonstrated by the fact that none of the states reduced the math achievement gaps among racial groups by a statistically significant amount.

11. The 1992 measures of Black-White between-school segregation are positively associated with the 1996 measures of the Black-White between-school achievement gap ($r = .39$). Specifically, a one-standard-deviation-unit increase in the between-school Black-White segregation could lead to a one-half-standard-deviation-unit increase in the between-school Black-White achievement at the state level. Reversed correlations are also significant when the 1992 Black-White achievement gap measures are related to the 1996 Black-White segregation measures ($r = .43$). Similar patterns of correlations are found between Hispanic-White within-school segregation and achievement gap measures ($r = .34$; $r = .50$).

12. Previous studies showed that the size of the racial achievement gap tends to be relatively large at the high school level, but changes in the racial achievement gap trends were fairly consistent across age or grade levels (Grissmer, Flanagan, & Willamson, 1998; J. Lee, 2002).

13. Previous studies showed that the extent of access to different levels of courses and course taking for various tracks varies among schools with different tracking policies (V. E. Lee & Bryk, 1988).

14. Information on student eligibility for free and reduced-price lunch (a proxy measure of family poverty) was not available until 1996 in NAEP. Moreover, includ-

ing this kind of proxy socioeconomic status (SES) variable in the analysis does not necessarily help reveal the relationship between racial segregation and the achievement gap. Because conventional measures of SES are poorly constructed, they fail to capture differences in family assets beyond income or in family background effects that span more than one generation. Further, because the conventional analysis of SES focuses on the attributes of individuals, such individual-level analyses make it difficult to assess the impact of the "social structure of inequality" (W. J. Wilson, 1998). Even if SES can be measured accurately and controlled fully in the statistical analysis, the interpretation of what remains unexplained in the observed effect of race may remain controversial (see Herrnstein & Murray, 1994; Jencks & M. Phillips, 1998; Neisser, 1998). All of the data limitations and analytical issues pose a challenge for research on the racial achievement gap.

15. The degree of correlation of racial segregation and the achievement gap may drop substantially if we were able to control for the effect of poverty statistically or eliminate socioeconomic segregation in schools practically (Kahlenberg, 2001; G. Orfield, 1996). However, previous studies of the long-term trend NAEP data suggest that the past reduction of the Black-White achievement gap was accomplished apart from poverty reduction (Grissmer, Kirby, Berends, & Willamson, 1994; Hedges & Nowell, 1998). Recent research indicates that socioeconomic disparities—that is, disparities in employment, housing, and health care among students' families—do contribute to achievement gaps, which are therefore susceptible to reduction through policy changes in these areas (e.g., Rumberger & Palardy, 2005; Rothstein, 2004).

16. For the counterargument that high-stakes testing has had a disproportionately harmful effect on minority students because they often have not had the opportunity to learn the material on which they are tested, see Heubert (2005).

17. The grand notion of reciprocity for social justice was advanced by Rawls (1971), who proclaimed through his "difference principle" that resources in education should be allocated so as to have the most advantaged group use its natural endowments, such as academic ability, in ways that help and improve the long-term expectation of the most disadvantaged. In practice, schools may take advantage of the existing achievement gap to facilitate cooperative learning or peer tutoring (e.g., Student Teams-Achievement Divisions, Peer-Assisted Learning Strategies). In reading instruction, "reciprocal teaching" was designed to capitalize on students' varying levels of competence in collaborative learning settings (Darling-Hammond, 1997). However, the effects of these race-neutral pedagogical strategies on racial achievement gaps remain to be examined.

New Dimensions of Integration

*The Growth of Non-Black
Minority Groups*

Adolescent Immigrant Students in U.S. Schools

Issues of Cultural Pluralism, Successful School Settings, and Intergroup Relations

M. Beatriz Arias, Christian Faltis, and James Cohen

The Latino and immigrant populations in U.S. schools have exploded. Since the 1960s, Latino population growth has accounted for half of all population increases. The impact of unprecedented immigration flows in the 1990s has resulted in immigrants representing one in nine of all U.S. residents and their children representing one in four of all school-age children who are low income (Capps, Fix, & Murray, 2005). The share of first-generation immigrant students, according to Capps, Fix, and Murray, increases in the upper grades and poses special challenges for secondary schools. Many foreign-born students enter U.S. schools with limited English proficiency and limited schooling in their home country. This essay addresses the challenges that the growth of the English Language Learner (ELL) immigrant population poses for secondary schools. These students are experiencing significant difficulty completing school successfully, much less in preparing for postsecondary education that is now so critical to achieving success in the American economy (Fry, 2005; Capps, Fix, & Murray, 2005). The current policy trends have cut back on special programs aimed at supporting language-minority children, ending bilingual education in several states and dissolving desegregation plans or other interventions, all the while subjecting these students to increasingly demanding, high-stakes English-language tests.[1]

This essay suggests that these trends are counterproductive. Forced assimilation of these students will likely fail and have serious consequences (Valenzuela, 1999). Instead, we suggest that the best alternative to educate this ever-growing segment of the public school population is a pluralistic strategy of linguistic and cultural inclusion in successful, multiracial schools. This approach could produce greater success for students at risk, as well as gains in understanding and adapting to a changing society for White students.

In the past thirty-five years, two significant events have occurred since the courts ordered public schools to address the language and academic learning needs of non-English-proficient immigrant and native-born students (*Lau v. Nichols,* 1974; *Castañeda v. Pickard,* 1981). First, bilingual education as a programmatic remedy has been made virtually illegal in California (1998), Arizona (2001), and Massachusetts (2001), where one-third of the entire school-age population of English learners nationwide resides and attends school (Waggoner, 1999). Additionally, support for minimal native language instruction has diminished in the remaining forty-seven states (Macias & Kelly, 1996), due in part to the regulations of the No Child Left Behind Act (2001), which favor English-immersion accommodations over bilingual education. Second, the population of school-age immigrant children and adolescents who speak a language other than English has burgeoned in recent decades, from 2.2 million in 1989–90 to more than 4 million at the beginning of the twenty-first century (Ovando, Collier, & Combs, 2003; García, 2004). These children and adolescents are the fastest growing segment of the school-age population in Arizona, California, Florida, Illinois, Massachusetts, New York, and Texas (Olsen & Jaramillo, 1999; Waggoner, 1999). Moreover, in recent years the number of immigrant students enrolling in grades 7 through 12 has increased at a proportionally greater rate than that at the elementary school level in states with large immigrant populations (Olsen & Jaramillo, 1999).

Adolescent Immigrant Students and Intergroup Relations in Schools

We focus here on adolescent immigrant students for the following reasons: (1) adolescent immigrants are the fastest growing segment of the student population nationwide (Olsen & Jaramillo, 1999; Waggoner, 1999); (2) very little is known about adolescent secondary-school immigrant students because nearly all studies in the past thirty-five years have been conducted at the elementary school level (Faltis, 1999); and (3) research on intergroup contact and intergroup relations has been primarily focused on adolescent and adult learners (J. A. Banks & McGee-Banks, 2004).

In the following sections we propose that intergroup contact and positive intergroup relations between immigrant and nonimmigrant adolescent students not only depend on providing all students with safe environments for learning but also on the philosophical stance a school takes toward cultural pluralism (Kjolseth, 1982), (or additive acculturation

[Gibson, 1995]), as opposed to cultural assimilation (Kjolseth, 1982). For the purposes of this essay, "cultural pluralism" refers to policies and practices that seek the integration and participation of students from diverse language and cultural backgrounds in ways to enable these students to maintain their language and cultural identities and practices while they acquire English and learn academic content. "Cultural assimilation" refers to policies and practices that seek the integration and participation of linguistically and culturally diverse students only under the condition that these students give up their cultural traditions, value systems, and language practices and replace them with those deemed to be American. From a cultural pluralism stance, providing immigrant students with quality programs that are safe and geared toward their educational and social needs in school requires at least that administrators, teachers, and support staff are credible models for and knowledgeable about the students and the communities they serve. To this end, we discuss ways that adolescent immigrant students who enroll in secondary school vary in terms of prior schooling experiences and transitions to the United States. In the final section we discuss the research literature on programmatic, classroom level, and curricular efforts that support positive intergroup contact and relations, with an eye toward recommending practices that may be especially effective for schools with large numbers of newly arrived adolescent immigrant students. The essay concludes with a discussion of practices implemented in diverse secondary schools to support positive intergroup relations.

Characteristics of Schools Receiving Immigrant Students

First- and second-generation Latino immigrants are by far the most populous group of immigrant students to have entered the United States in recent years (McArthur, 1993). Latino students are America's most segregated minority group and have steadily become more segregated since the late 1960s (as Latinos have continued to become a larger percentage of the public school enrollment). The average Latino student now goes to a school that is less than 30 percent White, where a majority of the children are poor, and where an increasing concentration of students do not speak English. In fact, according to Frankenberg, C. Lee, and G. Orfield (2003), Latino ELLs attend schools where over 60 percent of the students are Latino. By comparison, they found that the racial isolation is less severe for Asian ELL students, who attend schools that are, on average, only one-quarter Asian.

Several structural features, including socioeconomic status, neighborhood characteristics, and the schools immigrant students most frequently attend, shape opportunity for immigrant youth. The reality is that most immigrant youth enter highly segregated neighborhoods with large co-ethnic or minority populations. There is usually little contact with the mainstream middle class. McDonnell and Hill (1993) note that 78 percent of the newly arrived immigrants locate in the largest cities in California, Texas, New York, Florida, and Illinois. Data from the census of 2000 indicate that by several measures Latino immigrant students are the most segregated in the southern, northeastern, and western regions inclusive of these states. Almost four-fifths of Latino students in these regions are in schools where more than half of the students are non-White (Frankenberg, C. Lee, & G. Orfield, 2003, table 37). In every region of the country in 2000 there were fewer White students in the school of the average Latino student than two decades earlier (Frankenberg, C. Lee, & G. Orfield, 2003).

Compounding the societal segregation is the fact that most immigrant students live in poor neighborhoods where they are consistently exposed to gang activity and violence. Walqui (2000) has noted that a central feature of the social context for many immigrant students is the presence of gangs and violence. This contextual feature makes it imperative that immigrant students find safe havens from violence, and to some extent that schools can focus on developing safe zones for youths. Immigrant students need school settings that can help them cope with their social context, gangs, alienation, low social status, and prejudice. Schools that recognize and address these factors begin to provide settings in which immigrant students can thrive.

Providing a Safe Learning Environment

The decline of bilingual educational support services; the segregation of many immigrant students from White, middle-class, or native English speakers in schools and neighborhoods; and fewer accommodations for immigrant English learners, coupled with increases in this population, creates new problems for public schools seeking to provide quality education to all students regardless of their home language, race, ethnicity, or social class.

How students fare in school today affects their individual, cultural, and economic needs in the future. Schooling is especially decisive for immigrant students, a majority of whom hail from poverty or war-torn backgrounds (C. Suárez-Orozco & Todorova, 2003), because school achievement can offer these students more options for professional and economic development than were available to them in their home countries. Students who perform poorly in school, especially those who do not graduate, will have fewer options than those who perform well.

The reason why some immigrant English learners do well or poorly in school is a complex issue we will explore further in this essay. However, the most convincing evidence suggests that the answers lie, to a great extent, in how schools organize learning environments and how they view their immigrant student populations. Schools that acknowledge the educational and social needs of their students and families in ways that pay attention to and value their cultural identities and practices, home language and English proficiency, and prior as well as present schooling experiences are schools that are most conducive to immigrant student success (California Tomorrow, 2004; Faltis, 1994, 2005; Y. Freeman, D. Freeman, & Mercuri, 2002; T. Lucas, Henze, & Donato, 1990; Minicucci & Olsen, 1992; Olsen & Jaramillo, 1999; Walqui, 2000).

We expand the concept of "safe schools," usually meaning schools that are relatively free from racial hostility and violence, to include schools that encourage the development of ethnic and racial identity. We envision schools as safe havens for the development and explorations of diversity. When schools are organized to support and value students' life experiences, students are provided with a safe environment for learning. As a result, they are more likely to participate as members of school communities in which the learning environments are inviting as well as challenging, thoughtful, and culturally responsive to their specific needs as immigrant students.

A "safe haven" learning environment enables immigrant students who are learning English in U.S. schools to try on new identities as members of academic communities, to become readers and writers of English, and to grow into young adults as new Americans in ways that do not force them to lose their individual and group (including immigrant and transnational) identities as members of language and cultural groups to which they and their families belong across space and time (Brittain, 2002; Canniff, 2001; Olsen, 1997; Tse, 2001; Valdés, 2001).

Encouraging Positive Intergroup Relations

While safe learning environments are necessary, they are not sufficient to ensure successful schooling for immigrant students. Schools reflect society, and across the nation, especially since the September 11 attacks, attitudes toward immigrants in general—but specifically toward brown-skinned, non-English-speaking immigrants—have become increasingly and overtly negative. Accordingly, research in successful schools for immigrant students has illustrated the need for encouraging and sustaining positive intergroup relations between immigrant and nonimmigrant students as a way to develop acceptance and nurture intergroup contact and understanding (T. Lucas, Henze, & Donato, 1990; Olson & Jaramillo, 1999; W. G. Stephan, & C. W. Stephan, 2001). This need is especially critical in secondary school communities, where identity affiliations (the belief systems and practices to which students align themselves), peer groupings (the groups to which a students belongs and identifies with), transnational messages (remarks and statements that immigrant students hear about American education, and how others see them), and self-selected segregation along ethnic, language, gender, family income, and academic tracks often become highly divisive (Brittain, 2002). In some cases this can make both learning and positive intergroup relations in schools unsafe and, consequently, more difficult to achieve. In large urban high schools, for example, well-established ethnic gangs with competing interests seek out recent immigrant students to join them, which not only inhibits the potential for the development of positive intergroup relations among different ethnic and language groups but also can make schools dangerous places to be (Vigil, 2002).

Insightful educators and leaders, concerned with making today's schools places where all students can learn, have found it necessary to address how issues of race, class, gender, language, and ethnicity are reflected and reinforced by school practices and policies. These educational leaders recognize that students will learn in environments where they feel safe and not threatened by physical violence, slurs, and harassment based on ethnicity, language, religion, or race. These leaders also recognize that in today's increasingly multicultural school environments, students and adults need to learn how to learn together and from one another. In subsequent sections this essay will present approaches that educational leaders have successfully implemented in secondary schools across the nation to improve interethnic relations.

The Role of a Cultural Pluralism Stance

What any school with large numbers of immigrant students can accomplish with respect to providing a safe learning environment and positive intergroup relations is in no small measure tied to the philosophical stance that undergirds its raison d'être for preparing immigrant students.

In simple terms, schools that largely disregard the immigrant students' home language and prior schooling experiences fall under a general stance that can be referred to as assimilation. From this philosophical stance, a major role of school is to teach students how to be "American," by prohibiting home language use in school (other than as a foreign language) as well as any celebration of home country behaviors or interests, in order to learn standard English. Likewise, information and implied messages that students hear about their homeland through the media and other sources are ignored. Maintenance of home cultural ways of thinking, believing, acting, and using language undermines the school's goal of assimilation into the so-called mainstream. Ethnic community involvement in school matters is not sought, and any form of intergroup conflict is downplayed. The school and its faculty subtly and at times overtly stress the superiority of the English language and American society over non-English-speaking peoples and their cultures.

From an assimilationist perspective, English and the cultural content of academic work are placed above languages and cultures that immigrant students bring with them to school. In recent years, under the No Child Left Behind Act, the move toward academic standards, high-stakes testing for graduation, and state-adopted textbooks for elementary and secondary schools has worked in favor of an assimilationist perspective by standardizing the American curriculum in ways that favor a narrow view of what it means to be an educated American citizen.

At the other extreme from assimilation is the stance that there are many types of Americans and the school's role is to foster the civic development of immigrants without having them shed their individual and group identities as members of ethnic and language groups as they adjust to a new society and nation. This perspective is referred to as cultural pluralism, or additive acculturation.

Schools that promote cultural pluralism take a positive stance toward the attributes that immigrant students bring: their language and culture. Schools with a pluralistic stance often devise curricular programs where the language of the immigrant student is supported as a course of study, where immigrant students can serve as role models as native speakers of a target language of study, or where immigrant students are given credit toward graduation for their language proficiency. Dual-language programs, where students are developing language proficiency in two languages, provide a powerful opportunity to address linguistic segregation and provide an equal status contact setting for immigrant students (see Killen, Crystal, & Ruck, this volume).

As advocates for positive change, schools and teachers who work toward this philosophical stance seek ways to make transparent the differing interests between and among immigrant and nonimmigrant students. Additionally, they seek resolution of conflicts that arise when students of diverse language, social, economic, and ethnic group backgrounds are encouraged to physically and socially integrate in order to share experiences and draw on different voices as they learn and engage in academic practices in school and classroom settings.

Research has shown that the longer those immigrant students who are forced to lose their language, to learn standard English only, and to relinquish their cultural bonds and practices are in the United States, the more negative they become toward school and additive acculturation (Rumbaut & Cornelius, 1995; M. Suárez-Orozco & C. Suárez-Orozco, 1995; Waters, 1995). This is exactly the opposite of what the assimilationist model predicts. On the other hand, when schools embrace cultural and language variation, pay attention to the educational and social needs of immigrant students and children of immigrants, and encourage immigrant students to add on elements of the new culture to supplement their culture, many of these students fare very well in school (Canniff, 2001; Gibson, 1995; Olsen & Jaramillo, 1999; M. Suárez-Orozco, 1998; Trueba, 1998). In addition, their success in school translates into greater potential for occupational mobility and higher earnings than their parents (Portes, 1995; Trueba, 1998).

Variation among Adolescent Immigrant Students

Most of what is known and understood about adolescent immigrant students in school settings is relatively recent, with the bulk of research having begun in the 1990s. Even research journals geared toward bilingual education and ELLs have rarely included studies about adolescent English learners (Faltis, 1999). In educational research the main goal has been to better understand adolescent immigrant students' educational needs based on types and levels of prior home country schooling experiences upon arrival in the U.S. (Faltis & Wolfe, 1999; Y. Freeman, D. Freeman, & Mercuri, 2002; T. Lucas, 1998; Mace-Matluck, Alexander-Kasparik, & Queen, 1998; Minicucci & Olsen, 1992). More recently, the emphasis has focused on factors such as the ease or difficulty with which they arrived as immigrants (Phelan, A. L. Davidson, & Yu, 1998) and how their acculturation to U.S. settings relates to effective intergroup relationships that allow immigrant students to acculturate without necessarily severing ties to their home language and culture (Brittain, 2002; Canniff, 2001; M. Suárez-Orozco, 2000).

Faltis and Arias (1993) focus attention on the type of schooling immigrant students had experienced in their home country before they entered high school as parallel or nonparallel to U.S. students. They discuss immigrant students who had attended bilingual schools and learned English in their home country, pointing out that these students belong mainly to the elite class, and, accordingly, they have a relatively smooth transition to American high schools. Such students are often held up by mainstream society as exemplar immigrant students (the model minority). In contrast to these immigrants are students who received some formal schooling in their home country but are unprepared for U.S. schools. Many immigrant students, particularly those whose families had little education, arrive at secondary school with gaps in their literacy abilities and content knowledge, and are likely to be unsure of how U.S. schools operate academically and socially. These students have had nonparallel educational experiences, meaning that when they enter U.S. schools, they are usually two or more years behind academically. If they arrive in the elementary grades and are given no language or academic support, they are likely to become long-term English learners, or English as a Second Language (ESL) "lifers," as they are sometimes referred to disparagingly. Finally, Faltis and Arias (1993) discuss immigrant students who enter high school with fairly parallel academic abilities but lack English proficiency. These students need intensive ESL coursework, but once they are transitioned into grade level content classes, they tend to perform very well in school, because they bring with them strong academic and school knowledge foundations.

Immigrant students are challenged to succeed in American schools and to become "Americans." Studies indicate that the Americanization process is not smooth. Research conducted by Olsen (1997) and Phelan, A. L. Davidson, and Cao (1991) focuses on the factors that affect academic and social engagement for immigrant students within the school community. Olsen (1997) studied immigrant students at one high school to understand how they managed to fit into the complex system of assimilation that denied them full participation. She concluded that there were three components to the Americanization process that immigrant students in secondary schools undergo. These included academic marginalization and separation, the requirement to become English speaking, and the pressure to find a place in the U.S. racial hierarchy.

Phelan, A. L. Davidson, and Cao (1991) followed fifty-five immigrant students at four high schools. Based on their findings, they developed a "multiple worlds" model to illustrate the diverse ways in which meaning drawn from immigrant youths' family, peer, and school worlds combines to influence these students' identities and practices in and out of school. The multiple worlds model enabled the authors to understand variation

Table 1. Immigrant students' multiple worlds at school and in society

	Come from congruent experiences	Come from different experiences
Smooth transitions	These students move effortlessly from their home country to the U.S. and experience only minor differences between schooling at home and schooling in the U.S. Many of these immigrant students are from middle- to upper-middle-class, high-achieving backgrounds.	Some of these students are aware of and understand differences between their home country and the U.S.; they use adapting strategies to manage the new environment successfully, and usually perform well socially and academically in school. Others see their worlds as completely different, but are able to adapt to new settings effortlessly. These students tend to have multiple international experiences.
Transitions resisted	These immigrant students, who were high-achieving in their home country, may do well on standardized tests, but receive low or failing grades from their teachers because they resist adapting to U.S. schools and society. Teachers' explanations for failure are often rooted in deficit views toward the student, their family, and their cultural background.	Some immigrants understand differences between their home country and the U.S. but find transitions to the new settings to be very difficult. These students may do well in a few classes, but poorly in the rest. Others hold beliefs and expectations that are so discordant that they perceive differences as insurmountable, and thus, actively or passively, they resist transitions. These students tend not to adjust well to school and may affiliate with groups who operate in opposition to school expectations.

Adapted from Phelan, A. L. Davidson & Yu, 1998.

among adolescent immigrants' ability to be successful in school and in their own worlds by paying attention to the ease or difficulty of their transitions into school and whether they came from congruent or incongruent worlds (see table 1).

The relatively new fields of immigration studies (M. Suárez-Orozco, 2000; M. Suárez-Orozco & C. Suárez-Orozco, 1995; C. Suárez-Orozco & Todorova, 2003) and transnational studies of immigration (Albrow, 1998; Brittain, 2002; Portes, 1995, 1999; Portes, Guarnizo, & Landolt, 1999) have also contributed to our understanding of immigrant adolescents' lives prior to and once in school. Work in these fields shows that in addition to prior educational, world, and transitional experiences, students also come to school with and continue to develop transnational immigrant identities, affiliations, and practices—ways of being, interacting,

Table 2. Identities, prior academic experiences, and school success among new immigrant adolescents

	Transnational identity	Local identity
Technoskills and high degree of literacy	These immigrant students are likely to experience a high degree of success in secondary school. They have high levels of literacy and technological knowledge, and their identities cross economic, social, national, and cultural boundaries.	These immigrant students are likely to experience some success in secondary school because they have high levels of literacy and technological knowledge. However, because they create local identities affiliated with immigrants who tend to resist school, their academic success may be limited.
Manual skills and low degree of literacy	These immigrant students are likely to eventually succeed in school because they strive to balance their home language and cultural ways with those of new settings. Their identities as immigrants cross economic, social, national, and cultural boundaries.	These immigrant students are likely to experience social isolation in school and to develop local identities affiliated with compatriot immigrant students who tend to resist school practices. Moreover, since they also have low literacy abilities and experience with manual skills only, their success is school is likely to be limited.

Adapted from M. Suárez-Orozco, 2000.

and doing that "cross and overlap with boundaries between nation-states (e.g., transnational corporations, political agreements, and migrant labor markets)" (Brittain, 2002, p. 13). For instance, many immigrant youth maintain home country pop culture connections with music and dance, and yet participate actively in American pop culture as well. These transnational immigrant identities create and are created by social spaces in which some students learn to operate, based on their prior experiences with literacy, media, and types of labor. Together these transnational spaces, coupled with prior world experiences, have an impact on how some immigrant students relate and succeed in the academic world of U.S. secondary schools.

M. Suárez-Orozco (2000) posits that immigrant students who develop transnational as opposed to local identities as they adapt to the new society are likely to be more successful in school. By "local identities" we mean that these students look to and affiliate with ways of using language, acting, thinking, and being that are aligned more with local practices than with practices associated with their home country. Table 2 shows the relationship between identities and prior schooling experiences.

As can be seen in table 2, success in secondary school and in the work world may depend on the extent to which adolescent immigrant students create and nurture transnational or local identities and develop technoskills and proficiency in academic literacy. For our purposes, what is relevant about the work of M. Suárez-Orozco and others in this field is that it points to the possible influence that transnational and local social spaces and identities can have on the intergroup relations immigrant students develop in school. For example, through the multitude of venues by which immigrants are able to both obtain artifacts and live in an "Americanized" version of the life they had in their home country, immigrant adolescents are able to continue to live in both worlds, not necessarily adapting wholly to the new life of an "American." This may strain relations with other immigrant adolescent students who have taken another route, one of assimilation.

Secondary Schools for Immigrant Students

In this section, we present an overview of research on schools that provide positive educational experiences for immigrant students. We review the characteristics of successful schools and return to assess available research regarding the development of positive intergroup relations between immigrant and nonimmigrant students. And we conclude with recommendations about ways to incorporate positive intergroup relations practices, keeping in mind the variation among and multiple needs of today's adolescent immigrant students.

Most immigrant students enroll in schools that are not only highly segregated, as discussed above, but also have a severe mismatch between their organizational structure and meeting immigrant students' needs. In a 1992 study of California secondary schools, Minicucci and Olsen characterized the schools' organizational structure as being contrary to supporting the needs of immigrant youths. They stressed that the fragmented and rigid institutional structure of the typical secondary school could not accommodate the differentiated and individualized instruction needed by ELLs and students from diverse cultural backgrounds. The organizational structures of the typical secondary school—the scheduling of classes, prerequisites for classes, tracking of students, and range of offerings available to immigrant students—become barriers to the immigrant students' educational progress.

Olsen (1995) identified the following structural mismatches between immigrant students' needs and the organization of most secondary schools. They include: (1) the standard four-year high school model that presupposes levels of skill development and academic knowledge that is not applicable to immigrant students; (2) inflexible systems of earning credits that lock in a specified age-grade norm; (3) lack of support services; and (4) inflexible school schedules.

The standard comprehensive high school model assumes that students have successfully progressed through a pre-K through eighth-grade curriculum in which a basic proficiency in English and mathematics has been mastered. Until recently most high schools neither provided entry-level ESL courses nor addressed the needs of students who had not developed literacy skills prior to attending high school.

In some schools, course scheduling dictates the progression of students through course requirements. The system by which students earn credits presupposes that students have taken prerequisite courses in specific grades. For example, algebra, usually taken in the freshman year, is a prerequisite for geometry. In some schools, geometry is only offered to sophomores; consequently, if a student did not take algebra by freshman year, they are not eligible for geometry in sophomore year.

Immigrant students need support services that will help them navigate the culture of the American secondary school. Newcomer centers are helpful but not available at all schools. Services such as academic counseling and medical and community referrals are needed to assist immigrant students adjusting to a new culture and also to explain the needs of immigrant students to secondary-school teachers and administrators.

Immigrant secondary students often have responsibilities beyond school. They may hold part-time jobs or be responsible for caring for younger siblings. Inflexible school schedules make it problematic for these students to keep their part-time jobs or fulfill their care-giving responsibilities.

In addition to the structural features of secondary schools, Olsen (1997) noted that the curriculum in the schools she studied did not address immigrant students' needs. She characterized the schools as dependent on "sheltered-content" classes, taught by inadequately trained or prepared teachers. These secondary schools offered almost no primary-language instruction or support. Olsen chronicles the social isolation of immigrant students, the lack of support services in the students' home languages and conflicting faculty attitudes toward immigrant education.

Most researchers who focus on immigrant students in secondary schools have concluded that the secondary setting does not facilitate the assimilation of immigrant students. Mace-Matluck (1998) and her colleagues identified school structures that impeded secondary schools from serving the needs of immigrant students. These included:

1. a school structure that does not facilitate smooth transitions from program to program, school to school, or school to college or work;
2. an instructional program that fails to give ELLs grade appropriate access to academic concepts and skills;
3. few program and curricular alternatives for students with limited prior schooling and low literacy skills; and
4. a shortage of school personnel trained to meet these students' specified needs.

Characteristics of Schools That Promote Access for Immigrant Students

Research conducted by T. Lucas, Henze, and Donato (1990) identified the characteristics of schools in California and Arizona that were effective with Latino ELLs. Building on this work, T. Lucas (1998) described ways in which schools can help immigrant students succeed. She developed a checklist of effective elements of schools for language-minority students that focused on four major factors: school context, curriculum, staff, and longevity and pervasiveness of effective features.

Walqui (2000) has provided a profile of four secondary schools with significant immigrant student enrollment, which addressed issues of culture, language, and ethnicity. Two of these schools are particularly notable in that they significantly altered the structure of the traditional secondary school to provide opportunities and access for immigrant students.

Calexico High School, in Calexico, California, restructured its curriculum to create flexible instructional units that stressed high expectations for all students. Curricular restructuring included creating academies and institutes, detracking course offerings, establishing comparable curricula for native English students and English Language Learners with bilingual materials, and requiring a senior project. The clustering into four academies at the school occurs at the tenth grade, with approximately 150 students assigned to a specific team of teachers. One of the four academies is an ESL academy, which facilitates teacher collaboration. This means that the team can plan integrated units, exchange information about students, and share strategies. The clustering also assists students to feel connected in a smaller, more personalized unit. Institutes were also developed for the eleventh and twelfth grades to offer in-depth specialized concentration in an area of study that will lead to postsecondary education or work opportunities. These institutes include Business and Economics, Visual and Performing Arts, Human Services and Engineering, and Technology. An interdisciplinary team of teachers that supports a community dedicated to professional growth plans the institutes.

Similar to Calexico High School, New York's International High School focused on innovative instruction and curriculum to address the needs of immigrant students. International High School is remarkable in that while more than 75 percent of the students qualify for free and reduced lunch, every year more than 90 percent of the graduates apply and are accepted to college.

International High School addressed the needs of immigrant students by eliminating the departmentalized curriculum and established a thematic-based curriculum, increasing the relevance of education by linking internships with course offerings and supporting intensive teacher collaboration. While this school has been very successful in facilitating access to a high-quality curriculum for immigrant students, it has done so in a relatively isolated environment. It admits only students who have lived in the United States fewer than four years and who score in the lowest quartile on an English language proficiency test. International High School, then, is an example of a program designed specifically for immigrant students.

Walqui (2000) emphasizes that "the programs that seem to have the most success . . . are those that have been created specifically for immigrant students, not those that have reformed existing structures" (p. 197). She maintains that programs that temporarily separate educational arrangements for particular students are justified for their curricular benefit to ELLs.

Schools That Promote Additive Acculturation

Gibson (1995) notes that many first- and second-generation immigrant students are successful because they draw strength from their home cultures and from a positive sense of their ethnic identities. She stresses that successful immigrant students use a strategy of additive acculturation in accommodating to the new culture. In her study of Punjabi Sikhs in California, Gibson described processes that students use to fit into the official way of school, adopting desirable American ways yet resisting full assimilation by maintaining separate cultural identities. Parents encourage acculturation to a point. They support students' acquisition of English, but at the same time they discourage their children from participating in extracurricular activities or from mixing socially outside of school, wanting to maintain their children within the cultural fold.

Similarly, Rumbaut and Ima (1988) found a strong correlation between ethnic resilience (maintenance of home language and customs) and grades in their study of Southeast Asian refugees: the stronger the sense of ethnic resilience, the higher the grades. "Implementing a policy of additive ac-culturation, or multiculturalism in schools would help resolve the conflict that some students feel between acquiring new cultural competencies and maintaining their social identity. Schools have an important role to play in helping students feel they can become competent in many different cul-tures without forsaking their identity," concluded M. Suárez-Orozco and C. Suárez-Orozco (1995, p. 187).

This raises several questions: Can programs be designed that benefit both immigrant and non-immigrant students? Is it possible to address the needs of immigrant students in diverse schools? How can we further the accommodation of immigrant students so that they have opportunities to interact positively with non-immigrant students? The dual challenge is how to support schools that can create an additive school culture (one that encourages students to retain their language and culture) for immi-grant students while building and encouraging respect for diversity within the entire student body.

Schools That Promote Positive Intergroup Relations

Positive intergroup contact offers a means for alleviating prejudice, dis-crimination, and conflict (see Killen, Crystal, & Ruck, in this volume). W. G. Stephan and C. W. Stephan (2003) have noted that mixed groups working together cooperatively generate more positive attitudes than multicultural efforts alone. Personal contact offers a significant means of reducing intergroup prejudice. As Pettigrew (2004) has noted, "Peers, community leaders, adults in schools, church members, and coaches are important particularly for the adaptation of immigrant adolescents" (p. 778). These relationships provide immigrant youths with compensa-tory attachments, information about new cultural norms and practices, and tools vital to success in school.

Thus one more challenge for schools to promote positive intergroup relations is to strategically design highly involved cross-group exercises. Heterogeneous grouping has been shown to improve intergroup relations by increasing trust and friendliness. It teaches students skills for work-ing in groups that can be transferred to many student and adult work situations (E. G. Cohen, 1986). Cohen has asserted that if children have very little chance to interact with each other, cultural prejudices will have no opportunity to be challenged. In fact, highly diverse schools offer an optimal contact situation where positive intergroup relations could be structured. The diversity of today's schools presents an opportunity for promoting prejudice reduction. Equal-status group interaction offers a chance to attack these prejudices.

How can schools create a climate that combats prejudice, racism, and separatism? What kind of affirmative efforts connect students across lines of culture, language, and race? The following discussion relies heavily on Henze et al. (2002), who conducted a promising study of twenty-one schools across the nation believed to promote positive interethnic relations. The schools had at least three major ethnic groups, a history of racial or ethnic conflict or tension in the school or surrounding community, and leadership that employs a proactive approach to addressing these conflicts and building positive relations among ethnic groups.

These researchers document how schools responded to racial conflict situations. In each school the response began with a leadership team (principal, teachers, and sometimes community members) visioning positive interethnic relations. The process of promoting positive interethnic relations began by examining local data to improve equity and ethnic relations and address student and faculty needs. Core problems were identified, solutions proposed, goals were set, and action was taken. Often the vision was reflected in a mission statement that included equity, social justice, and positive interethnic relations embodied in policies and practices throughout the school.

Organizational changes occurred at many levels: many schools initiated structures such as houses, families or pods, and academies in order to cluster students into smaller groups and provide a more personalized school experience and equal status interaction. Many of the schools made diverse staffing and ongoing professional development basic objectives. Diverse staffing provided role models, improved communication with diverse students and parents, and provided more opportunities for staff and students to learn about diversity. Special events were the most common approach used to infuse information about ethnic groups in these schools where the events were not trivialized as a once-a-year event.

Curriculum modification was addressed at several levels. These schools provided programs that were optional additions to the regular curriculum—offered after school, during weekends, at lunchtime, or in the summer. They included mentoring and tutoring programs, conflict resolution programs, and extracurricular activities such as sports, arts, and student clubs.

Other curricular adaptations that support an additive school culture are dual-language programs, which serve language-minority (immigrant) and language-majority (nonimmigrant) students by enriching the curriculum with language development as well as language maintenance activities for both languages (Genesee, Hamayan, & Cloud, 2000). Dual-language programs are primarily found in K–8 schools. The compartmentalization of the comprehensive high school does not easily support the concurrent development of two languages. However, some charter schools and magnet programs have integrated the dual-language approach (students learning each other's language) as a component of the language arts curriculum. More efforts in this area are needed as students graduating from K–8 dual-language programs seek to retain their bilingualism and biliteracy.

Concluding Statements

We have reviewed research that identifies structural barriers embedded in secondary schools that promote the exclusion of immigrant students. Most secondary schools are characterized by an inflexible system of credit earning coupled with inflexible school schedules and a lack of support services (Olsen, 1995). We have identified characteristics of secondary schools that promote access for immigrant students. Schools that accommodate to students' culture, language, and ethnicity (Walqui, 2000) assure that immigrant students have access to the general curriculum by modifying the delivery of instruction, redesigning instructional modules, and providing smaller class size environments.

We have documented the benefits to immigrant student academic progress when schools support their developing ethnic identity (Rumbaut and Ima, 1988). It is notable that research shows that students who maintain their cultural identity do better in school. We have noted exemplary ways in which schools can respond to potential racial conflict through systematic support of student interethnic contact. We know it takes site leadership to initiate change in organizational structures, provide a diversified staff, support professional development, and implement curricular programs that build on students' language and cultural assets, such as dual-language programs.

This review has provided readers with an understanding of the context and efforts needed to support immigrant student access and develop positive interethnic relationships in secondary schools. The challenge of the changing demographics of American secondary schools is coming at a time when far too little attention is being devoted to issues of building successful intergroup relations and creating school environments where all students and parents feel welcome and respected. Existing research and experiences show ways that perceived problems can be converted into opportunities and suggest that doing nothing will have higher costs for the future of society and the economy. We are currently on a path that leads to growing polarization and mounting costs. It is time to seriously examine the alternatives and invest in strategies that will bring newcomers more effectively into our schools, thereby helping our schools better reflect and serve our changing society.

Note

1. See Valenzuela (2004) for an analysis of how current accountability policies particularly impact Latino students.

"Desperate to Learn"

The Schooling Experience of Latinas in North Carolina

María Teresa Unger Palmer

The previous essay documented the mismatch between secondary schools' philosophical and organizational structures and the needs of immigrant students (Arias, Faltis, & Cohen, this volume). This essay looks at how this reality is experienced by a small number of immigrant students in their first three years in the American educational system. The research conducted in one school in a North Carolina college town puts a face on the people discussed in broader terms in the rest of this volume, a necessary step if we are to answer the call to create schools where all students feel welcomed.

In the census of 2000, millions of Hispanic citizens were counted in areas that in the census of 1990 had not recorded a Hispanic presence, including many nonmetropolitan parts of the South. To the surprise of longtime residents, North Carolina had the fastest-growing Hispanic population in the country, estimated at a 394 percent increase from 1990 to 2000. Immigration was a new statewide phenomenon, with census numbers confirming what residents had not failed to notice: "the browning of America" (J. H. Johnson, 2001).

The North Carolina Department of Public Instruction (DPI) showed a 285 percent increase in enrollment of Hispanic students across the state from 1990–91 to 1997–98 (DPI and State Board of Education, 1999; Mikow-Porto, 1999). In the 2000–2001 school year, of 73,079 national origin minority (NOM) students—immigrant children or children of foreign-born parents—at North Carolina public schools, 48,358 came from Spanish-speaking households. This represents an increase of 9,949 students from the previous year. An estimated 83 percent of Spanish-speaking NOM students received English as a Second Language (ESL) services in 2001.

In the county where this research was conducted, the influx of Hispanic immigrants in the 1990s was unexpected. In the southern third of the district, for example, the census of 1990 counted 64 persons of Mexican origin; in 2000 there were 1,530. While the town had enjoyed the presence of international students and researchers for many years, their presence had little impact on the school. The Hispanic newcomers of the 1990s, most of whom were the children of young nonprofessional, non-English-speaking parents, posed a greater challenge.

The growth in the immigrant population in the 1990s coincided with North Carolina's implementation of a groundbreaking system of accountability. It also coincided with a period of economic boom followed by tightening immigration controls and rising unemployment in the wake of the September 11 terrorist attacks. Lacking experience and a research base for educating immigrant children, North Carolina's educational leaders did not know how to address the needs of Latino children during these educationally and socially turbulent times. My research study was a response to the urgent need to document the reality of the new Hispanic community in North Carolina.

Within the Hispanic community, cultural expectations unique to each sex affect the students' approach and response to schooling. Romo (1998), in her research on why Latinas leave high school, cites examples of gender-specific problems, including sexual harassment, gender bias, and mother-daughter relations. Valenzuela (1999) also documents the conflicts that Latina students experience between traditional roles and family responsibilities and academic success. The focus of my research was limited to young women in order to independently explore the particular experiences of Latina women.

Description of the Study

In this essay I summarize the original case study of Latina immigrant students in one high school, and the action research and community organizing efforts that followed. Over the course of one academic year, from fall 2001 to fall 2002, I observed and interviewed eleven students to learn about the students' understandings and responses to their schooling experiences. I was a regular presence in the school, documenting the daily interactions of students and becoming familiar with the everyday aspects of their school life.

Of the fifteen Latina immigrant ESL students enrolled, I interviewed the eleven who were willing to schedule interviews. The interviewees represented all the major Spanish-speaking countries represented in the school and the socioeconomic and educational levels of the families. They were in grades 9 to 12 and exhibited a range of academic achievement, from a college scholarship recipient to average and failing students.

While the focus was the students' experiences, I also interviewed ESL or ESL-cooperating teachers (teachers with groups of ESL students intentionally placed in their classes) and counselors. These members of the staff were chosen because of their close work with the students and the importance of ESL courses.

Study Context

School and Environment

I assigned the school and community fictitious names: Columbus High School (CHS) in Columbus, North Carolina. CHS is a comprehensive, four-year high school located in a college community. In 2002 it served 1,600 students: the student population of CHS was 75 percent White, 13 percent African American, 5 percent Hispanic (over 80 percent of these receive ESL services), and 7 percent Asian/other. Fewer than 10 percent of CHS students received free or reduced lunch.

With a spacious campus and abundant resources, CHS is a hub of academic and cocurricular activity. It offers one of the state's most complete college-preparatory curricula, including six foreign languages, vocal and instrumental music, visual and dramatic arts, and a wide range of Advanced Placement (AP) courses. In contrast, the Career and Technical Department is small and offers a very limited number of career sequences compared to other high schools in the region. Three "academies" in the department offer programs in information technology, finance, and health sciences for upper-level students. These selective programs of study have never enrolled English Language Learners (ELLs), and enrolled only three English-proficient Hispanics in their five-year history. The coordinator attributed this to the application process and the high level of parental involvement needed, as parents must be willing to attend after-school information sessions and commit to off-campus components. These three academies would be ideal for students needing marketable skills—students in the situation of most of the research participants, who have to work and contribute to the household income.

Post–September 11 Environment

Until 2001 Columbus was known as a haven for newcomers because of immigrant-friendly local governments and the abundance of employment. The September 11, 2001, attacks and changes in the economy brought new circumstances for Hispanics. During the fall of 2002 two families involved in the study had relatives detained and deported. In the school district the official unemployment rate climbed from 0.5 percent to 2.8 percent in eighteen months (Employment Securities Commission of North Carolina, 2003). The loss of permanent jobs by parents and extended family members produced family instability and the need for students to work. Those who remained in school did so with fewer resources and faced an uncertain future.

Student Context

The study included six students from Mexico, reflecting the predominance of Mexican immigrants in the region, two Colombians, and one each from Venezuela, El Salvador, and Argentina. The students varied in age from fourteen to twenty-one, and all but two were at least a year older than usual for their grade. At the beginning of the study, four students, varying in ages from seventeen to twenty-one, were in twelfth grade. There was one in eleventh grade, three in tenth grade, and three in ninth grade (see table 1).

The students shared several characteristics in common: problematic immigration status or histories, a positive attitude toward CHS, and difficult family economic circumstances. The common experience of these students (unlike most CHS ESL students prior to 1990) was that they belonged to families that had struggled because of war, poverty, or financial crises in their home countries and had moved at significant social and financial cost, and even at great personal risk.

For all the students, immigration concerns were never far from the surface. Many were concerned about what the school authorities might pass on to the Immigration and Naturalization Service (INS, now BICS). One student had to reveal that she could not work legally, which almost resulted in her losing her internship placement. In one instance where the father lost his job because of immigration issues, the daughter's language skills became critical to the family's survival, and little of the family's energy could be spent on her academic success; she was very much alone handling any school-related problems.

The majority of the students, including all but one of those with legal status, had spent a year or more separated from their parents while father, mother, or both established themselves in the United States. Some reported having had to be reacquainted after several years apart. Some had missed up to a year of schooling in the process of immigrating. Two students had moved to North Carolina from New York and Chicago, where

Table 1. Student characteristics

Name and age as of October 1, 2001	Grade	Lives with	Period of separation from parents	Academic path in high school
Rosario (20)	12	mother, siblings	2 years	second-year senior, graduated
Guadalupe (21)	12	husband	2 years	graduated
Juliana (18)	12	brother	1 year	remedial courses to pass state tests, graduated
Elvira (17)	12	mother, siblings	2 years	summer school and remedial courses to pass state tests, graduated
Paty (15)	11	father, mother, siblings	7 and 2 years	summer school and after-school class, on track to graduate at age 17
Raquel (18)	10	aunt, uncle	11 years	
Josefina (15)	10	father, mother, siblings	none	summer school, failed one class
Alicia (15)	10	father, mother, other relatives	unknown	
Olga (14)	9	father, mother	1 year	transferred to charter school, fall 2002
Rocío (15)	9	mother		failed ninth grade
Gabriela (14)	9	father, mother		low grades, chronic absenteeism

they followed relatives but where their families had not been able to find work or adequate housing.

The second characteristic the students shared was a positive attitude and a feeling of privilege at attending high school in a wealthy district. All the students believed that CHS offered the best educational opportunities available to them. One student's family had allowed her to marry and move to North Carolina at age sixteen because they believed there would be more opportunities away from the gangs and established Hispanic neighborhoods of Chicago. This student was committed to her studies, although she worked full-time and performed all the household chores; her husband had never attended high school in Mexico or the United States.

A third common characteristic of the students was the scarce financial resources of their families. All the students in the study lived in low-rent apartments, which was the case of 90 percent of the Hispanic students enrolled in this affluent district. None of the families owned their homes. The lack of space in itself affected the students' ability to do schoolwork at home, where they often shared a room with several family members. In addition to space limitations, computer access was a major problem.

Unlike many of their classmates, none of the students owned a car. Of the eleven students, six were working and contributing significantly to their families' financial support, two were working full-time. The others had part-time babysitting jobs or were indispensable for housework or the supervision of younger siblings and cousins.

All the students planned to attend college; yet none were in college-preparatory courses, despite having advanced skills, such as three years of accounting completed in Mexico by one of the seniors. Academically all the students were placed in a mixture of vocational and "sheltered" courses (regular classes taught specifically for ELLs) that would allow them to continue to learn English while fulfilling their graduation requirements. Moreover, they had been discouraged by their counselors from taking more than the basic requirements and instead were given electives considered less demanding, including sewing, or work internships in a child-care center. All of them took either an additional year or summer and after-school courses to graduate. Two things seemed to be of paramount importance in their placement: getting the courses required to graduate and passing competency exams. One student reported her frustration at the low-level courses and slow progress in English. She reported spending her first year sitting in the back of classrooms, not understanding anything and "desesperada por aprender" (desperate to learn). With minimal English skills, they felt unprepared for the regular classes, while finding the pace of sheltered courses too slow and the content unchallenging.

The students represented a wide range of academic commitment and performance. The freshmen had the most problems academically and in making meaningful connections with the school. One student failed every class for skipping school and was taken to court by the police, another made minimal academic progress, and a third chose to transfer to a charter school. They experienced the adjustment problems of most ninth graders moving into a new school; however, these problems were magnified by the lack of a supportive cohort and by having to function in ESL classes with older students. The three ninth-grade study subjects mentioned two classmates younger than fifteen who had given up: one became pregnant and dropped out during the year, and the other did not return to school in the fall of 2002 after failing every course and attempting a different high school for a few months.

Themes in the Schooling Experience

Seven themes appeared repeatedly in the students' interviews and in field notes. They are presented here in the order in which they were identified during the analysis. There are overlaps and connections among themes, as there are no clear boundary lines separating sections of the subjects' lives.

"No Sé": Student and Staff Lack of Competence

In the immediate and everyday experiences of students, I found "No sé" (I don't know) answers to such basic questions as "How much is the school lunch?" to "What is going on today?" When asked about her most difficult class, one student identified the subject but could not pronounce the teacher's name or the name of the course. This student was in her second year at Columbus High School.

The students' sense of "No sé" was much larger than simply lacking immediate information, although that was a component. The majority of students expressed a feeling that taking the right classes or passing the number of courses necessary for graduation was, in large part, a function of luck and not of planning based on accurate information. Students lacked information about everyday activities and cocurricular opportunities, but more seriously, they had a pervasive lack of understanding about the curriculum, course options, resources, and sources of information. One school visit will illustrate this theme.

I arrived at the school shortly before lunch to meet Juliana. On the way to the cafeteria we saw tables set up. As soon as the bell rang, the tables were mobbed by students. I asked my host what was happening, and she answered uninterestedly, "No sé." When I expressed surprise at her lack of curiosity, her response was, "Siempre hay algo, y te la pasas preguntando" (There is always something, so you spend your time asking). I asked the organizers how a student might have found out about the event (it turned out to be a Valentine "match" sale, where students received the name of their ideal "match") and was informed that announcements had been read over the intercom system; there were also posters and a newspaper article. Juliana was completely uninformed. She explained, "Cuando leen esos anuncios, yo no les entiendo nada. La verdad es que nadie escucha, todos están conversando" (When those announcements are read, I don't understand anything. Nobody listens, really; everyone is talking).

Amid the noise the decontextualized and fast-paced intercom announcements were almost impossible to decipher for an ELL. Teachers seemed to assume the information would get to the students by some other means. The implied message was that the announcements were not of critical importance. I asked my student-host what would happen if something very important were to be announced. She replied, "No sé. Ya me enteraré. Los maestros de ESL nos lo dirán" (I don't know. I'll eventually find out. The ESL teachers will tell us). Informing the students about school activities or events, however, was not a part of any ESL class I observed. I never saw teachers read or explain the announcements or even make reference to them. I also never saw the ESL teachers use the student newspaper in class. I never heard a student ask about an announcement or newspaper article.

Much of the information contained in the announcements was about extracurricular activities, organizational meetings and tryouts, sporting events, and student-led groups. While this information is not critical to students' academic success, participation in such activities provides students a low-anxiety environment to learn and practice English. Participation is also judged by teachers and counselors, potential employers, and college admissions officers as a reflection of a student's willingness to invest in the school community. Moreover, such activities allow students to become personally acquainted with teachers and find other students with interests similar to their own, enabling them to cross cultural barriers and racial divisions. In the case of most of the students I interviewed, their lack of participation in activities reflected their lack of knowledge of the opportunities available rather than a decision not to take part.

Not all the opportunities missed for lack of information were social or extracurricular. There were cocurricular activities that constituted important educational experiences. An example was a trip to Washington, D.C. The day I visited Elvira's Economic, Legal, and Political Systems (ELP) class, the roommate list for the Washington trip had just been posted on the bulletin board. When I asked Elvira who she would be rooming with, she explained, "A mi no me invitaron. Es sólo para los chicos de noveno" (I was not invited. It is only for ninth graders). According to the teacher, however, all ELP students were eligible to participate. He told me it would have been "impossible" for Elvira to miss all the announcements. In the announcements, though, the trip was referred to as "the ninth-grade trip to D.C." Since Elvira was taking the course out of sequence and was not in ninth grade, it had seemed clear to her that she was not invited.

At first it seemed that the students were passively accepting a sense of ignorance and powerlessness. I reacted with frustration. "What do you mean you don't know what courses you need to graduate?" I would ask, "When do you think you will know?" or "Where could you find out?" My attitude changed gradually. I realized that the students would agree with me out of politeness, or because they agreed that this was what they should do if they had the courage and the skills. However, it was clear, even in the same interviews, that asking teachers or administrators for information was not a strategy the students used, and that suggesting that they confront their teachers or demand answers only distanced me from the students.

A second reason I stopped suggesting that students demand answers from the staff is that I realized how much effort the students were already investing in trying to obtain information and how often they were unable get accurate answers. By the second semester I began seriously looking at where the students might find accurate answers or help in navigating school life. It was discouraging to see that I had not understood how difficult it was for them to navigate an environment where so much of the information was incomprehensible.

I presented this problem to the counselors: few students seemed able to obtain concrete answers about school procedures, their schedules, course requirements, and other important issues affecting their futures. One counselor's answers illustrate just how difficult it was to obtain information.

> Counselor: I never got any training on how to interpret the transcripts [to assign credit for students' previous work]. I'm sure the other counselors also wish there were someone. . . . Sometimes I only had partial information, then I realized it was wrong. It's mostly trial and error.
>
> María Palmer (MTP): You just said you sometimes only had partial information and it was wrong. Who gave you that information? . . .
>
> Response (R): Sometimes other counselors. For example . . . I told one of my sophomores that they could take a correspondence course, and then later I found out from another counselor that we only let seniors do that, so I had to go back and tell my student, "I'm sorry.". . . We don't have an orientation for new counselors. We don't even have a department head.

I received similar vague and inconclusive responses from counselors about transcript evaluations, testing issues, college admission requirements, and scholarship eligibility, among other issues.

This lack of accurate information was complicated because the confusion among the counselors was passed on, with some students convinced they had finally obtained the right answer and sharing the wrong information with friends. Ninth and tenth graders consulted older Hispanic students, who referred to their own experiences, not knowing that the rules were different for students in other classes. Then the students would ask the ESL teacher and the counselor, receiving two additional contradictory explanations.

The counselors' lack of expertise seemed to be an institutional problem with no foreseeable solution. There was the mistaken perception that providing any specialized counseling for students on the basis of their ELL status would constitute discrimination; thus the system of dividing students among counselors by the alphabet resulted in an absurd misuse of resources. The only counselor who spoke Spanish and who had, in another state, specialized in ESL students had only a handful of the Spanish-speaking students, and no opportunity to work with these students as a group.

Having "Confianza" with a Teacher: Someone to Talk To

Closely related to the "No sé" answer was the explanation offered by some students as to what was keeping them from soliciting assistance: lack of "confianza" in their teachers. The word *confianza* is translated in *Simon and Schuster's International English/Spanish Dictionary* (1973) as "1. Confidence, trust, reliance, faith. 2. Self-confidence, assurance. 3. Familiarity, informality." The phrase *en confianza* is rendered as "privately, confidentially." In Latin America the phrase *de confianza* implies a degree of familiarity that allows someone to discuss matters that are private in nature. In most cases students lacked confidence or boldness to approach the teacher and felt it would be presumptuous to request additional assistance.

Culturally it is not acceptable for a student to assume that she can approach a person in authority and ask for help unless that person has given the student permission in some way, has given her "confianza" to do so. Students might even feel that teachers would be offended by the implication that their teaching is inadequate and might retaliate. An example is Juliana, who reported being lost about both the content and the teachers' expectations. She explained that the math tutor her family was providing (a volunteer recruited through her brother) did not seem to make a difference, that her grades were still very low, despite her completing her homework assignments and studying with the tutor. In English class the situation was not much better. When I suggested that she should go to the teachers and ask for assistance, she explained that she would probably just wait until things started to make sense. The idea of approaching a teacher was intimidating. She commented, "Con esa profesora no tengo confianza" (I don't have *confianza* with that teacher).

That this is a common experience can be seen in the advice offered newcomers by two older students who had found relationships of confianza. Repeatedly they said they would tell newcomers to talk to their teachers and not to be afraid; to have confianza—to both be bold and to trust in somebody so they could get help. One of the more acculturated and successful students went as far as to suggest newcomers must act as if they had confianza even when they did not feel it, because to maintain a distance from their teachers would signal that they considered themselves inferior, presumably resulting in even less help.

Relationships of confianza happened occasionally and for only three of the students in the study. In these instances staff initiative played a major role by taking a step to breach the difference in rank, authority, or social position between student and teacher. Administrators and counselors invited confianza by joining students in such informal situations as breakfast or lunch, writing notes, speaking to students in the hallway, and by explicitly offering help and specifying times when they would be available.

One important factor in developing relationships of confianza was the presence of a community advocate. For example, one counselor, who expressed concerns about communicating and relating to ESL students, explained how she had developed a close relationship with two sisters because of the presence of an advocate/translator, which made it possible to counsel without feelings of inadequacy. She explained: "I remember when that meeting was set up, I was told there'd be a translator . . . and right away it became clear that the kids could understand me. I have a wonderful relationship with those students—both because I could communicate with them and because they needed my assistance and I could help them."

Some counselors and teachers discussed the need for students to seek help and become "self-advocates" in order to build relationships of confianza. However, students are not taught or encouraged to be self-advocates in the Hispanic community. If the teachers' and counselors' willingness or ability to develop close relationships with the students depends on the students' initiative and self-advocacy, then confianza will remain elusive.

Barriers to confianza mentioned by students included the lack of communication between teachers and the home, the lack of personal relationships between staff and some students, and "pena" (embarrassment) at talking to male teachers.

Two students reported meaningful relationships with bilingual Anglo (White, non-Hispanic) students, both from the advanced Spanish classes, which can be described as relationships of confianza. These students had formed friendships at the invitation of classmates who valued the opportunity to speak Spanish and regarded the Hispanic students as valuable resources and friends. At the same time, the Anglo students offered important help and cultural interpretation in navigating high school life. Given the lack of significant relationships of confianza with teachers and staff, successful Anglo students did, on occasion, act as counselors, tutors, and even advocates to the immigrant students. Such peer relationships at CHS were rare and always entered into at the initiative of the Anglo students.

Some Ill Will and Prejudice, and Considerable Misunderstandings

All the students interviewed reported incidents of discrimination, ranging from subtle offenses to overt harassment and threats from both Anglos and African Americans. Some dismissed such incidents as the result of ignorance. Other students reported insults designed to hurt, such as, "If you're going to live in America, you have to talk English" or "Go home, dirty Mexican." Most overt discrimination came from other students; however, some incidents involved teachers and staff.

Categorized as Hispanic and treated as if they were all Mexican (see the "Changing Identities" section below), the students were also alienated by the lack of adequate services they were offered and the expectation that they should be accepting of second-class treatment. One glaring example was the advising and placement services. The students reported waiting an average of four days to receive their schedules, even when they had registered weeks before the beginning of the school year. At the beginning of each semester a disproportionate number of the students waiting to see counselors or receive schedules were Hispanic. The students noticed this and attributed the poor services they received to their being foreign.

A counselor explained that she could not place ELLs in just any class; she must schedule them with teachers who would be welcoming and willing to work with the students, thus protecting the students from environments that might compromise their academic achievement or emotional well-being: "Some teachers would be here in five minutes telling me, 'You cannot put this student in my class.'" This counselor was developing a cohort of teachers whose classes were not "the college level–type courses that would be way too hard." This well-meaning counselor was in fact creating a more limited number of options for Hispanic ESL students, something they understood clearly and that reinforced their understanding of themselves as a subgroup without equal access to courses. On the other hand, the counselor might be increasing the chances of her particular students graduating, even though they might do so within a limited "ESL track."

The majority of incidents reported as acts of discrimination committed by staff I could easily attribute more to ignorance and carelessness than to ill will. The students, however, were not ready to believe that there was no malice or ill will involved when the results were sometimes so detrimental to their hopes of participating and feeling part of school life. One example, involving two students' ability to play soccer, illustrates this point.

Elvira and Paty, clueless about the process by which teams are selected for the school, arrived at the field for soccer tryouts at the beginning of the year. Neither student had the proper equipment (cleats, shin guards, etc.), which the coach said would keep them from playing any games. The students misunderstood the coach's explanation about the day the last cut and team roster would be announced, understanding instead that they must have their equipment by that date or risk not being allowed to play with the team. Since the purchase of this equipment represented a significant expense for the families, both girls delayed the purchase as long as possible while they worked to earn most of the money. Unfortunately, the day they brought their new equipment to practice was also the day they learned they had not made the team. In truth, neither student was competitive in soccer, something they did not understand. The coach had not addressed this issue during the two weeks of tryouts. This seemed a great injustice to the students, who felt the coach had not really wanted them on the team and had used their delay in purchasing the equipment as an excuse to dismiss them. Since the few African American students who tried out were also cut from the team, Elvira and Paty were convinced that the Anglo coach was prejudiced and that minorities had little chance to participate fully in a school run for wealthy whites.

As Lisa Delpit (1995) points out, when minority students are not taught the implicit assumptions and rules, they are disadvantaged. In the case of these students they had no understanding of the standards for team selection or what specifically they must do to meet the standard. They also did not know the importance of having appropriate equipment during the tryouts. The fact that the students who remained on the team were all Anglo girls—all of whom knew each other from soccer clubs—seemed too much of a coincidence.

When I visited classrooms where the students reported feeling "unwelcomed," the teachers were not rude to any students in my presence, but neither did they attempt to reach out to the students or make them feel comfortable.

Other students reported that their teachers were openly antagonistic, as in the case where a teacher complained about having "another Hispanic" added to her class in the first week of school. Later in the semester the teacher apologized to the student, explaining her remarks as based on previous negative experiences with Hispanic students.

> R: Fue como si hubiera visto dos ogros. Ya después empezó a cambiar, porque veía que no faltábamos. . . . Nos fue conociendo y le preguntamos. . . . Nos dijo: "Discúlpenme por el día que los recibí así, pero anteriormente había tenido tres hispanos," dice, "dos hombres y una mujer . . . fatales," dice. "Me sacaron canas verdes. Ya desde esa vez he tenido muy mala impresión de los hispanos. Pero ustedes dos me han cambiado la visión de los hispanos".
>
> (She later changed, because she could see we didn't skip class. . . . She got to know us and we asked her. . . . She said: "Forgive me for the day I welcomed you like that, but I had had three Hispanics," she said, "two men and one woman . . . terrible," she said. "They gave me gray hair. Since then I've had a bad impression of Hispanics. But you have changed my view on Hispanics.")

Many of the students reported hearing teachers' comments, even compliments, that revealed their low opinion of Hispanic achievement in general. Sadly, when students reported these comments, along the lines of "My teacher said a C is a really good grade for a Hispanic student," they were unquestioning of the teacher's perceptions. One student reported proudly that the principal was surprised to see how well she was performing, given that she is Mexican.

As was the case with this student, some of the prejudiced comments of teachers or administrators did not seem to bother all Hispanic students— some believed them to be true about Hispanics in general but not about themselves. They believed teachers to be justified in their low opinions and simply needed to be set right about particular students.

Some of the staff's seemingly discriminatory comments were reported to me in Spanish: "Nos dijo que nosotros somos los primeros hispanos que ella ha visto que quieran estudiar" (She said we are the first Hispanics she has seen who want to study). When I questioned the accuracy of their recollections and their understanding of the teachers' and administrators' intended meaning, the students were quite sure that they had understood the intended communication, even when they could not recall the exact words in English. Some conversations, exchanges, or classroom incidents were reported with significant detail, and the students could recall how they felt and what their reactions had been. Whether the majority of staff who made these comments were aware of how prejudiced they might sound is subject to interpretation.

Overt harassment from students, both Anglo and African American, was reported in the majority of the interviews. While the students reported not being physically afraid of violence, they described some hostile classroom environments. Except for one particularly disruptive exchange, the teachers in charge of those classrooms did not stop to address these problems. The students seldom reported any of the incidents to staff, often believing that the teachers already understood the situation. Most students seemed to believe that Anglo teachers and administrators simply did not want to pay attention to their struggles and that African American staff resented their presence.

I Am Not Who I Used to Be: Changing Identities and Becoming Hispanic

All the students interviewed who were in their first semester in the United States talked about themselves in terms of their nationality, referring to themselves as "Colombiana," "Argentina," or "Mexicana." It took less than a semester for students to begin including themselves in the "Hispanas" category in addition to their national origin identification. This was part of a complicated change of identity experienced as they adjusted to the social and ethnic designation of "Hispanic" by the community and the school. The changes the students experienced as a result of their struggles were sometimes gradual but often quite significant, noticeable to both students and their families.

The students had been, in their home communities, members of the racial and ethnic majority. While none of the students ever explained the changes they experienced due to immigration in terms of becoming part of a minority group, they did reflect on the way they were perceived and responded, often negatively, to the social pressures that cast them as "Hispanics."

The school played an important role in the construction of each student's group identity, and it affected their attitudes toward the school and, more significantly, their understanding of themselves and their futures. To minimize the effects of the perceived stigma of being an immigrant student, some students began to deny their national origin identity, choosing to identify more with American-born Hispanics and accentuating any differences they might have with people from their home countries and their cultural values and traditions.

Those students who were not embarrassed or did not seek to minimize their identification with their country of origin still had to negotiate new identities. Several students used to being identified by their compound names had to choose which one to adopt, as teachers invariably used only one name. One student who appeared on my list as "María" informed me that she had never used that name at CHS. "Habíamos muchas Marías" (There would be many of us Marías), she complained. It was an ironic comment because as María Teresa I had faced that same dilemma in college, learning to respond to "María," a name that is seldom used without a second name in Latin America. I remembered clearly that at the end of my first semester, upon hearing my parents call me "Maritere," I thought: "I have become two people."

The students I interviewed were, in many ways, two different persons: the daughter of a Colombian, Mexican, Salvadoran, Venezuelan, or Argentinean family and an immigrant Hispanic student. Their behavior and attitudes were not the same in both roles. The dutiful daughter who took care of the household responsibilities, translated for parents, and supervised siblings was also the student who skipped class, failed to turn in assignments, and impatiently endured misunderstandings and insults. More than once was I shocked to hear angry words and rough language used by students that I had met outside of school at a Hispanic community event and would have thought incapable of such conversation. Two students, who accepted as valid the school staff's prejudiced comments, tried especially hard to relate to their Anglo teachers and to prove that they were not "Mexicanas típicas" (typical Mexicans). In discussing faculty perceptions, one of them, herself a recent Mexican immigrant, attributed the problem of poor achievement and high dropout rates to the "bajo nivel económico, educativo y cultural" (low economic, educational, and cultural level) of the majority of the school's Hispanic population. In a follow-up interview this student explained that most Mexicans did not value an education and that their lack of achievement was responsible for the teachers' poor attitude toward Hispanics. Her dreams and aspirations included marrying "un Americano," becoming a citizen, and joining the U.S. Armed Forces.

At CHS, gradually throughout the year, new students seemed to accept that those differences that seemed so immense to them—accents, idioms, national identities—were unnoticeable to their classmates and teachers. They were simply "Hispanic." Moreover, they were easily confused with other Latina students with whom they shared little in common. On one occasion I was interviewing Josefina when an assistant principal interrupted to ask her a question. It was apparent immediately that the assistant principal had mistaken Josefina for another Hispanic student, a recent arrival from a different country. When I explained the mistake, the assistant principal asked me to deliver the message to the right student, assuming, I thought at the time, that I had routine communication with all Hispanic students.

Aware of Josefina's embarrassment and sadness at the scene, I attempted to excuse the administrator's behavior—it's easy to confuse students—and Josefina smiled sadly and said, "Yo sé. Pasa todo el tiempo. Pero ella fue mi assistant principal en middle school. Yo pensé que sabía quien era" (I know. It happens all the time. But she was my assistant principal in middle school. I thought she knew who I was).

The students interviewed accepted that the staff and students, Anglos as well as African Americans, viewed them as "Hispanic" and were not knowledgeable about their country or culture. They realized that the school community was developing a dominant stereotype of the Hispanic student as a poor- and low-achieving Mexican, and that it was their burden to prove that they did not fit that stereotype.

While constructing new ethnic identities, students faced the challenge of applying behavioral norms learned in another cultural context to gender roles in their school setting. Their parents were not a good source of guidance because they knew even less about American behavioral norms than the students did. My help was enlisted in trying to convince parents to allow participation in such activities as school dances, trips, and even a tutoring program where parents suspected their daughters were meeting boys. The area of gender relations was, for all the students, both at home and at school, an important area of conflict and negotiation.

During the research period the students were negotiating new identities, merging their self-concept as foreign nationals with what they saw themselves becoming in response to their schooling experience: Hispanic, North Carolina high schoolers. While some students could be explicit about changes in their personality, values, or opinions, the majority did not see the difference as a change within them, but reported ways in which their lives and expectations were changing due to their circumstances. However, as one mother pointed out, such adjustments invariably affected the students' self-concept and eventually their repertoire of behaviors and options. From changing career plans (from dentist to nurse) to giving up on the hope of taking a favorite class, the students were not only learning to see themselves as Hispanics but learning also to adjust their expectations of schooling and of their futures.

Latino versus Black: Conflict and Misunderstanding

As immigrant students developed a sense of Hispanic/Latina identity and a sense of belonging to a group, this created racial and ethnic intergroup tensions at the school, making it difficult for the students to move comfortably among existing racial groups or form friendships with both African American and Anglo students.

A recurring theme in the interviews was the tension and distrust between Latina students and African American students and teachers. These problems were different from the alienation and stereotyping coming from the Anglo students, as the relationship with African Americans was perceived to have an element of competition and resentment, perhaps informed by the Latina students' own prejudices. All but one student interviewed related some incident or problem, and some used generalizations about African American culture that suggested they were prejudiced against African Americans. The Latina students complained that African American students were loud and disrespectful to their teachers and that teachers would allow things to degenerate into chaos, that African American females in particular did not like them, and that they bullied and intimidated Latinas for sport.

One of the complaints, that African American women intimidated Latinas, was clearly evident in the hallways, bathrooms, cafeteria, and even in some classrooms. Whether the result of deliberate roughness on one side or unfounded fear and misunderstanding of the culture on the other was more difficult to determine. I observed a Latina student react in fear, almost hiding behind me, when an African American student, who was speaking to another friend, yelled a greeting in her direction. Because she could not understand the greeting, the Latina student had interpreted the action as aggressive.

Most of the African American students who shared classes with ELLs were among the lowest performing students in the school, and they shared some of the least capable teachers. I felt intimidated when I observed African American students being blatantly disrespectful while their teachers exhibited poor classroom management. In one remedial math classroom an African American female student arrived as the bell was ringing, sat at the teacher's desk, and started using the teacher's computer. When the teacher asked the students to clear their desks so they could take a quiz and asked the young woman to take a seat, she answered, "I'm checking on something," which caused laughter among the other African American students. The teacher eventually had to go to her desk and turn off the computer. My host that day commented: "Hacen lo que les da la gana" (They do as they please).

The lack of confianza with staff meant that when students encountered racial and ethnic tensions, these went unreported and unaddressed. The situation was more complicated when the teacher was African American and perceived to be anti-Latino, a situation that several students reported. Students identified the area of race relations, and specifically Black/Latino issues, as the area most in need of improvement and urgent attention. More than half of the students mentioned the need for teachers and administrators to stop the fights between Latinos and African Americans and to address the issue of disrespectful and disruptive classroom behavior.

The cultural differences, negative perceptions and stereotypes, and unaddressed conflicts between Latinas and African Americans challenged the immigrant students' social adjustment and negatively affected their academic performance, interfering with their feelings of safety and acceptance and their willingness to participate in classroom activities. While the students expressed their concern to me, it was never the topic of any classroom discussion, school forum, or conversation with school staff. From the students' point of view the administration was either not aware of or had chosen to ignore the problems.

Structured and Demanding Teachers versus Students Must Take the Initiative

All but one of the students could identify some classes in which they were experiencing academic success, which they defined sometimes as "aprendiendo mucho" (learning a lot) and more often as "sacando buenas notas" (getting good grades). When asked about these classes, the students could also explain their teachers' methods to ensure students were learning the material and prepared for tests. Unfortunately, the students could identify many courses where they were not succeeding and where they were unable to master the material or produce the projects, papers, or other required products. Often their participation in class and their receiving the instruction they needed to learn were dependent on their taking the initiative of asking for assistance. This posed a difficult problem for students used to more autocratic Latin American teachers, who demanded their involvement and performance, and educational systems where there is more structured and required classroom participation. Some students explained this in terms of needing or wanting teachers who "te hacen trabajar" (make you work).

The students offered examples of good teachers who provided a combination of encouragement and pressure, while adjusting instruction to meet the needs of ESL students. These teachers invariably provided considerable structure and controlled the learning process, including small-group exercises, pacing, classroom practice, peer editing, and exam reviews—in other words, they demanded student involvement and learning. One student described a geometry class where the two immigrant students were put into heterogeneous groups and made to participate "with charts, so she knew what we knew. . . . When she saw that we were quiet she made us participate."

Thus students became engaged, even if reluctantly. When teachers provided structure and forced participation, this also forced Anglo and African American students into collaborative groups and shielded students from being left out. High praise was offered for a social studies teacher, considered demanding by even English speakers, who pushed all students to participate and to overcome their feelings of inadequacy.

Praise was also offered for a teacher who demanded that ESL students in his class take their turn at reading and presenting, because he allowed them opportunities for trial runs, mostly during the lunch hour, when he offered instructional help. Olga explained:

MTP: El profesor favorito, ¿qué hizo para ganarse ese puesto?
(The favorite teacher, what did he do to earn that spot?)
R: El me ha ayudado mucho, me . . . dio también clases en U.S. History y siempre me decía tu puedes y a veces yo me pongo muy nerviosa y siempre decía, "No me gusta leer porque no me gusta leer en inglés," y el me decía, "Y si no practicas nunca vas a poder". Me hace participar. . . le gusta que cumplamos con las tareas y si no, va menos un punto, para que aprendamos que siempre tienen que ser responsables, le gusta que hagamos un trabajo en grupo y que todos trabajemos, es lo que más me ha gustado, porque muchas veces, unos trabajan y otros no. La calificación es grupal.
(He has helped me so much, he . . . taught me also U.S. history classes and he always said, "You can do it," and sometimes I get very nervous and I would say, "I don't like to read because I don't like to read in English," and he would say, "If you don't practice you will never be able to." He makes me participate. . . . and he likes for us to complete our home-

work, and if we don't then it's minus one point, so we learn you have to be responsible; he likes for us to work in groups and that everyone works, that's what I like best, because often, some work and others don't. The grade is for the group.)

MTP: Y ¿cómo sabe que hacen eso?

(And how does he know you're all doing it?)

R: Porque lo hacemos en la clase y él pasa a ver a cada uno y nos pide nuestras opiniones sobre el tema que estamos viendo. . . .

Hay gente que no les gusta . . . pero él les dice. . . . El es muy riguroso, entonces le dice que se salga. Entonces a uno le da miedo, "Entonces sí trabajo," porque hay maestros que dicen: "A la tercera te mando a sacar," pasan cinco veces y nunca lo sacó y él sí. Llama a los maestros si es nec-esario a los principales, manda a las oficinas y lo que dice es que "a mi clase vienen a trabajar y quiero que todos trabajen".

(Because we do the work in class and he goes around and checks on each one and asks our opinion on the topic we are working on. . . .

There are people who don't like him . . . but he tells them. . . . He's very demanding, so he tells them to leave. So then you get scared and "I better work" because there are teachers that say, "The third time I'll have you removed," and five times go by and they never had him removed, but he does. He calls other teachers if necessary or the principals; he sends students to the office and says, "To my class you come to work and I want everyone to work.")

The students appreciated the teachers who recognized that English skills might limit their achievement or their testing ability and who provided other evaluation opportunities as opposed to ignoring a student's poor performance.

Asked what good teachers did to help overcome language barriers, many of the students explained that there were teachers who used projec-tors or drawings or who tried to explain in different ways. When asked if it was common for teachers to check for understanding and offer such help, students identified only a few who practiced such "buena peda-gogía" (good teaching) consistently.

In some classes, teachers employed good strategies, but did not take into consideration the needs of ESL students. One student mentioned a science class, which she had failed. In explaining why she said the teacher was not very organized and that the class was not well structured, so none of her study techniques seemed to help. She explained how the teacher distributed study guides the day before exams—perhaps enough time to guide native speakers in their study but of no help to ESL students who must answer the questions aided by a dictionary and then find help with the grammar before attempting to memorize the answers. Thus it had not been enough to receive the study guide when she lacked the time and support needed to use it. One senior was clear that had she not enlisted the help of the librarian and the technology specialist, she would have failed a class because the teacher did not realize she lacked computer skills.

Requiring students to take the initiative assumes they feel empowered to demand services. At CHS, teachers expected that students would advocate on their own behalf, something that requires not only self-confidence and assertiveness but also communication skills immigrant ESL students lacked. Students knew what type of classrooms they wanted: structured and well-sequenced instruction that provided them with many inputs as well as teachers who were strict disciplinarians and who demanded participation and performance from all students but who realized when accommodations were necessary to ensure mastery and appropriate evaluation. Both students and teachers expected the other to take the initiative, which resulted in the students' needs not being addressed in many classrooms.

Diploma versus Education: Are We Here to Learn or to Graduate?

Graduation was the indisputable priority of the staff and the five juniors and seniors in the study. The staff saw graduation as the goal and the indicator that they had succeeded in their educational mission. The students saw a high school diploma as a requirement for entry into a "carrera profesional" (professional field) that would ensure them a better future and a comfortable life. Only one of the students had the financial ability and family support to go back and pursue a career in her country of origin; all the others lacked the resources, academic credentials, or Spanish skills to gain entrance to a Latin American university. Failing to graduate and attend college in North Carolina would mean accepting a future as unskilled workers.

While the students admitted learning important information and acquiring new skills in their classes, there was no connection drawn between their classroom experiences and any future careers, even when I tried to make the connection. Performing well in class was seen only as a way to get good grades and obtain a diploma. Only one student could mention a class in which she was receiving preparation that could be important in her chosen profession, a student taking advanced sewing who mentioned this had furthered her interest in fashion design.

All the students worried that they were unprepared for college. Two planned to take additional ESL classes at the community college before attempting any higher-level courses. They explained that obtaining a high school diploma meant taking many different classes, which interfered with focusing on language skills and learning English well. They saw high school as a necessary step in the process of obtaining further career training but did not believe that it would adequately prepare them for college, nor that their teachers could help make the transition possible.

Conclusions and Recommendations

At Columbus High School I observed the disempowering of Hispanic immigrant women. Students' language and culture were not made part of the school program; moreover, they were not expected to have any significant skills or giftedness that could qualify them for upper-level courses. The teaching, with few exceptions, did not promote active use of language to generate students' own knowledge, but focused on mastery of basic skills to graduate. While outside the school the students' families were consistently disempowered and disrespected, inside the school they simply did not play any role in the educational enterprise. A few committed educators offered Latina students empowering experiences, such as asking for Spanish lessons or involving them in planning classroom activities. The administrative personnel and most teachers did not advocate for the students, and rather than alter their practice, they regarded the students as the problem.

Immigrant young women learned that the school was not organized for their academic achievement, that it would take incredible perseverance and determination to overcome significant barriers to graduate, and that they would have to negotiate further education and training on their own because teachers and counselors were not preparing them or expecting them to go to college.

As these students acquired English language skills and learned to negotiate high school society, they also learned that they were not expected to be involved, contributing members of the high school community. In classrooms, cafeteria, gymnasium, and hallways, Hispanic immigrant students became members of an ethnic/cultural subclass created by the school system, for which graduation in the lowest academic track could be considered a success. At CHS I found a reproduction of the power relations encountered by the new Latino diaspora in North Carolina: Hispanics were second-class members of society—not citizens, but uninvited guests.

My commitment to recording, understanding, and reporting the experiences of students was driven by my hope to improve their educational opportunities. The members of the congregation I pastor supported my research because they believed research is a tool in the quest to achieve better educational opportunities for their children, and because this work will make me a better or more respected advocate. To them my research project could be justified only in terms of the positive changes it could bring about for the children of our community. Phrases I have heard from my parishioners include: "La pastora está yendo a la escuela para ayudar a los muchachos" (The pastor is going to the school to help the children).

The students themselves issued, in interviews and as my guests in community forums, their call for teachers and administrators to address their most pressing needs. Among them was the need for intervention to facilitate race relations, the assignment of Spanish-speaking teachers/mentors who could answer questions and guide students, and the use of "good pedagogy" in the classroom.

I continue to present the data to educators in the hope of moving teaching toward empowering pedagogy. I believe some of the presentations and discussions have helped teachers understand the need for redefining their roles in light of the presence of immigrant students and for the need to bring about systemic changes in the schools.

While university audiences have reacted positively to my presentations and my writing, I have been disappointed at the reaction of most high school administrators, those most able to bring about changes. I have encountered an attitude that could best be described as fear to disclose or study the problems their immigrant students face, reluctance to accept criticism, and a fatalistic view that there is not much that they can do. CHS's principal, after reading my dissertation, indefinitely postponed an invitation to provide staff development to the faculty based on the findings. One superintendent suggested that I will not be able to find employment in my region until I go back to the classroom for a couple of years to prove I am a "team player" and not a troublemaker. However, when I present the stories of the eleven students in the study, discussing their families and immigration experience, their successes and failures in school, and their dreams for the future, administrators begin to ask questions and share insights into their own situations. They recognize in these voices their own students' experiences.

I recently attended a high school orientation for rising ninth graders at a middle school in my district. One of the first words of advice given the students was, "In high school, you have to ask for help. You have to be a self-advocate." I was instantly transported to CHS and realized what a prevailing cultural expectation this is in North Carolina. The parents in attendance were upper-middle class and established members of the community. No Latino families, no public housing parents, no Spanish translation. Moreover, I was sure that the parents present had no intention of leaving their children to advocate for themselves—they would be vocal participants in shaping their children's educational experiences.

High school administrators need to abandon the practice of allocating resources on the basis of advocacy. We must monitor students' social and academic needs and organize the school's resources accordingly. This requires a commitment to know the students so that we can understand what they know and teach them what they need to know. In North Carolina the New High Schools Project holds some promise. With funding from the Gates Foundation, the state is sponsoring restructured schools with small enrollments and a focus on graduating students who are already started on a career path or are already enrolled in postsecondary institutions.

Traditional schools must deploy their staff in a manner that ensures the development of close relationships between students and faculty. Intensive staff development is needed to create an understanding of the unique needs of language minority students. There are many strategies to help teachers understand the affective and academic struggles of their immigrant students. I have facilitated small-group discussions of case studies based on real students' experiences. Staff development can enable teachers to overcome their insecurities and prejudices and enter into dialogue with immigrant students and their communities. This in turn can result in relationships of "confianza" that affirm and empower students.

Perhaps the most powerful result of this research has been in creating the opportunity for educators and parents to reflect on the schooling experience of immigrant Latinas, as described by the students themselves to a willing and sympathetic listener. It is a painful experience of limited opportunities and disempowerment. Perhaps it is also a call to a new civil rights struggle.

Interracial Status as a Double-Edged Sword

*The Educational Experiences
of Interracial Children*

Simon Cheng

While much attention was consumed by integrating children of different races in school in the years after *Brown v. Board of Education of Topeka* (1954), teachers are confronting a racially ambiguous yet distinct population in their classrooms: students of interracial backgrounds. Interracial students are an inherently diverse group, with roughly half considering themselves Latino, a group that itself encompasses people from more than one race. Some interracial students may not obviously resemble their multiple racial heritages, while others may distinctly appear to have mixed racial traits. Understanding how these students and their families interact in school settings is essential in order to effectively integrate this rapidly growing group in our nation's schools. There are projected to be, in 2050, 21 percent of Americans who may identify themselves as multiracial (J. Lee & Bean, 2004).

Many have suggested that "race" is an ambiguous term with changing definitions (Omi & Winant, 1994). This makes the study of interracial students a complex task. Not surprisingly, although research on racial differences in education has attracted a great deal of scholarly attention, scholars have mostly ignored interracial students in their research on family, school environments, and children's educational experiences (Gibbs, 1989; Kao, 1999; Radina & Cooney, 2000; Xie & Goyette, 1997). Because most teachers lack a clear understanding of interracial students, the experiences of this group in school become largely dependent on how they interact with, and are treated by, their (mostly) monoracial peers.

In this essay I seek to fill this gap by examining the educational experiences of interracial children.[1] Noting the increase in racial diversity in school environments over the past few decades, I wish to advance the current discussion on how multiracial children fare educationally compared to monoracial students, particularly in varying school racial environments. At present most teachers and policymakers have little practical

Table 1. Population by race, for all ages, for 18 years and over, and for under age 18 for the United States

Subject	All ages	
	Number	Percent of total population
Race		
Total population	281,421,906	100.0
One race	274,595,678	97.6
White	211,460,626	75.1
Black or African American	34,658,190	12.3
American Indian and Alaska Native	2,475,956	0.9
Asian	10,242,998	3.6
Native Hawaiian and Other Pacific Islander	398,835	0.1
Some other race	15,359,073	5.5
Two or more races	6,826,228	2.4
Hispanic or Latino (of any race)	35,305,818	12.5

Source: U.S. Census Bureau, Census 2000 Redistricting Data (P.L. 94-171) Summary File for States, tables PL1, PL2, PL3, and PL4. Internet Release date: April 2, 2001.

information concerning the impact that this increasing population will have on future school environments. Consider, for example, a child who has one White and one Black parent.[2] How will the child's Black/White interracial status affect his or her educational experiences?

Given the substantial body of existing research centering on racial differences of students in schools (e.g., academic achievement, peer interactions) and families (e.g., parental investment in children's education), this essay considers the dynamics of interracial children's experiences, both in schools and in families. I will first discuss the growing body of research about interracial youth and the complications involved in this line of study. After discussing relevant research, I present the major findings from my own study on the educational experiences of interracial children and their families. Because the diverse cultural experiences of multiracial populations may present different challenges for educators, the empirical findings from current research on interracial students have profound research and policy implications. These are addressed in the essay's final section.

	18 years and over		Under 18	
Number	Percent of population 18 years and over		Number	Percent of population under 18
209,128,094	100.0		72,293,812	100.0
205,158,752	98.1		69,436,926	96.1
161,862,337	77.4		49,598,289	68.6
23,772,494	11.4		10,885,696	15.1
1,635,644	0.8		840,312	1.2
7,777,999	3.7		2,464,999	3.4
271,656	0.1		127,179	0.2
9,838,622	4.7		5,520,451	7.6
3,969,342	1.9		2,856,886	4.0
22,963,559	11.0		12,342,259	17.1

Spotlight on the Multiracial Population

Both the rates and the absolute numbers of interracial marriages have been rising steadily in the past few decades, particularly after the U.S. Supreme Court's 1967 ruling that declared laws forbidding racially mixed marriages in Virginia to be unconstitutional (P. M. Brown, 1990; Gibbs & Hines, 1992; Kalmijn, 1993; Qian, 1997; Root, 1992; Xie & Goyette, 1997; for details about the *Loving v. Virginia* case [1967], see Wadlington, 1966). U.S. census records indicate that the number of interracial marriages more than quadrupled from 1970 (310,000) to 2000 (1.5 million) (U.S. Census Bureau, 2001a).[3] Correspondingly, the population of multiracial children younger than eighteen has also grown dramatically, increasing sixfold during this same time (Waters & Eschbach, 1995). As shown in table 1, the census of 2000 reveals that multiracial individuals younger than eighteen constitute approximately 4 percent of America's youth, making multiracial children the fourth-largest racial/ethnic group in the American youth population.

Various studies have suggested that distinct educational experiences exist for different racial groups, in part because of the structural barriers that may disadvantage minority students in schools. J. U. Ogbu (1978), for example, observed that Black and Latino students often face gloomy educational prospects and thus develop a culture that is opposed to societal norms. S. Cheng and Starks (2002) reported that both Asian students and their parents have higher educational expectations than their counterparts of other racial backgrounds. Admittedly, individual differences prevail within all racial groups. To the extent that race affects the transmission of social inequalities to children, however, biracial populations offer quite different but important challenges for our understanding of children's schooling experiences. While multiracial children may encounter problems with peer affiliations, in some cases, their appearance or skin color may force them to be more sensitive to racial issues than other same-age children, which might be viewed as an asset in an increasingly diverse society (Bradshaw, 1992; Gibbs, 1987, 1989; Park, 1931). Additionally, within multiracial families, parental decisions regarding children's education often involve negotiation between at least two sets of racial traditions (Cooney & Radina, 2000; Herring, 1992). The two parents' sex, coupled with racial differences, may further complicate the dynamics of these environments (Chew, Eggebeen, & Uhlenberg, 1989). As a result, understanding the educational experiences of multiracial children becomes even more complicated if we take family into consideration.

Prior Research on Multiracial Individuals

A handful of scholars have argued that potential advantages may exist for interracial individuals (P. M. Brown, 1990; Gibbs & Hines, 1992; Poussaint, 1984; Stephan, 1992). In their view, although multiracial individuals tend to suffer problems of peer isolation and internal struggle over an integrated racial identity, they are also more likely than monoracial people to develop insights into, and an understanding of, racial issues. Recognizing that race is a social construct that may delineate social boundaries, multiracial children may identify their race differently according to various social contexts (see Harris & Sim, 2002; Root, 1992).[4] This allows them to better deal with peers of different backgrounds in racially diverse environments.

Aside from these positive perspectives, however, most multiracial studies since the 1970s have tended to focus on multiracial children's potentially problematic life experiences, particularly on three disadvantages considered to be especially detrimental to their schooling (Brandell, 1988;

Figure 1. Factors affecting multiracial youths' life and schooling experiences

Category A: School	Category B: Racial identity	Category C: Family
Group affiliation		Family strain
Racial makeup of student body	Identity ambivalence	Parental educational practices
	Self-esteem	
Racial segregation	Psychological distress	Parental investment in *economic capital* *cultural capital* *social capital*
School embeddedness	Behavioral adjustment	
Friendship network	School failure	
		Parental school involvement
	Multiracial youths' educational and life experiences	

Chiong, 1998; Collins, 2000; Rosato, 1997; Sebring, 1985). First, multiracial students are more likely to experience peer isolation in their schools than are monoracial students (Comas-Diaz, 1996; Feld & W. C. Carter, 1998; Gibbs, 1987, 1989). Second, interracial children may have difficulty forming an integrated racial identification. With dissimilar physical traits or skin color compared to one or both parents, these children lack a reference person to identify with, and thus go through an emotional process of confusion and conflict (Hardesty, 2001).

Third, because prejudice often exists against mixed-race marriages, interracial couples are more likely than monoracial couples to experience stigmatization or discrimination (Foeman & Nance, 1999; Fu, Tora, & Kendall, 2001; Majete, 1997; Radina & Cooney, 2000). Family instability in biracial homes might disadvantage children by diverting the potential time and resources that parents can devote to their children.[5]

Most recently, the addition of multiracial categories into the census of 2000 has elicited a new wave of research inquiry into multiracial individuals.[6] Facilitated by new data sets that contain detailed racial information to identify biracial children and their families, these newer studies assess educational and psychological profiles of biracial youths. In figure 1, these studies are grouped into three broad categories to reflect the theorized multiracial disadvantages outlined above. I first discuss research related to biracial children's school environments (see category A in figure 1).

I then extend this discussion to include biracial/monoracial differences in educational and psychological outcomes and the educational practices of biracial families (categories B and C) based on the empirical findings from other scholars and my own research.

Current Research Developments

Social Isolation, Multiracial Status, and School Environments

A potential disadvantage of interracial students considered in the litera-ture is the issue of peer isolation. This has a strong influence on inter-racial students' schooling experiences because a weak sense of belong-ing at school is often associated with risk-taking behavior and negative school outcomes (M. K. Johnson, Crosnoe, & Elder, 2001; R. F. Marcus & Sanders-Reio, 2001; Mouton & Hawkins, 1996). This section explores interracial students' sense of belonging at school (or school attachment), its effect on school-related outcomes, and the influence of school racial context on the school attachment of students with different interracial status.

Past research has shown that being multiracial may hinder a student in his/her attempts to fit in with others (Comas-Diaz, 1996; Feld & W. C. Carter, 1998; Gibbs, 1989). At the individual level this peer isolation may be caused by perceptions of monoracial students that their biracial peers are physically and culturally different. This is particularly true for bi-racial students who display physical traits from both of their racial heri-tages. The effect of a student's interracial status is further compounded by structural barriers, such as racial segregation, caused by social preju-dice toward multiracial individuals.[7] Because structural barriers tend to result in social marginality, children of interracial backgrounds are more likely than monoracial students to experience disrupted social ties (e.g., broken friendships because of clique peer pressure) or peer isolation.

As suggested, however, biracial students may possess a more consid-ered understanding of racial issues than their monoracial peers because of their experiences in two racial worlds. Additionally, because peer af-filiations are often influenced by children's perceived similarity of demo-graphic backgrounds (Kandel, 1978; Sykes, Larntz, & Fox, 1976), it is possible that monoracial children see more similarities between them-selves and biracial children than with students from different mono-racial backgrounds. Biracial students may, in fact, occupy a social position that allows them to develop peer affiliations with students of different monoracial backgrounds.

This suggests being biracial could be both a disadvantage and an advantage for multiracial students. This advantage or disadvantage may depend on the degree of their "whiteness" because of the social privilege that is often granted to Whites. For White biracial students, their White and racial minority heritages may allow them to affiliate with peers from both White and minority groups. For non-White biracials, due to their lack of White heritage, their social marginality may be alleviated only in schools with large racial minority populations.

Empirical evidence is required for examining the aforementioned discussion about multiracial students' interactions with monoracial students in schools. Three questions arise. First, does multiracial students' sense of belonging in schools (or school attachment) differ by their interracial status? Second, how does students' attachment to school affect their school and behavioral outcomes? And finally, how does a school's student body racial composition affect students of different biracial statuses?

To answer the first question, I analyzed the school attachment index formed by six items measuring students' sense of belonging in schools (e.g., "You feel close to people at your school") from the National Longitudinal Study of Adolescent Health, 1994–95 (for more details, see panel B in the appendix). Note that although the category "Hispanics" consists of individuals from different racial backgrounds, survey data have often used the term as either a racial or an ethnic category. Because the Adolescent Health study identifies Hispanic students as an ethnic group, with no information for their multiracial heritage, these students are not considered in this section's analyses (Harris & Sim, 2002, p. 617).[8]

As shown in figure 2, Asian monoracial students displayed the highest school attachment score, followed by White monoracial, White biracial, Black monoracial, and non-White biracial students. These findings suggest that White biracial students feel more accepted in school environments than non-White biracial adolescents. While not all students may fit these patterns, the results are generally consistent with the stereotypical impression that Asian American youth are more attached to their student life than other racial groups,[9] and that Black students tend to feel more alienated in school settings (Kao & Tienda, 1998; J. U. Ogbu, 1978).

Next I examined the general relationships between school attachment (or sense of belonging in school) and twelve school and behavioral outcomes for all adolescent students. In virtually all of the outcomes that were analyzed, a close bond to school helped to promote positive schooling experiences, regardless of racial background. This pattern remained even after taking into account adolescents' characteristics and family

Figure 2. Predicted scores for adolescents' school attachment

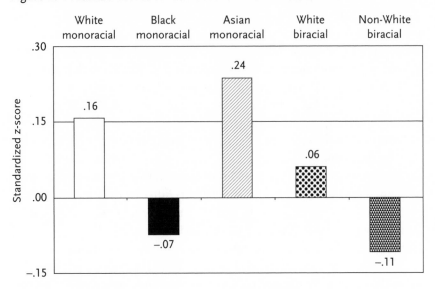

Data source: National Longitudinal Study of Adolescent Health, 1994–95.
Note: Predicted values are calculated from weighted regression analyses. Differences between racial groups are all significant at the .10 level, with the exceptions of (1) monoracial Asian versus monoracial White and (2) non-White biracial versus monoracial Black. Group sizes: Monoracial White = 5,690; monoracial Black = 980; monoracial Asian = 518; White biracials = 455; non-White biracials = 206.

backgrounds. Figure 3 compares the effects of a sense of school belonging on students of various biracial and monoracial backgrounds. As an illustration, the top-left panel suggests that, for White biracial students, one-standard-deviation increase in a positive sense of belonging in school is associated with an increase in their English grades by .27 points on a scale of 1 to 4. In other words, when a White biracial student's school attachment score changed from one standard deviation below the average to one standard deviation above the average, the associated change in her English grade is approximately a half grade.[10]

Of the twelve variables examined in figure 3, school attachment had a greater positive association with ten outcomes for White biracial adolescents than for monoracial students (skipping school and feeling support from friends were the two exceptions). Although the patterns for non-White biracial adolescents were not as uniform, school attachment had greater effects on five of the twelve measures for non-White biracials than for monoracial students.[11]

Admittedly, students' sense of belonging in school and the twelve school-related outcomes shown in figure 3 are likely to have mutual

Figure 3. Racial differences in the effects of school attachment on educational and behavioral outcomes

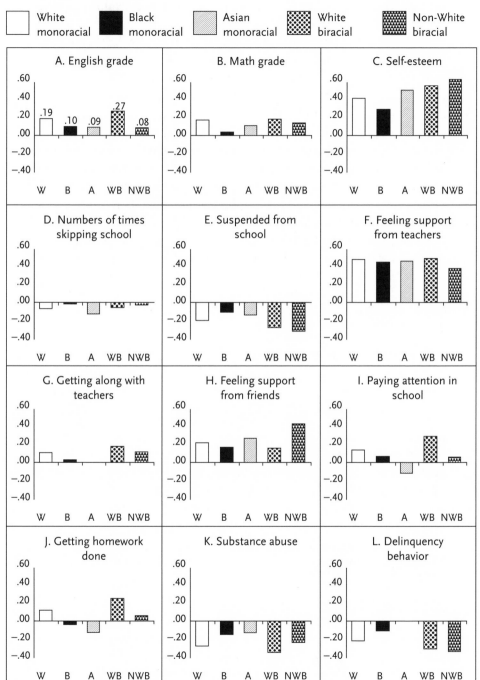

Data source: National Longitudinal Study of Adolescent Health, 1994–95.
Note: To facilitate comparisons, all coefficients (that is, y-axis) are fully standardized.

influences, as past research has shown that consistent discipline, supervision, and reduction in delinquency behaviors among students may help to promote school attachment (Liska & M. D. Reed, 1985). Such mutual influence, however, does not change the general conclusion that school attachment is relatively more important for interracial adolescents than for monoracial youths. More importantly, the analyses presented in figures 2 and 3 suggest two implications. First, a strong sense of belonging in school is important for positive schooling experiences, especially, but not exclusively, for adolescents of interracial backgrounds. Thus to improve outcomes for these students, schools should try to foster a greater sense of attachment for these students and their families. Second, treating biracial youth as a homogeneous group may blur the differences between students of various interracial backgrounds.

Finally, I examined the influence of school racial composition on the sense of belonging in school of the five groups of monoracial and biracial adolescents.[12] As shown for model 1 of table 2, the school attachment of White and Black monoracial students increases in schools that have higher proportions of students from their own racial backgrounds ($p <$

Table 2. Effects of school racial composition on adolescents' school attachment

Adolescents' racial status	Model 1 (before control)		Model 2 (after control)	
School racial composition	Coef.	S.E.	Coef.	S.E.
Reference: White students	−.01	(.069)	−.01	(.069)
Proportion of White students	.23	(.091)**	.23	(.092)*
Black students	−.31	(.089)**	−.28	(.094)**
Proportion of Black students	.41	(.166)**	.34	(.179)+
Asian American students	.02	(.067)+	.05	(.064)
Proportion of Asian American students	.06	(.168)	.03	(.172)
White biracial students	.00	(.091)	.00	(.089)
Proportion of racial minority students	.00	(.169)	.01	(.160)
Non-White biracial students	−.53	(.209)**	−.52	(.199)**
Proportion of racial minority students	.85	(.285)**	.85	(.278)**

Data source: National Longitudinal Study of Adolescent Health, 1994–95.
Note. Control variables include mother's education, age, employment, family income, students' gender, school year, grades, membership in sport teams, regions (student level; N = 5,948 children from two-biological-parent households), private school, and the average parental education of the school (school level; n = 131).
$+ p < .10$ $*p < .05$ $**p < .01$ (2-tailed)

.01). In contrast, the school's racial composition has little influence on White biracial adolescents' school sense of belonging. For non-White biracial adolescents, an increase of White monoracial students in a school has a greater negative impact on their school attachment than for any other students, perhaps due to the combination of their non-White and interracial statuses. These patterns remain even if we consider students with similar family and school characteristics, as shown in model 2. Note that although the results reported here are based on all biracial adolescents included in the Adolescent Health survey, the effect of school racial composition on each individual student may vary according to their physical appearance. An increase in the proportion of Black students in school, for example, may have different effects on the school attachment of Black/White children who look White, Black, or display physical traits of both Blacks and Whites.

The finding that White and Black monoracial adolescents' school attachment increases in schools with more same-race peers requires further discussion. While most scholars agree that desegregated school environments promote students' achievement and long-term attainment outcomes (Bankston & Caldas, 2000; Entwisle & K. L. Alexander, 1994), research has shown a mix of findings regarding the effects of interracial contact on adolescents' psychological well-being (Hallinan & S. S. Smith, 1985; Longshore, 1982; Longshore & Prager, 1985). These inconsistent findings are not evidence against desegregated schools. Rather, they suggest that, despite racial diversity in many U.S. schools, more remains to be done in order to establish a true racially integrated schooling environment for multiracial as well as for monoracial students.

In additional analyses I examined the influence of school racial compositions on adolescents' mental health. The results suggest that, as in the case of school attachment, school racial composition has no statistically significant effect on White biracial students' psychological state; in contrast, non-White biracial students' psychological well-being significantly improves in schools with a higher proportion of non-White students (S. Cheng, 2004). However, perhaps because adolescents' psychological well-being stems from their experiences from a variety of sources, including family, school, peer groups, and neighborhood (Jessor, 1992, 1993), the effects of school racial composition on students' general psychological health are generally small. Note that the analyses presented here focus on adolescent students. The effects of school racial composition on young children's school attachment and psychological well-being may be different, because the level of cognitive maturity may affect young children's interpretation of racial information (Holmes, 1995).

Taken together, these analyses provide evidence that school racial environments interact with individual racial status to influence adolescents' psychological states.[13] The magnitudes of these influences depend on whether the psychological outcomes are directly related to school context, as shown in the analyses of school attachment and adolescents' mental health. Most important, these analyses also suggest that, when placed in multiracial school contexts, White biracial students feel more comfortable than any other students in their interactions with different peer groups. This implies that educators and school counselors must take into account students' racial status and the racial composition of social contexts in order to understand multiracial youths' schooling experiences and their psychological well-being. However, "flexibility" of multiracial students' comfort in school may vary by the adolescents' racial identifications or their physical appearance (e.g., skin color). Unfortunately, there is not currently data to evaluate how students' physical appearances may affect the trends reported above.

In sum, past research concerning multiracial students has suggested that all multiracial youth are disadvantaged in school because of their interracial status. This section shows that the school disadvantage for multiracial students is more applicable to non-White biracial students than to White biracial adolescents, perhaps because of their double-minority status as interracial and as non-White. Additionally, the results highlight the importance of focusing on biracial children's sense of belonging in schools, as school embeddedness (or attachment) has greater positive effects on the school outcomes for these adolescents than on those for students from other racial backgrounds.

Psychological and School Outcomes: Revisiting the Pessimistic Portrayal of Multiracial Youths

The experiences of interracial children are obviously contextual. As noted, the increase in the number of multiracial students has been notable since the 1970s. This trend was accompanied by a growing multiracial movement in recent years, which seems to be gaining favor particularly on college campuses (K. M. Williams, 2005). Given this change in social context, it is important to reconsider the early literature on the marginality of multiracial youths. Earlier multiracial studies typically offered pessimistic portrayals of the academic and psychological profiles of multiracial youth. These studies suggested that biracial students might mask their identity ambivalence behind issues such as poor school performance and truancy, which in turn leads multiracial children to display more behavioral and academic problems than do monoracial students (McRoy & Freeman, 1986; McRoy & Zurcher, 1983).

Empirical studies, using nationally representative data, have recently tested the contention that multiracial children are socially and psychologically disadvantaged by their identities. Regarding racial identity, scholars generally find support for the postulation that interracial youths' racial identities exist in a fluid state and may change according to the social contexts they face, including family, school, or even larger social settings. Xie and Goyette (1997), for example, examined whether Asian biracial children are more likely to identify with their Asian or non-Asian parent. Using 1990 census data, they suggested that the concentration of the Asian population in a certain geographic area interacts with other sociodemographic variables (e.g., parental education) to affect Asian biracial children's racial identities. Similarly, Harris and Sim (2002) analyzed whether White biracial students have closer affiliations with their White or racial minority identities. They concluded that regional and neighborhood contexts (e.g., living in the South) affect adolescents' racial identifications. In this sense, racial ambiguity may be a source of marginality as well as an interactional leverage that allows multiracial youth to navigate different situations.

A direct implication from the above discussion is that, in contrast to the early literature, the inconsistency in multiracial youths' racial identification may not necessarily translate into worse school outcomes or higher psychological distress than for monoracial youth. In arguably the first comprehensive study on the educational profiles of biracial youth, Kao (1999) compared the biracial/monoracial differences in adolescents' school performance and self-esteem and found little evidence that biracial youth do worse academically or have lower self-esteem than their minority or White counterparts. In another study, Cooney and Radina (2000) examined nine indicators of adolescents' school adjustment problems.[14] Although biracial adolescents are more likely to be retained in a grade level, to be suspended from school, to have higher levels of depression, and are less likely to use counseling than White monoracial students, the differences from their monoracial minority peers on these outcomes are minimal.[15] Zill (2003) reported that the school readiness of Black/White biracial kindergartners is below that of monoracial White children but ahead of monoracial Black children. In all of these studies the authors concluded that the negative impression that dominated the early literature on multiracial populations was overstated.

Most of the studies reviewed above either focused on a specific biracial group (e.g., Black/White biracials) or analyzed multiracial children as a homogeneous group. In reality, as discussed, much heterogeneity exists within the pan-category of multiracial Americans. The blurring of multiracial categories in these studies stems largely from data limitations. More specifically, to fully identify biracial children, researchers must identify the racial status of children's biological parents.[16] Most existing data sets, however, do not provide complete racial information of children's biological parents, especially when the children do not live in two-biological-parent households.[17] This said, the studies reviewed here represent the best research efforts to date on the educational and psychological issues associated with multiracial youth until more data are collected on this fast-growing youth population.

Educational Practices of Biracial Families

Finally, since each child's education consists of both what happens in the school as well as out-of-school experiences, schools ideally would be supportive of how families from all backgrounds supplement the school's curriculum. Social and behavioral scientists have documented that positive parenting styles and family educational investment can benefit children's educational and life chances (Schneider & J. S. Coleman, 1993; Steelman, B. Powell, Werum, & S. Carter, 2002). Although a high correlation exists between a family's socioeconomic status and parental investment in children's education, researchers have also suggested that parental educational practices may vary across family type, individual cultural backgrounds, and the levels of conflict between spouses (Astone & McLanahan, 1991; J. S. Coleman et al., 1966; Steelman & B. Powell, 1993). If families' educational practices can lead to either benefits or disadvantages for children, it is important to understand whether biracial families might uniquely affect multiracial children in school.

Past research on intermarriage has suggested that although interracial couples, on average, have comparable or higher educational attainments and socioeconomic statuses than monoracial couples, they are more likely to experience family strain. With potential conflict between partners of interracial couples, then, do biracial children receive less parental support than do monoracial students? Existing empirical studies offer little evidence to answer this question. Given that family instability may divert parents' time and energies from their children, one could hypothesize that parents' investments to children from biracial families lag behind those of monoracial families.

Three additional possibilities exist for biracial families' investments in their children's education. First, biracial families' educational investments may lie between those of the two monoracial groups that comprise the interracial couple. Second, it is also possible that interracial parents are cognizant of their children's marginalized social position in monoracial environments. In order to compensate for this putative disadvantage and to increase their children's chances of success in school, parents from biracial families may invest more in their children's education than their same-race counterparts in monoracial families. Third, some scholars argue that racial disparities in family resources and in educational outcomes may be caused by the socioeconomic/class backgrounds of racial minority families (Blau, 1977; Hedges & Nowell, 1999). This explanation need not be seen as denying the importance of race per se but rather as offering an alternative rationale behind the racial differences. If true, differences between biracial and monoracial families should be explained by socioeconomic and other factors.

To evaluate which of the above scenarios is most consistent with the educational practices in biracial families, I compared the biracial/monoracial differences in family educational investments using data from the Early Childhood Longitudinal Study: Kindergarten Class of 1998–99 (ECLS-K) (S. Cheng & B. Powell, 2002). For each interracial combination, I determined whether the parental investments of the interracial families are higher than, lower than, or in-between those of their same-race counterparts (e.g., Black/Asian families compared to monoracial Black and Asian families). Figure 4 summarizes the results of economic, cultural, and social resources, both with and without sociodemographic controls (e.g., family income, parental education).[18] For the purpose of illustration, I use "Higher" in figure 4 to indicate that the biracial families invest more in their children's education than both groups of monoracial families related to the interracial couples. "Lower" signifies that biracial families' educational investments are lower than both groups of monoracial families. "Middle" suggests that the biracial families' investments fall between those of the two monoracial groups; and "Non-sig" indicates that the statistical analyses show no significant differences between the biracial and monoracial families.

The results from figure 4 suggest that the biracial/monoracial differences in parents' educational investments differ between economic, cultural, and social capital resources. For family resources over which the parents have greater control—such as children's possession of educational goods (or economic capital resources) or visiting cultural settings (or cultural capital resources)—the educational investments of biracial families tend to exceed those of monoracial families. This biracial advantage does not extend to social/interactional capital resources (e.g., talking to other students' parents or participating in children's school activities).

Figure 4. Biracial/monoracial differences in educational investments: Do biracial families invest more or less in their children than monoracial families?

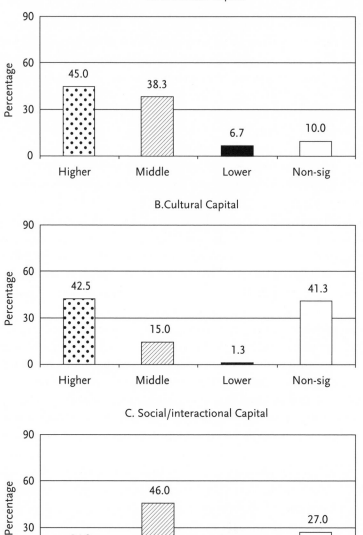

A. Economic Capital

B. Cultural Capital

C. Social/interactional Capital

Data source: Early Childhood Longitudinal Study: Kindergarten Class of 1998–99.
Note: Comparisons are based on 240 statistical models of ten categories of biracial families, and twelve sets of economic, cultural, and social/interactional resources (with and without sociodemographic controls). Three indicators are used for comparisons of economic capital investment; four indicators for cultural capital; and five indicators for social/interactional capital. In each case, comparisons are made between ten groups of biracial families and their corresponding monoracial groups. For details of all measures, please see the appendix.

As shown in figure 4, parents from biracial families show no greater investment than their counterparts from monoracial families in this type of family resources. This general pattern also remains after taking into consideration the influences of family sociodemographic factors, such as parental education and family income. Perhaps interracial couples' social marginality and their disrupted social networks may cause them greater difficulties in developing beneficial social/interactional resources for their biracial children. More empirical evidence, however, is required to test this possibility.

The inconsistent patterns of biracial/monoracial differences in family investments of economic, cultural, and social/interactional resources imply two potentially distinct but complementary mechanisms regarding the educational practices of biracial families. First, because parents from biracial families are cognizant of differential treatment in public settings, they may alter their parenting practices in order to compensate for their children's putative disadvantages in schools. Consequently, their educational investments may be greater than those of their monoracial counterparts with similar socioeconomic backgrounds. Second, interracial parents' abilities to increase their educational investments may be constrained or altered by factors such as family instability and racial prejudice toward interracial marriages.

The two mechanisms proposed above remain speculation until we further examine the motivations behind interracial parents' higher investments in their children's education. To investigate interracial couples' educational decisions for their children, and to further understand the circumstances involved in how they develop beneficial social capital for their children, I explored whether and how the racial backgrounds of parents in interracial families affect their decisions to participate in their children's school activities. Although social capital has been defined in different ways, this analysis using data from the ELCS-K focuses on the extent to which parents build social ties that broaden their children's educational opportunities, measured by parents' participation in open house, PTA meetings, parent-teacher conferences, student activities (e.g., plays, sports), fund-raising, and school volunteer work (J. Coleman, 1988; Kao, 2004; Portes, 1998). My hypothesis is that if interracial parents are indeed aware of racial prejudice and want to develop useful social ties for their children in school, they may send the spouse with higher racial status (e.g., White parents in White/minority interracial families, regardless of the spouse's gender) to attend their children's school events, particularly if the school enrolls a large number of White students.[19]

Analyses of ECLS data suggest that, all else being equal, fathers in

White father and minority mother families are more likely than fathers in monoracial White families to attend school events, whereas fathers in minority father and White mother families are less likely than their counterparts from monoracial minority families to participate in their children's educational activities. Similarly, mothers in minority father and White mother families are more likely than mothers from monoracial White families to attend school events. Further, mothers in White father and minority mother families are less likely than their counterparts from monoracial minority families to participate in their children's educational activities. These general patterns hold across the six school events in the analyses. These findings confirm my hypothesis that the racial status of interracial parents has a significant influence on which parents attend their children's school activities. The results also imply that, when forming parenting strategies, interracial parents are keenly aware of the social privilege that is often granted to Whites in our society.

Before concluding this section, it is worth noting that the general patterns reported from the two studies outlined above may vary by the mixture of racial backgrounds of interracial parents. For example, compared to other interracial households, Black/White interracial families tend to have lower investments in their children's education. Past research has indicated that White/Black parents often suffer more racial prejudice than other interracial combinations (Kalmijn, 1993). Future research is required to investigate whether and how family dynamics may differ by the racial backgrounds of the parents. Taken together, these analyses offer evidence that multiracial children are not educationally disadvantaged by the practices of their families.

Syntheses and Implications

Nearly forty years have passed since the *Loving v. Virginia* (1967) decision. While much research has been done to understand the growing population of interracial couples and their children over the past four decades, scholarly efforts have been mostly concerned with examining factors facilitating interracial marriages, issues of identity formation, and the fluidity of the concepts "biracial" and "multiracial" (Blau, Blum, & Schwartz, 1982; Kalmijn, 1993; Harris & Sim, 2002). These studies have certainly laid a foundation for educators to understand the schooling experiences of interracial youths, but their research findings may be less relevant today given the increasing visibility of multiracial students in classrooms and perhaps the change over the years in the nation's sentiment about race.

Early scholars have suggested that being multiracial is a double-edged sword. This remains true even in today's society. Note, however, that it is not being interracial that is the "double-edged sword," but rather it is the way in which multiracial students may be treated in schools. As we have seen in this essay, most adolescent students are uneasy when affiliating with peers of different races. This makes multiracial youth a potentially disadvantageous group because they constitute a small proportion of the student body in most schools. At the same time, however, the putative disadvantage caused by their ambiguous yet distinct racial status may motivate interracial populations to use their dual racial heritage as a potential resource in multiracial environments. This may explain why White biracial students' school attachment, on average, is less affected by school racial composition than are other students. For interracial parents the White spouse in a White/minority family is more likely than his/her counterpart from monoracial families to participate in their children's school activities.

The ability of interracial students and their parents to use their racial ambiguity as potential resources suggests that a multiracial status is not necessarily a negative characteristic. As shown in this essay, although most multiracial studies prior to the turn of this century suggested a pessimistic life prospect for multiracial youths, recent studies indicate that students of interracial backgrounds do not appear to be worse off than other monoracial minorities in school outcomes (in many cases, better than monoracial minorities). On the other hand, the finding that non-White biracial adolescents seem particularly alienated in school settings suggests that the experiences of interracial youth in schools are contingent upon the type of their interracial status. This implies that, although much school racial desegregation has been achieved since the *Brown* case, much remains to be done by educators and policymakers to develop a racially integrated schooling system.

Three additional policy implications follow directly from this essay's findings. First, it is necessary to correct the misperception from early studies that interracial youth are more psychologically disoriented than monoracial children. Teachers and principals may foster positive attitudes toward interracial populations by including positive multiracial characters in children's curricula and encouraging cross-racial contacts among students. Second, as educational policymakers continue to implement policies to encourage parental school involvement, future efforts should be made to reduce the racial factors that may affect interracial as well as racial minority parents' decision in participation in their children's school activities, perhaps by creating more racially friendly environments. Third, educators should consider how to assist non-White biracial students so that they feel a greater sense of belonging. Whenever necessary, therapeutic intervention should be designed to help non-White biracial students to deal with their stressful experiences regarding peer affiliations, especially in schools formed mostly by White students.

Finally, it is worth noting that the educational experiences of interracial students may differ in schools with different socioeconomic composition. These issues are, however, not addressed in this essay. Our lack of understanding in these issues stems largely from data limitations. Currently, only a few nationally representative data sets permit the analysis of interracial youths' educational experiences. Yet the small samples of interracial students in these data often limit the scope of analyses researchers can do. To more fully document how multiracial children fare in school, government agencies should collect more data on multiracial children and their families. This would facilitate empirical research on multiracial children's schooling experiences and thus help educators to better address the issues that this growing population faces.

Appendix

Description of variables in the analyses

Panel A. Variables from Early Childhood Longitudinal Study: Kindergarten Class of 1998–99

Variables	Notes / Question wording / Coding
Biracial families	
White father, Black mother = 32	Single-parent households are excluded
Black father, White mother = 111	from analyses.
White father, Hispanic mother = 303	
Hispanic father, White Mother = 298	
White father, Asian mother = 102	
Asian father, White mother = 72	
White father, other mother = 94	
Other father, White mother = 97	
Black and Hispanic = 56	
Hispanic, Asian = 51	
Economic capital	
Possession of educational goods	Composite variable, mean = 0, std = 1
Child has a home computer?	1= yes, 0= no
Private school?	1= yes, 0= no
Cultural capital	
Cultural activities: Reading and book-related	Composite variable, mean = 0, std = 1
Cultural activities: Non-reading	Composite variable, mean = 0, std = 1
Participate in art classes/lessons	Composite variable, mean = 0, std = 1
Visit cultural settings	Composite variable, mean = 0, std = 1

Variables	Notes / Question wording / Coding
Social/interactional capital	
Parental educational aspirations	1 = less than high school, ~6 = doctoral
Positive parent–child interactions	Composite variable, mean = 0, std = 1
Number of close grandparents	Continuous variable
Number of other students' parents talk with	Continuous variable
Parental involvement in school activities	Composite variable, mean = 0, std = 1
Parental school involvement	
Since the beginning of this school year, which adults in your household:	
Attended an open house or a back-to-school night?	Nominal variables; 1 = mother, 2 = father, 3 = both, 4 = neither
Attended a meeting of a PTA, PTO, or Parent-Teacher Student Organization?	
Went to a regularly scheduled parent-teacher conference?	
Attended a school or class event, such as a play, sports event, or science fair?	
Acted as a volunteer at the school or served on a committee?	
Participated in fund-raising for (CHILD)'s school?	

Panel B. Variables from National Longitudinal Study of Adolescent Health, 1994–95 (N = 7,849)

Variables	Notes / Question wording / Coding
Biracial/monoracial students	
White = 5,690	
Black = 980	
Asian = 518	
White biracials = 455	
Non-White biracials = 206	
School attachment index	
You feel close to people at your school.	Composite variable, mean = 0, std = 1
You feel like you are part of your school.	All responses ranged from 1 (strongly
You are happy to be at your school.	disagree) to 5 (strongly agree)
The teachers at your school treat students fairly.	
You feel safe in your school.	
Other outcome variables from Adolescent Health	All items below are standardized
English grades	4 = A, 3 = B, 2 = C, and 1 = D or lower
Math grades	4 = A, 3 = B, 2 = C, and 1 = D or lower
Self-esteem	Composite variable
Number of times skipping school for a full day without an excuse	Continuous variable
Suspended from school before	1= yes, 0= no
Feeling support from teachers	1 (not at all) to 5 (very much)

Variables	Notes / Question wording / Coding
Getting along with teachers	0 (never) to 4 (everyday)
Feeling support from friends	1 (not at all) to 5 (very much)
Paying attention in school	0 (never) to 4 (everyday)
Getting homework done	0 (never) to 4 (everyday)
Substance abuse	Composite variable
Delinquency behaviors	Composite variable

Notes

I would like to thank Prudence Carter, Erica Frankenberg, Michael Mulcahy, Gary Orfield, Brian Powell, Kim Price, Genevieve Siegel-Hawley, and Wesley Younts for their helpful comments. This research was supported by grants from the University of Connecticut and from the Program in Positive Interracial Outcomes in the Classroom. Direct all correspondence to Simon Cheng, University of Connecticut, Department of Sociology, Storrs, CT 06269–2068; E-mail: simon.cheng@uconn.edu.

1. Children with parents from two different races are biracial. When one of the parents is biracial or multiracial, the child is multiracial. Since almost all (93 percent) multiracial children are biracial, I use "biracial" and "multiracial" interchangeably. I acknowledge, however, that "biracial" is a subset of "multiracial."

2. Throughout the essay, the term "White biracial children" indicates children who have a White parent and a parent from a different racial background. "Non-White biracial children" refers to children with parents from two racial minorities, such as Black/Asian and Black/Hispanic children. Please see the appendix for the distribution of White and non-White biracial children included in this analysis.

3. Multiracial individuals are highly concentrated geographically. For example, the state of California contained approximately 12 percent of the U.S. total population in 2000, but contained approximately 24 percent of the national multiracial population (R. Kim & Ness, 2001).

4. Despite the lack of biological distinction in the definition of race, the social construct of race has powerful connotations in U.S. society. Today race does not only exist in people's perceptions; it also affects government policies and delineates social inequalities (Omi and Winant, 1994). Therefore, understanding the social construction of "race" is essential for understanding the current schooling system.

5. Because families headed by interracial couples are by definition two-parent households, the comparison here is between children of interracial and monoracial couples. While the relative dis/advantages between children from interracial homes and families headed by single parents may be of interest to some readers, this focus is beyond the scope of the present study.

6. The census of 1990 used four racial categories: White, Black, American Indian or Alaska Native, and Asian and Pacific Islander. The census of 2000 intro-

duced Hawaiian as a new race category, and, for the first time in American history, allowed people to identify themselves as more than one race. Since 1970 the Bureau of the Census has also included a separate question specifically on Hispanic origin. In most cases, however, Hispanics are treated as an ethnic rather than a racial category in census reports.

7. Stanton-Salazar (1997) defines "structural barriers" as "features in school environments that prevent, impede, or discourage students from engaging fully in learning—social or academic" (p. 24). Structural barriers are often inherent in the policies and procedures of the institution and appear in such things as racial segregation and tracking.

8. In analyses using the Early Childhood Longitudinal Study: Kindergarten Class of 1998–99 (discussed later in this essay), "Hispanic" is used as a racial category. In additional analyses I estimate models excluding Hispanics. These analyses yield similar findings.

9. For example, Southeast Asians may not fit the "Asian" stereotype mostly derived from Japanese, Korean, and Chinese Americans. For a more detailed discussion of this issue, see Goyette and Xie (1999).

10. In this example, $.27 \times 2 = .54$; from a B to a B+ average.

11. These five measures were self-esteem, being suspended from school, getting along with teachers, feeling support from friends, and delinquency behavior.

12. School racial composition was calculated using the entire in-school sample from the Adolescent Health study. The variable was then linked to the core sample to examine the influence of school racial context on adolescents' school embeddedness. In supplementary analyses I also examined whether students did better in schools that were not solely composed of White or racial minority students. The results suggest that both biracial and monoracial students have higher math grades in schools with approximately equal proportions of White and racial minority students. Due to their sample sizes, however, the relationship for biracial students is not statistically significant at the .10 level.

13. While my discussion focuses on biracial students, the analyses and the conclusion can be extended to include monoracial students as well. For a similar argument, see Cole, in this volume.

14. Like the 2000 Census, the Adolescent Health survey data used by Cooney and Radina asked separate questions about race and Hispanic origin. This two-question approach makes it problematic to code Hispanics as a racial group, because it is often unclear what respondents meant in their selection of a Hispanic origin and race. For a brief discussion of this issue, see Harris and Sim (2002, p. 617).

15. The other five school adjustment outcomes are delinquency behavior, substance abuse, school performance, school problems (e.g., getting along with teachers and students, paying attention in class), and general feelings in school. Analyses focusing on these indicators show no statistical differences between biracial and monoracial children.

16. The term "biracial children" refers to children whose biological parents are

from different races. "Children of biracial families" consists of children whose current parents (who may or may not be the children's biological parents) are from different races. These two groups do not completely overlap with each other because many children do not live with their biological parents.

17. Three nationally representative data sets contain information that permits analyses of multiracial children and adolescents: (1) the ECLS, (2) the Adolescent Health study, and (3) U.S. census data. Of these, only the ECLS provides the racial status of biological parents for children who do not reside in two-biological-parent households.

18. The no-control models examine whether biracial families' educational investment in their children differ from those of monoracial families. The with-control models explore whether these group differences are the function of family sociodemographic characteristics. The pattern reported in figure 4 remains consistent regardless of whether sociodemographic controls are included.

19. Because of the unclear status hierarchy between non-White interracial couples, non-White interracial families are excluded from this analysis.

Toward an Integrated Future of Schooling

Possible Solutions

Preparing Teachers for Multiracial and Historically Underserved Schools

Christine E. Sleeter

Teacher preparation should be nested within a vision that values diversity, equity, and social justice. Fundamental to that vision is conceptualizing its purpose as preparing everyone who qualifies for admission into teacher education to teach well in someone else's community. Regardless of whether one is located in a predominantly White area, a diverse urban area, an American Indian reservation, a rural area, or anywhere else, all teachers should learn how to cross cultural borders, gain knowledge from diverse community contexts, recognize brilliance in children who differ from themselves, and build productive interpersonal and academic learning environments for diverse children.

This vision represents a paradigm shift from most teacher preparation programs. Many programs reflect the belief that difference should not matter and that teachers need to learn generic teaching practices presumed to apply universally. Others reflect the belief that while differences do matter, teacher education coursework alone can prepare anyone to teach in diverse contexts. I will argue that the vision demands a more far-reaching response. Teacher education should facilitate the entry into teaching of those who genuinely want to learn to teach cross-culturally and then provide them with ongoing support to do so. This entails recruiting and welcoming diverse preservice teachers, involving preservice teachers in cross-cultural community-based learning, offering multicultural and bilingual education coursework, and nurturing pedagogy in the classroom from preservice through the first years of teaching. In this essay I develop recommendations that are informed by research studies and filtered through my thirty-year history with teacher preparation, first as a White teacher prepared in a field-based urban education program, then as a teacher educator and researcher working with teachers at the preservice level (preparation prior to obtaining a teaching position) and the inservice level (continued professional development after obtaining a teaching position).

It is widely recognized that the demographic gap between schoolchildren and teachers is large and growing. In 2002–3 enrollment in U.S. public elementary and secondary schools was, in round numbers, less than two-thirds White (59 percent) and more than one-third students of color (18 percent Latino, 17 percent African American, 4 percent Asian/Pacific Islander, and 1 percent American Indian/Alaskan Native) (G. Orfield & C. Lee, 2005). Thirteen percent of students spoke a language other than English at home. By contrast, the teaching force was 84 percent White, 9 percent African American, 5 percent Hispanic, 1 percent Asian/Pacific Islander, and 1 percent American Indian/Alaskan Native, and it had changed little since previous years (National Center for Education Statistics, 2002). Those who have recently entered teaching are a little more diverse than the profession as a whole (78 percent White, 22 percent of color), with teachers of color concentrated in urban schools with high proportions of students of color (Shen, Wegenke, & Cooley, 2003). Nevertheless, the majority of teachers and those entering teaching are still White and female.

Most White preservice teachers bring to teacher education very little cross-cultural knowledge and experience, although they often possess a naive optimism that coexists with stereotypes that reflect racial and ethnic biases, such as believing that African American and Latino families do not value education. For example, Schultz, Neyhart, and Reck (1996) surveyed more than one thousand preservice teachers in Pennsylvania, 92 percent of whom were White. About one-quarter of those surveyed indicated interest in urban teaching and tended to agree that urban children are much like themselves. At the same time, about half added various caveats, such as the belief that urban children's cultural background hinders learning, or that urban children are violent or "slower." Other researchers have found that White preservice teachers are willing to teach cross-culturally, but are also uncomfortable with cultural differences, including some reporting discomfort with experiences with others from different cultural backgrounds (Barry & Lechner, 1995). White preservice teachers generally bring little awareness or understanding to issues of discrimination, especially racism, and try not to "see" racial or ethnic differences in order to cope with their fear and ignorance (e.g., Avery & Walker, 1993; McIntyre, 1997; Su, 1997; Valli, 1995). Significantly, White preservice teachers' lack of cross-cultural knowledge is a direct result of the racial isolation in which most White people grow up and live.

Preservice teachers of color tend to bring a richer multicultural knowledge base than their White counterparts. They are more likely to bring a commitment and sense of urgency to multicultural teaching, social justice, and providing children of color with an academically challenging curriculum, and they tend to have positive attitudes toward racial and cultural diversity (J. R. Dee & Henkin, 2002; Knight, 2004; Rios & Montecinos, 1999; Su, 1997), although not necessarily toward other forms of difference, such as sexual orientation.

The teaching profession needs to recruit and prepare preservice teachers from a variety of backgrounds for several reasons. Teachers from diverse backgrounds (White and of color) can help to educate each other about backgrounds of children from communities with which they are familiar. Diverse teachers offer diverse role models to young people. Evidence suggests that sometimes students achieve better when taught by a teacher of the same race (T. S. Dee, 2004). Although the race of any given teacher does not predict anything—ability to teach, knowledge, sensitivity, and so forth—the more closely the teaching profession reflects student populations, the more likely a well-prepared teaching profession will have the repertoire of knowledge to teach diverse students well.

Predominantly White institutions, which prepare the majority of U.S. teachers, have generally responded slowly to the need to prepare a teaching force that can teach well in racially diverse contexts. Fifteen years ago, for example, 94 percent of the faculty and students in nineteen midwestern teacher preparation programs were White, and only 56 percent of these institutions required elementary preservice teachers to complete a coursework designed to prepare them for diverse students (Fuller, 1992). Many programs offer disjointed preparation that depends on the interests of individual professors. Some topics may recur in several classes, such as textbook bias (that is, the quality and quantity of representation of diverse racial, ethnic, or gender groups), while other topics are never addressed, such as how to identify students' cultural strengths or how to make education accessible to second-language learners. Field placements and cooperating teachers during student teaching too often are selected without regard for how well they will prepare novices to learn to teach diverse or historically underserved students. Student teachers from such programs have been found completely unprepared for urban students, often encountering great difficulties. For example, student teachers often interpret urban students' attempts to participate in class as discipline problems, reprimanding students rather than engaging them academically. Student teachers often fear urban students and avoid establishing constructive communication with them and their families (Davis, 1995; Goodwin, 1994; S. M. Miller, K. L. Miller, & Schroth, 1997; Parker & Hood, 1995).

Predominantly White programs also too often reinforce White perspectives and comfort levels while disregarding the perspectives and comfort of educators of color. For example, White preservice teachers sometimes gang up on peers or faculty of color, either harassing them or ignoring them when they speak. This not only has the effect of maintaining the power of White viewpoints (e.g., Agee, 1998; Burant, 1999), but also discourages students of color from entering such programs. When teacher education programs do not address race and other forms of diversity, they not only fail to teach what teachers can do but also fail to interrupt the predominance of perspectives that continues to make schools most responsive to students from White, English-speaking, middle-class backgrounds.

Currently the teaching profession is not attracting and retaining strong teachers for diverse populations as well as it could. Teacher education programs generally attract and serve a predominantly White female population. Although various factors outside the purview of teacher education account for this, teacher education programs themselves are often less attractive to students of color than they could be, as will be discussed below. Further, once certified, almost half of beginning teachers leave the profession after five years; those most likely to leave are from schools that are in poor, urban areas. Some of the reasons for leaving include lack of support and inadequate preparation, factors that teacher education can help to address (Ingersoll, 2003). In the remainder of this essay I will develop recommendations for reworking teacher education to attract and welcome diverse preservice teachers, then prepare them to teach crossculturally by including as part of teacher education community-based learning, coursework on culture and equity pedagogy, and extended support while learning to teach in the classroom.

Attracting and Welcoming Diverse Preservice Teachers

After discussing problems with attempts to prepare overwhelmingly White cadres of preservice teachers, I will discuss how teacher education programs can be more intentional about attracting and welcoming diverse preservice teachers, including Whites who want to learn to teach cross-culturally. Most preservice teacher education programs are constructed mainly for traditional students who can attend school full-time without holding a job simultaneously and for whom the university campus is a convenient and reasonably welcoming location. Although students apply for admission into teacher education programs, admission decisions are made primarily on the basis of grade point average and other required tests; admission is rarely denied on the basis of willingness to learn to teach diverse students. While many programs try to recruit students of color, most continue to take as given the continued predominance of a predominantly White female student population. Faculty with strong interest in preparing teachers for cross-cultural teaching and social justice, then, expend tremendous energy attempting to convince this overwhelmingly White population that racism and other forms of discrimination still exist and need to be challenged and that community cultures of students from historically marginalized backgrounds serve as assets on which to build.

It is unclear, however, the extent to which overwhelmingly White cadres of preservice teachers become the excellent teachers that schools need. Throughout the literature on multicultural education coursework, one finds frequent reference to novice teachers (mostly White) who resist multicultural perspectives (e.g., VanGunten & R. J. Martin, 2001), do not apply pedagogical strategies they were taught (e.g., Guillaume, Zuniga, & I. Lee, 1995), or adopt a few teaching strategies but not the deeper cross-cultural understanding necessary for good teaching (Arias & Poynor, 2001). Sometimes called "resisters," these are novice teachers who refuse to learn to teach diverse students well, assuming that discussions of culture, language, and equity (that is, reduction of school-based barriers to learning) are unnecessary and taught for political rather than educational purposes.

Further, the small amount of research on the impact of such coursework questions its effect on some prospective teachers. For example, R. W. Smith (2000) studied two White preservice teachers to examine the relative influence of life experiences prior to entering teaching and teacher education coursework. He found that the student teacher with prior diversity experiences used awareness of culture as a tool for relating to students and constructing lessons in ways that built on what students had learned from life outside school. The other student teacher, who was a caring person, lacked awareness of culture and therefore was unable to use cross-cultural teaching strategies her program taught as teaching tools. Causey, C. D. Thomas, and Armento (2000) followed two White teachers three years after they had completed their teaching credential. Their teacher education program had emphasized how to address educational equity issues—school and classroom barriers students encounter due to race and class, such as lower academic expectations or curriculum that does not relate to students' experiences. The researchers found one teacher to have forgotten equity issues from previous coursework, and to have reverted to stereotypical notions about her students, while the other continued to develop an activist approach to equity. The authors speculated that the main difference between the two was their disposition to learning about culture and equity and to reflecting on personal beliefs in order to grow.

Both studies suggest that while teacher education can build on life experience and predispositions that novice teachers bring, novices who lack predispositions or experiences for learning to work cross-culturally reject or forget their teacher education. Predisposition to working with culture, language, and equity makes a difference. Consider the teacher who knows algebra well and knows how to teach it to children much like herself, but believes that her low-income Black and Latino students are not only too far behind to learn algebra but also too disinterested and too lacking in home support. This is not a problem of the teacher lacking teaching methods or content knowledge, but rather it is one of understanding students through a cultural deficiency worldview that results in low expectations and teaching geared accordingly. Resisters like this teacher should either not be admitted into teacher education or be actively selected out early on.

Rather than admitting preservice teachers on the basis of grade point average and test scores alone, an alternative approach is to specifically recruit and admit into teacher education only those (both White and of color) who (1) want to learn to teach students who are culturally different from themselves or live in poverty-stricken communities, (2) bring dispositions that enable them to learn to teach such students well, and (3) demonstrate academic ability. Then design the teacher education program primarily for this population rather than for predominantly White cohorts who may not want to teach cross-culturally. Doing this will attract a more diverse and often a more mature mix of people into the teaching profession. Although it would screen many people out of teaching, it would potentially attract those who otherwise do not enter teaching. Further, if coupled with the rest of the recommendations in this essay, more teachers would be successful in the classroom and less likely to leave the teaching profession.

Haberman (1995; 1996) developed an interview process that helps to identify prospective teachers who have dispositions (such as strong belief in children, capacity to learn from mistakes, and willingness to explore and try alternatives) that will enable them to learn to teach well in urban schools. He developed it based on his observations of star urban teachers. Preservice teachers who bring these dispositions are generally older (thirty to fifty years of age). In urban areas the majority are of color and from the local area, and most have raised children or held other jobs. Adopting his interview process is not a panacea, but it offers a way of conceptualizing admission based on willingness and ability to learn to teach cross-culturally.

Recruiting a diverse population into teacher education should imply welcoming and supporting that population. Teacher education programs designed for teachers of color offer clues about how to reconceive teacher education to make it more welcoming and supportive. Many of these are alternative programs (Shen, 1998). For example, the University of Southern California has an alternative program, the Latino and Language Minority Teacher Projects, established "to increase the number of Latinos(as) and language minorities in the teaching profession by creating a career track for practicing language minority paraeducators" (Genzuk, 2003). Throughout its ten-year history the program has certified scores of Latino and other language minority teachers. Another example is the Elementary Certification for Ethnic Colleagues for the Elementary School (EC3), an alternative certification program that existed for four years in Wisconsin to recruit and prepare prospective teachers of color (Shade, Boe, Garner, & New, 1998). It was created through collaboration between two predominantly White universities and a local school district; it successfully certified three cohorts of teachers of color, mainly African American.

Other such programs are part of established colleges of education. At Sacramento State University two departments prepare teachers: the Teacher Education Department and the Bilingual/Multicultural (B/MED) Department. Faculty members who are primarily of color established the latter ten years ago "to prepare bilingual/multicultural teachers to work effectively" with culturally and linguistically diverse students (Cintrón, 2004). Faculty members argued that the existing teacher education program was so established within mainstream ways of teaching and learning that a different program focusing explicitly on culture and language was needed. The B/MED program attracts a high proportion of preservice teachers of color because of this focus and how it informs course content, its faculty to whom students of color can relate, and the program's commitment to working with communities of color. Another program, Project TEAM (Transformative Educational Achievement Model) at Indiana University, in existence since 1996, serves undergraduate students of color who are preparing to become teachers. It addresses concerns of students of color that are often ignored in predominantly White programs, such as how teachers of color can negotiate predominantly White schools when teaching there (Bennett, Cole, & Thompson, 2000).

These programs share several characteristics that make them attractive to diverse prospective teachers. The program directors assume that prospective teachers of color and other adults who want to teach in racially diverse schools are in the community and potentially interested in teaching, but engaged in other activities, such as working (e.g., as paraprofessionals in schools) or attending community college. Therefore, to accommodate them, classes are often scheduled in late afternoons and evenings, in places that are convenient to them (which may not be the university campus). Programs frequently offer paid internships so students will not have to stop working to return to college. Some programs provide books and access to technology. Many offer pathways to help prospective teachers complete their undergraduate degrees as well as teacher certification. Some also offer intense academic assistance in reading, writing, and math for prospective teachers who graduated from academically weak public schools.

The predominantly minority context of many such programs provides "safe space" for discussing schooling in relationship to the lived experiences of preservice teachers of color. Coursework presumes that students bring knowledge of and commitment to working in diverse schools. Rather than attempting to convince them that racism exists or that cultures of diverse groups can be viewed as assets, coursework focuses on how to capitalize on diverse cultures, address various manifestations of racism, and teach well. I taught one semester in EC3 while teaching simultaneously in a predominantly White program. Because the EC3 students, who were mainly African American, could "fast forward" through fundamentals of multicultural education, we were able to focus intensely on teaching strategies and curriculum planning for culturally diverse classrooms.

Cross-Cultural Community-based Learning

Most teachers—particularly those who are White but also many teachers of color—grow up in relatively culturally and racially homogeneous settings, a direct result of persistent housing as well as school segregation. Most have had little experience learning how to learn from someone else's community; yet this is exactly what teachers need to do in order to build pedagogy that is culturally and contextually relevant to their students. Well-structured cross-cultural community-based learning should be part of teacher education at preservice and inservice levels. Cross-cultural community-based learning means learning about a community that is culturally different from one's own by spending time there, equipped with learning strategies such as interview questions, active listening skills, and guidance in what to observe. This is immensely beneficial in many ways.

It helps teachers learn to gain insights about what their students know and how they learn. It also helps teachers learn to interact with parents and other adults from unfamiliar communities and develop awareness of their own cultural assumptions and perspectives.

One can think of cross-cultural community-based learning experiences as lying on a continuum of intensity levels. On one end of the continuum are immersion experiences in which one lives in another cultural context for a period of time; on the other end are short visits to someone else's community or neighborhood. Experiences of varying levels of duration and intensity can have value if they are structured to promote reflection, learning, and pedagogical insights. Extended immersion experiences have potential to promote the deepest learning, mainly because when one lives in another cultural context for a period of time, one cannot retreat to what is familiar or comfortable. One must deal with discomfort and confusion; generally, one must learn from other people in the host cultural context. In short cross-cultural visits (say, for a few hours or a day), one returns to what is known and comfortable at the end of the visit and may never need to question one's fundamental assumptions. Nonetheless, it is usually more feasible to require shorter, less intensive experiences. Every preservice or inservice teacher should be required to engage in at least one cross-cultural community-based learning experience, and if possible, multiple experiences in different communities.

Immersion experiences can vary in length. Indiana University has had semester-long cross-cultural immersion experiences since the mid-1970s in placement sites that include the Navajo Nation, the lower Rio Grande Valley, inner-city Indianapolis, and overseas. The academic year prior to their immersion experience, students complete intensive preparatory coursework in which they study the culture, history, lifestyle, and education of the group with which they will be placed. Stachowski and J. M. Mahan (1998) noted that this preparation serves as an "effective self-screening device in that applicants whose primary motivation may be to play 'tourist' are discouraged by the intensive preparatory work" (p. 156). During the immersion experience, students complete their student teaching while engaging in ongoing substantive community involvement in a project they co-plan with a community member. According to follow-up surveys of graduates, this experience has a strong impact on attitudes, knowledge, and ability to teach cross-culturally; graduates report interaction with community residents as particularly significant to their learning (J. Mahan, 1982; Stachowski & J. M. Mahan, 1998).

Shorter immersion experiences also have value, although they probably promote less extensive learning. For example, Aguilar and Pohan

(1998) took students from Nebraska to the Southwest for four weeks, where they lived in Mexican households and worked on a children's arts program. Riojas Clark and Bustos Flores (1997) took teacher education students to Monterrey, Mexico, for a week, where they studied and experienced the schooling of Mexican children who have immigrated to the United States.

Immersion experiences, when carefully planned to guide learning and help students reflect on what they experience, make a powerful impact on teaching. For example, Noordhoff and Kleinfeld (1993) studied the impact of student teachers' semester-long immersion experience in a small indigenous Alaskan community. The student teachers lived in the community and became involved, for example, in sewing or beading groups, local churches, or cross-country skiing. Videotapes over the semester showed the student teachers learning to shift from teaching as telling to teaching as engaging students with subject matter, using culturally relevant knowledge to connect academic knowledge with what students know. For example, by the end of the semester, one student teacher developed a science unit that engaged students in observing condensation and evaporation of water during steam baths (which were popular in the community) to learn about the relationship between temperature and water state. Further, many teachers who are prepared in community-based cross-cultural programs take teaching positions there. For example, Sconzert, Iazzetto, and Purkey (2000) found that 33 percent of the graduates of a program based in Chicago take teaching jobs in Chicago Public Schools subsequently.

The least intensive type of community-based learning does not involve living in another community. Preservice or inservice teachers visit neighborhoods or communities that differ from their own by factors such as social class, ethnicity, race, or primary language. While there they have a role to play (such as tutoring) or a specific learning activity (such as interviewing senior citizens or constructing a community portrait). These duties often take the form of service learning experiences, in which the teacher's role serves a community-identified need, such as assisting in a food bank or a homework center (M. Boyle-Baise, 2002).

Moll and González have used community-based learning to help inservice teachers improve their teaching (Moll, Amanti, Neff, & González, 1994). After instructing teachers to conduct interviews, they have teachers identify children whose families they would like to visit in order to learn more about the family. Moll and González work with the teachers to arrange nonintrusive home visits. While in the home, teachers learn about household "funds of knowledge"—areas of expertise that family members have as a part of everyday life, such as carpentry, cooking, or mechanical repair. Teachers also try to find out about family social networks to become acquainted with various people in the community who interact with children in the family. After the home visits, Moll and González help teachers to build curriculum to connect academic knowledge with the knowledge family members can teach their children. For example, after discovering that a local Mexican mother was an excellent candy maker, a teacher had students compare ingredients in U.S. and Mexican candy to explore nutrition (connected with their health unit). Then she invited the mother to demonstrate candy making in the context of a discussion on food consumption, nutrition, and food production.

Before novice teachers enter someone else's community, I recommend teaching them some of the community's history, as well as ethnographic research skills to use as tools for learning, such as interviewing, active listening, and careful observation. Throughout the experience the instructor should help them make sense of what they are learning and link it to teaching. For example, for several years I had preservice teachers in my multicultural education course work thirty to fifty hours in predominantly African American or Latino community centers, where they tutored children, provided recreational support, or assisted in other ways. After teaching them how to engage in active listening during interviews, I assigned them to interview adults with whom they were working, assisting them in selecting interview topics and questions. An African American novice teacher explored bilingual education in the Latino community, and a White novice teacher explored reasons youths join gangs, for instance. I also taught observation skills, such as how to discern cultural differences in interpersonal interaction styles. In addition, some students explored the community, including services available, community history, and community events. A Mexican immigrant novice teacher who entered class with negative stereotypes about African Americans discovered that Mexicans and African Americans shared low-status jobs in the local community, which helped her to identify common concerns of both groups. Throughout the semester, as students brought data into the classroom, I helped them translate what they discovered into pedagogically relevant instruments, such as how to link curriculum concepts with what children do in the neighborhood or on weekends (see also L. Boyle-Baise & Sleeter, 2000; Narode, Rennie-Hill, & K. Peterson, 1994; Olmedo, 1997; Sleeter, 1996).

Community-based learning must include planned reflection, such as discussing the significance of what one experienced or learned, connecting what one learned with teaching strategies, or examining one's own earlier assumptions about a community in light of what one has learned. Armaline (1995) and Brookhart (1997) found that when extended reflection sessions were connected with urban field placements, students gained more than those in field placements without structured reflection.

Most research studies on community-based learning have found that it helps novice teachers to develop more positive attitudes toward diverse communities and improve their skill in teaching diverse students. I have found community-based learning to be helpful in challenging deficit perspectives and in teaching how to build on students' cultural strengths, because it involves teachers in becoming acquainted with people in the school's environment. For example, hearing low-income African American and Pacific Islander parents in a community center discuss their strong interest in their children's education is much more powerful than reading about it in a book. But community-based learning, by itself, is not a universal remedy for preparing teachers. Some researchers have noted White preservice teachers' reluctance to contextualize communities within broader relations of power, particularly racism (e.g., Murtadha-Watts, 1998). Sometimes the experience only confirms students' stereotypes (Haberman & Post, 1992; Ross & W. Smith, 1992), particularly if reflection is not planned well or if the placement site reveals little about the community. Cross-cultural community-based learning will not make students who are unreceptive to diversity into good teachers of all children. It is, however, a powerful learning process for those who want to learn to teach cross-culturally.

Coursework on Culture and Equity Pedagogy

Considerable development of multicultural and bilingual education coursework has occurred in the past twenty years, particularly at the preservice level. Coursework can provide conceptual and research background in areas such as the dynamics of privilege and oppression; patterns of institutionalized inequity in schools; second-language acquisition, bilingual education, and biliteracy (literacy in two languages); relationships between culture, identity, and learning; multicultural curriculum development; assessment procedures that are fair for students from different cultural and language backgrounds; and how to build positive relationships among students from diverse social groups (such as ethnic groups or between special education and general education students) in the school and classroom. As much as possible, such study should be integrated into teacher education coursework across the program as a whole, for example, by considering how to teach science in culturally relevant ways or considering human development from diverse cultural perspectives.

In coursework on culture, language, and equity, particularly useful teaching strategies engage novice teachers in reflecting on their beliefs and experiences in relationship to those of others. Shared journaling is one such process. The instructor pairs students and then assigns them to write reflections that connect reading assignments or class discussions with their own experience. Pairs exchange and read their partner's journals, writing reflections back to the partner. The instructor also may read and respond to journal entries. Those who have studied effects of shared journaling report that it prompts considerable constructive reflection on novice teachers' beliefs and assumptions (Milner, 2003; Garmon, 1998; Pewewardy, 2005). Other helpful active learning and reflection strategies connect conceptual frameworks with personal experience, examine diverse points of view, and apply pedagogical strategies.

Preservice teachers seem to learn most from courses that blend substantive learning about concepts—such as racism, multicultural teaching strategies, and second-language acquisition—with open discussions in which honest questions are taken seriously. For example, Torok and Aguilar (2000) examined what students learned from a multicultural education course they taught to preservice teachers, most of whom were White. The course focused on the following core concepts: culture, ethnicity, race and racism, social class and classism, gender and sexual orientation, religious diversity, language diversity, and disability. Students were expected to read, write daily reflective journals, complete an in-depth project about a self-selected issue, and engage in a short, self-selected cross-cultural experience. The researchers found considerable growth in students' attitudes. Students attributed most of their growth to the course's open environment, in which students could discuss controversial issues, and its encouragement of students to learn from each other. Not recommended are sustained, didactic presentations about different racial or ethnic groups, which are likely to teach stereotypes and generalizations (McDiarmid, 1992).

Similarly, for inservice teachers, multicultural and bilingual coursework is helpful when it prompts reflection on classroom practice. For three semesters I have taught a graduate-level multicultural curriculum design course for practicing teachers. In addition to engaging them in reading and discussing foundational issues like those mentioned above, we also work directly with curriculum and teaching strategies that the teachers can apply in their classrooms. For example, teachers perform mini investigations in which they interview their students to unearth what students know about topics they plan to teach, then revise lessons or units based on their findings. Teachers analyze their textbooks for representation of diverse sociocultural groups and then design a unit that uses resources they already have (such as the textbook and literature selections), supplemented with additional resources such as research material or books from the school library, to address textbook limitations. Researchers have found that teachers learn to improve their daily classroom practice when graduate coursework is linked with classroom practice and includes critical inquiry in which teachers gather data on their practice and reflect on what the data show (Exposito & Favela, 2003; Jennings & C. P. Smith, 2002).

The more diverse the novice teachers in a course or program, the more productively they can learn to work with diversity through their interactions with each other. When admitting teachers into the Master of Arts in Education program at California State University, Monterey Bay, my colleagues and I consider applicants' experiences and commitments (such as their previous work in low-income communities or with child advocacy groups) that would enable them to become advocates for culturally and linguistically diverse students. Our courses, as a result, are highly diverse, usually with no racial or ethnic majority. We work to build a sense of community, as well as supportive space where complex issues can be discussed. We find ourselves modeling teaching strategies and personal relationships that we believe should be part of K–12 education. The teachers of color tell us that our courses strengthen their ability to advocate for their students, and everyone, White teachers included, learns a good deal from peers with differing backgrounds (Sleeter et al., 2005).

Support in the Classroom

One learns to teach while working with students in the classroom, but extended classroom experience alone does not generally produce excellent teachers, particularly for students in historically underserved communities. In addition to classroom experience, teachers need the professional preparation that credential programs provide.

Probably the most well-known program currently preparing teachers largely through classroom-based "on-the-job" training is Teach for America (TFA), which is premised on the idea that individuals who bring strong subject-matter preparation from top universities need mainly classroom experience in order to learn to teach. TFA-certified teachers have as little as five weeks' formal training in education before being placed in classrooms as novice teachers. To examine this model's effectiveness, Laczko-Kerr and Berliner (2002) compared 109 matched teacher pairs of newly hired teachers in five low-income school districts in Arizona. Matched pairs were teaching in the same school or, if that was not possible, the same or a similar school district. One member of the pair had been certified in a regular teacher education program, and the other was undercertified (e.g., having an emergency certificate or having been prepared through TFA). Laczko-Kerr and Berliner compared the teachers on the basis of their students' scores on a standardized test of achievement in reading, language arts, and math. They found that students of fully certified teachers achieved about two months more (with scores about 20 percent higher) than those of the undercertified teachers, including TFA-trained teachers. The researchers concluded that on-the-job training lacks professional knowledge preparation and reflection about practice that helps novices link classroom practice to guiding theories and principles. In other words, experience in the classroom needs to be connected with professional knowledge about teaching and learning. Ongoing guided reflection helps novice teachers make connections.

Classroom experiences with guided reflection should begin early in the preservice level and extend into the first years of teaching. Preservice teachers benefit most from classrooms that model and support exemplary practice. One challenge is offering novice teachers access to classrooms of excellent teachers of multiracial or historically underserved students. It is imperative that novice teachers see excellent real teaching, so that they can believe it is possible as well as conceptualize what it looks like. Because excellent teachers are usually in short supply, they can be videotaped to serve as examples. I have videotaped several exemplary local teachers (Sleeter, 2001) and periodically use the tapes in courses and workshops. As students in a preservice course finished watching a tape featuring an early career teacher teach a wonderful interdisciplinary unit on immigration, one exclaimed, "Well, if she could do that, then so can I!"

When selecting placement sites, excellent cooperating teachers are preferable, but positive results can emerge from placing novices with average teachers who are receptive to learning and growing themselves. Goodman and Fish (1997) studied the impact of a teacher education program that was designed around a progressive teaching philosophy. Preservice teachers worked in classrooms of teachers who were open to and supportive of the child-centered approach taught in the teacher education program. The researchers found that even in classrooms of teachers who were only moderately skilled in using child-centered strategies, the preservice teachers learned not only how to apply child-centered and socially critical strategies but also how to negotiate the freedom to try these strategies within the constraints of the school.

Cochran-Smith (1991) studied school-based inquiry teams composed of teachers and preservice teachers who were involved in reforming culturally diverse urban schools. The experienced teachers had considerable teaching skills, but they were also interested in improving their practice. Teams pursued questions, using school or classroom data to help generate solutions, such as how to handle children who had been in kindergarten two years but were not yet ready for first grade or how to develop specific children's reading skills. The teachers and preservice students talked regularly about what it means to teach real students well. In addition, the preservice students observed good teaching modeled, and they engaged in rich conversations with practicing teachers about their methods, the reasons for their methods, and what questions or problems they were grappling with.

In both of these examples a core of teachers and university faculty (with some expertise in child-centered, cross-cultural teaching) created school-based environments where novice teachers could ask questions, try ideas, and be supported as they learned. Mutual respect between the classroom teacher and the preservice teacher is particularly important when they are of different cultural backgrounds or when the preservice teacher brings expertise the classroom teacher lacks. Paraprofessionals in teacher certification programs sometimes find cooperating teachers ignore their expertise and lock them into low-level classroom assistance tasks (Rueda & Monzó, 2002), a problem that teacher education programs should be prepared to notice and address.

To develop teachers' pedagogical skill with diverse students, I recommend extended (preferably yearlong) student teaching or an internship in a school that serves children who are different from the novice teacher by race, ethnicity, social class, or language, with ongoing support by good teaching coaches. A story of a recent experience with a novice teacher will illustrate why. I visited the classroom of a novice White teacher in a low-income school in which most of the children were African American or Latino. A student in one of my graduate courses, she had mentioned struggling to use active, hands-on pedagogical strategies. When she tried to use small-group work, she was not able to control the class, and teachers in her school told her that "this population" needs structure. As a result, she abandoned the small-group, hands-on learning in favor of a whole-group didactic approach. While in my course she developed a short unit that included a carefully planned role-play with discussion and problem solving. I visited her classroom twice to observe the unit. During the first visit she used mainly didactic whole-class teaching, and I saw considerable off-task student behavior; trying to keep students quiet and attentive then took up much of her attention. During the second visit, which included the role-play lesson, I saw students highly engaged, much less off-task, and participating in ways that showed they were thinking about the lesson's content. In a discussion afterward I helped her to recognize that she had carefully planned the second lesson for student engagement, and because it was interesting to the students and well thought-out, they got "into" the lesson rather than playing around. Their poor classroom behavior was not due to characteristics of "this population" but rather to the teaching they were offered.

With my encouragement as a classroom-based coach, she was able to rethink stereotypes that were affecting her teaching. Without good coaching many novice teachers develop understandings of their students or behavior patterns that obstruct good teaching, particularly if they absorb cultural deficiency beliefs about children that may permeate their schools.

Learning to teach in a different cultural context very often involves going through some degree of culture shock, a reality that is rarely discussed in teacher education literature. Consider the experiences of interns in a master's degree program that focused on urban and multicultural teaching and included a full-year internship in a low-income urban school. Through case studies of White interns, Rushton (2001) documented a growth process that began with culture shock and moved through various conflicts and difficulties and finally toward a sense of teaching efficacy by the end of the internship. Rushton noted that the full year allowed for support through a difficult period of culture shock and painful feelings of dissonance, so that by year's end the interns were able to collaborate with other teachers and focus on students' needs more than their own personal struggles.

Too often veteran teachers socialize novice teachers into deficiency views of the students and their communities to help these teachers through culture shock, as was the case with the novice teacher whose classroom I had visited. Periodically, novice teachers tell me that experienced colleagues inform them what "this population" needs or cannot do. Including a cultural broker (a community-based teacher or counselor) as part of teacher education would help novice teachers learn to interpret students more accurately. A cultural broker is a member of one sociocultural community (such as an adult who works with young people, a religious leader, a community center director, or a recreation director) who acts as a liaison with other sociocultural communities. A broker helps to induct outsiders into the new community and interprets the community from an "insider" point of view. When teachers learn to teach in communities that are culturally different from their own, they may receive pedagogical help from other teachers but not help interpreting teaching through the cultural frame of reference of the community. Persistent misinterpretations of students and communities result in poor teaching in historically underserved schools. Classroom-based coaching is crucial for developing novices' teaching skills, particularly when combined with cultural brokering that directly confronts misinterpretations of children.

Beginning teachers are much more likely to learn to teach well if they have sustained support over the first two or three years of teaching. Support during the first two or three years of teaching is most effective when it combines sustained workshops about pedagogy with classroom coaching. There is evidence that this model not only helps teachers develop practice but also improves student learning. J. Johnson and Kean (1992) developed and evaluated an intensive summer workshop on teaching science in multicultural settings, followed with classroom-based coaching and group meetings to provide teachers with support. The workshops focused on cultural awareness (e.g., classroom-based processes for identifying strengths of one's students), problem solving in science, and cooperative learning. Project staff then visited each teacher's classroom twice per month during the academic year, and general meetings of participants were held quarterly for discussion and problem solving. The researchers documented positive changes in teacher-student interactions, increased student-centered pedagogy and use of cooperative learning, more communication between some of the teachers and community members, and increased attempts to make science relevant to students (see also Lindley & Keithley, 1991, for research on a similar model).

Induction programs that include these components are becoming common. California has a Beginning Teacher Support and Assessment (BTSA) program, in which new teachers are assigned mentors who coach them on classroom practice. However, new-teacher mentors are not always good culturally responsive teachers who themselves know what good teaching looks like and have high expectations for students. Reis (2001) investigated California's BTSA program as a vehicle for helping new teachers use culturally relevant strategies for teaching literacy. She found that while BTSA is built on classroom support in the context of the novice teacher's daily work of teaching, most of the support providers lacked the background to effectively coach beginning teachers on culturally relevant pedagogy. Thus it is imperative that new-teacher support programs locate and work with teachers and teacher educators who understand, model, and give feedback on excellent teaching in diverse classrooms.

Conclusion

We can, and should, recruit and prepare a more diverse teaching force. What has become institutionalized as "teacher education" tends to benefit schools that are largely White and middle class because the products of traditional teacher education are mainly young White women. Programs designed to recruit and certify teachers of color or older urban adults offer models for redesigning teacher education. It may be that the greatest redesign barrier is not a lack of potential teachers of color but rather the institutionalized ways of higher education, as well as faculty who do not see compelling reasons for change.

At the same time, we can take stronger action to prepare teachers for racially diverse classrooms. The most promising approaches discussed here immerse prospective teachers in communities that are culturally different from their own. This immersion teaches them to learn from adults in those communities and then to shape curriculum, pedagogy, and interactions in ways that build on cultural assets. How much immersion is feasible varies widely (most people cannot move to another part of the country for a semester), but well-designed, shorter, or localized experiences matter. The most promising programs engage novice teachers with observation and coaching by exemplary teachers, to the greatest extent possible, rather than by whoever signs up. Ideally classroom support is longer than one semester of student teaching because, when learning to teach cross-culturally, teachers require support while moving through culture shock and disorientation. It appears that without support many lose their optimism and give up, or they revert to teaching based on control and stereotypical interpretations of students and their homes. With preparation and support, novice teachers can become the excellent teachers children need and develop a sense of teaching efficacy that keeps them from leaving the teaching profession.

Addressing Race and Racism in the Classroom

Julie Milligan Hughes and Rebecca S. Bigler

The treatment of race has been debated within all major societal institutions (e.g., business, government, and military organizations). Such debates have occurred regularly within the field of education. The *Brown v. Board of Education of Topeka* case in 1954 is one well-known example. A more recent illustration of the debate about race and its treatment within educational systems is California residents' vote on a proposition that would have prohibited the state from classifying "any individual by race, ethnicity, color, or national origin in the operation of public education" (*Proposition 54*, 2003). In this essay we focus on two current controversies related to the way in which race is addressed in elementary school classrooms. The first issue concerns whether race should be labeled; the second concerns whether racism should be discussed. Our goal is to provide educators (and others) with information that will help them to promote positive racial attitudes and intergroup relations among students within both segregated and integrated classrooms.

We begin the essay by introducing the controversial issues and describing what is known about elementary school-age children's racial attitudes and intergroup relations. Next we summarize research within developmental psychology that bears on the controversies, highlighting reasons to expect that racial labeling and discussions of racism might be associated with both positive and negative outcomes for children. To preview our conclusion, we argue that racial labeling—in the absence of clear and explicit rationale for doing so—is likely to facilitate the development of racial stereotyping and prejudice, especially among young children. In addition, we argue that discussions of racism are likely to foster improved racial attitudes, although such discussions may also produce negative emotions (e.g., guilt, anger). Next we present findings of two of our own studies specifically aimed at elucidating the debate surrounding these two issues, and, finally, we make recommendations for social and educational policies.

Racial Labeling and Racism Discussion

The debate about whether and when it is appropriate to label individuals by race is illustrated by two conflicting public messages that appeared in Austin, Texas, in the spring of 2004. The National Underground Railroad Freedom Center sponsored citywide billboards that stated simply, "He's a very articulate ~~black~~ man." Billboards with similar messages about the inappropriateness of labeling race were placed in other cities throughout the United States. At the same time that these billboards appeared, downtown Austin was festooned with flags celebrating African American writers. Each flag contained an author's portrait and bore a "Great Black Writers" caption. The decision about whether to label race affects educational institutions in significant ways (see Pollock, 2004). Educators must decide, for example, whether curricular programs (e.g., Black History Month) and materials should include racial and ethnic labels.

In addition to deciding whether to label the race of individuals and groups, educators must decide whether, and if so when and how, to address issues related to racism. Racism (that is, the belief that people of some races are by nature superior to people of other races) characterizes most of the history of human interaction. Should elementary school-age children be taught about the history of racial and ethnic prejudice and discrimination in the United States and abroad? In the Executive Summary of the 2001 World Conference against Racism, Racial Discrimination, Xenophobia and Related Intolerance, United Nations members were called upon to "introduce anti-racism education in early childhood" and to "rewrite educational texts to include histories of the oppressed" (United Nations, 2001, p. 2). The conference report did not, however, outline when or how to teach children the complex history of racial discrimination. Many educators remain uncertain of the developmental appropriateness of teaching the concept of racism to young children (see Kohl, 1995).

Racial Attitudes among Children

Although some individuals have viewed racism as a problem only among adults, racial stereotyping (that is, attributing characteristics to individuals on the basis of their racial group membership) and racial prejudice (that is, negatively evaluating others on the basis of their racial group membership) are common among children and adolescents (Aboud, 1988; Aboud & Levy, 2000; Bigler & Liben, 1993; Katz, 1988). Research indicates that children, even as early as age five, negatively evaluate unfamiliar others on the basis of race and ethnicity (Aboud, 1988; Ben-Ari & Amir, 1986; Bernstein, Schindler-Zimmerman, Werner-Wilson, & Vosburg, 2000; Bigler & Liben, 1993; Black-Gutman & Hickson, 1996; Doyle, Beaudet, & Aboud, 1988; Katz, 1973; Ritchey & Fishbein, 2001). Psychological studies indicate that the formation of racial prejudice involves a complex set of mechanisms, but these mechanisms are not well understood. Given young children's propensity to develop racial and ethnic biases (that is, stereotypes and prejudices) and the lack of knowledge about specific mechanisms of attitude formation, some individuals have argued that explicit talk about race and racism should be avoided when addressing children.

Additional complexity arises from the presence of age-related changes in children's thinking about race and racial discrimination. Children show increasing levels of racial stereotyping and racial prejudice across the early elementary school years. However, beginning at about age seven or eight, racial stereotyping and prejudice typically decrease due to age-related increases in cognitive abilities, such as the ability to classify people and objects along multiple dimensions simultaneously and to consider the perspective of other individuals (Aboud, 1988; Bernstein, Schindler-Zimmerman, Werner-Wilson, & Vosburg, 2000; Bigler & Liben, 1992; Inhelder & Piaget, 1964; Katz, 1973). Additionally, recent work from Killen, Crystal, and Ruck (this volume) suggests that children's understanding of racial discrimination also undergoes developmental change. This line of research suggests that the way in which children respond to racial labels and teaching about racism may vary across age.

Although stereotyping and prejudice typically decline across childhood, these racial biases remain high among some individuals throughout childhood and adolescence (Black-Gutman & Hickson, 1996; Ritchey & Fishbein, 2001). Because racial stereotyping and prejudice are associated with negative outcomes, including impaired academic performance (Steele & J. Aronson, 1995), limited social networks (Aboud & Mendelson, 1998; Killen, Lee-Kim, McGlothlin, & Stangor, 2002), and intergroup apathy and violence, it is important that effective intervention strategies aimed at reducing racial stereotyping and prejudice are implemented within schools and communities. Myriad intervention programs are used across the country, and they vary considerably in their treatment of race and racism. Some intervention programs aim to reduce racial prejudice without ever explicitly mentioning race or racism (E. Aronson & Osherow, 1980; Bruer, 1993; see also D. W. Johnson & R. T. Johnson, 2000; Slavin & Cooper, 1999), whereas other interventions explicitly label race or discuss racism with children. (We review these programs in greater detail later in this essay.) Understanding the consequences of labeling race and teaching about racism will help us identify the key components of effective intervention programs.

Consequences of Racial Labeling

Psychological research on children's racial attitudes suggests that the explicit use of racial labels to refer to individuals may promote increased racial bias. Simultaneously, there are reasons to expect the opposite (that is, labeling may promote decreased racial bias).

Negative Effects of Racial Labeling

Several areas of research directly or indirectly support the notion that racial labeling leads to increased racial prejudice. One area of relevant work concerns the role of labeling on children's category learning. Infants and toddlers use object and property labels to categorize unfamiliar objects (Waxman & Booth, 2003; Waxman & R. Gelman, 1986; Waxman & Markow, 1998). Among preschool-age children, classification of stimuli into hierarchical groups is aided when labels are given to novel objects (Waxman & R. Gelman, 1986). Applied to race, this suggests that very young children will form race-based categories more readily when individuals are presented with accompanying labels than when presented without labels.

Children also appear to use labels to infer shared properties of category members. In a study by S. A. Gelman and Heyman (1999), five- and seven-year-old children learned about characters who were described either with noun labels ("She is a carrot eater") or with verbal-predicate labels ("She eats carrots whenever she can"). Children who learned noun labels inferred that the given trait (e.g., carrot eating) was more stable over time and context (that is, permanent) than children who learned verbal-predicate labels. The results suggest that children treat noun labels about people as indicative of stable, nonobvious characteristics. Such thinking is likely to facilitate racial stereotyping.

Studies by Bigler and colleagues concerning children's intergroup attitude formation directly support the notion that labeling affects children's thinking about people (Bigler, 1995; Bigler, C. S. Brown, & Markell, 2001; Bigler, L. S. Jones, & Lobliner, 1997). In these studies, elementary school-age children attending summer school programs were assigned to novel social groups (e.g., "yellow" and "blue" groups, denoted by colored T-shirts). Various classroom conditions (such as whether teachers explicitly labeled the groups) were then manipulated. In one study, teachers in some classrooms used the novel groups to label children (e.g., "Good morning, blue and yellow groups" and "The yellow group can line up") and organize their classrooms (e.g., grouped desks into "yellow" and "blue" sections). In other classrooms, teachers ignored the novel groups or took a "color-blind" approach. Results indicated that children in "labeled" classrooms—but not in "color-blind" classrooms—developed biased attitudes (e.g., they believed their group to be superior to the other group). The findings suggest that teachers who frequently use racial labels may facilitate the development of racial biases among their students.

Positive Effects of Racial Labeling

Racial labeling may promote increased tolerance and understanding about ethnic and cultural differences in the increasingly diverse United States. Racial labeling is most likely to be associated with positive outcomes among older children, in part because they are capable of thinking about race with greater cognitive sophistication and in part because racial labeling may faciliate racial identity formation.

According to the work of Phinney and colleagues, ethnic identity among adolescents is associated with an understanding of and appreciation for ethnic diversity, positive racial attitudes, and positive self-esteem, although these components of ethnic identity are conceptually distinct (Phinney, 1990, 1996; Phinney, Cantu, & Kurtz, 1997; Phinney, D. Ferguson, & J. D. Tate, 1997). Because the first step in developing ethnic identity is the ability to label one's own ethnic group (Aboud, 1988), racial labeling may lay the groundwork for tolerant interethnic attitudes.

Work on memory also supports the notion that racial labels may promote positive racial attitudes. It has been well established that individuals' memories for events are affected by their preexisting attitudes (Alba & Hasher, 1983; Bartlett, 1932; Fiske & S. E. Taylor, 1984; S. E. Taylor & Crocker, 1981). Information that is consistent with individuals' stereotypical beliefs is remembered more accurately than information that contradicts such beliefs. Children show especially high rates of forgetting and/or distorting counterstereotypical information (Bigler & Liben, 1993). Labeling of group membership may, however, promote recall of counterstereotypical information (see Liben & Signorella, 1993). For example, Hirschfeld (1993) read children vignettes that contained either racial labels for story characters or illustrations that indicated the characters' racial backgrounds. Children were better able to recall characters' racial group memberships when they had been given verbal rather than visual information. This finding suggests that children will better recall counterstereotypical information about race when the individuals' racial or ethnic backgrounds are explicitly labeled.

There is, however, an important caveat to the work on race and memory. Some work suggests that exposure to counterstereotypical evidence about race and ethnicity is insufficient to reduce prejudice, even when it is remembered accurately (see Bigler, 1999; Hewstone, Macrae, Griffiths, & Milne, 1994). That is, exposure to a limited set of counterstereotypical models within the classroom is unlikely to offset the impact of the far greater number of stereotypical models found within children's typical environments (e.g., within television shows, books, and magazines). Thus relying on depictions of racially and ethnically diverse individuals, without addressing race and its social meaning, is unlikely to reduce bias.

Conclusions about Racial Labeling

We believe that the routine use of race to label individuals within educational environments, without an accompanying explanation of the practice, is likely to facilitate racial stereotyping and prejudice among elementary school-age children. That is, racial labeling is likely to lead children to infer that members of a racial group are innately different in deep and meaningful ways from members of other racial groups (see S. A. Gelman, 2003; Hirschfeld, 1993, 1995). At the same time, it is true that all children recognize racial categories, and most children show evidence of racial bias by the time they start school. In order to reduce children's racial stereotyping and prejudice, and to encourage the formation of positive racial and ethnic identities, it appears necessary to engage in racial and ethnic labeling. As Pollock's (2004) analysis of the treatment of race within an American high school elegantly shows, adults' refusal to label race (being "color-mute") does little to solve—and sometimes worsens—problems of racial bias and inequality.

Consequences of Discussing Racism

There is relatively little research on the consequences of discussing racism with children. Existing studies primarily address parents' (rather than teachers') talk about racial prejudice and discrimination. This literature indicates that European American (White) parents rarely discuss racism with their children (Katz, 2003) and that there is considerable variation in the frequency with which African American (Black) parents talk to their children about racism (Bowman & Howard, 1985; D. Hughes, 2003; Marshall, 1995; M. B. Spencer, 1985). Researchers tend to agree, however, that

African American parents are more apt to talk to their children about racial pride than discrimination (Boykin & Toms, 1985; D. Hughes, 2003), perhaps because many parents expect discrimination discussions to be associated with negative outcomes (e.g., fear or anxiety as a result of the belief that they, too, may become victims of discrimination).

Negative Effects of Discussing Racism

Some educators consider detailed information about racism to be irrelevant, possibly even harmful, to young children (see Peters, 1985; D. Williams, 2004a, 2004b). There are several possible reasons for the concern, including the timing of such discussions. Educators may base their decisions about whether to discuss racial discrimination with children on the perceived developmental appropriateness of such discussions. Although there is little research on the subject, the preschool and elementary school years are characterized by a host of cognitive constraints (such as limited perspective-taking ability and social comparison skills) that are expected to limit children's ability to understand and perceive discrimination (see C. S. Brown & Bigler, 2005; Quintana & Vera, 1999).

Other researchers and educators have argued that antiracism education might produce unintended negative emotions (McGregor, 1993; Weiner & Wright, 1973). The specific negative emotions aroused are likely to differ, however, among racial and ethnic minority children and European American children. Among European American children, for example, learning that members of one's racial group have been responsible for racial discrimination may cause guilt (Monteith, 1993; W. G. Stephan & Finlay, 1999) or defensiveness (McGregor, 1993). The content of the lesson (e.g., occupational discrimination versus genocide) is likely to affect the intensity of such reactions. Furthermore, some negative emotional reactions (e.g., guilt) may facilitate attitude change (Monteith & Walters, 1998), whereas others (e.g., defensiveness) are unlikely to support attitude improvement.

Among children from racial and ethnic minority groups, learning about racism is also likely to be troubling. Learning about racism has the potential to stigmatize racial and ethnic groups as powerless victims of European American oppression. Racial and ethnic minority children may, as a consequence of such lessons, fear future victimization (Mansfield & Kehoe, 1993). In addition, learning about racism may affect ethnic pride. Young children often endorse the view that individuals receive treatment that is deserved or fair (referred to as the "just world hypothesis," Lerner & Simmons, 1966; Stein, 1973). Racial and ethnic minority children who endorse the just world hypothesis may believe that their racial group was deserving of oppression by European Americans. This belief, in turn, may reduce children's ethnic pride.

Positive Effects of Discussing Racism

There are many educators and researchers who believe it is important to discuss racism and its pernicious effects with young children from all racial backgrounds (Derman-Sparks, 1989; Sefa Dei, 1996; Tatum, 1997).

According to some educators and researchers, discussions of racism may increase children's ability to cope with racial bias. Many African American parents provide information about racial prejudice to their children in an effort to prepare them for future experiences with prejudice (D. Hughes, 2003). Research suggests that—despite parental concern— racial and ethnic minority children often respond positively to information about racism, especially when it is embedded in other positive messages about race. Racial socialization (that is, messages about cultural knowledge and pride) has been linked to the formation of positive ethnic identity development among minority children and adolescents (Stevenson, 1995; A. J. Thomas & Speight, 1999) and with the development of positive interethnic attitudes (Romero & Roberts, 1998). According to the principle of self-congruity, positive attitudes about one's social ingroup "provide the base for the acceptance of others" (Ehrlich, 1973, p. 130), and thus accepting one's ethnic group may cause an individual to accept ethnic outgroups as well (Quintana, 1994).

European American children may also benefit from talk of racism. According to Helms (1990), those European Americans who have developed a positive White racial identity are more likely to have positive attitudes toward other racial groups than those European Americans who have not developed such an identity. Importantly, the achievement of such an identity requires that European Americans acknowledge the existence of racism and their racial group's role in its existence. It is not clear, however, how an understanding of racism leads to reductions in racial stereotyping and prejudice. Learning about racism may produce racial guilt, which in turn motivates individuals to hold nonprejudiced racial attitudes (Monteith & Walters, 1998). Research supports such a process among European American adults (Devine, Monteith, & Zuwerink, 1991), but little work has investigated the relation between racial guilt and racial attitude change among European American children.

Conclusions about Discussing Racism

We believe that discussing racism with children is likely to reduce children's racial stereotyping and prejudice for several reasons. Discussions of racism are likely to provide children with an explanation for racial and ethnic groups differences within American society. Specifically, lessons about racism teach children that environmental conditions, rather than innate differences, produce racial and ethnic group differences. Lessons about racism are likely to produce increases in the desire for racial fairness and racial empathy. Nonetheless, we believe that lessons about racism have the potential to trigger negative emotional reactions that may block attitudinal change, and thus they should be carefully studied before being adopted.

Addressing Race and Racism in Intervention Programs

The most commonly used interventions aimed at reducing racial prejudice among children refrain from explicitly using race to label individuals and organize information. They are often referred to as "color-blind." Such programs follow the philosophy that race differences are superficial, irrelevant, and uninformative bases to make judgments of people; thus discussions of race should be avoided in the classroom (see Schofield, 1986, 1997; Frankenberg, this volume, for a review of such approaches).

One example of a color-blind approach is cooperative learning, in which small, racially diverse groups of children work together to learn class material (E. Aronson & Osherow, 1980; Bruer, 1993; D. W. Johnson & R. T. Johnson, 2000; Slavin & Cooper, 1999). Ironically, cooperative learning programs are implemented by teachers who use race to group students (that is, who are not acting in a color-blind manner) but who do not discuss with students the basis for grouping. In other words, the program is aimed at addressing a problem (that is, racial prejudice) of which the students are not explicitly made aware via the use of a strategy that is covertly "race sensitive."

In contrast to the color-blind approach, a number of racial attitude interventions explicitly label race in an effort to encourage children to appreciate cultural and ethnic diversity. Such approaches often include "multicultural curricula" and are founded on the belief that race and culture should be discussed and celebrated (see Sardo-Brown & Hershey, 1995). Although multicultural interventions vary widely in their methods of application, the vast majority include information that labels race and/ or ethnicity.

Studies have found that both color-blind and multicultural interventions sometimes reduce racial bias among children and sometimes do not (see Aboud & Levy, 2000; J. A. Banks, 1995). Thus the literature does not conclusively indicate whether racial labeling in the context of racial attitude interventions is beneficial or harmful to children's racial attitudes.

In contrast to the color-blind and multicultural approaches, some researchers and educators believe that exposing children to curricula that highlight the negative effects of racism is an effective method of racial attitude improvement (Derman-Sparks & C. B. Phillips, 1997; Sefa Dei, 1996). Some interventions teach about racism through literature and dramatic films, while other programs employ more explicit discussions about children's own prejudice experiences (Derman-Sparks, 1989; Reeder, Douzenis, & Bergin, 1997; Tatum, 1997).

Studies of the effects of antiracism lessons on children's racial attitudes have also yielded mixed results, with some indicating positive changes (McGregor, 1993) and some showing a lack of change, or negative changes, in children's attitudes (see Schofield, 1986). Conclusions about the consequences of discussing racism are, therefore, difficult to draw.

New Empirical Data on Racial Labeling and Discussions of Racism

To study the effects of racial labeling and discussions of racism on children's racial attitudes, we conducted two studies in which children received lessons about the lives of several African American and European American historical figures, such as Jackie Robinson, Babe Ruth, Barbara Jordan, and Jeanette Rankin (see J. M. Hughes, Bigler, & Levy, in press, for a description of some of these data). The first study examined the effects of such lessons on European American children, whereas the second study examined the effects of such lessons on African American children.

Intervention among European American Children

Seventy children attending a summer school program in the Midwest were assigned to one of three conditions in which the biographies of several famous African Americans and European Americans were presented, with (a) no explicit labeling of race (race-blind lessons), (b) explicit labeling of race (race-based lessons), or (c) information about the racial discrimination the African American historical figures had experienced at the hands of European Americans (antiracism lessons). Educational and logistical constraints required that children be assigned to classrooms of similarly aged peers prior to the start of the study. We matched classrooms by age and randomly assigned each classroom to one of the three conditions. Lessons occurred every day for six consecutive school days, lasting approximately twenty minutes each day. Abbreviated sample lessons appear in appendix A. At each daily lesson's conclusion, a brief questionnaire assessed children's (a) perceptions of within racial- and between racial-group variability, (b) counterstereotypical beliefs about race, (c) desire for racial fairness, (d) racial defensiveness, and (e) racial guilt. The specific questions are presented in appendix B.

When the lessons were completed, we examined children's attitudes toward African Americans and European Americans. Specifically, participants rated the proportion (that is, "all," "a lot," "some," "not very many," or "none") of African Americans and European Americans characterized by five positive and five negative traits. Recent research suggests that children's attitudes about their own racial groups are independent from their attitudes about other racial groups (Aboud, 2003; Cameron, Alvarez, & Ruble, 2001). Thus presenting European American children with counterstereotypical information about a racial outgroup (e.g., successful African Americans) may reduce outgroup biases while leaving ingroup favoritism unchanged. Because antiracism education provides children with positive information about African Americans and negative information about European Americans (that is, European Americans' history of anti–African American discrimination), we expected such interventions to have a greater effect on children's racial attitudes than interventions that presented only positive information about African Americans.

Daily testing revealed that the three lesson forms had different cognitive and affective consequences for children. Those who received antiracism lessons expressed desire for racial fairness more frequently than did children who received race-blind or race-based lessons. Children who received antiracism lessons also expressed racial defensiveness more frequently than did children who received race-based lessons. Finally, older children (nine- to eleven-year-olds) but not younger children (six- to eight-year-olds) who received antiracism lessons expressed racial guilt more frequently than did children who received race-blind or race-based lessons.

Results also indicated that children who received antiracism lessons had significantly more positive attitudes toward African Americans than did children who received nearly identical lessons that did not include explicit information about racism. The antiracism condition was, in fact, the only one in which children—at the group level—endorsed completely nonbiased views of African Americans and European Americans. This pattern of findings held for all ages in the sample, suggesting that providing information about racism may be effective for reducing bias among European American children across a broad range of ages.

Interestingly, lessons that explicitly labeled race but did not provide information about racism proved to be the least effective for reducing racial prejudice. Overall, children exposed to these lessons showed markedly biased views, attributing European Americans with more positive, and fewer negative, traits than African Americans. Although pursuing the laudable goal of educating children about the positive contributions of different groups, highlighting race may increase children's belief that race is an important dimension along which individuals differ. Children who receive messages that make explicit use of race—without an accompanying explanation of why race is being highlighted—might construct their own reasons for the authority figures' attention to race. Specifically, we hypothesize that children who are exposed to environmental messages that highlight race begin to categorize on the basis of race and believe that the people in these categories differ in deep, stable, and innate ways from one another (Hirschfeld & S. A. Gelman, 1997). Such views are likely to be associated with the endorsement of racial stereotypes (see S. A. Gelman, M. G. Taylor, & Nguyen, 2004, for a discussion of similar issues concerning gender).

Intervention among African American Children

Results from our initial study suggested that European American children benefit from learning about racism, despite its association with increased guilt and defensiveness. As members of a racial group that has been (and remains) the target of discrimination, African American children are likely to have a different set of cognitive and affective responses to learning about racism. We examined this possibility in a second study of children's responses to discussions of race and racism.

In this study sixty-nine African American children (thirty-four girls, thirty-five boys; ages six to eleven) attending either a summer camp program or an after school program completed measures of their (a) empathy skills, (b) endorsement of equitable treatment of underprivileged children, and (c) racial attitudes. Children were then assigned randomly to one of two conditions in which the biographies of several famous African Americans and European Americans were presented with either (a) explicit labeling of race (race-based lessons) or (b) information about the racial discrimination the African Americans had experienced at the hands of European Americans (antiracism lessons). The race-blind condition was omitted for logistical (that is, we lacked enough participants to include all three of the conditions used in the earlier study) as well as theoretical reasons (that is, race is salient among racial and ethnic minorities members irrespective of whether it is labeled).

One or two days after the lessons were completed, children's reactions to the lessons were assessed.

To gauge children's emotional responses, participants answered questions designed to tap (a) overall lesson satisfaction, (b) civil rights activism, (c) desire for racial fairness, (d) anger toward European Americans, and (e) desire for amends for prior discrimination. To assess children's racial attitudes, participants rated the proportion of African Americans and European Americans characterized by positive and negative traits (as in the previous study).

Results from the emotional responses questionnaire indicated that children in the antiracism condition were more satisfied with the lesson series and expressed a greater desire for racial fairness than children in the race-based condition. Younger children in both conditions expressed a greater desire for amends for prior discrimination than did older children. Additionally, older children expressed higher levels of anger toward European Americans and higher levels of civil rights activism than younger children, regardless of lesson condition.

The attitudinal data showed a complex pattern of findings. Patterns of attitude change from pretest to posttest differed by the target racial group (that is, African Americans or European Americans). Children's trait ratings of African Americans did not differ between lesson conditions but did differ between age groups. The youngest children (six to seven years old) in our study rated African Americans both more positively and less negatively from pretest to posttest. Children aged eight to nine years old also rated African Americans less negatively from pretest to posttest. The trait ratings of African Americans by the oldest children (ten to eleven years old) did not change from pretest to posttest. Children's ratings of European Americans also did not differ across conditions. Children's rating became both more positive and more negative from pretest to posttest.

In summary, despite concerns about the possible negative effects of learning about racism, the results indicated that both types of experimental lessons (race-based and antiracism) improved African American children's attitudes toward their racial ingroup and produced more differentiated (that is, more positive and more negative) views of European Americans.

Summary and Conclusion

In this essay we investigated whether European American and African American children are positively or negatively affected by adults' use of racial labels and discussion of racism. Previous work within the field of psychology led to conflicting expectations. That is, there are reasons to expect that racial labeling and racism discussions produce both positive and negative outcomes among children. We expected, however, that discussions of racism with children were especially likely to produce reductions in racial stereotyping and prejudice, primarily because such lessons induce empathy and a desire for racial fairness among European Americans.

To investigate the matter further, we conducted two studies that tested whether lessons that incorporated either racial labeling or information about racism reduce children's racial prejudice. We also examined children's emotional and cognitive responses to the content of the lessons. Among European American children, results indicated that discussing racism leads to reductions of racial prejudice against African Americans, whereas racial labeling has no positive effects on racial attitudes. Among African American children, results indicated no differences in racial attitudes among children in the two lesson conditions. Lessons that incorporated information about racism, as well as lessons that made use of racial labels, were found to produce more (a) positive views of children's own racial group (that is, African Americans), especially among younger children; and (b) differentiated (that is, more positive and more negative) views of European Americans.

Our primary conclusion, therefore, is that children benefit from learning about racism in the context of lessons that discuss the positive achievements of European American and African American individuals.

Children's emotional reactions to the antiracism lessons revealed both positive and negative outcomes. The primary positive effect of learning about racism was an increased desire for racial fairness, which was exhibited by both African American and European American children. Negative emotional consequences among European American children included elevated feelings of racial defensiveness and, among older European American children, elevated levels of racial guilt. In addition, the oldest African American children in our sample (ten- and eleven-year-olds) expressed slightly more anger toward European Americans than did younger children, regardless of condition.

Although some readers might believe that the existence of negative emotional reactions among the children in our studies argues against discussing racism with children, we disagree. Despite increased levels of anger among the older African American children, this group showed racial attitudes that were no more negative toward European American than younger children. Indeed, it is possible that negative emotional reactions are sometimes a necessary component of the process of racial attitude improvement. European American children who experience racial guilt in response to learning about racism may, for example, be motivated to become less prejudiced (see Tatum, 1992, 1997). Clearly, additional research on this issue is needed.

Teaching children about racism is important for many reasons, regardless of its effect on racial stereotyping and prejudice. Knowledge about racism is crucial for understanding world history and the history of the United States. A basic understanding of racism is, for example, a necessary component in lessons on the Civil War, World War II, and the civil rights movement. Additionally, addressing racism is an inextricable component of teaching children the histories of non–European Americans in the United States and for understanding contemporary race relations.

There is much left to learn about the effects of learning about racism on children. It is particularly important for future research to examine the links between children's emotional responses to learning about racism and subsequent attitudinal and behavioral change. Future research should also examine individual differences in children's responses to lessons about racism. Children's level of self-esteem, reasoning about justice, and peer relations (e.g., number of same- and other-race friends) may affect the likelihood that they experience positive versus negative emotional reactions in response to learning about racism. Future research should also focus on means of preventing negative emotional reactions (e.g., defensiveness) that might block positive racial attitude change.

Another important issue concerns the settings in which lessons about racism occur. Children's responses to antiracism lessons may vary as a function of the racial composition of the classroom and the characteristics (e.g., race) of the teachers involved. In our studies, intervention groups were racially homogeneous, and those who conducted lessons were trained individuals with a strong commitment to racial equality. As Sleeter (this volume) has highlighted, teachers' commitment to embracing racial diversity in their classrooms directly influences the success of classroom discussions of race and racism. An additional question for future research to answer is whether discussing racism in a multicultural context produces a similar pattern of emotional and attitudinal effects in children. It is feasible that introducing the topic of racial discrimination in a diverse context would intensify children's emotional reactions to the lessons. Alternatively, discussing racism in a setting that facilitates interracial discourse may improve children's attitudes more so than discussing racism in a racially homogeneous setting (see Killen, Crystal, & Ruck, this volume). Effects of a classroom's racial composition and teacher characteristics on the consequences of learning about racism need to be investigated before we can generalize the findings of this study across educational settings and other racial and ethnic groups.

Finally, we would like to highlight the finding that teaching children about racism was associated with elevated levels of desire for racial equity among African American and European American children. If this desire remains elevated over time, children's behaviors may mirror their desire to achieve racial fairness. For example, children who value racial fairness may be motivated to have interracial friendships, which are related to higher levels of self-esteem and social competence among elementary school-age children (Fletcher, Rollins, & Nickerson, 2004). They may also be motivated to address racial prejudice and discrimination within their schools and communities. Thus the potential benefits that might accrue from all children having a good understanding of racism are likely to be great.

Appendix A: Race-blind, Race-based, and Antiracism Sample Lessons

Race-blind Lesson

Today we're going to learn about Jackie Robinson, a famous baseball player. When he was a little boy he lived in Georgia, and he was good in many sports. He went to college, where he played baseball, football, basketball, and ran track. After college he served in the U.S. Army as a lieutenant. After he was in the Army, he played professional baseball for the Kansas City Monarchs and the Montreal Royals. Then in 1947 he joined the Major Leagues of baseball and played on a team called the Brooklyn Dodgers for ten seasons. He was inducted to the Baseball Hall of Fame because he played so well on the Dodgers. After he retired from professional baseball, he did a lot of work for the public good, like opening a bank, and he was also the vice president for the Chock Full O'Nuts Coffee Company, which still makes coffee today.

Race-based Lesson

Today we're going to learn about Jackie Robinson, a famous *African American* baseball player. When he was a little boy he *lived in a mostly White neighborhood* in Georgia, and he was good in many sports. He went to college, where he played baseball, football, basketball, and ran track. After college he served in the U.S. Army as a lieutenant. After he was in the Army, he played professional baseball for the Kansas City Monarchs, *which was a team in an all–African American baseball league,* and for the Montreal Royals. Then in 1947 he joined the Major Leagues of baseball and played on a team called the Brooklyn Dodgers for ten seasons. *He was the first African American Major League baseball player.* He was inducted to the Baseball Hall of Fame because he played so well on the Dodgers. After he retired from professional baseball, he did a lot of work for the public good, *like opening a bank for African Americans,* and he was also the vice president for the Chock Full O'Nuts Coffee Company, which still makes coffee today.

Antiracism Lesson

Today we're going to learn about Jackie Robinson, a famous African American baseball player. When he was a little boy he lived in a mostly White neighborhood in Georgia, *and his White neighbors teased him because he was African American.* Jackie Robinson was good in many sports. He went to college, where he played baseball, football, basketball, and ran track. After college he served in the U.S. Army as a lieutenant. After he was in the Army, he played professional baseball for the Kansas City Monarchs, which was a team in an all–African American baseball league, and the Montreal Royals. *The reason he played in an all–African American baseball league was that the White people in charge of the Major League back then were racist. They didn't let any African Americans play on a Major League team, no matter how good they were, just because they were Black.* In 1947 Jackie Robinson joined the Major Leagues of baseball and played on a team called the Brooklyn Dodgers for ten seasons. He was the first African American Major League baseball player, *and after that more African Americans were allowed to join.* Jackie Robinson was inducted to the Baseball Hall of Fame because he played so well on the Dodgers. After he retired from professional baseball, he did a lot of work for the public good, like opening a bank for African Americans *that didn't treat African Americans unfairly, like so many banks owned by Whites did back then, and working for equal rights for African Americans.* He was also the vice president for the Chock Full O'Nuts Coffee Company, which still makes coffee today.

Appendix B: Cognitive and Affective Reaction Questionnaire

1. Did today's lesson make you wish Black people were treated more fairly and given what they deserved (desire for fairness)?

2. Was today's lesson unfair because it made White people look meaner and more unfair than they really are (racial defensiveness)?

3. Did today's lesson make you feel bad about being White (racial guilt)?

4. Did today's lesson make you think that Black people are unique, special, and different from each other (perceptions of within-group variability)?

5. Did today's lesson make you think that Black people and White people have a lot in common and aren't very different at all (perceptions of between-group variability)?

6. Did today's lesson make you think that Black people are really smart and hardworking (receptiveness to counterstereotypical information)?

Classroom Integration and Accelerated Learning through Detracking

Carol Corbett Burris and Kevin G. Welner

Although more than fifty years have passed since the landmark desegregation decision, *Brown v. the Board of Education of Topeka* (1954), a sizeable achievement gap between the academic performance of African American and Latino students and White students persists (American Educational Research Association, 2004). In the 1970s and 1980s the gap narrowed as African American and Latino student achievement test scores in mathematics and reading improved at an even faster rate than their White counterparts (J. Lee, 2002). However, that improvement abruptly stopped in 1990, and after two decades of progress the gap is now widening (R. F. Ferguson & Mehta, 2004; J. Lee, 2002). Indeed, reducing the test score gap while improving the academic performance of all students is one of the major goals of the No Child Left Behind Act of 2001. Calls for equity of opportunity, initiated by the *Brown* decision, are now joined by calls for equity of outcome.

The root causes of the gap are continually discussed, studied, and debated by educators and policymakers alike. From the large and disproportionate number of uncertified and inexperienced teachers in inner-city schools to the sorry state of the facilities serving at-risk youths, a variety of factors that may influence the achievement gap has been identified and explored (National Commission on Teaching and America's Future, 2004). Singham (2003) speaks for many when he suggests that the gap is a symptom of broad educational problems and that those who are the furthest behind will gain the most from instructional improvements. Among other problems, Singham identifies lower teacher expectations and unchallenging curricula, especially in mathematics, as two important reasons for the achievement gap.

In fact, among policymakers and researchers there exists an overwhelming consensus that high student achievement is linked to a rigorous curriculum with high expectations for student learning (Adelman, 1999;

American Educational Research Association, 2004; Levin, 1997). Yet, despite this knowledge, the vast majority of American secondary schools engage in the practice of tracking, limiting access to rigorous curriculum (Oakes, Gamoran, & R. Page, 1992). Tracking is a system that provides stratified curriculum and instruction to groups of students by placing them in different classes, or tracks, based on perceived ability. In theory, instruction is tailored to students' needs. In practice, high-track classes are characterized by enriched or accelerated instruction while low-track classes follow a remedial curriculum (Oakes, 2005). The connection between tracking and the racial achievement gap includes the intentional use of tracking as a way to undermine desegregation orders (Welner, 2001). Schools, forced by courts to desegregate schools, used tracking to resegregate students within those schools—what some scholars have labeled "second-generation discrimination" (K. J. Meier, Stewart, & England, 1989). Research has repeatedly established that low-track classes result in lower student achievement (Heubert & Hauser, 1999). Because African American and Latino students are consistently overrepresented in low-track classes, the effects of tracking must concern educators interested in closing the achievement gap (Welner, 2001). This essay describes how Rockville Centre, a diverse suburban district on Long Island, New York, narrowed the gap by offering its high-track curriculum to all students through detracked classes.[1]

The Politics of Detracking

When minority and majority students have different educational experiences within the same school, due to the sorting of curriculum, practices, and expectations in tracked classes, within-school achievement gaps are a predictable result (Wenglinsky, 2004). Yet the popularity of an educational policy among policymakers and the public is only loosely tied to its empirical success. Tracking is but one example; grade retention is another (Heubert & Hauser, 1999; Shepard & M. L. Smith, 1989). That tracking remains widespread in the face of research and logic pointing to counterproductive outcomes may be because detracking is as much a normative and political reform as it is a technical one (Oakes, 1992; Welner, 2001). For example, Oakes and Wells (1996) describe how the detracking reforms in ten secondary schools they studied were scaled back and undermined when the reformers "ran headlong into deeply held beliefs and ideologies about intelligence, racial differences, social stratification, and privilege" (p. 40).

Oakes and Wells, in fact, describe reforms that share key features with the reform we describe in this essay. For instance, the detracking was initiated by school-level and district-level educators who recognized the harmful effects of their tracking systems—especially the academic, racial, and socioeconomic divisions tracking created. Although specifics differed in the various schools, Oakes and Wells (1996) found common-alities in their reforms, including the following: the elimination of the lowest-level classes, the addition of support classes for former low-track students, proactive enrollment of students of color in higher-level classes, and the development of teaching strategies appropriate for heterogeneous groups of students.

Oakes and Wells (1996) also noted that stiff resistance to detracking arose in each of the ten school districts in their study. Opposition to de-tracking is common—even likely—in districts where ability grouping "has served as a proxy for racial and social class segregation" (George, 1992, p. 26; see also Wells & Serna, 1996; Welner & Oakes, 2000). Resis-tance to detracking typically comes from the parents of high-achieving students, who believe that their children are advantaged by tracking, even when they are reassured by school leaders that all students will be chal-lenged in high-quality heterogeneous classes (Oakes, 2005; Oakes, Wells, M. Jones, & Datnow, 1997).

Part of why tracking is thought to benefit high achievers is that the lit-erature on tracking shows mixed results for high-achieving students when schools detrack. Some studies report that the learning of higher achiev-ers decreases in detracked, heterogeneous classes (D. J. Brewer, Rees & Argys, 1995; Epstein & MacIver, 1992; Kulik, 1992), while other studies report no significant differences (Burris, Heubert, & Levin, 2004; Figlio & M. E. Page, 2002; Mosteller, Light, & Sachs, 1996; Slavin, 1990; Wel-ner, 2001). Even in those studies that show a tracking benefit for high achievers, the researchers cannot disentangle the effects of tracking from curriculum and other factors associated with high-track classes, such as better instruction and more qualified teachers (Kerckhoff, 1986; S. Lucas, 1999; Oakes, 1982, 1986; Slavin & Braddock, 1993). This study and other studies (e.g., Burris, 2003; Boaler & Staples, 2005; Burris, Heubert, & Levin, 2004) show, however, that all students, including high achievers, benefit if the high-track curriculum is provided to all learners in hetero-geneously grouped classes.

Tracking and the Achievement Gap

Among those who suggest that the literature on tracking is inconclusive are scholars who argue that tracking should be reformed rather than abandoned and that there is no clear connection between tracking and the achievement gap (R. F. Ferguson, 1998; Hallinan, 1994). Indeed, some proponents of tracking assert that its resulting racial stratification is an artifact of achievement differences and that, when prior achievement is controlled for, African American students are statistically more likely to be placed in high-track classes. Loveless (1998, 1999), citing a 1989 study by Gamoran and Mare, contends that the abolition of tracking may, in fact, depress the achievement of high-track African American students, who, he reports, are more likely (by a factor of 10 percent) to be placed in high-track classes. The results of the Gamoran and Mare study that Loveless cites, however, were reevaluated in 1993 by Lucas and Gamoran, and this advantage was found not to exist when course-based indicators, rather than student self-reports, were used (S. R. Lucas & Gamoran, 1993).[2]

The strong connection between tracking and the achievement gap was recently confirmed by the National Research Council (Heubert & Hauser, 1999), the research division of the National Academy of Sciences. Heubert and Hauser concluded that the negative achievement effects of low-track classes were dramatic and have a disparate impact on minority students who are overrepresented in low-track classes and underrepresented in high-track classes, even after taking students' prior achievement into account (see also Burris, 2003; Mickelson, 2001; Slavin & Braddock, 1993; Welner, 2001). Based on the Third International Mathematics and Science Study's (TIMSS) comparison data, Cogan, Schmidt, and D. E. Wiley (2001) concluded that, for children of America's lower-income families, tracking limits students' access to rigorous curriculum, which directly damages our ability to compete internationally (see also Kifer, 1993; Schmidt, 1993; Schmidt, Houang, & Cogan, 2002; Schmidt et al., 1999).

A study by Yonezawa, Wells, and Serna (2002) concluded that even when students are allowed to choose their track, the same social stratification results (see also S. Lucas, 1999). In racially mixed schools, disproportionately few African American and Latino students from low- and middle-track classes opt to move into high-track classes, even after prerequisites have been removed. According to the authors the complex interactions between class, race, tracks, and aspirations persisted, even when the barriers for movement to higher tracks were dismantled (Yonezawa, Wells, & Serna, 2002). From placement by parental and student choice to placement by test scores, the same patterns resulted.

If lower-tracked classes are instructionally weaker, then students who are enrolled in those classes are disadvantaged. This remains true even if one accepts the assertions of Loveless (1999) and others that the pattern of disproportionate enrollment of students of color in lower-tracked classes is justified by, for example, prior measured achievement. Whatever the reason for placing students of color in lower-tracked classes, the result is that these children are offered diminished learning opportunities (Oakes, 2005). Accordingly, even if a district has nondiscriminatory rationales for the disproportionate placements of minority students in lower-tracked classes, such placements exacerbate the achievement gap (Welner, 2001).

If we acknowledge that there is a relationship among tracking, curriculum, race, and achievement, what changes are needed to close the achievement gap? Some believe that the solution is encouraging more minority students to take high-track classes (J. Ogbu, 2003). Others suggest that it is critical to provide all students with rigorous academic curricula (Singham, 2003; Barth & Haycock, 2004). Many who carefully study the relationship between curricular rigor and tracking argue that no students—whatever their race, wealth, or prior achievement—should be placed in classes that have the watered-down curriculum associated with low-track and remedial classes. These researchers believe that the solution is to replace the tracking system itself (Oakes & Wells, 1998; Yonezawa, Wells, & Serna, 2002). In this essay we provide evidence for the success of this latter approach. Dismantling tracking and providing the high-track curriculum to all students can close the achievement gap on important measures of learning.

Providing "High-Track Curriculum" to All Students

In 1993 Rockville Centre School District Superintendent William H. Johnson and the Rockville Centre Board of Education established an ambitious goal: by the year 2000, 75 percent of all graduates of South Side High School would earn a New York State Regents diploma. This goal reflected the superintendent's strong belief in the assessment of student learning by an objective, outside evaluation, and it also reflected the district's commitment to academic rigor. At that time the respective Regents diploma rates for the district and the state were 58 percent and 38 percent. To qualify for a New York State Regents diploma, students must pass, at a minimum, eight end-of-course Regents examinations including: two in mathematics, two in laboratory sciences, two in social studies, one in English language arts, and one in a foreign language.

Regents exams are linked with coursework; therefore, the district gradually eliminated low-track courses that did not follow Regents curriculum. South Side High School (the only high school in the district, serving students in the ninth through twelfth grades) eased the transition by offering struggling students instructional support classes while carefully monitoring these students' progress. The support classes were taken every other day and were not remedial in nature. Rather, teachers engaged in pre- and post-teaching of the Regents curriculum. At the same time the "gates" to study honors courses were opened, and any student who wanted to take a high-track class could do so. The high school replaced a three-track rigid tracking system with one that had two tracks with open enrollment.

South Side is a diverse suburban high school. Twenty percent of South Side High School's approximately twelve hundred students are African American or Latino, about 12 percent of all students receive free or reduced-price lunch, and approximately 10 percent are special-education students. Of those students who receive free or reduced-price lunch, virtually all are minority students (in a typical year, approximately 90 percent are African American or Latino). Furthermore, over half (56 percent) of all African American and Latino students participate in the subsidized lunch program. During the years of the study, 1995–2004, the district was remarkably stable with no shifts in the demographic composition of the district.

Although the overall number of Regents diplomas increased after the lowest tracks were eliminated during the early 1990s, a disturbing profile of students who were not earning the diploma emerged. These students were more likely to be African American or Latino, receive free or reduced-price lunch, or have a learning disability. In other words and as discussed in the following section, while majority, middle-class, regular-education students made great progress in earning the Regents diploma after the school eliminated the lower track, students of color and poverty, as well as students with learning disabilities, were left behind. If all graduates were to earn the Regents diploma, systemic change would need to occur to close the gaps and ensure that the needs of all students were met.

Accelerated Mathematics in Heterogeneous Classes

Upon closer inspection of the data, educators noticed that the second math Regents exam presented a challenge for African American and Latino students in earning a Regents diploma. Students earning this advanced diploma needed to take and pass at least two Regents math courses, one of which emphasizes algebra and a second of which emphasizes geometry. Further, they had to pass the external examinations corresponding with each course. While high-track students met the math requirement by the end of ninth grade and enrolled in the third Regents math course in the tenth grade, low-track students did not even begin the first Regents math course until grade ten.

In order to provide all students with ample opportunity to pass the needed courses, in 1995 Superintendent Johnson decided that all students would study the accelerated math curriculum formerly reserved for the district's highest achievers. Under the leadership of the assistant principal, Delia Garrity,[3] middle school math teachers revised and condensed the curriculum. The new curriculum was taught to all students, in heterogeneously grouped classes. To assist struggling learners, the school initiated support classes called math workshops and provided after-school help four afternoons a week.

The results were remarkable. More than 90 percent of incoming freshmen entered the high school having passed the first Regents math examination. The achievement gap dramatically narrowed. Between the years of 1995 and 1997 only 23 percent of regular-education African American and Latino students passed this algebra-based Regents exam before entering high school. After universally accelerating all students, in heterogeneously grouped classes, the percentage more than tripled—up to 75 percent. The percentage of White and Asian American regular-education students who passed also greatly increased—from 54 percent to 98 percent. This has remained the pattern throughout Rockville Centre's detracking reform: higher achievement for all plus a narrowing of the achievement gap.

Detracking South Side High School

When universal math acceleration began, the district was cautious. Some special-education students, while included in the class, were graded using an alternative assessment. This 1998 cohort of special-education students would not take the first ("Sequential I") Regents math exam until they completed ninth grade. Upon entering high school these students with learning disabilities were placed in a double-period, low-track Sequential I ninth-grade math class, along with low-achieving new entrants. Consistent with the recommendations of researchers who have defended tracking (e.g., Hallinan, 1994; Loveless, 1999), this class was rich in resources—a mathematics teacher, a special-education inclusion teacher, and a teaching assistant provided instruction and assisted students. Yet the low-track culture of the class remained not conducive to learning. Students were disruptive, and teachers spent considerable class time addressing behavior management issues. Students were acutely aware that the class carried the "low-track" label.

Table 1. Detracking courses by grade level and year, South Side High School

Detracked cohort	Detracked course(s) in grades 6–8	Year of entry into grade 9	Detracked course(s) in grade 9	Detracked course(s) in grade 10
	English, social studies, foreign language	1995–97	foreign language	foreign language
Year One	English, social studies, foreign language, math	1998	foreign language	foreign language
Year Two	all subjects	1999	English, social studies, foreign language	foreign language
Year Three	all subjects	2000	English, social studies, foreign language, science	foreign language
Year Four	all subjects	2001	all subjects	foreign language
Year Five	all subjects	2002	all subjects	foreign language, English, social studies
Year Six	all subjects	2003	all subjects	foreign language, English, social studies
Year Seven	all subjects	2004	all subjects	foreign language, English, social studies, math

District and school leaders decided that this low-track class failed its purpose. The class was eliminated, and the district boldly moved forward with several new reforms the following year. All special-education students in the ninth-grade year of entry (YOE) cohort of 1999 took the math Regents exam in the eighth grade. (This is the cohort of students who would normally graduate in June 2003.[4]) The YOE cohort of 1999 also studied science in heterogeneous classes throughout middle school, and it became the first cohort to be heterogeneously grouped in ninth-grade English and social studies classes (see table 1).

Ninth-grade teachers were pleased with the results. The feeling tone, activities, and discussions in the heterogeneously grouped classes were academic, focused, and enriched.[5] Science teachers reported that the heterogeneously grouped middle school science program prepared students well for ninth-grade biology.

Detracking at the high school level continued, paralleling the introduction of revised New York State curricula. Students in the YOE 2000 cohort studied the state's new biology curriculum, entitled "The Living Environment," in heterogeneously grouped classes. This combination of new curriculum and heterogeneous grouping resulted in a dramatic increase in the passing rate on the first science Regents exam—especially for minority students, who were previously overrepresented in the low-track biology class. After just one year the passing rate for African American and Latino students increased from 48 percent to 77 percent, while the passing rate for White and Asian American students increased from 85 percent to 94 percent.

The following September the YOE cohort of 2001 became the first class to be heterogeneously grouped in all subjects in the ninth grade. The state's new multiyear "Math A" curriculum was taught to this cohort in heterogeneously grouped classes in the eighth and ninth grades.

In 2003 some tenth-grade classes detracked. Students in the YOE cohort of 2002 became the first to study a heterogeneously grouped pre–International Baccalaureate (IB) tenth-grade curriculum in English and social studies. To help all students meet the demands of an advanced curriculum, the district provided every-other-day support classes in math, science, and English language arts. These classes were linked to the curriculum and allowed teachers to pre- and post-teach topics to students needing additional reinforcement. The teachers of the support class also taught the corresponding course. The average support class size was eight students.

Closing the Gap on the Earning of the Regents Diploma

In 1995 New York State issued a mandate requiring that local school diplomas would be phased out and all students would be required to pass Regents exams in order to graduate.[6] Notwithstanding this momentous change, New York's statewide racial achievement gap in the earning of Regents diplomas has persisted. In 2000 only 19.3 percent of all African American and Latino and 58.7 percent of all White and Asian American twelfth graders graduated with a Regents diploma. By 2003, the year in which those high school completers who entered ninth grade in 1999 (YOE 1999) graduated, the percentage statewide of students in both groups earning the Regents diploma had increased (26.4 percent of African American and Latino students and 66.3 percent White and Asian American students), but the gap did not close (figure 1).

In contrast, Rockville Centre students have increased their rate of earn-

Figure 1. South Side High School and New York State Regents diploma rates by year of entry cohort (South Side High School) and by ethnicity

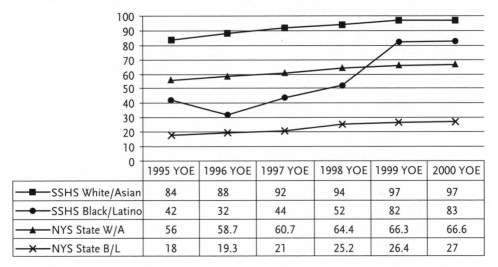

	1995 YOE	1996 YOE	1997 YOE	1998 YOE	1999 YOE	2000 YOE
■ SSHS White/Asian	84	88	92	94	97	97
● SSHS Black/Latino	42	32	44	52	82	83
▲ NYS State W/A	56	58.7	60.7	64.4	66.3	66.6
✕ NYS State B/L	18	19.3	21	25.2	26.4	27

Note: The New York State data are reported by graduating class; the state does not report year of entry data for Regents diploma rates. Therefore, the state data also fail to reflect dropouts and to show higher Regents diploma rates than would be reported if given by YOE cohort. (Rockville Centre has a dropout rate near zero.) For these reasons, the trends shown in this figure are informative but cannot provide exact comparisons.

ing a Regents diploma, and the gap has decreased (figure 1). For those students who entered ninth grade at South Side High School in 1999, the gap had nearly disappeared: 82 percent of all African American and La- tino and 97 percent of all White and Asian American graduates earned a Regents diploma. In fact, a close inspection of figure 1 shows that for this 1999 cohort (the first to experience detracking in all middle school and most ninth-grade subjects), the Regents diploma rate for the district's minority students surpassed New York State's rate for White and Asian American students. At the same time the percentage of students who were noncompleters (dropouts or transferred to a GED program) remained very low. During the years that the three detracked cohorts graduated, the noncompleter rate was 0.1 percent (2002), 0.3 percent (2003), and 0.1 percent (2004).[7] During the three prior years the rate ranged from 0.3 per- cent to 0.7 percent. This result should help assuage the fears of those who see detracking as leading to imbalanced competition that may harm the self-esteem of lower-ability students (Loveless, 1999).

Further Analysis of the Reform

Descriptive statistics, such as the percentages of students earning a Regents diploma, are often used to show changes in student performance and to assess the effects of reforms. However, additional factors may contribute to a change in school performance. Factors such as demographic changes in the community, for example, may be partly responsible for a changed outcome measurement. In order to ensure that the decrease in the gap was not attributable to a changing population, we used binary logistic regression analysis to compare the probability of earning a Regents diploma before and after detracking.[8] In addition to membership in a detracked cohort, the regression model controlled for the effects of the following factors: race/ethnicity, socioeconomic status (SES), and special-education status. The inclusion of these terms allowed us to isolate the effects of detracking by controlling for three key demographic factors. Those students who were members of the YOE cohorts from 1995 to 1997 were compared with members of the YOE cohorts of 1998 to 2000. We found that even after accounting for the effects of SES status, special-education status, and ethnicity, membership in a cohort subsequent to the detracking of middle school math was a significant contributor to earning a Regents diploma ($p < .0001$).

As mentioned earlier in the review of the literature, some researchers believe that when studies control for prior achievement, the achievement gap associated with tracking disappears. Could it be that the increases we found in the rate of minority students earning a Regents diploma were attributable to higher-achieving African American and Latino students attending the school district? In order to rule out that possible cause for the observed increases in achievement, we added a measure of general cognitive aptitude to the regression model: tenth-grade Preliminary Scholastic Aptitude Test (PSAT) verbal and math scores (M. C. Frey & Detterman, 2003).

Since Rockville Centre School District pays for its students to take the PSAT and gives the exam during school hours, nearly all students (with the exception of members of the YOE cohort of 2000, whose results are unavailable) had tenth-grade PSAT scores in their records. In order to balance the number of African American and Latino students, as well as the number of low socioeconomic status students, in the pre- and post-tracking groups, we compared the earliest two tracked cohorts, YOE 1995 and YOE 1996, with the first two detracked cohorts, YOE 1998 and YOE 1999. We controlled for ethnicity (UNDERREP), socioeconomic status (SES), special-education status (SPED), and math and verbal PSAT scores

(MATH, VERBAL). The final covariate (that is, the variable that may influence whether a student earns a Regents diploma) of interest was a binary value, PREPOST, which indicated whether the student belonged to a cohort subsequent to the detracking of math. The inclusion of PREPOST would allow us to understand the unique contribution that detracking made to the earning of a Regents diploma after controlling for the other factors we included in the model.

Results

When we added PSAT scores to the regression model, the model became a better predictor of obtaining a Regents diploma. In addition, as shown in table 2, the model shows students in detracked cohorts to be more than 7.4 times as likely to earn a Regents diploma than students in the earlier, tracked cohorts, per the value of $\exp(\beta)$.[9] This "boost" provided by being a member of a detracked cohort was equal to the "boost" provided by about seven additional PSAT points, or seventy points on the Scholastic Aptitude Test (SAT).[10]

Reform initiatives are sometimes divided into excellence and equity categories, with the former designed to benefit all students and the latter designed to benefit the most needy. Ideally excellence reforms should benefit all, while providing the most benefit to those who began furthest behind (J. Ogbu, 2003). In order to determine if detracking had a different effect on those who were the furthest behind, we ran the regression model two more times—first with only the combined group of African American and Latino students and then with only the combined group of White and Asian American students. We controlled for prior achievement, SES, and special-education status. We found that while detracking

Table 2. Factors that contributed to earning a Regents diploma for Rockville Centre students

Variable	B	$\exp(\beta)$
UNDERREP	−0.5743	.5631
SPED	−2.3988****	.0908
SES	−1.1264*	.3242
VERBAL	.0732***	1.0760
MATH	.1093****	1.1155
PREPOST	2.0030****	7.4114

*$p < .05$ ** $p < .01$ *** $p < .001$ **** $p < .0001$

Table 3. Contributions of variables to the probability of earning a Regents diploma: African American or Latino students and White or Asian American students

Variable	B	exp(β)
African American or Latino students		
PREPOST	2.1248***	8.3716
SPED	−1.8596**	.1557
SES	−.8458	.4292
VERBAL	.0601	1.0619
MATH	.1062**	1.1121
White or Asian American students		
PREPOST	1.6111***	5.0083
SPED	−2.7396****	.0646
SES	−2.4951**	.0825
VERBAL	.1056****	1.1114
MATH	.1365****	1.1462

*p < .05   ** p < .01   *** p < .001   **** p < .0001

benefited both groups, the benefit for the African American and Latino group was greater: these students were 8.4 times more likely to earn a Regents diploma if they were members of detracked cohorts, while White and Asian American students were five times more likely to do so (see table 3). The Rockville Centre detracking reform therefore fit the definition of an excellence reform—benefiting all, with the most benefit for those furthest behind.

We then asked a second, related question to explore the relationship between the achievement gap and tracking. Prior to detracking were African American and Latino students less likely to obtain a Regents diploma even after SES, special-education status, and achievement were taken into account? If so, what happened after detracking? In order to answer these questions, we ran two additional models—one with the earliest two tracked cohorts and one with the two detracked cohorts for which PSAT scores were available. The results are given in table 4.

In tracked cohorts the probability of not earning a Regents diploma was associated with being African American or Latino (UNDERREP), even when controlling for SES, special-education status, and prior achievement.[11] However, for the cohorts that experienced detracking, the contribution of UNDERREP was no longer significant—in fact, its small contribution to the model was positive, indicating that when all covari-

Table 4. Contributions of variables before and after detracking to the probability of earning a Regents diploma

Variable	B	exp(β)
Tracked cohorts: YOE 1995–96		
UNDERREP	−1.3177*	.2678
SPED	−3.0549****	.0471
SES	−.9966	.3691
VERBAL	.0891**	1.0932
MATH	.1061**	1.1119
Detracked cohorts: YOE 1998–99		
UNDERREP	.2752	1.3168
SPED	−2.0769***	.1253
SES	−1.3575	.2573
VERBAL	.0524	1.0538
MATH	.1201**	1.1276

*$p < .05$ **$p < .01$ *** $p < .001$ **** $p < .0001$

ates were held constant, being African American or Latino was associated with a small, insignificant increased probability of earning a Regents diploma. In other words, detracking appeared to be the factor that helped close the gap in the earning of a Regents diploma after accounting for special-education status and the effects of poverty.[12]

The results of detracking in Rockville Centre offer a compelling challenge to the belief that the achievement gap associated with tracked minority students can be explained away as an artifact of general cognitive aptitude or poverty. These children achieve at high levels when given high-quality educational opportunities (Burris & Welner, 2005).

Detracking helped "narrow the gap" in other ways as well. The cohorts in which all students were detracked and accelerated in middle school math (YOE 1998–2000) showed significant increases in minority students studying in advanced math courses. African American and Latino student enrollment in trigonometry, pre-calculus, and Advanced Placement (AP) calculus increased (Burris, 2003). Moreover, even as more students from those cohorts studied AP calculus and as the race or ethnicity achievement gap in these classes decreased from 38 percent to 18 percent in five years, the AP calculus scores of all students significantly increased ($p < .01$) (Burris, Heubert, & Levin, 2004).

Finally, the recent detracking in the tenth grade, combined with teaching all students pre-IB curriculum in English and social studies, was associated with higher scores and increased passing rates on the New York State Global Regents exam[13] for all students and, in particular, for African American and Latino students. After heterogeneously grouping the YOE 2002 cohort and providing all students with a demanding curriculum to prepare them for IB courses in the eleventh grade, the district witnessed two key improvements. Performance on the tenth-grade Global Regents increased, and the following year 72 percent of all students, and 50 percent of minority students, chose the IB curriculum in English and in History of the Americas. Remarkably, 91 percent of these students achieved a score of mastery (85 percent or above) on the six-hour English Language Arts (ELA) Regents in January 2005. By way of comparison, in 2001, when only 43 percent of the cohort of 1998 studied the IB English curriculum in the eleventh grade, their mastery rate on the ELA Regents was 60 percent.[14] While gaps still exist, they are unmistakably closing as the school continues to detrack. As more students study the high-track curriculum, more students of all racial and ethnic groups are demonstrating high academic achievement.

Detracking as a Process

As mentioned earlier in this essay, detracking reforms usually meet with stiff resistance, especially at the high school level.[15] Why has the Rockville Centre School District, a racially and socioeconomically diverse district, been able to detrack its high school when so many other schools have failed in their attempts or abandoned the reform shortly after implementation? We identify the following as essential components of this detracking success:[16]

Stable school district leadership, committed to achieving excellence and equity. The reform greatly benefited from the support, encouragement, and leadership of a twenty-year veteran superintendent who deeply believed that all students were entitled to the best curriculum that a school has to offer. He hired administrators who shared these core beliefs.

Elimination of the lowest track to begin the process. This resulted in an immediate improvement in school culture and higher achievement. The elimination of the lowest track is a key step in the detracking process because it is the track that has the most profound negative effect on student achievement (Heubert & Hauser, 1999).

Commitment to a high-track curriculum plus support for struggling learners in heterogeneous classes. Such support is a key component to this strategy's success (Rubin & Noguera, 2004).

Teachers eased into heterogeneous classes. Because there was already open enrollment in high-track classes, teachers had adjusted to teaching a more heterogeneous group of students, making for a smoother transition when the ninth and tenth grades later moved to only heterogeneous classes with high-track curriculum.

External forces provided opportunity for change. Changes in New York State standards and testing provided natural opportunities to revisit grouping practices. With the strong support of Superintendent William H. Johnson and Assistant Superintendent Delia Garrity, the high school principal leveraged changes in the state curriculum to continue detracking, such as the heterogeneous ninth-grade curriculum in math and science. Detracking was never done for the sake of detracking; it was always tied to a change in curriculum and standards, helping parents to understand why the school changed its grouping practices. Detracking is a reform that many parents have difficulty understanding because of its counterintuitive nature. On the surface, dividing students into groups and providing different curricula based on perceived "ability" makes sense. The new standards accountability context, which expects high achievement from all students, has helped parents understand why detracking, combined with rigorous curricula, is needed.

Steady, determined progress. The school did not fall into the trap of waiting for everyone to get onboard. Reforms that challenge the status quo and privilege will never garner full support. While the process was gradual and paced, administrators did not wait until all teachers and all parents agreed.

Collection and dissemination of achievement data. School and district leaders consistently collected, analyzed, and communicated data. The collection and dissemination of achievement results move the discussion from opinion to fact. Data analysis showed time and again the following effects of detracking: achievement improved, curriculum was not "watered down," and the performance of high achievers did not decline (Burris, Heubert, & Levin, 2004). Large studies of tracking that do not control for the effects of curriculum, school, and community are not as helpful when communicating with parents and teachers because groups opposed to change emphasize that each school and district has unique needs and resources. Often this becomes the rationale for rejecting a reform. District data are the most credible data with the school community.

Careful selection and evaluation of staff. Whenever a teacher retired or left, the principal carefully chose a replacement who believed that all students can be high achievers. While beliefs can change and be shaped by experience, teachers who do not buy into a detracking school's philosophy will not easily internalize and practice the strategies needed to make heterogeneous grouping successful.

Methodical creation of truly heterogeneous classes. School administrators ensured that classes were truly heterogeneous and did not allow de facto tracking to occur. Classes were carefully constructed so that equal numbers of high achievers were in each class. Music programs such as school orchestras, research programs that prepare students for competitions, and special-education support classes can cause clusters of high achievers or low achievers to follow the same schedule. Only careful creation of class rosters can ensure true heterogeneity.

Attention to school culture. Due to positive experiences with detracking, school culture became even more favorable to the reform. As ninth graders became more successful, teachers became strong supporters of the reform—especially those teachers who previously had taught the lower-track class. Thus the culture of the building began to change, and detracking gained strong support among the faculty.

Earnest response to parental concerns about learning and achievement. Parent concerns were never dismissed. While issues of both achievement and equity were paramount in school leaders' minds, they clearly understood that learning and scores on achievement tests were of greater concern to parents. When parents objected to the move to heterogeneously grouped tenth-grade classes, school leaders and teachers spent time listening to parent concerns. The concerns expressed by parents generally reflected traditional beliefs about the efficacy of tracking, with a few parents expressing thinly disguised racial and social class prejudices. In response school leaders and teachers carefully explained the new heterogeneous classes. They ensured that the curriculum developed for the course was a true honors curriculum with support classes that would pre- and post-teach content to struggling learners. Data collected at the end of the year showed across-the-board (at each achievement level: low, medium, and high) elevated scores on the New York State tenth-grade Regents exam. When the next school year started, parents did not question the detracked classes.

Support for and engagement of school staff. The district provided generous support to teachers. The assistant superintendent provided continuous staff development on the differentiation of instruction and literacy (Garrity, 2004). The principal praised teacher efforts while communicating and celebrating student achievement with the staff. All achievement gaps were discussed, and strategies for closing them were developed.

Increasing the achievement of all students by "leveling up"—giving all students the high-track curriculum—continues to be a goal of the district. During the decade of detracking reform, the school became a U.S. Department of Education Blue Ribbon School of Excellence and one of *Newsweek*'s "One Hundred Best High Schools in the United States." The school has produced both Intel and National Merit Student finalists. Its International Baccalaureate Program is now the thirteenth largest in the world, with the percentage of students earning the diploma exceeding the world average. In sum, detracking has brought substantial academic benefits to students of color and poverty, without adversely affecting the achievement of any student group (Burris, Heubert, & Levin, 2004).

Implications of This Study and the Need for Further Research

What, then, are the contributions of this study of one school to the literature on tracking and its relationship to the achievement gap? Unlike previous studies of the achievement effects of tracking, this study does not examine the effects of grouping practices on student performance on only one test; rather, it follows cohorts of students and measures achievement as the earning of the New York State Regents diploma, for which students must demonstrate competence on multiple exams that meet external standards. Accordingly, it provides a measure that goes beyond one testing event, using measures of achievement growth in all academic areas over the course of the high school years. Changes in the rate of earning a Regents diploma can be compared not only within the district for the years of study but also with data across the state of New York.

In addition, this analysis makes a unique contribution to the literature on tracking by documenting its relationship to the achievement gap in the district of study. Previous studies have demonstrated the effects of tracking on achievement, while others have demonstrated the relationship between race and track placement. This study ties together these two strands in the literature by showing how a district with tracked classes stratified by race was able to (1) detrack and thereby eliminate that stratification, (2) institute a high-track curriculum for all students, and (3) increase achievement for all students while narrowing the gap.

It is important, then, to consider the generalizability of these findings to other districts with different demographics or resources. Are the positive effects of detracking in Rockville Centre transferable to schools with greater numbers of students of poverty or with fewer resources for students? Although we can offer no definite proof, we have good reason to believe that they are.

First, this study does not stand in isolation from other studies examining the effects of acceleration and detracking. For example, many studies demonstrate that an enriched, accelerated curriculum is more beneficial to at-risk learners and low-achieving students than a traditional, remedial curriculum that slows instruction (Bloom, Ham, Melton, & O'Brient, 2001; Mason, Schroeter, Combs, & Washington, 1992; J. M. Peterson, 1989; White, Gamoran, Porter, & Smithson, 1996). Several of these studies were based in diverse, urban schools with a large number of students from low-socioeconomic households. Furthermore, the implementation of detracking as a "leveling up" process is hardly new. Slavin and Braddock (1993) advocated a detracking process whereby the "top-track" curriculum "becomes accessible to a broader range of students without watering it down" (p. 15; see also Wheelock, 1992). Thus the Rockville Centre School District's strategy builds on a strong research foundation.

Furthermore, the demographic and socioeconomic diversity of the Rockville Centre student body, and the consistent benefit to all groups, provide evidence that detracking, along with the culture of high expectations with support, can effectively be used to close gaps in achievement. While most of the student body in Rockville Centre is drawn from upper-middle-class families, the average proportion of all students receiving free or reduced-price lunches in the high school during the years of this study was 12 percent. During the years of this study, African American and Latinos comprised 20 percent of each cohort, and 56 percent of these minority students received free or reduced-price lunch. Most of the low-income students live in a housing project located in the school district. These low-income students, therefore, are representative of those around the nation who are typically written off as least educable.

Would detracking be as effective in a district with fewer resources to support struggling students or in a district in which more students struggle academically? While there is little doubt that such conditions would make the reform more difficult to implement, such challenges can be partially or fully overcome. Implementation will differ in each new context. Gains may even be reduced. But there is little reason to believe that districts with greater numbers of poor students would not gain substantial achievement benefits from comparable detracking initiatives. In fact, a recently completed longitudinal study in an urban American high school with a far greater proportion of students from low-income households shows results that are remarkably similar to those of this study—when detracking was combined with a common rigorous curriculum in mathematics, student achievement increased (Boaler & Staples, 2005).

Rockville Centre is a district committed to closing the achievement gap. By providing all students with heterogeneous classes and high-track curriculum along with support for low achievers, this district has made substantial progress. All groups of students—majority, minority, special education, and students of all socioeconomic backgrounds—have experienced increases in achievement. This evidence can now be added to the larger body of tracking research that has convinced the Carnegie Council for Adolescent Development (1989), National Governors Association (1993), and most recently the National Research Council (2004) to call for the reduction or elimination of tracking. The Rockville Centre reform confirms common sense: closing the "curriculum gap" that results from tracking is an effective way to close the "achievement gap."

Notes

1. Dr. Burris currently serves as a high school principal in the school district.

2. S. R. Lucas and Gamoran (1993) found that earlier results were due to erroneous "overreporting" of track assignment by Black students.

3. Ms. Garrity is presently the Rockville Centre School District's assistant superintendent for curriculum and instruction.

4. We use ninth-grade YOE to identify the students because a small number of students take 4 and a half or five years to graduate. Since our concern is the particular phase of the detracking reform that a student experienced, the YOE approach is the most accurate.

5. Feeling tone is the "emotional climate" in the classroom, which can be either positive, negative, or neutral. According to Madeline Hunter (2005), students learn best in classrooms that are pleasant, to a lesser degree in classrooms that are unpleasant, and almost nothing of what occurs when there is a neutral feeling tone (see Hunter, 2005, for an extensive discussion of the Hunter instructional model). Low-track classes tend to be characterized by either negative (punitive) feeling tones or the neutral feeling tone that comes from boring drill and skill activities.

6. The mandate was phased in beginning with the YOE cohort of 1996. Since that time, modifications have been made, and the acceptable score for graduation has remained at 55 percent on five examinations.

7. During the years of study, total school enrollment was approximately one thousand students. Therefore, 0.1 percent represents one student, 0.3 percent three students, and so forth. There are no racially identifiable trends in the numbers.

8. Logistic regression is a model used to make statistical predictions. Binary logistic regression is used when, as in this case, the dependent variable can have only two possible outcomes (e.g., obtaining or not obtaining a Regents diploma). The model estimates the probability of either of the two events occurring. The coeffi-

cients selected for the model are likely to also affect the outcome, and so the model shows their contribution to the event (obtaining or not obtaining a Regents diploma) (see Menard, 1995, for further discussion of logistic regression analysis).

9. Logistic regression analysis provides a statistic, Exp(β), that allows us to estimate the contribution of each of the variables to the probability of earning a Regents diploma. Also, table 2 provides the odds ratio for each of the variables, given as the value exp(β).

10. In the model the effect of achievement is measured by the exp(β) values for MATH or VERBAL. The comparison in the text is simply a comparison of those values with the exp(β) for PREPOST.

11. The negative beta value (-1.3177) tells us that the contribution of the variable decreased the probability of the outcome. Calculating the exp(β) for this beta yields a value of .2678, meaning that for the tracked cohorts a White or Asian American student was 3.73 times more likely to earn a Regents diploma than an African American or Latino student. To explain the effect of an exp(β) that is less than one, 1 is divided by the exp(β) value.

12. Low SES status also ceased to be a significant contributor when only two cohorts were included in each model. It is likely, however, that given the small number of free and reduced-priced lunch students in the two detracked cohorts ($N = 73$), there was simply not enough power to see a significant effect in either the tracked or detracked group.

13. This is a Regents exam that tests students' knowledge of world history following a two-year course of study. It must be passed to earn a New York State Regents diploma.

14. Burris, Welner, E. Wiley, & J. Murphy have prepared an extensive analysis of the effects of detracking on the school's IB program. This analysis will appear in a special issue on detracking in the Spring 2007 *Teachers College Record*.

15. For an excellent discussion of why this is so, see Attewell (2001).

16. This list, and a more detailed discussion of these issues, is set forth in Welner & Burris (in press).

Fostering an Inclusive, Multiracial Democracy

How Attorneys, Social Scientists, and Educators Made the Case for School Integration in Lynn, Massachusetts

Richard W. Cole

The educational success of the voluntary integration plan of the public school district in the city of Lynn, Massachusetts, and the theories and methodologies successfully applied in defending the constitutionality of its integration plan in *Comfort v. Lynn School Committee,*[1] provides a road map for educators and policymakers committed to promoting the racial integration of students, and for the lawyers advising them. In this case, Lynn has established the importance of voluntary efforts by school districts to integrate their students and the necessity of taking race into account as central to the achievement of its educational mission.[2]

This essay provides practical guidance to educators, policymakers, and lawyers in designing effective integration plans, modifying existing plans, and defending policies from constitutional challenge and offers educators and community leaders strategies for success in desegregating schools and integrating students.[3] It does so by examining the defense in the *Comfort* case from both a litigation and educational perspective and by summarizing the expert evidence in *Comfort,* which provides a social science and psychological explanation for understanding why K–12 integration matters, and by supplying a specific structure to guide school districts in developing vibrant, high-quality integrated schools.

The *Lynn* case was the first trial in the United States that focused on whether public school districts are constitutionally permitted to voluntarily integrate their schools to meet the educational and race relations needs of their students.[4] Primary and secondary schools are often the first and only place where children from different racial backgrounds have the opportunity to interact with each other, disarm racial stereotypes, develop positive racial attitudes, build cross-race relationships, and prepare for success in multiracial workplaces and communities. However, once a child develops racial stereotypes and racial distrust, these attitudes are almost impossible to dislodge.

As our nation becomes increasing racially diverse, a growing number of school districts have turned to voluntary plans that take race into account when making school assignment and transfer decisions to protect students from racial isolation and segregation and to provide them the important educational and race relations benefits of a racially integrated education. Even in racially diverse school districts, such as Lynn, without race-conscious school assignment or transfer policies, segregated housing patterns and other local conditions often result in predominantly White or minority elementary and secondary schools.

In the *Comfort* case a handful of Lynn parents sued the City of Lynn's school system in August 1999, claiming that the U.S. Constitution and federal civil rights laws prohibit Lynn from continuing to implement its twelve-year-old voluntary integration plan (the "Voluntary Plan for School Improvement and the Elimination of Racial Isolation," or "Lynn Plan"). The Lynn Plan uses race as a decisive factor when approving certain requests for school transfers to integrate Lynn's schools and prevent the racial isolation and segregation of its students. Plaintiffs also argued that the U.S. Constitution forbids the state of Massachusetts from providing financial incentives to encourage communities to desegregate their schools under the Commonwealth's Racial Imbalance Act (RIA).[5] Currently twenty Massachusetts communities, including most of the large and medium-sized cities in Massachusetts, have race-conscious voluntary desegregation plans under the RIA.

In order to prove the constitutionality of a voluntary integration plan, a school district must first establish that integration in its elementary and secondary schools matters. Once a district establishes the educational and race relations benefits of integration in its K–12 schools, the question becomes whether it is constitutionally permissible for K–12 educators to take voluntary steps to integrate their schools and what steps must be taken to stay within the "narrow tailoring" requirements of the U.S. Constitution.

Although the Supreme Court has recognized the substantial educational benefits that derive from racial diversity in higher education in its landmark decision in *Grutter v. Bollinger* in June 2003, in finding constitutional the University of Michigan Law School's affirmative action admissions program, it has not yet directly addressed the constitutionality of voluntary, race-conscious efforts to provide racially integrated education in K–12 schools. The Supreme Court's recognition of significant educational benefits from racial diversity in higher education, however, provides powerful support for Lynn's governmental interest in racially integrating its K–12 schools through race-conscious means.[6]

Because of the importance of the issues and the richness of the trial record, the *Comfort* case was closely watched by school districts, education experts, and educational equity advocates nationally. They recognized not only the powerful impact the case would have on the quality of education in Lynn but also the significant role the case may have in determining the future of integration in K–12 education in our country.[7] Whatever the ultimate result of voluntary integration litigation in the Supreme Court, however, Lynn's extraordinary record of success provides powerful support for the proposition that learning in racially integrated schools offers children fundamentally important educational and citizenship skills, improves race relations, and instills values essential for maintaining the social fabric of schools and the community they serve, while contributing to the goals of an inclusive, democratic society.

Background about the City of Lynn and Its Integration Plan

Lynn is an urban school system with over 15,000 students attending its twenty-four schools: eighteen elementary schools, three middle schools, and three high schools. It is a racially and ethnically diverse city of approximately 89,000 people, located on the coast of Massachusetts, nine miles north of Boston. According to the census of 2000, the city's overall racial composition is 68 percent White and 32 percent non-White. Hispanics comprise 18.4 percent, African Americans 10.5 percent, and Asian Americans 6.4 percent of Lynn's population (U.S. Census Bureau, 2001b). Non-Whites, however, comprise a majority of the students in its public schools. At the time of trial in June 2002, 42 percent of Lynn's students were White and 58 percent non-White—29 percent Hispanic, 15 percent African American, and 14 percent Asian American. The racial composition of Lynn's schools reflects population trends similar to many urban communities, with higher birthrates, larger family sizes, and comparatively younger ages of minorities as compared to Whites living in the community (McArdle Tran.).

In 1987, with its schools deeply troubled and plagued by racial divisions, Lynn adopted a voluntary plan to integrate its schools. The plan, approved by the Massachusetts Board of Education in 1988 under the RIA, governs the assignment of students to each of Lynn's schools. To desegregate their schools, the Lynn Plan encourages parents to voluntarily transfer their child to a school outside their neighborhood while it guarantees every Lynn parent the ability to send his or her child, regardless of race, to that child's neighborhood school. The Lynn Plan is one of the least intrusive types of desegregation plans because it promotes integration by encouraging desegregative voluntary school transfers while maintaining a neighborhood-based school system. It does not permit coercive or involuntary school transfers. A student's race is considered and used as a decisive factor only when Lynn is approving parents' voluntary requests for school transfers, and only then in certain circumstances. Lynn only denies a parent's request for a voluntary transfer, space permitting, when the transfer would exacerbate "racial isolation" or "racial imbalance," as defined by the plan, in a particular school. So long as a school's racial composition falls within 30 percent (elementary) or 20 percent (middle and high schools) of the district's overall racial composition, there are no limits on transfers for that school. For example, since 1992 the plan's transfer restrictions have been applicable only to Lynn's elementary and middle schools. Lynn's three high schools have remained integrated without the transfer restrictions. Moreover, before race is used in a transfer decision, Lynn accounts for a number of individualized, race-neutral factors. Parents can appeal transfer denials, and where they document a concrete hardship from the denial, Lynn will grant the appeal. Before the plan almost all children were required to attend their neighborhood school.

The Legal Environment

When Lynn first implemented its plan in 1987, the legal landscape was far different than it is today. In the 1980s school districts like Lynn were concerned with potential legal liability for policies and practices that courts could find constituted evidence of intentional, de jure racial discrimination (where school or government officials knowingly assist in establishing or maintaining segregated schools). They were not concerned with any possible legal risk for efforts to desegregate voluntarily.

In 1987 the Massachusetts Department of Education was pressuring Lynn to adopt a voluntary desegregation plan, under the state's Racial Imbalance Act, citing certain actions and inactions by Lynn that placed it at substantial legal risk of being sued for de jure discrimination (see *Comfort*, 2003). The resolve of Lynn city officials to avoid potential desegregation litigation was only reinforced by the long-standing judicial oversight of Boston public schools, located only nine miles south of Lynn. The federal courts were just completing twelve years of close oversight and control over the desegregation of Boston's schools (*Morgan v. Nucci*, 1987).[8] Lynn was also evaluating its policy options during a time when the U.S. Supreme Court was expressing its general approval of state and local governments promoting racial integration in education and redressing racially segregated K–12 schools through voluntary means (see *Wygant v. Jackson Board of Education,* 1986, p. 291; *Crawford v. Board of Education,* 1982, pp. 535–536; *Washington v. Seattle School District No. 1,* 1982, pp. 472–473; *Bustop, Inc., v. Board of Education,* 1978, p. 1383), although there is debate as to whether the Court's statements in these cases are legally binding.

By 1999, however, the legal landscape had dramatically changed. The language used by the Supreme Court in its affirmative action decisions (in noneducational contexts) beginning with *City of Richmond v. J. R. Croson* in 1989 led many to question the continued constitutional viability of the government's voluntary use of race-conscious policies (see also *Adarand Constructors, Inc. v. Peña,* 1995), even though no subsequent Supreme Court decision questioned the line of cases expressing general approval of state and local officials acting voluntarily to prevent racial isolation and promote racial integration of public schools. When approving the University of Michigan Law School's affirmative action admissions program, the Supreme Court noted in *Grutter* that language in *Croson* and other prior affirmative action decisions led to the misapprehension that remedying past discrimination was the only constitutional justification for race-based government action (*Grutter,* 2003, p. 332).

Additionally, when reviewing K–12 voluntary integration plans, lower federal courts were engaging in the most exacting scrutiny of the use of race, as the Supreme Court had applied with racial classifications by other governmental entities. Although one federal circuit court concluded that racial classifications could never be used except to remedy past discrimination (*Hopwood v. Texas,* 1996), other federal courts found the use of race in K–12 assignments or admissions unconstitutional because it was not narrowly tailored, while assuming, without deciding, that diversity could constitute a compelling interest in the K–12 context (*Wessmann v. Gittens,* 1998; *Tuttle v. Arlington County School Board,* 1999, 2000; *Eisenberg v. Montgomery County Public Schools,* 1999, 2000; but see *Brewer v. West Irondequoit Central School District,* 2000; *Hunter v. Regents of University of California,* 1999).

Lynn had a heavy legal and evidentiary burden under a strict scrutiny standard; it had to demonstrate that the benefits that flow from its race-conscious plan are compelling and that the plan is narrowly tailored to achieve its compelling interests. The federal courts would carefully examine whether Lynn's students, through its plan, actually obtained compelling educational and race relations benefits from integration and whether

Lynn could demonstrate that it had accomplished the plan's identified educational goals with objective, quantifiable evidence of success. The federal courts would also carefully examine whether the Lynn Plan satisfies the exacting narrow tailoring requirements (discussed later in this essay).[9]

Narrow tailoring requires that Lynn:

(1) Demonstrate that the means it employs for approving elective school transfer requests are calibrated specifically to accomplish its asserted purpose and that it does not use race more than necessary to achieve its compelling goals;

(2) Show that its plan does not "unduly harm members of any racial group" or innocent third parties;

(3) Establish that the plan is not overbroad by using only White and non-White racial classifications, rather than treat all Lynn's racial and ethnic subgroups separately in its plan;

(4) Demonstrate its good faith consideration of workable race-neutral alternatives (which would achieve the racial diversity in Lynn schools about as well as its plan produces). A court will take into account the expertise of Lynn's educators, however, in determining whether race-neutral alternatives will effectively generate racial integration in its schools; and

(5) Establish that the plan is limited in time and scope, that it updates and modifies its policies to address changing conditions, and that it reviews the plan's operation to determine whether changes in circumstances might limit or render unnecessary using the plan's race-conscious components. (See, generally, *Grutter*, 2003; *Comfort*, 2005a)

Additionally, after the Supreme Court decisions in *Grutter* and *Gratz v. Bollinger* (2003), Lynn had to establish why narrow tailoring does not require it use an individualized-type assessment for its school transfer decisions, as mandated in *Grutter* and *Gratz* for evaluating candidates for admission in competitive, race-preferential, higher education admissions programs.

Litigation Background

In June 2002 the district court held an eleven-day bench trial.[10] In an expansive decision issued in September 2003, the district court found overwhelming evidentiary support for Lynn's educational need for its plan, while finding the plan was narrowly tailored to achieve its compelling goals. The plaintiffs appealed. On appeal a three-judge panel of the First Circuit Court of Appeals concluded that "defendants have made a persuasive case that a public school system has a compelling interest in obtaining the educational benefits that flow from a racially diverse student body" (*Comfort,* 2004a, p. 34). The unanimous panel held, however, that the Lynn Plan was not narrowly tailored.[11]

The state and Lynn defendants petitioned for a rehearing en banc (requesting all active judges of the First Circuit to rehear the case). The First Circuit granted the motion (*Comfort,* 2004b). The parties reargued the case. In June 2005 the First Circuit issued its opinion holding that the Lynn Plan met constitutional requirements. The First Circuit, relying on *Grutter,* unanimously held that Lynn had a compelling interest in obtaining the substantial educational benefits that flow from its school integration plan. Except for one ground the five members of the en banc court also unanimously agreed that Lynn's integration plan was narrowly tailored. The two dissenting judges stated that Lynn erred by using race as a decisive factor in school transfer decisions, rather than as "a strong but non-determinative 'plus' factor" (*Comfort,* 2005a, p. 31).[12] The First Circuit Court, however, concluded that individualized consideration of each student is unnecessary in this educational context.

In December 2005 the U.S. Supreme Court rejected plaintiffs' request to hear their constitutional challenge to the Lynn Plan; and, in July 2006, the Court turned down plaintiffs' motion to reconsider its rejection and revive the case, ending the litigation with Lynn prevailing with its plan intact.

Presenting a Compelling Case through a Comprehensive Examination and Evaluation of a School District

Litigation Strategy: Proving Integration Matters

Success at trial and on appeal was highly dependent on making tight connections between the social science research and the specific, concrete workings of the Lynn Plan. The First Circuit, in its *Wessmann* decision, had articulated a high threshold for expert testimony to justify the use of race in the K–12 context when rejecting the race-based admissions policy of the Boston Latin School. Although the context and interests advanced by Lynn's school transfer program are far different than in *Wessmann* (where the court reviewed a competitive, race-preferential, secondary school admissions policy), Lynn, to ensure success, could not risk making only broad assertions about the educational benefits that flow from an integrated school (or the harms from racial isolation and segregation). Instead, it had to demonstrate that the general benefits identified in the social science literature were applicable to the specifics of Lynn's school system. The First Circuit Court of Appeals stated, "only solid evidence will justify allowing race-conscious action; and the unsystematic personal observations of government officials will not do, even if the conclusions they offer sound plausible and are cloaked in the trappings of social science" (*Wessmann*, 1998, p. 808). The evidence an expert relies on must be "of the quality necessary to satisfy the methodological rigor required by [the relevant] discipline" (*Wessmann*, 1998, pp. 804–805). The first challenge, however, was to develop persuasive evidence demonstrating the favorable educational conditions in Lynn's schools to justify its use of race.

The parties stipulated at trial that, "The government interests identified by Lynn in its Plan include fostering integrated public schools and what Lynn believes are its positive effects; reducing minority isolation and avoiding segregation and what Lynn believes are their negative effects; promoting a positive racial climate at schools and a safe and healthy school environment; fostering a cohesive and tolerant community in Lynn; promoting diversity; ensuring equal educational and life opportunities and increasing the quality of education for all students" (*Comfort,* 2005a, p. 14). Based on the governmental interests identified in the plan, and the evidence collected and developed, Lynn advanced five separate but interrelated compelling governmental interests for integrating its schools through race-conscious means: (1) promoting racial and ethnic diversity; (2) improving the quality of education and increasing educational opportunity for all students; (3) ensuring safety; (4) preventing racial isolation; and (5) implementing the clear promise of *Brown v. Board of Education of Topeka* (1954) by eliminating segregated schools.

Preparing to Prove That Integration Matters

To persuade the court of the plan's success required an interdisciplinary approach that applied and integrated developmental and social psychology with social science research and study in the fields of education and school desegregation, with the study of housing and demographic trends and patterns of racial change in Lynn. The experts' interdisciplinary presentations would need to effectively explain why racially integrated schools generate positive educational, academic, social, developmental, and race relations benefits. The experts would then need to measure Lynn's success based on a broad array of objective criteria, with test performance serving as only one of many factors. As a result, an effective defense necessitated retaining experts who could systematically study the impact of the Lynn Plan on its school system and its students and who could persuasively establish (if conditions warranted) that by racially diversifying its schools, Lynn achieves concrete, compelling benefits and prevents serious educational and race relations harms.

Legal counsel for Lynn identified experts who could emphasize the rich developmental and social psychological research that explains the positive social and moral development of children and adolescents in integrated schools; how children form and overcome racial and ethnic stereotyping and prejudice; and the conditions that foster or impair positive racial attitudes and behavior among children from different racial and ethnic backgrounds. A social psychologist with expertise in intergroup relations could explain how racially motivated school disruptions and violence would again likely become prevalent in Lynn schools with the return of segregated and racially identifiable schools, with the most significant safety-related effects on Lynn's middle and high schools. A desegregation expert would then explain the well-established harms of segregation, racial isolation, and racially identifiable schools on minority children, and the benefits they receive from school integration, while identifying the more recent desegregation research findings about the beneficial effects of school integration on White children. A housing and racial population change expert would study the segregated residential housing patterns and population change in Lynn and the impact on Lynn schools of terminating the plan. In order to enhance the likelihood of success at trial and on appeal, Lynn's experts were nationally renowned in their respective fields.[13]

To assist the experts, Lynn engaged in a concerted effort to identify, collect, and analyze relevant data the school district and the Massachusetts Department of Education maintained about Lynn's schools, its students, and the history of school conditions before and after the plan's implementation. The relevant data included, but was not limited to: (1) student academic performance as reflected in standardized test scores (including increases in scores over time and a performance comparison to school districts with comparable racial and socioeconomic composition); (2) discipline rates (including by race, by school, by year); (3) attendance rates; (4) private and parochial school attendance rates; (5) rate of racial incidents, and incidents of violence, by school (from Lynn's discipline records, high school peer-mediation records, and school-related incident reports from the Lynn police department); (6) evidence of White flight (rate of population change of Whites with school-aged children residing in Lynn, White and minority birthrates, stability of White enrollment, and rate of change in Whites attending Lynn schools); (7) graduation rates; (8) dropout rates; (9) trends in teacher selection of schools based on seniority; (10) the racial and socioeconomic background of each student and the racial and socioeconomic composition of each school and the district; (11) student participation in special education and bilingual education programs (including by race); (12) statistics about immigrant students by country; (13) simulations determining the consequence of returning to a neighborhood school assignment plan or adopting other race-neutral assignment plans; (14) desegregative school transfers by race; (15) record of segregative school transfer requests by race and by school requested; (16) record of appeals from transfer denials; and (17) record of success of appeals by race.

The experts' task was not simple. They needed to comprehensively assess the current educational and race relations conditions in Lynn schools, compare the current conditions to the conditions before the plan (stark differences in conditions before and after the plan could serve as dramatic proof of integration's benefits), provide social science explanations for changes in the educational and race relations conditions, and determine which improvements were attributable in whole or as a substantial contributing factor to integration, and not solely from race-neutral factors (e.g., curricula changes, physical plant and resource improvements, and increased professional training).

At trial Lynn introduced testimony from ten witnesses, along with Lynn's vast archive of information and data about its school district and its students. Four of Lynn's witnesses were school and district administrators and educators with twenty-six to nearly forty years of experience in the Lynn schools who described the dramatic improvement in Lynn schools because of the plan. The plaintiffs relied on the testimony of one Lynn parent, who was also one of the plaintiffs, and Dr. Christine Rossell, their sole expert witness. For a number of reasons the district court found that Dr. Rossell's testimony was not credible. For example, Dr. Rossell "made no firsthand observation of Lynn's schools and conducted no surveys of Lynn's students, teachers or parents" and "made sweeping conclusions without reviewing demographic or socioeconomic data and without having an accurate understanding of the Plan itself" (*Comfort*, 2003, pp. 359, 382).

Lynn's four experts based their testimony on their systematic study of Lynn's local conditions and the extensive data about Lynn's schools and its students. As part of their examination of the Lynn Plan, Drs. Dovidio and Killen each visited eight elementary, middle, and high schools. The experts had complete control over determining the schools they would visit (while making sure they examined a representative sample of schools at all levels), the parts of each school they would observe, the classes they would attend, and the administrators, teachers, staff, and students they would interview. The defense experts employed a methodology to assess students and school climate that was consistent with peer-reviewed research and publications in leading social science journals, including Dr. Killen's study funded during this same time frame by the National Institutes of Health.[14] The experts also relied on authoritative studies and publications in peer-reviewed journals in their fields of expertise to support their expert opinions (*Comfort,* 2003; *Comfort,* 2005a).

Additionally, Dr. Orfield surveyed the entire class of Lynn juniors in spring 2000, using a seventy-two-question "Diversity Assessment Questionnaire" designed by leading school desegregation experts to determine the success of school desegregation nationwide. Finally, demographics expert Nancy McArdle performed a comprehensive study of demographic and housing trends in Lynn.

What Did the Evidence Show?
Before Its Plan, Lynn Was an Educational System in Crisis

When Lynn first adopted its plan in 1987, its school system was in educational crisis.[15] Beginning in the early 1980s a large number of Hispanic and Asian American families, many of whom were recent immigrants to the United States, moved into Lynn. The district's racial composition changed from 9 percent minority in the late 1970s to 26 percent minority in 1987. As the percentage of minority students increased, they became more racially isolated and segregated, concentrated in four of Lynn's eighteen elementary schools and one middle school. The schools were not prepared to educate large numbers of students from diverse racial and socioeconomic backgrounds.

Lynn's segregated schools were plagued by racial strife and interracial violence between its White and non-White students, with high levels of student self-segregation by race, poor academic performance, low attendance rates, high rates of discipline, and low community confidence in the school system. For example, during the 1987–88 school year, Lynn had attendance rates at 89.3 percent, significantly below the average rate in schools statewide. Lynn experienced an alarming rate of White flight, with White enrollment declining an average 5 percent each year for the ten years preceding the plan (from 1977 to 1987). White families with school-aged children were moving out of the City of Lynn at high rates. Because of educational and school climate issues, White students were opting to leave the school system for private and parochial schools in increasing numbers. In 1987 the percentage of students attending nonpublic schools in Lynn was 17.4 percent.

Compared to Lynn's predominantly White schools, schools with high minority student concentrations had significantly inferior educational conditions, including older and poorly maintained school facilities, over-crowded classes, lower funding and fewer resources, outdated books, high teacher turnover, and less experienced teachers who were not provided the specialized training needed to teach effectively students from racially and linguistically diverse backgrounds. Under rights granted through their union contract, "wherever possible, teachers with seniority—who had priority in choosing new openings—transferred out of minority schools into the identifiably white, wealthier schools, where the school climate was more conducive to learning and teaching" (*Comfort,* 2003, p. 344). Lynn's experience mirrored the fate of many schools with high concentrations of low-income and minority students. As Dr. Orfield explained, in minority identifiable schools almost all the important educational conditions are usually inferior or produce obstacles to providing an adequate education, students are less prepared for success, with much lower graduation and college admission rates. Additionally, minority students risk negative stereotypes from attending minority identifiable schools with lower achievement levels (Orfield Tran.).[16]

Today Lynn Is an Urban School System Thriving

Today, by all measures, Lynn's school system is remarkably successful. In a district with a significantly higher percentage of minority and low-income students than before the plan, Lynn has improved the quality of education for all its students.[17] Lynn has achieved significant educational and academic achievement gains throughout the school system, most particularly for students attending schools in Lynn's urban center. It has improved students' motivation to learn and learning outcomes. Lynn students scored above average on the mandatory, statewide high stakes MCAS (Massachusetts Comprehensive Assessment System) tests, compared to students in other urban school districts.[18] Lynn provides a safe learning environment necessary for Lynn students to achieve positive academic gains. Schools have uniformly high attendance rates and declining suspension rates, with extraordinarily low levels of student conflict, crime, and violence, as documented in school, police, and high school peer-mediation records. Students are much more prepared to succeed in racially diverse colleges and workplaces and live in racially diverse communities. Additionally, Lynn schools have a stable White student enrollment, with a rate of decline averaging less than 1 percent per year from 1987 through 2002, despite declining White birthrates. Further, the share of students attending private and parochial schools was 10 percent in 2001, declining from over 17 percent in 1987. Plaintiffs' expert Dr. Rossell admitted that the low rate of White enrollment decline since the plan's adoption was highly unusual (Rossell Tran.).

Race relations among students are very positive. According to the witnesses, students generally maintain many cross-race friendships and comfortably integrate by race in classroom and informal school settings, such as in the school cafeteria. Throughout the Lynn schools, students from diverse backgrounds are well represented in student government, peer-counseling roles, and extracurricular activities. Lynn has also addressed the facility, resource, and staff inequities existing for minority students before the plan's implementation.

As the district court stated, "Indeed, [plaintiffs] agree that Lynn schools are considerably better . . . than they were before the plan was instituted" (*Comfort,* 2003, p. 376; *Comfort,* 2005a, p. 15). The parties, however, disagree about the cause for the remarkable transformation of Lynn schools.

How to Explain the Transformation of Lynn's Schools?

Lynn transformed its schools by eliminating its students' racial isolation and segregation. Contrary to the experience of Lynn's educators, the parents challenging the plan solely attribute the educational crisis in Lynn schools in the 1980s to the inequitable educational conditions and educational resources and lack of specialized training of teachers in Lynn schools, rather than the racial isolation of Lynn's minority students or to the racial identifiability of its schools. In response, Drs. Dovidio, Killen, and Orfield identified racial isolation, segregation, and racially identifiable schools as the essential factors in generating Lynn's myriad education and race relations problems in the 1980s. In support of their opinions, the experts emphasized that when adopting and implementing its plan, Lynn educators identified racial isolation of its students and its schools as a priority goal to reduce the conflicts and violence between Whites and minorities and to enable Lynn to achieve all of the hoped-for educational improvements.

As Dr. Orfield explained, racial isolation and segregation have "an adverse impact on school attendance and performance [of minority students], with long term consequences" (*Comfort,* 2003, p. 355). He continued, "These effects, [however], can be combated by racial integration"

(*Comfort*, 2005a, p. 14). Additionally, as Dr. Orfield established, "as a result of racial isolation and segregation, [White children] forfeit the opportunity to learn from other groups and are less prepared to handle interracial settings as an adult" (*Comfort*, 2003, pp. 355–356). Drs. Dovidio and Killen further explained that socially, feelings of racial distinctiveness often produce lower performance motivation. They also detailed how racially isolated minority children become highly sensitive to evidence of racism and discrimination and how Lynn's racially isolating school conditions before the plan bred racial hostilities between its White and non-White students. Relationships become characterized by distrust and suspicion. Based on extensive expert testimony, the district court found that because a large number of Lynn's children had few interracial experiences or social relationships, racial distrust and conflict permeated race relations in the schools, particularly in the middle and high schools.

The district court concluded, based on Drs. Dovidio, Killen, and Orfield's testimony, that no amount of facility renovation, resource improvement, programmatic innovation, or professional training would address effectively a child's development of racial stereotypes, fears, and distrust from learning in racially isolated or segregated school environments. Nor would these improvements address the rise of rigid, racially distinct social cliques beginning in the sixth or seventh grade. As Drs. Killen and Dovidio emphasized, race is often the dominant factor in governing who joins which clique, unless students have preexisting interracial relationships. Once students from different racial backgrounds sort themselves into separate cliques, the opportunity to avoid racial polarization and overcome racial stereotyping through cross-racial interaction is lost (*Comfort*, 2003).

Critical to litigation success was providing social science evidence that persuasively established at trial the reasons for the transformation of Lynn's schools. Drs. Dovidio and Killen provided the district court with the framework for understanding how the significant change took place. They presented the "intergroup contact model" and explained that it is the only social science explanation for Lynn's transformed educational and race relations conditions that began with the plan's implementation. They summarized the five decades of developmental and social psychological research, study, and experience that has established the intergroup contact model's validity across cultures and contexts. They explained that it is the fundamental strategy for fostering for both White and minority children important cognitive, social reasoning, citizenship, and race relations benefits. They also described how personal interracial contact enables children to overcome the fear and anxiety that exist around interacting with members of other racial groups (see also generally, Killen, Crystal, & Ruck, this volume).

Further, as Drs. Dovidio and Killen explained, as the years have passed since the plan was first implemented, integration has produced increasingly positive effects. The longer a child experiences intergroup contact in integrated schools, the more likely the child will internalize attitudinal changes. The effects became cumulative, and self-reinforcing, with a multiplying effect. For example, Lynn's graduating classes of 1999 through 2002 received their entire education through the plan, and they reaped the most benefits from the plan.

To transform desegregated (racially diverse) schools into racially integrated learning environments, the intergroup contact model requires educators to satisfy four essential conditions (Aboud & Levy, 2000; Dovidio, Kawakami, & Gaertner, 2000; Pettigrew, 1998; Pettigrew & Tropp, 2000):

1. Authority sanction and supportive norms. The adult authority figures of a school community consistently promote personalized interracial contact and establish supportive norms conveying the value of diversity, a commitment to equality and fairness, and the wrongfulness of exclusion and discrimination.
2. Equal status and egalitarian principles. Equal status is maintained between the different racial and ethnic groups within the schools, without any group dominating, exerting too much influence, or being treated more favorably.
3. Common goals and cooperative learning activities. Common goals and cooperative activities are employed to enable students, who, while recognizing their own racial and ethnic identity, connect to and identify with the larger school community.
4. Promoting personalized intergroup contact. Students are provided frequent opportunities for personal contact with substantial numbers of children from other racial and ethnic groups in a variety of school settings to catalyze positive intergroup relations and disarm stereotypes.

Similarly, the district court emphasized Dr. Orfield's testimony that "the [Harvard] survey's conclusions about the Lynn experience neatly align with the underlying theory of a new area of desegregation research: that benefits accrue to all children, not just minority children, as a result of school integration." Further, as the court stressed, Dr. Orfield cited recent studies that have found that "where integration has been achieved (as it has in Lynn) . . . side-by-side learning with other races confers substantial citizenship benefits on all students." The district court also highlighted Dr. Orfield's testimony that desegregation research has established that if schools implement desegregation with complementary elements, including teacher training, with a positive, supportive atmosphere, both White and minority children obtain "'benefits in the way of thinking, understanding of the society, [and] the ability to function in society,' as well as gains in academic achievement across the board" (*Comfort,* 2003, p. 355). Dr. Orfield explained that integration also opens a full range of middle-class opportunities for minorities, including increased networking, enhanced opportunities for higher education, and improved occupational status and employment opportunities. Further, minorities who attend integrated schools are more likely to live in integrated areas as adults.

At trial Lynn's educators authoritatively described race relations and the educational conditions of its schools before and after the plan and attested to integration's instrumental role in the district's remarkable educational transformation.

Lynn transformed its schools by providing benefits that flow from racial integration. The City of Lynn fully satisfied the four conditions of the intergroup contact model for achieving racial integration. The experts found that Lynn provided the essential ingredient for satisfying the intergroup contact model, that is, sufficient levels of racial diversity in all Lynn schools (the fourth condition of the intergroup contact theory). Based on expert testimony the district court concluded that for intergroup contact to be successful and for the benefits to flow from it, White and minority (African American, Hispanic, and Asian American) students should comprise a "critical mass," or at least 20 percent of a school's student population. Intergroup contact's benefits cannot be achieved with only token numbers of minority and White students in a school. The experts established that the significant benefits from intergroup contact are triggered when Whites and minorities constitute 20 percent or more in a school. It is the "critical mass" that is the essential ingredient in generating "the quality and quantity of interactions, the frequency of interactions that allow all these [intergroup contact] processes to operate" (Dovidio Tran., p. 82).

Lynn attracted both White and minority student transfers to desegregate its schools by creating magnet schools with special educational themes and programs (although Lynn's magnet schools do not offer the type of unique educational programs that magnet schools traditionally provide) and expanding educational themes and programs into its non-magnet schools. It also built extensions to increase classroom space in predominantly White schools to make space available for minority transfers, while constructing new schools and modernizing dilapidated schools and educational facilities. More than one-third of all Lynn students attend a non-neighborhood school under the plan. Lynn received financial assistance from the state that allowed it to improve the condition of its school buildings; to expand the number of available seats in many of its schools through the financing of new school construction; and to develop, maintain, and offer magnet programs, staff, and resources. Lynn also employed certain administrative tools to effectively desegregate its schools, including centralizing student enrollment and assignment procedures, regularly monitoring desegregation progress, and maintaining a parent information center to coordinate and track student assignments and transfers and to perform extensive data collection and analysis.

Lynn satisfied the other conditions of the intergroup contact theory by encouraging interracial contact, promoting educational equity, and instituting comprehensive race-neutral educational changes. Their educators enriched and standardized the curricula used throughout the school system. They organized programs to improve parental involvement and instituted new instructional programs. School administrators implemented rigorous performance evaluation measures for its schools, staff, and students. They provided leadership opportunities and training to provide students the skills necessary to address effectively racial tension and conflict. Lynn's educators also applied cooperative learning techniques and employed innovative strategies to teach a multiracial student body. Lynn expanded professional development and training of administrators, teachers, and staff. It also established solid partnership relationships with area colleges and businesses for academic and programmatic assistance.

The *Comfort* courts found strong and systematic evidence that Lynn transformed its schools into integrated learning environments by satisfying all four conditions of intergroup contact, adopting both race-neutral improvements and its race-conscious transfer policy that desegregated its schools.[19] The plaintiffs did not dispute that Lynn met the first three conditions of intergroup contact.

Lynn satisfied condition 1: Authority sanction and supportive norms. Lynn's leaders adapted the plan to fit the local conditions in their community at that time. Lynn's leaders also wanted to distinguish its plan from the desegregation remedies ordered by the federal court for Boston's schools, which resulted in forced busing and involuntary transfers. Lynn promoted its plan as an effort to improve the overall quality of education and provide equal educational opportunities for all students, while improving race relations. Rather than adopting a controlled choice plan, where involuntary transfers would likely be imposed to prevent school segregation, all transfers were voluntary, with Lynn guaranteeing the right of students to attend their neighborhood schools.

Lynn began desegregating its schools in the late 1980s with little, if any, student, parent, or community resistance or turmoil. Lynn's political and educational leaders convinced the Lynn community to support its comprehensive educational improvement and integration plan. Their public support for the plan demonstrated "authority" approval for the goals of integration and helped prevent either organized community resistance or White flight from its schools (which occurred in other communities, like Boston).

Lynn's policies, rules, mission statement, and norms support principles of equal treatment, fairness, and the wrongfulness of prejudice and discrimination. The signs, posters, and written messages on the walls in hallways and classrooms promote mutual respect and tolerance for others who are different. Curricula and instruction fosters positive intergroup attitudes. Lynn's administrators, teachers, guidance counselors, and staff members consistently encourage students from diverse racial backgrounds to interact together and develop friendships.

Teachers received extensive training to enhance the education of its students from diverse racial and linguistic backgrounds and address feelings of racial isolation and alienation of minority students and students who do not speak English as a primary language. Lynn also implemented a teacher performance evaluation system with ratings on how effectively they teach children from diverse backgrounds. Students said "that [integration] is what they liked about Lynn, and when they contrasted it to other communities around them, they felt that Lynn has a special place in terms of multicultural support, and it being a . . . long-term value of the community. . . . [P]eople felt that this was central to what Lynn is and what their school was" (Dovidio Tran., p. 63).

Student responses to the Harvard survey reflect that classroom discussions have made them much more comfortable in learning about people from other racial and ethnic groups. Over 90 percent of students feel prepared to work in a job setting with people of a different racial or ethnic background. The majority of students also state that their school experiences have increased their commitment to civil rights and to reducing inequality.

Lynn satisfied condition 2: Equal status and egalitarian principles among groups. To foster equal status among racial groups, Lynn's school personnel motivate students from all racial groups to fully participate in all aspects of the school community, do well in school, and show special interest in students regardless of their race. Teachers received extensive training to increase their commitment to and promotion of equal status among students. They were also trained to assign responsibilities and respond to students from different racial and ethnic groups in equitable ways. (In circumstances where the status of one group is actually or perceived to be higher than another, children interact in ways that confirm stereotypes and perpetuate biases.) Students from all racial groups are encouraged to participate in classroom discussions, take advanced placement courses, and attend college. Teachers consistently show warmth to and positive physical contact with all students, regardless of their race.

School administrators make conscious efforts to promote equal status and prevent the rise of racial cliques. For example, one Lynn high school maintains rotating lunch schedules, preventing students from sitting with the same students each day. Shifting high school student lunch schedules serves to foster development of important social skills and a sense of independence in students. It compels them to learn how to meet, identify common interests, and socialize with students whom they do not know from various racial and ethnic backgrounds and learn how to enter and become part of a group that is already established. Other schools redesigned their lunch cafeterias to promote more interracial communication by using round lunch tables and by preventing use of chairs at the head or foot of their large rectangular lunch tables.

When students interact at recess, children play without observed hierarchies differentiated by race. Students play together and take leadership roles equally. Teachers encourage students to exchange roles in sports activities. Participation in school activities and student leadership positions are quite mixed racially. Throughout Lynn's schools, students from diverse racial backgrounds are well represented in student government positions, peer counseling roles, and in extracurricular activities. Further, school sports teams reflect the same diversity.

Lynn's disciplinary records show that discipline imposed during the three-year period prior to trial was applied equally. That is, the rates of suspensions for White, African American, Hispanic, and Asian students are consistent with their percentage of the student population during those three years.

Data from the Harvard survey of Lynn's eleventh-grade students reflect that students from all racial groups perceive that they maintain equal status within Lynn's schools. Lynn students have equivalent aspirations and expectations about what they could achieve while attending Lynn's schools and after graduation. In addition, consistently across racial groups students believe if they try hard they can do well in school. The students themselves report that they are being treated fairly by teachers and administrators.

Lynn satisfied condition 3: Common goals and cooperative learning activities. To promote common goals and cooperative activities, Lynn teachers adopt strategies encouraging team learning and cultivating student interdependence. They organize classroom activities and after-school projects and assignments to foster positive interracial relationships.

For example, school administrators at Ingalls Elementary School organized a two-way bilingual education program for grades K–4. The children who spoke primarily Spanish had tended to segregate themselves, and the two-way language program was effective in getting all the children to interact and develop interracial friendships. Cooperative learning activities diminish ingroup and outgroup differences, foster cross-race friendships, and reduce prejudice by promoting interdependence among children, for they must interact, exchange ideas, and rely upon each other to complete their joint assignments and projects successfully (see also Hawley, this volume).

To foster collective identity and cooperative interdependence, some Lynn schools divide faculty and students into learning "clusters," sharing several classes and teachers together, in ways that make them racially and ethnically heterogeneous. The cluster memberships "cross-cut" racial and ethnic group members, a strategy that has been shown to improve intergroup relations.

The Harvard survey data of the eleventh-grade students reflect the success of cooperative learning strategies in Lynn schools. The majority of student respondents in all racial groups reported that teachers encourage them to work with students of other racial and ethnic backgrounds, and substantial portions of these students indicated that they worked on school projects or studies with students from other racial groups at least once or twice a month.

Lynn satisfied condition 4: Promoting personalized intergroup contact. Combined with the application of policies and practices that promote personalized interracial contact and friendships, Lynn satisfied the intergroup contact model's requirement that its students interact with a critical mass of children from diverse racial backgrounds in a variety of settings for sustained periods.[20]

In every possible school setting students interact on a personal and friendly basis with students from other racial backgrounds. Even in informal settings—in the cafeteria, in the gymnasium, in the hallways between classes, and outside the school where students walk to and from school—students regularly interact with members of other racial groups. Racial cliques are not evident, and students appear to comfortably join established groups in both formal and informal settings.

Students reported having friends through school who were members of other racial and ethnic groups, having often visited these friends' homes, and feeling free to date members of other racial and ethnic groups. When a dispute or fight arose between a minority and a White student, they viewed it as an interpersonal dispute and not as an interracial conflict. In classes students from different racial and ethnic groups were observed by defense experts sitting and working well together. In describing his observations, Dr. Dovidio stated: "So the schools have really established a relationship where people are interacting at a very personal level, often at an intimate level in a way that is, I found, profound and in a way that I didn't expect, in a way that I really wasn't prepared to encounter" (Dovidio Tran., p. 67).

Legal Conclusions of the Federal Courts in *Comfort*

Lynn Has a Compelling Interest in Racial Integration and Preventing Racial Isolation

The district court concluded that the benefits that flow from Lynn achieving racially integrated schools and avoiding racial isolation and segregated schools through its plan are compelling interests (*Comfort*, 2003). In affirming the district court's legal conclusions, the First Circuit Court of Appeals found that the interests Lynn advances in this K–12 educational context "bear a strong familial resemblance" to many of the educational interests the *Grutter* Court found compelling for higher education (*Comfort*, 2005a, pp. 14–17). The Court in *Grutter* cited findings that "the Law School's admissions policy promotes cross-racial understanding, helps to break down racial stereotypes, and enables [students] to better understand persons of different races" (*Grutter*, 2003, p. 330). The *Grutter* Court further relied on the "numerous studies show[ing] that student body diversity promotes learning outcomes and better prepares students for an increasingly diverse workforce and society, and better prepares them as professionals" (*Grutter*, 2003, p. 333, internal citations omitted).

The First Circuit also found that the benefits that flow from the racial integration of Lynn's schools are distinct from those in higher education and are even more compelling in the K–12 educational context, summarizing expert testimony that established that, "It is more difficult to teach racial tolerance to college-age students; the time to do it is when the students are still young, before they are locked into racialized thinking" (*Comfort*, 2005a, p. 16). The court also emphasized the evidence Lynn presented establishing the "positive impact of racial diversity on student safety and attendance," which are important and distinctly different educational interests from those that institutions of higher education advance for promoting racial diversity (*Comfort*, 2005a, p. 16). Moreover, the court recognized Lynn's compelling interests in preventing racial isolation and segregation, because they adversely affect the school attendance and academic performance of minority students, and found that "these effects can be combated by racial integration" (*Comfort*, 2005a, p. 14). The First Circuit concluded that the Lynn Plan not only improved educational opportunities for all students but also generated "higher attendance rates, declining suspension rates, a safer environment, and improved standardized test scores—since the Plan's inception" (*Comfort*, 2005a, p. 14).

The Lynn Plan Is Narrowly Tailored to Achieve Its Compelling Governmental Interests

In light of the Supreme Court's *Grutter* decision recognizing the benefits of diversity in education, school districts are in a much more favorable legal position in establishing their compelling interest in promoting integration through a race-conscious student assignment or transfer plan. A district's ability to successfully defend against a constitutional challenge, however, will often turn on whether a desegregation plan also satisfies the rigorous requirements of narrow tailoring as applied by the First Circuit in *Comfort*. To prevent legal challenges and to succeed if subject to litigation, school districts with race-conscious plans should, therefore, carefully evaluate whether they have satisfied each narrow tailoring requirement and take immediate steps to address any identified deficiency. Below is a review of these requirements and how in practice Lynn met its legal burden under narrow tailoring.

Does the Lynn Plan Use Race Too Much?

The social science evidence established that to achieve the benefits of integration the racial composition of schools matters. In accordance with *Grutter*, Lynn's integration efforts would constitute unconstitutional racial balancing, however, if race was used merely to attain proportional racial representation for its own sake, and not for achieving the educational benefits the specific levels of racial diversity its plan is designed to produce (*Grutter,* 2003, pp. 335–336).

First, Lynn demonstrated the need for a critical mass of White and minority students in each of its schools to catalyze the positive benefits from integration. For example, in schools with more equal representation of Whites and non-Whites, children with nascent racial stereotypes are unlikely to continue to view members of other racial groups as all alike; they will no longer assume that when children from another racial group think or act in a way different from a stereotype they are merely an exception, or when a child exhibits behaviors consistent with a stereotype, they no longer will use it to confirm or strengthen their stereotype (Dovidio, Tran.; Killen Tran.).

Second, Lynn established the educational benefits that accrue from maximizing racial integration. As Drs. Killen and Dovidio explained, and the district court found, the developmental and social psychological research has established that the significant benefits of intergroup contact accrue along a continuum, beginning as school districts attain critical mass or 20 percent of Whites and non-Whites in its schools. The benefits then increase as the percentage of Whites and non-Whites in schools move closer to 50 percent. Establishing critical mass is only the beginning, for as racial diversity increases (as a school moves closer to racial balance), students experience a linear increase in benefits. More racial diversity leads to increased racial harmony and understanding and reduced racial stereotypes and tension (*Comfort,* 2003; *Comfort,* 2005a; Dovidio Tran.; Killen Tran.).

Third, school districts should maximize racial integration to avoid the damaging effects of racially identifiable schools.[21] Lynn's strong interest in preventing racially identifiable schools arose from its experiences in the 1980s. In 1987, when the plan was first adopted, four of its elementary schools were minority identifiable, with minorities constituting 50 percent to 55 percent of the student population, while four other elementary schools had at least a 95 percent White student population, and three more were about 90 percent White. Students attending the four elementary schools that were racially balanced (50 percent to 55 percent minority) should have experienced the benefits of integration (assuming the other necessary conditions of intergroup contact were present). Instead, because these four schools were minority identifiable in the context of the racial composition of the Lynn community and Lynn's racially changing neighborhoods and schools, the minority students felt isolated, ignored, and excluded. These schools experienced high levels of racial tension and conflict (*Comfort,* 2003; Orfield Tran.; Dovidio Tran.).[22]

Lynn's ability to prevent schools from deviating too much from the school district population's overall racial composition, however, is constrained by the plan's voluntary nature. Lynn's percentage ranges are, in effect, aspirational. Lynn does not use "coercive assignments or forced busing" when its schools, as they inevitably have, fall outside its plus or minus 10 percent and 15 percent ranges (*Comfort*, 2003, pp. 334–335). Nevertheless, Lynn's flexible ranges enable it to identify and deny segregative transfer requests to maximize integration, while preventing segregation, racial isolation, and racially identifiable schools as existed before the plan.

Does the Lynn Plan Unduly Burden Third Parties?

The First Circuit concluded that the Lynn Plan minimally burdens third parties because it does not involve evaluating a student's qualifications or merit or loss of a significant benefit, such as admission to a unique or selective educational institution. Rather, the plan involves the grant of a noncompetitive transfer request to an educationally comparable school. The plan does not govern initial student assignments, and students may always attend their neighborhood schools. When Lynn denies transfers, it offers alternative assignments that parents generally accept. A parent may appeal a denial of a transfer request, and when reviewing appeals, Lynn employs flexible standards. Relatively few appeals are filed and roughly 50 percent of appeals are successful (*Comfort*, 2003; *Comfort*, 2005a).

Do Social Science Research and the Local Conditions in Lynn Support Lynn's White and Non-White Racial Classifications under Its Student Assignment Plan?

As part of their attack on the plan, plaintiffs challenged Lynn's use of only two racial classifications in the Lynn Plan, White and non-White, rather than employing classifications that recognize the existence of the many subgroups within each racial category. The Lynn Plan defines minority or non-White as a student who is African American, Asian, Hispanic, or Native American. The courts in *Comfort* concluded, however, that the two racial categories are narrowly tailored to address the precise issues present in Lynn schools (*Comfort*, 2003; *Comfort*, 2005a).[23] In *Grutter* the Court found similar White and non-White categories in the University of Michigan Law School's admission program constitutional (*Grutter*, 2003, pp. 324, 333–335).

Before the plan's implementation, an intergroup relations crisis existed in Lynn between White and minority students but not between students from different minority groups or subgroups or from different national origins.[24] Further, the plan's use of its White and non-White categories is consistent with developmental and social psychological research, which has found substantial similarities in how African Americans, Latinos, and Asians experience segregation, racial isolation, and racial and ethnic exclusion, as compared to Whites. Additionally, for a child who is a minority, the presence of children from other racial minority groups other than their own reduces the impact of stigmatization and feelings of racial isolation and distinctiveness (*Comfort*, 2003; Killen Tran.; Dovidio Tran.).

Has Lynn Made Good Faith Efforts to Consider Feasible Race-Neutral Alternatives to Lynn's Race-Conscious Plan?

Lynn's administrators carefully examined race-neutral alternatives and determined that no workable or feasible alternative exists for Lynn to achieve the plan's compelling goals without the race-conscious means it currently employs and without sacrificing its neighborhood-based school system and other important educational and practical objectives.[25] The First Circuit concluded that Lynn met its legal burden here, for it "seriously considered, and plausibly rejected, a number of race-neutral alternatives" (*Comfort*, 2005a, p. 22). Lynn examined the viability of (1) a strict neighborhood-based assignment plan without transfers, (2) a freedom of choice assignment plan, (3) a lottery-based assignment system, (4) a district assignment plan with magnets, (5) a socioeconomic-based assignment system, (6) a controlled choice plan (which may require involuntary transfers), and (7) redrawing school attendance zones (*Comfort*, 2005a; *Comfort*, 2003).

The *Comfort* courts determined that none of these race-neutral alternatives are feasible because of the segregative housing patterns in Lynn and the wide geographic separation between the predominantly White and minority sections of Lynn, combined with the persistent pattern of segregative school requests by Lynn parents (*Comfort*, 2005a; *Comfort*, 2003).

Some alternatives, such as a lottery-based assignment system or redrawing attendance zones, would sacrifice Lynn's neighborhood-based school system, disregarding the wishes of many Lynn parents who want their children educated in their neighborhood school or requiring students to travel long distances to attend so-called neighborhood schools located far away from their neighborhood (*Comfort*, 2003). Further, if Lynn implemented any race-neutral alternative, its minority children would be adversely affected. According to simulations, because of Lynn's housing patterns, regardless of the alternative adopted, schools located in Lynn's densely populated urban center would become overcrowded, unfairly placing the burden of school transfers, mostly involuntary, on the minority children who reside in these school attendance zones.

As the district court found, without its plan Lynn schools would resegregate, and racial segregation would intensify. Indeed, because of patterns of residential housing segregation and other local conditions, without its plan Lynn's schools would become highly segregated. Moreover, given the current poverty levels in Lynn's minority community, without the plan housing segregation in Lynn would accelerate and the schools would become increasingly racially segregated, "with a host of pernicious consequences" (*Comfort*, 2003, p. 334). It is probable that racially motivated school disruptions and violence would again become prevalent in Lynn schools, with the most significant safety-related effects on the middle and high schools. Without safe schools, academic gains for both Whites and minority students would be lost, and racial stereotypes and conflicts would reemerge as significant barriers to learning. Moreover, the adverse effects of terminating the Lynn Plan would likely have cumulative, cascading effects over time (Dovidio Tran.; Killen Tran.; *Comfort*, 2003).

Plaintiffs argued, however, that Lynn did not consider several viable alternatives and therefore failed to satisfy narrow tailoring. They pointed to the City of Boston's recently (2000–2001) implemented race-neutral assignment plan as an option. No evidence was presented, however, that Boston's race-neutral assignment plan would achieve integration about as well, as *Grutter* requires, or that housing patterns or other local conditions in Boston and Lynn are sufficiently similar for Lynn to adopt Boston's plan while maintaining integration. As the First Circuit held, although "Lynn must keep abreast of possible alternatives as they develop . . . it need not prove the impracticability of every conceivable model for racial integration. It is sufficient that it demonstrate a good faith effort to consider feasible race-neutral alternatives, as it has done here" (*Comfort*, 2005a, p. 23; see also *Grutter*, 2003, pp. 339, 342–343).

Does Lynn Employ Mechanisms to Enable It to Determine Whether Changes in Conditions Should Limit or Eliminate Its Use of Race in School Transfer Decisions?

Lynn satisfies the narrow tailoring requirement that a plan "be limited not only in scope, but also in time" by performing "periodic reviews to determine whether racial preferences are still necessary to student body diversity" (*Comfort*, 2005a, 22; quoting *Grutter*, 2003). Lynn regularly reviews the extensive data collected about every component of the plan's operation, its schools, and its students and regularly analyzes its extensive data to determine the effect of terminating the plan on school integration. Lynn updates and modifies its policies to address changing conditions. Lynn also applies a built-in mechanism for limiting or ending its use of race, resulting, for example, in the plan's restrictions not applying to Lynn's high schools since 1992. Moreover, although it has not set a specific termination date, Lynn will limit the plan's duration, as events warrant, which is demonstrated by Lynn's record of reducing its use of race-conscious components (*Comfort*, 2005a).[26]

Does *Grutter*'s Individualized Assessment Requirement for Competitive, Race-Preferential Higher Education Admissions Apply to Lynn's Race-Conscious School Transfer Decisions?

The Supreme Court in *Grutter* and *Gratz* held that narrow tailoring mandates that competitive higher education admissions programs must individually assess the background characteristics and qualifications of candidates, where race serves as a "plus" factor (*Grutter,* 2003, p. 336; *Gratz,* 2003, pp. 270–274). The First Circuit held, however, that "if a non-competitive voluntary student transfer policy is otherwise narrowly tailored, individualized consideration of each student is unnecessary," stating that "the concerns motivating the individualized consideration requirement in a competitive, race-preferential admissions context that focuses on diversity along a number of axes (e.g., the *Gratz* and *Grutter* policies) are simply not present in a non-competitive K–12 transfer policy aimed at racial diversity" (*Comfort,* 2005a, pp. 32–34).[27] The First Circuit concluded that the interests at stake in *Comfort* are quite different from those in *Grutter* or *Gratz.* Lynn's interests are, quite simply, to achieve racial integration (to realize its benefits) and avoid racial isolation and segregation (and their adverse consequences) (see also *Comfort,* 2003). This case is also distinguishable from affirmative action cases involving competitive admissions or distribution of a limited benefit—including noneducation cases—where some form of preferential treatment of non-Whites, some might argue, may reinforce the stereotype that non-Whites cannot compete with Whites on the basis of merit or that they need special governmental assistance to succeed (*Comfort,* 2005a; *Comfort,* 2003; *Grutter,* 2003, p. 317). Instead, the Lynn Plan, "by reducing racial isolation and increasing intergroup contact," has "ameliorated racial and ethnic tension and bred interracial tolerance" (*Comfort,* 2005a, p. 19).[28]

Lynn's use of race does not reinforce racial stereotypes or heighten the risk of bringing attention to racial differences among students. To the contrary, students' racial differences must be recognized and confronted to increase racial understanding and overcome racial divisions. As the district court recognized in highlighting Dr. Dovidio's testimony, "Race is the elephant in the room that does not go away until it is confronted" (*Comfort*, 2003, p. 378). Lynn's use of race "is not a form of stereotyping, but a method to prevent the formation of stereotypes" (*Comfort,* 2003, p. 379, citing *Comfort,* 2000).

Barring Lynn from using race as a decisive factor when making its school transfer decisions would have had the practical effect of precluding the use of the only means at its disposal to achieve integration and its benefits, that is, denial of segregative transfers. Consideration of other background characteristics apart from race, such as socioeconomic status, whether a child is a recent immigrant to this country, or from a single parent home, will not enable Lynn to prevent racial isolation and segregation.

Lynn's individualized review of transfer requests is, moreover, consistent with *Grutter* and appropriate for this educational context and the interests Lynn advances. Lynn takes into account individualized, race-neutral factors, including a student's place of residence, school attendance zones, a sibling's school assignment, whether a "neutral transfer" applies, class size, space availability, and the student's language or special education needs before race is taken into account in transfer decisions (*Comfort*, 2003).

Conclusion

The Supreme Court in *Grutter,* in declaring constitutional the University of Michigan Law School's affirmative action admissions program, recognized that race matters in educating students in schools of higher education. But we would continue to forfeit much of integration's benefits if we fail to provide integrated learning experiences in K–12 schools, before Whites and minorities develop entrenched stereotypes, racial fears, and distrust. Developmental psychological research demonstrates that racial stereotypes, once established, are quite difficult to dislodge. And racial stereotypes spur the development of attitudes and behavior that can permeate not only our schools but our workplaces, our neighborhoods, and our communities.

Recent studies reveal that Americans of different races often live separately from one another and that children from different races rarely have sustained, meaningful contact with one another (Logan et al., 2001). They often reside in different neighborhoods and communities and largely attend separate elementary and secondary schools. Most incoming college students rarely have had significant experiences across racial lines (Frank-enberg, C. Lee, & G. Orfield, 2003).

As the chief judge of the First Circuit recognized, "The goal of the Lynn plan . . . is not unlawful; the attack is upon the means." The chief judge continued,

> Yet given the goal, it is not easy to see how it can be achieved in a commu-nity like Lynn without using race as a touchstone. The problem is that in Lynn, as in many other cities, minorities and whites often live in different neighborhoods. Lynn's aim is to preserve local schools as an option without having the housing pattern of *de facto* segregation projected into the school system. (C. J. Boudin, concurring opinion, *Comfort*, 2005a, pp. 28–29)

Finding unconstitutional voluntary, race-conscious efforts at school in-tegration would, in essence, reject the import and continued relevance of *Brown v. Board of Education* to the twenty-first century. As the district court stated in *Comfort:*

> To say that school officials in the K–12 grades, acting in good faith, can-not take steps to remedy the extraordinary problems of *de facto* segrega-tion and promote multiracial learning, is to go further than ever before to disappoint the promise of *Brown*. It is to admit that in 2003, resegregation of the schools is a tolerable result, as if the only problems *Brown* addressed were bad people and not bad impacts. Nothing in the case law requires that result. (2003, p. 391)

The evidence from Lynn, Massachusetts—and other districts that have pursued similar, voluntary race-conscious assignment or school transfer policies—demonstrates that successfully integrating our children in our schools beginning at the youngest ages is not some outdated, ill-conceived notion, but a practical necessity if we are to successfully prepare the next generations of children for work and life in our increasingly diverse com-munities, country, and world. Indeed, we need to recognize the essential role of integration in educating our children, instilling values essential for maintaining the social fabric of our country and ensuring full participa-tion in our democratic system.

Notes

The views expressed in this essay are solely those of the author and do not neces-sarily reflect the views of the Attorney General or the Office of the Attorney Gen-eral of Massachusetts. The author wishes to thank David Beck, Assistant Attorney

General and Deputy Chief of the Public Protection Bureau, for his assistance in editing this essay.

1. On September 5, 2003, the federal district court issued its opinion holding that Lynn's race-conscious school transfer policy was constitutional (*Comfort,* 2003). On June 16, 2005, the First Circuit Court of Appeals, sitting en banc, affirmed the district court's judgment by a three to two majority, concluding that the plan meets constitutional requirements (*Comfort,* 2005a). The First Circuit is the first federal appeals court to uphold a K–12 school district's voluntary integration plan; two other circuit courts have since upheld other voluntary integration plans.

2. Whenever this essay discusses Lynn's defense at the trial or appellate levels, it means all Lynn and state defendants, who adopted a joint defense, with the Commonwealth's attorneys serving as lead trial and appellate counsel.

3. The discussion below relies on the testimony of expert witnesses and Lynn's educators at trial, trial stipulations, the results from the Harvard survey of Lynn students, and trial exhibits. (See Kurlaender & Yun, 2002, for more on the Harvard survey.) Due to space constraints, however, specific citations to the trial transcript or record are generally not included. (References to "expert testimony" at trial are designated as, for example, "Dovidio Tran.") The parties agreed to extensive stipulations of fact in lieu of proving these facts through testimony of many additional fact witnesses and introducing many more trial exhibits, which would have extended the trial by weeks or months.

4. In a case involving high school assignments only, the federal district court in *Parents Involved in Community Schools v. Seattle School District No. 1* (2001) relied on affidavits rather than a trial in finding constitutional the City of Seattle's voluntary school desegregation plan. The en banc Ninth Circuit upheld the constitutionality of Seattle's plan (*Parents Involved,* 2005). After trial, the federal district court in *McFarland v. Jefferson County Public Schools* (2004) found the City of Louisville's K–12 voluntary desegregation plan constitutional; a Sixth Circuit Court of Appeals panel upheld the district court's decision (*McFarland,* 2005). On June 5, 2006, the U.S. Supreme Court agreed to review the constitutionality of the voluntary integration plans used by the Seattle, Washington, and the Louisville, Kentucky, school systems (see *Community Schools v. Seattle District No. 1* [2001], and *Meredith v. Jefferson County Board of Education* [2006]). When this book went to press, these cases were pending before the Supreme Court, and it is anticipated that the Court will issue a decision in the cases in spring 2007.

5. The Massachusetts legislature enacted the RIA in 1965. As originally enacted, the RIA gave the Massachusetts Board of Education power to order the integration of public schools. In 1974 the legislature amended the RIA to encourage school districts to adopt desegregation plans voluntarily in exchange for increased education funding (Massachusetts General Laws [M.G.L.] c. 15, § 1I), including funds for magnet schools and programs, parent information centers, certain transportation costs, and 90 percent reimbursement for school building renovation and construction to reduce racial imbalance (see M.G.L. c. 71, §§ 37I and 37J; *Comfort,* 2003).

6. *Grutter* recognized that race still matters in educating students. "Just as growing up in a particular region or having particular professional experiences is likely to affect an individual's views, so too is one's own, unique experience of being a racial minority in a society, like our own, in which race unfortunately still matters" (*Grutter*, 2003, p. 335).

7. On September 14, 2005, counsel for plaintiffs filed a petition with the U.S. Supreme Court requesting that it allow an appeal (certiorari) from the First Circuit's en banc decision. On November 4, 2005, the Lynn and state defendants filed an opposition to the Petition for a Writ of Certiorari. On December 5, 2005, the U.S. Supreme Court rejected plaintiffs' request to review the constitutionality of the Lynn Plan (*Comfort*, 2005b). On June 9, 2006, the Lynn plaintiffs asked the Supreme Court to reopen the Lynn case after it granted requests to review the lower court decisions in the Seattle, Washington, and Louisville, Kentucky, school cases. On July 31, 2006, the Supreme Court denied plaintiffs' request for it to reconsider its refusal to hear the Lynn case.

8. In 1974 the federal district court found that the Boston School Committee maintained an unconstitutional, racially segregated public school system (*Morgan v. Hennigan*, 1974).

9. Lynn argued in *Comfort* that the plan required only intermediate level scrutiny to determine its constitutionality because Lynn's school transfer decisions do not involve a competitive process based on merit or the distribution of limited benefits or resources. Lynn, however, exercising caution, planned their defense based on the courts' likely examination of the plan under the strict scrutiny standard. Intermediate scrutiny would only require Lynn to show that the means chosen by the Lynn Plan are substantially related to serving "important government objectives" (citations omitted) (*United States v. Virginia*, 1996, p. 533). The First Circuit concluded that intermediate review was foreclosed by a recent Supreme Court decision (*Comfort*, 2005a, citing *Johnson v. California*, 2005).

10. In the original *Comfort* complaint, neither the Commonwealth of Massachusetts nor any state official was named a party defendant. A few months after the case was filed, however, the Commonwealth, through its Attorney General, decided to intervene to defend the constitutionality of the state's RIA. The intervention decision was made months after the City of Boston decided to eliminate race as a factor in its school assignments, following a legal challenge to Boston's student assignment plan by the same group of lawyers who filed the *Lynn* case and who, after Boston's response, had publicly declared their intent to challenge the constitutionality of voluntary desegregation plans in other Massachusetts communities. Although the district court dismissed most of the *Comfort* case in 2001, the constitutionality of the RIA and the Lynn Plan was challenged again by parents of six other Lynn schoolchildren in a new action, *Bollen v. Lynn School Committee*. The Court then consolidated for trial the remaining parts of the *Comfort* action with the *Bollen* case. The later filed *Bollen* complaint named members of the Massachusetts Board of Education as defendants, requiring, under state law, the Office of the Attorney General to serve as their legal counsel.

11. The panel held that the Lynn Plan was not narrowly tailored because of (1) its "mechanical use of race"; (2) because it took into account the race of students more than necessary to obtain a critical mass of 20 percent White and non-White students in each of its schools (which it incorrectly asserted was Lynn's integration goal); (3) "the failure fully to explore the feasibility of race-neutral alternatives [consistent with the need for only a 20 percent representation of Whites and non-Whites in each school]; and (4) the absence of a commitment to periodic review" (*Comfort,* 2004a, pp. 47–48).

12. The First Circuit's opinion was joined by two appellate judges, with the chief judge writing a concurring opinion. The two dissenting judges were members of the original three-judge *Comfort* panel. (One member of the three-judge panel was a visiting appellate court judge sitting by designation.)

13. Lynn's experts were Dr. John F. Dovidio, a nationally prominent educational and social psychologist with a specialty in intergroup and interracial relations; Dr. Melanie Killen, a developmental and education psychologist and one of the leading national experts on how racial integration and racial segregation influence the social and moral development of children and adolescents; Dr. Gary Orfield, a political scientist and a nationally renowned expert in education, desegregation, and educational equity; and Nancy McArdle, a well-recognized expert on demographic and housing trends.

14. The observational methodology Dr. Killen employed when viewing schools included a detailed analysis of children's interactions; their discourse styles, including the way they speak to one another; their facial expressions, emotional displays; and their nonverbal and verbal behavior (Killen Tran.).

15. Unless otherwise indicated, the discussion in this section is drawn primarily from the district court and the en banc First Circuit decisions (e.g., *Comfort,* 2003; *Comfort,* 2005a).

16. As used in *Comfort,* a "racially identifiable school" in a racially diverse school district is either predominantly White or has a concentration of non-Whites that is highly unrepresentative of the district's overall racial composition (a "minority identifiable school").

17. Minorities constituted 58 percent of the overall student population in the 2001–2 school year, compared to only 26 percent in the 1987–88 school year; and 65 percent of its students' families lived at or near the poverty level in the 2001–2 school year, compared to approximately 30 percent to 35 percent in the 1987–88 school year.

18. Dr. Rossell, plaintiffs' expert, concurred: "When there are academic gains from desegregating, it appears that the gains come for both minority and White students" (Rossell Tran., p. 149).

19. The evidence the *Comfort* courts relied on to determine that Lynn had satisfied the four conditions—and the evidence that will be used in the following discussion of the four conditions except where noted—was the testimony of the experts (Dovidio Tran.; Killen Tran.; McArdle Tran.; Orfield Tran.) and Lynn's educators, the stipulations agreed to, and the Harvard survey (Kurlaender & Yun, 2002).

20. A few Lynn schools have not invariably maintained a critical mass at all times, but students for all or the most substantial parts of their education attend schools with a critical mass. As Lynn's experts established, however, in these circumstances students do not forfeit the long-term educational and race relations gains of integration when they then attend a school with a relatively short-term or marginal deviation from critical mass (*Comfort*, 2003; *Comfort*, 2005a).

21. Federal courts, educators, and social scientists throughout the United States adopt similar percentage ranges that Lynn applies (plus or minus 10 percent or 15 percent), to minimize the number of racially identifiable schools and to promote effective desegregation (see Orfield, Tran., *Comfort*, 2003, pp. 386–387, citing *Belk*, 2001, p. 319; see also *Morgan*, 1987, p. 320 ["We decline to decide whether 80 percent or 90 percent is a better gauge of racial identifiability in the Boston schools"]).

22. Neither the authority sanction nor the equal status conditions of the intergroup contact model are satisfied when school districts maintain racially identifiable schools. The failure to meet two of the four essential conditions of intergroup contact explains why a racially identifiable school does not generate the anticipated benefits from a racially diverse school (Dovidio, Tran.; Killen, Tran.).

23. Even if White immigrant students from Europe attended Lynn schools in large numbers (rather than approximately 1 percent of the district's student population), social science supports Lynn's decision to treat them as White under its plan. Once a White immigrant student learns the language and the culture, they assimilate in ways different from Blacks, Latinos, and Asians, "because they don't have the visual distinctiveness to go along with it" (Dovidio Tran., pp. 147–148; *Comfort*, 2003, pp. 379–380; see also Killen Tran.).

24. Nevertheless, based on a district's history, intergroup relations dynamics, the population size of racial groups, and other local factors, a school district may determine that to meet its educational goals it is necessary to maintain a critical mass of each minority group—African American, Asian American, and Hispanic—in each school and therefore treat them separately under its student assignment plan.

25. In adopting alternatives, the law school need not "effectively sacrifice all other educational values" or "a vital component of its educational mission" (*Grutter*, 2003, p. 340).

26. This is "tak[ing] Law School at its word that it . . . 'will terminate its race-conscious admissions program as soon as practicable'" (*Grutter*, 2003, p. 342).

27. The two dissenting judges maintain that the Lynn Plan is not narrowly tailored because of Lynn's inflexible use of race. The dissent maintained that a student suffers harm when Lynn denies transfers "for the *sole* or determinative reason of race—an immutable condition that a student cannot change" (*Comfort*, 2005a, pp. 65–66).

28. In support of its conclusion, the First Circuit cited to the recent decision in *Johnson v. California* (2005, p. 1147), involving a state prison policy that required the racial segregation of new prisoners, where the Supreme Court, in holding the

prison policy unconstitutional, explained that "by insisting that inmates be housed only with other inmates of the same race, it is possible that prison officials will breed further hostility among prisoners and reinforce racial and ethnic divisions," while recognizing that "racial integration . . . tends to diffuse racial tensions and thus diminish interracial violence (*Comfort*, 2005a, pp. 18–19).

Future Directions

The Common Schools Democracy Requires
Expanding Membership through Inclusive Education

john a. powell and Rebecca High

Today our society faces a future of sweeping changes and increasing interconnectedness both domestically and globally. No longer insulated, we cannot be isolated from developments in the wider world; economic, demographic, physical, and political changes demonstrate that the ability to build cross-cultural understanding is now a crucial survival skill. A strong system of integrated public schools is our best hope for increasing understanding among the people of our diverse nation as well as the best protector of our common dream—shared around the globe—of a society with liberty and equality for all.

The U.S. Supreme Court declared in 2003 that "effective participation by members of all racial and ethnic groups in the civic life of our Nation is essential if the dream of one Nation, indivisible, is to be realized" (*Grutter v. Bollinger*, p. 332). The importance of effective participation by all groups means that an education that prepares every child for democratic life is "pivotal to 'sustaining our political and cultural heritage' with a fundamental role in maintaining the fabric of society" (*Grutter*, pp. 331–332). The democratic process requires that society accept its fundamental responsibility for public education. Indeed, the *Brown v. Board of Education of Topeka* decision recognized in 1954 that "education is the very foundation of good citizenship" and that "where the state has undertaken to provide it, is a right which must be made available to all on equal terms" (*Brown*, p. 493). Yet even today this foundation of democratic life remains far from secure, and the right to education remains contested.

Schools cannot make the dream of full citizenship for all a reality in isolation from each other or from the larger society, but a backward-looking, fragmented, and exclusive education system surely will not serve. To fulfill the critical role of enabling effective participation, schools must be accessible to and inclusive of students from all walks of life. If democracy is to flourish in the years ahead, schools must offer a model of universal membership.

The issue of full membership and effective participation, the defining of who is able to shape the nation's laws and institutions, was passionately debated at the framing of the new government and pointedly asked again in *Dred Scott* (1857), which questioned whether free Blacks or slaves could be considered part of the community. After the abolition of slavery it was contested under Jim Crow segregation and in *Plessy v. Ferguson,* wherein the Supreme Court opined that if segregation stamped the excluded with a badge of inferiority, this was "solely because the colored race chooses to put that construction upon it" (*Plessy,* 1896, p. 551). In 1954 a unanimous Supreme Court overturned *Plessy* and insisted that America's strength depended on a united system of public schools that build membership for all. Today, however, the questioning continues in the contexts of national origin, religion, and immigration status as well as race, and the nation's schools are more segregated than they have been in more than thirty years (G. Orfield, 2005).

Progress toward the ideal of full participation has been made since the founding of the republic, but the struggle for and achievement of equality is often met with new, more subtle forms of disenfranchisement, in which even though membership is extended, the meaning is lost or changed and new members are left to negotiate restricted and narrowed institutions and arrangements. Education is an example of this problem. Education was held out as the best, if not only, hope for African Americans liberated essentially property-less into a struggle for full citizenship in the society they had helped to build (McAfee, 1998; Morris, 1981). But this hope was betrayed by the institution of separate schooling, which guaranteed that Black students would be kept distinct from Whites as a class and race (e.g., Margo, 1990; Anderson, 1988). Successful negotiations for this institutionalization of a racial caste system in the public schools were quickly followed by the denial of voting rights and the imposition of wide funding disparities between White and Black schools. *Brown* finally pronounced these separate schools, which had by then educated generations of students, "inherently unequal" (*Brown,* 1954, p. 495)—not because of differences between the schools themselves, or even, as some have suggested, because of differences between Black and White students, but rather because, in an era in which education had already become critically important, separate education conferred full citizenship only on certain members of society.

Racially separate schools continue to deny citizenship, or perhaps more poignant, membership, to disfavored groups, but they also distort the meaning of membership to favored groups. As Dr. Martin Luther King Jr. explained, "Segregation distorts the soul and damages the personality. It gives the segregator a false sense of superiority and the segregated a false sense of inferiority" (King, 1963). Moreover, the way membership is distributed not only defines who has access to the political process, but also frames the dominant concepts of fairness and equality. In this way, segregated schools perpetuate fragmentation and a lack of understanding within and between communities.

The Supreme Court in *Brown* discussed the importance of physical presence in integrated schools. Referring to a decision in which a segregated graduate school setting impermissibly deprived a student of "intangible considerations: '. . . his ability to study, to engage in discussions and exchange views with other students'" (*Brown,* 1954, p. 493, quoting *McLaurin v. Oklahoma State Regents for Higher Education,* 1950, p. 641), the Court noted that "such considerations apply with added force to children in grade and high schools" (p. 494). The Court thus recognized that the opportunity for exchange of ideas is a critical aspect of equal educational opportunity at the K–12 level and beyond, and that denial of it represents an impermissible inequality.

The more recent *Grutter* decision on intentional diversity in a public law school underscored the importance of educational settings in creating universal membership by affirming that in pursuit of this goal, integrated educational settings offer more than an absence of exclusion; they alone offer opportunities for the development of the ability to work effectively across cultures and to communicate respectfully from diverse viewpoints. Such schools, by bringing together, in a context of equality, students from many different backgrounds, provide an opportunity for students to experience a society in which all may participate, both in its imagining and in its making. And, as the Supreme Court has repeatedly affirmed, not only in *Grutter* but also in *Brown* and other cases, these efforts toward fuller realization of democratic ideals must begin early in children's education.

Children, of course, arrive at school with different backgrounds and resources. To effect the transformation needed in K–12 education, schools will need to reach out to individual children and their families and help communities bridge rising levels of inequality and segregation. This essay reviews some of the challenges involved in such efforts and what communities are doing to meet them. We first examine specific impediments such as the effects of racial segregation, growing economic inequality, and inadequate social supports. We then review some of the characteristics and benefits of diverse educational settings and describe some of the forward-looking educational policies that communities have adopted to obtain them.

Structural Impediments to the Creation of Inclusive Public Schools

To a much greater degree than when the *Brown* Court made its judgment, when children are denied an equal and meaningful education, their ability to participate effectively in the job market is also diminished, and their chances of impoverishment or incarceration are increased (G. Orfield, 2004). Our failure to protect and educate children is therefore reflected in startling measures of human suffering: the United States posts the highest mortality rates for children under five, when economic capacity is taken into account (Lane, 2000); poverty rates twice the average for all developed nations (Institute for Policy Studies and Cities for Progress, 2005); and a rate of imprisonment five times that of the next highest nation (McDonough, 2005).

Most Americans agree that we should do more to improve the educational opportunities that would dramatically improve these measures of social well-being: over the course of the seventies, eighties, and nineties, the National Opinion Research Center recorded an increase from 51 to 73 in the percentage of Americans who think that the government is spending too little on education (Teixeira, 2000). Yet over the past twenty years, state spending on prisons grew at two and a half times the rate of spending on education (Western, Schiraldi, & Ziedenberg, 2003), and the nation's prison population quadrupled as funding to education and other sources of social support were cut along with taxes for the wealthiest, even as wealth remained essentially untaxed.

Racial and Economic Inequality and Segregation

Between 1945 and 1975 the income levels of the top and bottom 20 percent of the world's population shifted from a twenty to one to a forty to one ratio (Barlow, 2003). Over the past three decades, economic inequality in America has only grown, as the top 1 percent of the population doubled its share of income to equal nearly the total amount paid to the lowest 40 percent of earners—in spite of the increased hours logged by lower-wage workers (Shapiro, 2004). This rising inequality is even more extreme globally: the incomes of the richest four hundred people now exceed those of 45 percent of the world's population combined (Barlow, 2003).

The racial income gap in the United States has declined somewhat over this period, but it remains profound, with the average Black family's earnings reaching only 64 cents for every dollar earned by the average White family in 2004 and that of Latino families, 56 cents (DeNavas-Walt, Proctor, & C. H. Lee, 2005). Poverty rates, moreover, especially for families with children, are increasing. At the 2006 signing of the reauthorization of the 1996 changes to aid for needy families, President George W. Bush announced that "real after-tax income is up nearly 8 percent per American since 2001" (Bush, 2006). But the 8 percent per American did not reach every home: poverty rates for children, having declined from 22.7 percent in 1993—the highest level since 1964—to 16.2 percent in 2000, were climbing again, reaching 17.8 percent by 2004. Poverty rates for African American and Latino children were nearly three times those of non-Hispanic Whites (10.5 percent), with fully one-third of African Americans and 28.9 percent of Latinos under eighteen living below the poverty line (U.S. Census Bureau, 2005).

Inequalities in wealth—or accumulated resources—also increased in the 1980s and 1990s to the extent that in 1998, 80 percent of Americans shared just 16 percent of all financial assets (Wolff, 2002, p. 12). Within this overall structure, the White/Black wealth ratio remained approximately ten to one. This disparity often feeds into race-coded outcomes when a family confronts a financial crisis such as job loss or health problems, but it is also key for access to education. Depending on the ability of an extended family to provide help at critical moments, families with similar incomes may experience dramatically different abilities to secure housing in areas in which schools are well funded and high achieving (Pattillo-McCoy, 1999; Shapiro, 2004). The continuing White/Black wealth disparity means that even when their incomes are the same, White families are ten times more likely to be able to move—financially, socially, and educationally—beyond the level to which their personal success and earnings could have taken them than are Black families, who must, to achieve equal results, not only earn the same income as Whites, but also try to build up the kind of financial reserves on which Whites can often draw in times of crisis. In other words, Blacks must "outearn the wealth gap" (Shapiro, 2004, p. 2).

Although this gap is partly historically derived, it also reflects the ongoing impact of racially limited and devalued housing markets on African Americans' ability to build assets (Oliver & Shapiro, 1995; Massey & Denton, 1993). This problem is rooted in the lending policies of the federal government, which provided massive support for the construction of explicitly segregated White suburbs in the postwar boom of the 1950s (Massey & Denton, 1993; Barlow, 2003). The government's role in the development of residential segregation and the difference it makes in current levels of accumulated assets and educational access dramatically undermine the reasoning of recent Supreme Court cases in which school segregation is attributed to "private decision-making and economics" (*Board of Education of Oklahoma City Public Schools v. Dowell*, 1991, p. 243). And yet such decisions allow, or in some cases compel, school districts to abandon desegregation plans even as current housing segregation levels decline (Chemerinsky, 2005; Reardon & Yun, 2005; Frankenberg, C. Lee, & G. Orfield, 2003). This reversal of assignment policies that were designed to overcome segregated housing patterns created by both federal policies and public school segregation encourages racial separation and inequality to become more entrenched across many metro areas, hardening localism around equity issues and contributing to regional fragmentation nationwide. Rather than encouraging communities to reach across boundaries in the interest not only of a constitutionally mandated end to segregated schooling and the stigma that such schooling serves to maintain, but also of a better America, these decisions enshrine "choice," for those who can afford it, and deem marginalization or exclusion acceptable for the less fortunate other.

In this way the freedom of markets is repeatedly conflated with true liberty interests in decisions affecting the public schools. This results in decisions that undermine the crucial role of schools in maintaining the social fabric and strengthening the democracy. And racial segregation must certainly be considered a poor product of free markets, even if this result were not in fact so profoundly related to state action. Allowing this kind of "freedom" to perpetuate ongoing segregation of schools and housing severely limits efforts to build true democracy in this country—just as it most certainly would have defeated efforts to end the institution of slavery itself had demands for marketplace freedom been allowed to trump those of human freedom and equality in that era.

Segregation makes a dramatic difference in the nature of the public education to which low-income students of color have access, because racially segregated schools are high-poverty schools. Black and Latino students make up 80 percent of all students in schools with poverty rates of 90 percent or more (G. Orfield & C. Lee, 2005), and almost half of all Black children attend schools in which 75 percent or more of the students are eligible for free or reduced-price lunch. Only 5 percent of White students attend schools this dramatically impoverished (National Center for Education Statistics, 2004). Decades of research demonstrate that high-poverty schools impose severe constraints on students, in addition to denying them the benefits of diverse schools (see, e.g., J. S. Coleman et al., 1966; G. Orfield & C. Lee, 2005). Concentrating low-income students lowers student achievement and increases teacher turnover, which in turn depresses teacher quality (Hanushek, Kain, & Rivkin, 2004b). It is a cycle that can be ended not with carrots or sticks, but with a willingness to finally open the schoolhouse doors to all American children, regardless of their family background, and create an integrated system of public education that will enrich the entire nation.

The Politics of Inequality

Dramatic inequality in the distribution of education, income, or access to opportunity violates generally held beliefs about fairness and democracy. A September 2002 survey by Public Agenda, a nonpartisan, nonprofit public opinion research group, revealed that 65 percent of the Americans questioned about the Constitution and democracy believe that the rich or powerful now have more rights and freedoms than do other citizens, and a majority think that the number of poor and homeless people represent a failure to live up to our national ideals. So it is unsurprising that widening inequality has corresponded with a drop in the percentage of Americans who believe that the federal government is run for the benefit of all, rather than for a few powerful private interests—from 55 percent in 1964 to below 20 percent in 1992 (Lane, 2000). Wealth today is a key to political access and increasingly drives the management of and access to our society's resources.[1]

Our national story—as the land of opportunity, in which a good dream, hard work, and a little luck are all that's really needed for success and full citizenship—affects most Americans' ideas about poverty in ways that encourage a blind belief in the success of the society in fulfilling its democratic mission. This framing of the story tends to place the blame for inequality on the people who suffer its effects, rather than recognizing it as a consequence of social and economic policies. Even low-income Americans express a belief that ours is an open and mobile society, often in complete disregard of their lived experiences (Scott & Leonhardt, 2005). In recent years globalization of economic activity and the escalating power of corporations in society have increased the shifting upward of resources and so contributed to the decline of the middle class. Non-Whites trying to earn a place in this shrinking space now encounter an ever more fearful White population that is scrambling to hoard its diminishing opportunities (Barlow, 2003). Stagnation of income and wealth for lower- and middle-income families has, moreover, taken place against rising educational levels and decreasing educational inequality in America (Wolff, 2004), leading to questions about why such merit and achievement are not producing the expected financial rewards.

Ready answers to these fearfully and often angrily posed questions have been crafted through the refinement of symbolism in politics in recent decades, which has to a large degree successfully obscured structural shifts in explaining the current reality. For the 80 percent of the population perhaps unaware that they share 16 percent of the nation's wealth, these answers have led to bitter zero-sum calculations that ignore the general welfare or even withdraw support from those most in need. But much of the hostility toward and disapproval of the poor is shaped by "politics and indoctrination, not by reality" (Alesina & Glaeser, 2004, p. 187). A racial strategy pitting nearly every other interest group against low-income African Americans has long been used to create a tension and unwillingness to invest in social resources, including education. One recent study of the differences between the redistributive policies of the United States and those of more supportive nations found that about half are attributable to the use of race by those seeking to limit benefits to the poor in America: a visually identified low-income minority acts as a foil to low- and middle-income Whites, who then differentiate themselves through support of policies that favor the wealthiest, making life harder for all low-income people and reducing the overall quality of the society (Alesina & Glaeser, 2004).[2]

Portraying wealth and poverty as merit-based and ignoring or disparaging the roles of luck, history, and inheritance unfairly stigmatizes the efforts of those barely getting by and disregards the facts about how the current economy is structured (Lane, 2000; Alesina & Glaeser, 2004). Moreover, contrary to the negative myths circulated about the effects of aid to poor families, low-income members of societies with stronger social supports actually tend to increase their incomes more than do similar groups in the United States; recent research indicates that support seems to lift, rather than weaken, its recipients.[3]

If this finding would seem self-evident, at least in relation to the large percentages of children—especially children of color—living below the poverty line, it has yet to trigger an effective response. Indeed, African Americans in particular often serve as the image of the "undeserving poor," creating both a terrible irony and a measure of just how far the society needs to go to free itself of racial stereotypes and their social consequences. Moreover, although it provides a national excuse for centuries of forced labor and economic exploitation, this message takes a continuing toll on Whites themselves, since stirring up racialized resentments provides such a successful diversion of inquiry away from the true causes of scarcity, such as slow rates of increase in wages and tax policies favoring the richest Americans over the middle class and the poor, especially since the early 1980s (Wolff, 2004).

These economic trends and racialized politics are intertwined. Equal protection language created after the Civil War to counter the most egregious forms of institutionalized racism has been successfully appropriated by the threatened White middle class in recent years. This false cry raised against efforts in schools and workplaces to transform the nation's deeply embedded racial structure is in some ways the same as the White backlash to Reconstruction. In the decades following the Civil War, powerful elites used fear to control both Whites and Blacks in orchestrating their own return to power (Foner, 1988). But today's complaints also represent fears arising in a complex and vulnerable state in which slogans about personal responsibility excuse governmental irresponsibility and individuals fear a collapse of the collective. The force of these protests and fears, as well as the power of race in our society, can best be diminished, therefore, by increasing investment in the common good and the expansion of opportunities for meaningful participation for all.

Inadequate Societal Support for Children and Families

As he accepted the Nobel Peace Prize in 1993, Nelson Mandela proclaimed that the reward of the struggle for human freedom and democracy is best measured "by the happiness and welfare of the children, at once the most vulnerable citizens in any society and the greatest of our treasures." Judging ourselves on that basis we must conclude that we have much to do and that a great deal of the work needs to be centered in our schools. Both inequality and segregation undermine our ability to give our children a well-founded belief that they are equally important to the ongoing strength of the society and equally prepared to contribute. Students' family incomes have important independent effects on achievement as well as educational quality and are highly correlated with race in this country (G. Orfield & C. Lee, 2005; Kahlenberg, 2001).

Access to books, for example, is critical to the development of reading skills. But a recent survey of the number of books stocked by the children's departments of bookstores in and around Philadelphia demonstrates the impact of racial and economic inequality on literacy: there were 1,300 books per one hundred children in a mostly college-educated area, 30 per one hundred children in a mostly White blue-collar area, 10 in a multiethnic area, and less than 1 book per one hundred children in a predominately Black area. Even the public libraries offered six times more books for children in upper-income areas, although these children are far more likely to have many books in their homes (Rothstein, 2004). Low-income students are also much more likely to attend schools in which there are fewer and lower-quality reading materials (Duke, 2000).

Richard Rothstein (2004), in an analysis of the economic aspects of the achievement gap, reports that proper treatment of vision problems, elimination of chronic environmentally caused illnesses, and access to adequate health care in general could cause the gap as currently measured to virtually disappear—especially if it were combined with support for housing and employment for low-income families. Other researchers have found that even modest increases in family income can make a decisive difference for low-income children. Mental health problems among Cherokee children, for example, showed marked improvement when the distribution of casino income raised a number of families out of poverty over the course of a study already in progress. Researchers were able to correlate the change primarily with increased parental supervision and interaction resulting from a decrease in hours spent generating income (Costello, Compton, Keeler, & Angold, 2003). The correlation between freedom from dire need and overall mental health, including good decision making and productivity, is well established (e.g., Lane, 2000).

Cultural and educational activities comparable to those experienced by middle-class students during summer months would also do much to reduce the achievement gap between low- and middle-income students, which tests have shown to develop primarily over summer breaks rather than during the school year (P. Alexander, D. R. Entwisle, & L. S. Olson, 2004; Rothstein, 2004). This kind of enrichment, moreover, by helping students lead fuller lives and develop a fuller range of abilities, would go much further toward closing the real gap in learning—measured from the top rather than the bottom of achievement levels—than does intensive drilling on test material in summer school.

So we do know a number of ways to remedy the educational problems of the children currently being left behind. What we need to learn is how to push past the often racialized resistance and fear that we face in doing so and how to, instead of developing incremental modifications to the system, reshape our larger structural arrangements with more productive and equitable practices. This is not an easy task, as it requires not only improvements in social planning and spending, but also direct confrontation of the ways that race affects how we think about social structures and our own roles. Charles R. Lawrence (2005) talks about the way segregated schools put walls between the children of the wealthy and privileged and those with too little, which allows the most powerful members of the community to ignore the reality, if not the existence, of these children. Taking those walls down would allow instead conversations, empathy, and negotiation. It would afford the possibility of a citizenry educated in integrated, equitable settings, who share the accompanying set of expectations.

Limitations within Schools

The Social and Educational Harms of Exclusion

Racially and economically segregated schools and classrooms create a sense of exclusion for many students today, inviting them to know their place, rather than their world, and impacting achievement in ways other than by limiting access to higher-level curricula. This social exclusion's effects are suggested by a series of experiments in which participants were randomly chosen to be told that they had not been selected as workmates by a newly introduced peer group. The rejected suffered a 25 percent drop in IQ scores and a 30 percent decrease in their ability to recall a complex reading passage or to answer questions that required higher-order thinking skills. They were also far more likely to behave aggressively, even toward innocent strangers, and dramatically less likely to be helpful to others than were those told they had been selected (Twenge & Baumeister, 2005). They were (temporarily, it is hoped) socially and intellectually diminished by an isolated experience of exclusion. Inclusive schools demonstrably counteract this problem. In Lynn, Massachusetts, for example, suspension and dropout rates reflect district demographics rather than the national average (see Cole, this volume), which is roughly twice as high for Blacks as for Whites (U.S. Department of Education, 2000) and even higher for Latinos (Kaufman, Alt, & Chapman, 2004).

Standardized testing can function in tandem with racial segregation and stereotypes to sort students within and between schools, often subjecting them to the harms of exclusion and rewarding or punishing them for attributes beyond their control (Deever, 1994, quoted in Clotfelter, 2004, p. 137). Students' test scores, after all, closely correlate with family income levels, reflecting both the educational attainments of parents and guardians and the lower quality of the educational opportunities generally available to low-income children (College Board, 2004).

The reporting of group-based levels of proficiency also requires racial and economic labeling of students. Recent work by Lewis (2003) and

Palmer (this volume) demonstrates that racial role assignments, rather than being preexisting factors with which schools merely must cope, often originate within school walls. Students from locations as different as California and Cambodia, the Bahamas and Iowa, or Venezuela and Texas thus become "Asian," "Black," or "Latino," frequently without any level of critical inquiry and, many times, under protest as to their true identity. Combined with the stereotypes so pervasive in society, this "racing" of students can depersonalize and predetermine much of an individual student's school experience, even transcending test scores when they do not validate racial and ethnic expectations for students. Roslyn A. Mickelson (2005), for example, after taking prior achievement into account, compared the English-class placements of White and Black eighth-grade students in Charlotte-Mecklenburg schools. Of those who scored in the top decile of the California Achievement Test, 72.3 percent of White students, but only 18.7 percent of Black students were assigned to the highest-level classes.

Mickelson's study suggests that unobtrusive and diagnostic testing might be helpful in ensuring access to higher-level or additional help for struggling students. Other researchers have found, however, that often it functions as a cause of retention and lower graduation rates (Heubert, 2005) or leads to a narrowing of the curriculum to those subjects that are tested (Sunderman, Tracey, J. Kim, & G. Orfield, 2004). This narrowing, combined with the drill and test practice instituted to defend against the testing program's sanctions, runs counter to most of what we know about preparing students to function effectively in modern society. Enriched curricula, discussion of ideas, critical thinking, teamwork, and student-initiated study are important for all students, not only for the elite, but it is these areas that are often hardest hit by the demands of the testing programs.

Test scores need to be handled more thoughtfully outside the school context as well, because publicizing scores that reflect students' past access to opportunity more than present school quality is feeding stereotypes and encouraging flight from more diverse schools (Wells & Holme, 2005). The No Child Left Behind Act of 2001 labels even highly effective diverse schools in high-income areas "failures" if even one testing subgroup falls short of externally imposed yearly testing goals (Heubert, 2005; Wells & Holme, 2005). This mislabeling of schools, given the current emphasis on testing, can lead parents to choose schools on very narrow measures of quality, even when those measures conflict with their broader social values. It also directly and indirectly pressures schools to "push out" struggling students who might trigger testing sanctions, especially when those students are beyond the age of compulsory schooling (Bridgeland, DiIulio, & Morison, 2006).

Disparate Access to Higher Education

Only 75 percent of White students in the high school class of 2001 graduated, and far fewer students of color did so: 50 percent of African Americans and 53 percent of Latinos (G. Orfield, Losen, Wald, & C. B. Swanson, 2004; C. B. Swanson, 2004). In an era in which a high school education is a necessary beginning, not end, of preparation for adult life, these numbers represent our continuing failure to fully implement an effective national system of public education. They also represent dreams denied for millions of Black and Latino families. A 2000 survey of American parents revealed that 47 percent of African American and 65 percent of Latino parents believe that a college education is the most important requirement for a young person's success, as do 33 percent of White parents (Immerwahr & Foleno, 2000). Yet only 17 percent of Black eighth graders eventually receive undergraduate degrees, half the rate of Whites (National Center for Education Statistics, 2003). In addressing the barriers that keep these college numbers low, both institutions of higher learning and the state must increase planning and resource allocation for K–16 public education. Colleges and universities can expand opportunities for students to earn college credit while still in high school, for example, which serves both as an incentive to stay in school and as a channel to increase access to higher education (Vail, 2004).

There is also an acute need to expand access to elite institutions of higher education for minority students. In 2003 Black enrollment averaged only around 7 percent in the 146 most selective schools, and even among these students, there were troubling disparities in levels of preparation, largely due to the ongoing effects of segregation (Century Foundation, 2003). Race is, however, only part of the problem; only 3 percent of freshmen at these schools came from families in the bottom quarter of the income scale, and another 6 percent from the second lowest. In other words, almost all first-year students at elite schools were from the top half of the income scale (Century Foundation, 2003). Reflecting the upward movement of resources in our society generally, this proportion of high-wealth, high-income students is larger today than it was two decades ago (Leonhardt, 2005).

So although higher education is increasingly important for full membership in society, unequal access to excellent and inclusive schools at the K–12 level serves to limit access to higher education. Moreover, even policy discussions that address alternative ways to design or interpret admissions criteria typically fail to question the role of social structures and institutions. Consequently, affirmative action continues to be seen by many as a process that allows lesser candidates entry to the institution, rather than a means to achieve the mission of higher education and fulfill colleges' and universities' stated goals (Guinier, 2003). This perspective both stigmatizes those students of color who make it to the doors of the university and distorts the worldview of Whites, who then recast integration as some kind of reparation to people they perceive as less qualified, rather than the realization of the promise of democracy and a necessity for a diverse society. Thus, despite, or perhaps, in part, because of the *Grutter* decision, the process by which we can best achieve diversity in higher education is still under contention, and many questions remain about the goals of higher education and the nature of merit.

In considering the relationship of merit to justice, the economist and Nobel laureate Amartya Sen notes that modern meritocracies tend to be "biased (often implicitly) toward the interests of more fortunate groups" (Sen, 2000, p. 14), which tends to increase inequality. While acknowledging the rationality of incentive systems, Sen points out the importance of defining merit in a way that helps generate valued consequences (p. 9). The Court in *Grutter* similarly encouraged a more comprehensive look at merit that includes potential that may or may not be measured in standardized tests.

The *Grutter* decision's support for the Michigan law school's valuing of diversity has not, however, stopped a "chilling" of efforts to recruit and support minority students in graduate education (Woodrow Wilson National Fellowship Foundation, 2005). Both federal support and fellowships and other aid to racial and ethnic minorities that is not replaced by aid for low-income students have been reduced in recent years, and this has occurred even as Blacks and Latinos together constituted only 7 percent of Ph.D. recipients in 2003, while comprising 32 percent of Americans of similar age (Wilson National Fellowship Foundation, 2005). Acquiescing in this and similar policies today all but guarantees similar problems going forward, as educational and intellectual leadership positions remain less accessible to students of color. Achieving the fundamental purpose of public education and attaining educational and cultural fairness—the mandates of *Brown*—will require that we summon the courage to look beyond short-term admissions games and to redirect resources, away from institutions designed to catch the fallout of our faulty education system, such as prisons, and toward serious investment in our future—our common schools.

A Renewed Commitment to Common Schools

Community Support for Inclusive Public Schools

Communities across the nation, acting from a variety of motives, are indeed developing or adapting plans to make the public schools of their communities more equitable and inclusive. Whether they are future-oriented plans for enhancing students' education through the benefits of diversity, plans designed to avoid the harms of segregation and concentrated poverty, or plans to preserve the overall health of a metro region—or all of the above—they have in common a willingness on the part of the communities that create them to acknowledge the effects of racial policies of the past and to take affirmative steps to minimize their impacts on the future. Under these plans school districts have taken steps to make their assignment, transfer, and school-siting policies move them toward these goals, by continuing policies adopted under court order, adapting such plans to new conditions, or by devising new integration plans (NAACP Legal Defense and Educational Fund, 2004; NAACP Legal Defense and Educational Fund, the Civil Rights Project at Harvard University, & the Center for the Study of Race and Law at the University of Virginia School of Law, 2005). Lynn, Massachusetts (Cole, this volume), and Rockville Centre, New York (Burris and Welner, this volume), offer examples of this work. Two other communities with similar goals, Louisville, Kentucky, and Seattle, Washington, have comprehensive metro-area plans that have been approved by federal courts of appeal, and the plan of another community, Berkeley, California, has been affirmed under state law.

One of the nation's largest school districts, metropolitan Louisville (Jefferson County), uses magnet schools, open enrollment, and transfers in a managed-choice plan designed to provide "'substantially uniform educational resources to all students' and to teach basic skills and critical thinking skills in a racially integrated environment" (*McFarland v. Jefferson County Public Schools,* 2004, p. 842). A majority of students (57.5 percent in 2002–3) attend their residentially assigned school, but students may apply to a number of specialized programs. Schools decide whether to accept students based on criteria ranging from performance to family hardship to available space to place on a random-draw list, although the district's integration plan requires that all schools aim for Black student enrollments ranging between 15 and 50 percent. When the plan's consideration of race was challenged, a federal district court applied strict scrutiny in assessing its constitutionality, and it agreed that the district had demonstrated compelling reasons for its use: "(1) a better academic education for all students; (2) better appreciation of our political and cultural heritage for all students; (3) more competitive and attractive public schools; and (4) broader community support for all JCPS schools" (*McFarland*, 2004, p. 850n29).

Louisville's voluntary integration of its schools has, as the court pointed out, encouraged continued public support for educational excellence and equity across the district, "invest[ing] parents and students alike with a sense of participation and a positive stake in their schools and the school system as a whole" (*McFarland*, 2004, p. 854). It also represents a community's resolve to protect the results of court-ordered integration and expand them through the efforts of a democratically elected board of education. The district court noted this issue in its comment that "it would seem rather odd" if concepts like equal protection, which helped desegregate schools, and "local control," which was often used as an argument against desegregation, were reversed in meaning to the point of prohibiting the flexible use of race as one of the many factors in student assignment planning—especially when the "harm" that is caused by the use of race is an assurance that every seat in a district's schools will be equally good (*McFarland*, 2004, pp. 851, 860). The Sixth Circuit Court of Appeals affirmed the decision in 2005 (*McFarland*, 2005); in 2006 the Supreme Court agreed to hear the case.

Another community plan for integrated schools that will be reviewed by the Supreme Court was developed in Seattle, which has a history of voluntary school integration. Its current plan is intended to provide diverse and equal educational opportunities across the district. The plan uses four tiebreakers in its noncompetitive-choice, high school assignment plan: a sibling preference; an "integration tiebreaker," triggered only if a student's first-choice school is becoming atypical for the district, in terms of racial or ethnic makeup; distance; and a lottery. The plan is intended to secure for students the benefits of diverse classrooms—especially as they improve critical thinking skills and understanding of people from different backgrounds—to ensure access to equal educational opportunity, and to increase the range of opportunities available to students after high school.

When the plan was challenged under Washington State's Civil Rights Act, the Equal Protection Clause of the Fourteenth Amendment of the Constitution, and Title VI of the Civil Rights Act of 1964, the Seattle district's goals were evaluated under strict scrutiny because of the consideration of race in one of the tiebreakers. In Seattle the Ninth Circuit Court, after reviewing the history and goals of the school system, found that the integration tiebreaker was minimally intrusive and helped the district provide educational excellence in spite of persistent residential segregation (*Parents Involved in Community Schools v. Seattle School District No. 1*, 2005).

Berkeley, California, also created, in 1968, a voluntary integration plan to combat school segregation growing out of housing segregation. A recent update to the plan uses student choice, location, siblings, socio-economic status, and race or ethnicity to help the district provide educational opportunities consistent with the "fundamental importance of education" and the "distinctive racial harm traditionally inflicted by segregated education" (*Avila v. Berkeley Unified School District*, 2004, p. 7, quoting *Crawford v. Board of Education*, 1976, p. 297). When the plan was challenged under Proposition 209's ban on "preferential treatment" on the basis of race, the Alameda County Superior Court found that "a race-conscious school assignment plan that seeks to provide all students with the same benefit of desegregated schools" was not prohibited by Proposition 209 (*Avila*, 2004, p. 8, quoting *Crawford*, 1976). Instead, the court noted that school boards were explicitly empowered under the state constitution to create voluntary school integration plans and that the district had a constitutional duty "to undertake reasonably feasible steps to alleviate school segregation regardless of cause" (*Avila*, 2004, p. 3, quoting *Crawford v. Board of Education of the City of Los Angeles*, 1980, p. 651). This duty, moreover, was to be fulfilled "even if such segregation results from the application of a facially neutral state policy" (*Avila*, 2004, p. 7, quoting *Crawford*, 1976, p. 297).

The Berkeley outcome demonstrates the value of a constitutional right to education, present in many states but denied under current federal law, in spite of national performance mandates and sanctions. Efforts to provide equal educational opportunity under the federal Constitution are currently limited by a Supreme Court case finding no explicit or implicit right to education (*San Antonio v. Rodriguez*, 1973). School-funding schemes, then, need only survive the lowest level of judicial scrutiny, offering some rational basis for their legitimacy rather than the compelling interest that strict scrutiny would trigger if education were protected as a "fundamental right"—as are voting, travel, and marriage, for example. American students, under *Rodriguez*, are entitled only to some education, not equality. This means that federal requirements for testing, teacher quality, tutoring, and student transfer options are superimposed over a patchwork of different and unequal local standards and unequal access to high-quality schools and high-level curricula. Moreover, because most schools are funded primarily at the state and district levels, access to public education is grossly inequitable across the nation (e.g., Kozol, 1991). Affirmation of the right to equal educational opportunity under federal law is therefore a critical step in the building of a truly effective public school system.

Community efforts, however, can play a critical role in generating and supporting the kind of thinking needed to transform our schools to better support a democratic society. Many local factors, after all, have major impacts on educational access: transportation, housing, and tax policies; metropolitan governance; as well as antidiscrimination efforts all dramatically affect educational access. And public school quality and equality have dynamic effects on the well-being of their communities. Recognizing this, the Raleigh, North Carolina (Wake County), metro area developed a plan that balances student socioeconomic status in pursuit of some of the same goals as those of voluntary integration plans that take race into account. The countywide plan uses roughly block-sized assignment "nodes" to create schools in which target poverty rates are no higher than 40 percent, and failure rates on the previous year's state tests, 25 percent (Finder, 2005; Flinspach & K. E. Banks, 2005). The county's plan to maintain a whole community of "healthy" schools makes it easier to share the challenge of educating all children in a rapidly growing school system (Flinspach & K. E. Banks, 2005, p. 276). The district's attention to reducing racial and economic segregation represents the continuation of a long-standing commitment to leadership in integrated education, but its efforts have yielded practical results as well: the percentage of African American students achieving proficiency on state tests has doubled over the past decade, from 40 to 80 percent, as the overall district percentage increased from 79 to 91 (Finder, 2005).

Communities can also support better schools by helping to monitor efforts to increase equity, develop policy, and educate the public about the benefits of diversity. They can increase support and resources available for school programs by forming connections with local foundations, institutes, corporations, and government agencies. Communities can also exert pressure on administrators and those in political office to adopt policies that improve educational access and equity. Local businesses and institutions of higher education can adopt particular schools and school districts and provide links to internships and equal employment opportunities. Spiritual leaders can mobilize to support racial equality and interracial contact within their congregations as well as throughout the community. Every concerned citizen can, moreover, visit a local public school and offer to lend a hand.

Inside Diverse Schools

Inviting All Families In

Because education continually increases in importance, parental under-standing of the significance of diverse school communities cannot be left to chance or taken for granted. In an immigrant society such as ours, there is always a tension between the nature of the public school sys-tem—one goal of which is the development of social cohesiveness—and parents' wishes to maintain their children's loyalty to their culture of ori-gin (Gradstein, Justman, & W. Meier, 2005). This tension occurs across social class, race, ethnicity, and length of time in the United States, and, although it is to be respected, it should not be seen as a cause for resis-tance to shared schools and programs. Indeed, the goal of such programs is greater protection of the freedoms that people from all walks of life value.

To promote understanding, schools need to involve parents in school-based and community-wide multiethnic activities early in their children's educations and provide them with information and opportunities for contact with the school (Hawley et al., 1983). Parent orientation, for ex-ample, should include discussion of explicitly stated school goals for ra-cial and cultural diversity and inclusiveness and options for participation. Within such a context, parents can be invited to contribute their educa-tional, professional, and experiential resources. In addition to attending administrative meetings or helping out with or attending student presen-tations, parents, grandparents, and guardians can also strengthen their relationships with teachers and become part of the school community by providing support ranging from helping students with reading to moni-toring of lunchrooms, buses, and playgrounds.

Because parental presence is so important, attention must be paid to how it is solicited, supported, and structured. Families with low incomes may need transportation or scheduling accommodation, for example. And parents of color need to help with the structuring of involvement, to ensure that it will be broadly accessible. Communication of opportuni-ties must be effective for all families, and schools must ensure, with the help of community organizations and booster clubs, that no student is barred from participation in extracurricular activities because of a lack of family resources. Schools should not overlook the value of casual or celebratory social and cultural events in which all families feel welcome as equals as ways of building familiarity and comfort within the school community.

Creating Inclusive Curricula and Programming

In efforts to bring all students up to high levels of understanding and participation in their coursework, addressing the effects of negative stereotypes that have served to diminish student achievement can be of great value (C. Steele & J. Aronson, 1998). Researchers have found, for example, that students subject to stereotypes—in one study, girls in the context of math and low-income students of color in the context of reading—when given information about brain function and learning, or taught that students can overcome major challenges and succeed, achieve significantly higher test scores than comparison groups (C. Good, J. Aronson, & Inzlicht, 2003). A sense of racial or cultural isolation can depress achievement as well, so some schools have encouraged students to establish peer study groups to discuss difficult problems, reduce anxiety, and encourage one another as part of a learning community (Gordon & Bridglall, 2005).

In the competitive and highly stratified American educational context, it is also worth remembering that some of the world's highest-achieving cultures offer virtually no identification of "giftedness"—just very high standards for all, as in Scandinavian countries. Others—for example, Japan—view all children as similar in potential but with differing achievement levels based on effort, perseverance, and teacher quality (J. Freeman, 2005). By adopting such attitudes and the practices that support them, even within schools in districts that have not made the kind of wholehearted commitment to every child described in the essay by Burris and Welner (this volume), teachers and school administrators can encourage higher achievement. By identifying giftedness across a broader range of abilities and expanding the use of "gifted" education, schools can help previously languishing students reach their full potential. Such strategies are exemplified by a "guest" program in a Durham, North Carolina, elementary school in which African American students with high test scores just below the "gifted" level were moved into advanced classes, where they had previously been dramatically underrepresented. This plan for "nurturing giftedness" was accompanied by a lifting of the level of expectations for all students, diversity training for teachers, and regular mandatory meetings with parents. The program recorded the elimination of a White/Black achievement gap of about 30 points for reading and 20 points for math for students in the grade level that had been in the program for the first three years of its existence (Jolla, 2005).

Middle and high school students can be encouraged to stay on the path to higher education through offerings and structures that ensure that they are able to develop and be recognized in areas of special interest and ability. Projects on subjects of great interest to them can combine the development of authentic research and presentation skills with internships that enable them to "appropriate the tools of the research community" and strengthen their relationship to academic work (e.g., Oakes, Rogers, Lipton, & Morrell, 2000, pp. 18–19). As is suggested in the essay by Hughes and Bigler (this volume), students in today's learning communities also need authentic educational materials that explicitly address racism and race relations in the United States. Moreover, a deeper understanding of constitutional rights and social policies on issues such as integration, affirmative action, concentrated poverty, and racial equality is critical to a more democratic future and has tremendous public support (e.g., Public Agenda, 2002).

Students learning to live in—indeed, create—a just, democratic society can only do so in a humane and disciplined school environment that fosters a sense of trust that problems can be examined and solved and not just exacerbated by punishment or denial. Rules and procedures governing schools must therefore be clear, fair, consistent, and responsive to students' needs. They must be administered with persistence and without racial bias. The principal's ideological commitment to the fostering of positive interracial contact, moreover, is crucial. Students are more likely to interact in the lunchroom and at recess, for example, in schools in which the principal values such contact (Wellisch, A. H. Marcus, MacQueen, & Duck, 1978). Schooling for democracy also includes students in the process of rule or decision making and ensures that all students have an equal role status, regardless of racial or ethnic background (Slavin, 1995a).

Helping Students Learn from One Another

As the *Grutter* opinion reminds us, our society is already part of a global, information-based economy. To be effective members of such a society, students need both the enriched thought processes best developed in diverse educational settings and the "soft skills" such settings foster—teamwork, responsibility, and the ability to communicate with others across lines of race, class, or culture. Business interests support diverse educational settings because they know that diverse teams are more productive and more able to avoid the pitfalls of "group think," such as illusions of invulnerability, unanimity, or moral superiority; censorship; pressure to conform; and rationalization (Janis & Mann, 1977). Similarly, leading businesses have been moving away from the traditional layered structure of decision making to a team-based model because the latter is more effective and successful. This more inclusive and less hierarchical decision-making structure is also better suited to a democratic society. Giving students such experience as a part of the learning process helps them develop an expectation that their own insights stand to be enriched by those of their fellow students, as well as an ability to move past opposing viewpoints toward solutions strengthened by analysis from diverse points of view.

Students preparing for futures in a global society must also have access to teachers and other students who hold and can share both reinforcing and divergent viewpoints and beliefs. Within diverse classrooms, students consciously and unconsciously strive to make sense of expressed or perceived differences of opinion, thus becoming more racially and culturally fluent. In engaging in this process of "perspective taking," students must alter or expand their own thinking and develop more complex reasoning and problem-solving abilities (P. Gurin, Dey, Hurtado, & G. Gurin, 2002; Piaget, 1965). Experiences of dissonance and disequilibrium stimulate higher levels of cognitive function and help students avoid "automaticity" and expand both their understanding and their intellectual capacities. It is in such learning contexts that students are most likely to perceive and cross barriers between themselves and others and to become aware of and transcend the limiting aspects of their own cultural traditions or beliefs, even as they learn to appreciate more fully their singularity and connections with others (Giroux, 2005). This kind of work is, therefore, a core benefit of inclusive, diverse school settings.

Bridging Cultural and Social Divides Outside the Classroom

Extracurricular activities that encourage equitable diverse groupings have a stronger influence on interracial friendships and cooperative involvement than almost any other educational variable (Patchen, 1982). Efforts therefore should be made to promote diversity in school group memberships and to heighten a sense of connection to grouping that includes students from different backgrounds. Activities can be structured to be attractive to a wide range of students when adult supervisors are aware of this goal. When participation in enrichment opportunities is left to chance, however, there can be negative results, as described by Palmer (this volume), or as in Minnesota, where St. Paul school officials have acknowledged the need to increase Latino students' participation in extracurricular activities (*Garcia et al. v. St. Paul Independent School District 625*, 1976). Schools can improve their participation levels by consciously monitoring membership in school groups, encouraging underrepresented students to join and already involved students to be welcoming, as well as ensuring that transportation and equipment do not present obstacles to participation.

Integrated athletic teams are a strong source of positive intergroup attitudes and reduced prejudice (Braddock, Dawkins, & G. Wilson, 1995), even among those who are not themselves athletes (Schofield, 1977). And although competitive sports, by their very nature, impose some limitations on opportunities for participation, intramural sports can provide a popular option for students to form teams of varying ability levels. Creative problem-solving competitions offer another arena for teamwork in which diversity itself is a positive element, since diverse teams tend to produce more creative solutions, as discussed above (Janis & Mann, 1977).

Student-formed groups can provide opportunities to identify and clarify racial and ethnic assumptions, intervene in ethnocentrism, and help school communities avoid the harms of stereotyping (P. T. Coleman & Deutsch, 1995). By tutoring low-income students, for example, students can help close achievement gaps in local elementary schools while simultaneously dismantling stereotypes on both sides. Through presentations on the nations of origin of students and their families, they can develop appreciation of one another's cultural differences and similarities or provide educational outreach on these issues. Diverse student organizations can also explore and share practices ranging from mediation to support for human rights. All of these activities can help students form positive connections with one another and with the larger community.

Securing Our Future in Inclusive Public Schools

Loosening the constraints into which each of us is born, whether those constraints limit by deprivation, intolerance, social isolation, or complacency, is the essence of education. Yet the free-market fundamentalism (Munck, 2005) and competition that have come to dominate our culture have combined with economic pressures on the majority to create a great deal of confusion and strife about "choice" and have caused many to push, perhaps unwittingly, for a scenario too closely resembling Michael Young's satiric meritocracy, in which a fortunate few are "identified at an early age and selected for an appropriate intensive education, and there is obsession with quantification, test-scoring, and qualifications" (1961, p. 7). Schools, however, have a much larger role to play in a democracy; they are central to the struggle to define and maintain our cultural values. Americans do know this. In spring 2004, the one most important goal of education chosen by the highest number of Americans in eighteen "presidential battleground states" surveyed by the Educational Testing Service was producing "literate, educated citizens who participate in our democracy" (26 percent, and 29 percent of parents), followed closely by preparing students for continuing their education (25 percent, and 27 percent of parents). This same survey revealed once again that Americans do care about the disenfranchised: funding for schools in low-income areas was a "major concern" of 55 percent of these citizens, 60 percent of whom thought that such schools were "inadequate" or "in crisis" (Educational Testing Service, 2004).

Replacing these schools with inclusive diverse schools will provide common ground and opportunities for both students and members of the wider community. This common ground will help build membership and participation in the democracy and may also allow us to ask one another why it is that our public schools are so focused on forms of work that are inherently isolating and competitive rather than exploratory or forward looking, why public policy seems increasingly at odds with public opinion, and why the distribution of America's vast wealth benefits fewer and fewer of its citizens. Perhaps our children, born into an era of instantaneous global connections, can help us figure out how to reverse some of the trends toward greater isolation and inequality that threaten our democratic ideals, both here and around the world. Perhaps they will even meet the challenge of opening the doors to education to the one hundred and forty million children around the world who are not in school at all or the many others—many here among us—who are not receiving adequate educations (United Nations Educational, Scientific, and Cultural Organization, 2005). At the very least, as explained by Roia Ferrazares, a parent intervener in the case upholding the Berkeley schools' integration plan, "When our children learn together, we are filled with hope for a better world" (NAACP Legal Defense and Educational Fund, 2004).

Our nation is founded on and sustained by the efforts and beliefs of dreamers and dream keepers, both free and unfree, rich and poor. People all over the world, moreover, struggle toward its common dreams of equality, freedom, and democracy. Addressing the world from Oslo, Norway, Nelson Mandela (1993) asked that we

> Let the strivings of us all, prove Martin Luther King, Jr. to have been correct, when he said that humanity can no longer be tragically bound to the starless midnight of racism and war.
> Let the efforts of us all, prove that he was not a mere dreamer when he spoke of the beauty of genuine brotherhood and peace being more precious than diamonds or silver or gold.

All of our children will live the future that current policies are shaping. Will they stare out at one another, unknowing, across impenetrable racial and financial divides, or will they develop the capacity to reach out to other valued members of their extended, global family? Will we provide them with an education that equips them to recognize and benefit from diverse viewpoints and to address conflicts in a spirit of respect and co-operation? Policies and practices that support important changes in our schools are well within our reach, and the promise and obligations of *Brown v. Board of Education* stand as a beacon for us even today, as the Supreme Court recently reaffirmed in *Grutter v. Bollinger*. Our children do have a right to know one another, confer with one another, and "disarm stereotypes" about one another for the benefit of the whole society (*Comfort v. Lynn School Committee,* 2005a). They have a right to an equal and integrated education that truly prepares them for productive lives and full citizenship—a fundamental right in any truly democratic society.

Notes

1. Two legislative actions in 2005 reflect this pattern: the Senate, which has increased its own pay by $28,500 over the past five years, declined to give the lowest-paid workers their first raise in eight years, from $5.15 an hour to $7.25 an hour, phased in over two years (Labaton, 2005). The yearly income of a minimum-wage earner working forty hours a week for fifty-two weeks is $10,712, almost $7,500 below the poverty level for a family of four. The Senate also passed a bill limiting the ability of families to file for bankruptcy, requiring them to continue to pay the credit card companies who wrote the legislation. These measures seem to represent what one commentator calls "a steady erosion of the protection the government provides against personal misfortune, even as ordinary families face ever-growing economic insecurity" (Krugman, 2005, p. A23).

2. Testing their conclusion against a specific program, Alesina and Glaeser (2004) find that controlling for state income levels, Aid to Families with Dependent Children payments in the fifty states fell by $138 per month with each 20 percentage point increase in a state's Black population. For more on this problem and its history, see also Guinier, 2004.

3. Alesina and Glaeser's (2004) study compared the United States with Italy and Germany. The lowest-income Germans worked far fewer hours than comparable Americans and overwhelmingly declined to place blame for poverty on low-income people.

Conclusion

Challenges for This Generation: Integration and Social Transformation

Gary Orfield

Our society is going through sweeping demographic changes that are transforming our schools. Thousands of elementary and secondary schools are passing through difficult and complex changes that have major consequences, and they are without any strategy or help. This threatens a democratic society in which common schools have traditionally played a central role in helping diverse groups of students and their broader communities get to know one another and our common societal values. Ignoring issues of race (and class) has only resulted in increasing segregation in every region of the country (G. Orfield & C. Lee, 2005).

In spite of resegregation there are still many schools—some the result of desegregation policies and some from minority out-migration or gentrification—that are racially diverse. In fact, a growing percentage of students attend multiracial schools, although students in these schools are still a minority (G. Orfield & C. Lee, 2006). There are many new issues for schools that include Latino, Asian, and White students or traditionally Black schools now receiving a tide of immigrant children.

There are few resources to deal with issues of race and very little attention is given to them. Many teachers and administrators feel the tensions and, sometimes, recognize the failures, but do not know what to do. Rote celebrations of Martin Luther King Day or Cinco de Mayo or Black History Month don't help much (e.g., in schools where King's dream is revisited amid conditions of concentrated poverty and racial segregation). Simpleminded workshops by consultants about the way various groups learn or emotional encounters about racism seldom contribute much. A half-hour inservice on dealing with language-minority children and their parents is virtually useless (see Gándara, Maxwell-Jolly, & Driscoll, 2005).

Most adults in schools are products of segregated lives (Freeman, Brookhart, & Loadman, 1999), and few have well-developed knowledge and skills in racially integrated environments. In a society with deep and long-standing racial divisions, it is extremely unlikely that individual schools will devise effective solutions on their own, although we have seen a few exemplary schools' solutions in this book. Without thoughtful, research-based programs and policies, stereotypes can far too easily be reinforced and opportunities to use the considerable educational potential of diversity lost. This often happens even in situations where people are trying their best to do what they believe to be the right thing and to be fair to all students.

In this book and in other related recent research, particularly that done for the Supreme Court's affirmative action case in 2003, data show that integrated classrooms where there is positive student contact produce higher academic achievement and access to networks of information and opportunities and that integrated schools tend to lead to integrated lives (G. Orfield, 2001). The fact that White students are the most segregated group (G. Orfield & C. Lee, 2005) means that their broader learning and understanding of their society are accordingly limited, which makes them less competent to deal with our society's interracial future. The importance of this problem has been recognized by school districts that fought to defend desegregation in Lynn, Massachusetts; Seattle, Washington; and Louisville, Kentucky, and by the federal courts that approved these districts' integration policies.[1]

The demographic transformations since the most recent period of serious desegregation research mean that we can no longer proceed in thinking about successful integration without fully considering issues of immigration, language, national origin, class, and generational differences within Latino and Asian communities (G. Orfield & C. Lee, 2006). We must also think about the situations of millions of students from multiracial families who do not fit into any traditional categories. In some districts, already overwhelmingly segregated, regional solutions must be found to overcome the inequality imposed by district boundaries. Since we all benefit from the education of our future citizens and workers, we need to commit to providing appropriate schooling opportunities regardless of the fragmented nature of educational institutions that currently determines educational opportunity.

Recent research suggests ways that we can better train professionals to succeed in diverse settings and ways that teachers, principals, counselors, and district officials can contribute. We must place a high priority on recruiting strong, experienced, racially diverse teachers, and teachers who understand students' language and culture, for the schools that most need them. We should explicitly and effectively train and support teachers to work across their own racial and ethnic lines with more extensive high-quality, hands-on experience and mentoring. Some of the actual techniques teachers could use to more effectively reach students and resolve racial problems are explored and documented here. We need to get them into schools.

We have learned, in these studies, about the growing diversity in our public schools and the new educational dimensions of multiracial schools as well as ways in which students from diverse backgrounds can best contribute to and benefit from inclusive schools. We have seen a powerful case showing possibilities of eliminating tracking, at least in a district with strong resources and leadership, raising issues rarely discussed by educational leaders in this conservative era. This book also provides an example of collaboration among researchers, litigators, and local educational leaders in developing evidence on a wide range of benefits from policies that created successful and stable integration in what had been an unstable and resegregating inner suburban community. We continue to learn about the important benefits to individual students and to our larger society of inclusive integrated environments. In all of these ways and more, this book's authors have moved forward the agenda of research and policy.

The research reported in this book is far from complete and definitive, but it begins to fill a vacuum created in the generation since there were serious funding and policy initiatives for desegregated public schools. Our project lacked funds to initiate any major new research, but we found many researchers who had access to data and experience and were eager to produce usable knowledge for today's multiracial schools. We hope that these studies help reopen a long interrupted dialogue over positive programs for integrated education in a time when it is folly to ignore the issues and possibilities.

It is encouraging to note that the new findings in this book are largely consistent with studies a generation earlier and that it was possible to substantially expand the frontiers of this field relatively quickly. This does not mean that major national studies are not needed, as well as many studies of individual subgroups and types of schools and regional issues, but it does mean that we can begin to learn, to act, to define research and policy agendas, and to initiate better preservice and inservice training along with more comprehensive school-based strategies and programs.

The questions our policy discussions have omitted for a generation, and that this book addresses, remain very important—far more important, in fact, than they were in the past—as the proportion of minority students grows rapidly and the consequences of unequal education deepen for these students and our society. In such a diverse and ever-changing society, Whites need much more to know how to work effectively with non-Whites. The history of socially divided nations warns us that it is foolish to ignore inequalities and separation in a society where more than two of every five students are non-White. The results discussed here suggest that the challenges in diverse schools are far from intractable—that in fact these schools offer considerable opportunities that may not be available in homogeneous White or non-White schools with appropriate leadership in the school and district.

The best evidence is that desegregation is far from the zero-sum game that its critics allege, claiming that the gains of minority students come at the cost of the Whites. Properly done, it is a positive-sum game where both groups receive substantial gains as does the community as a whole. These are findings teachers and administrators need to know about and implement, even as researchers are encouraged to dig deeper toward more precise and fully documented findings. It is also important that parents, community leaders, and judges know about this evidence so that they can all make informed choices that will help to create and sustain stable, viable diverse schools.

Racial transformation will not wait; we are in the last period of a White majority in our schools. We have very little time in a historic sense before our schools must learn to effectively serve a majority of young people whose ancestry is not European. We will need to successfully operate such schools in a country of amazing diversity. Thousands of suburbs, which, until now, have had almost no experience with racial diversity, will need to learn how to successfully operate multiracial schools or suffer the consequences of failure—destructive transformation like the kind of ghettoization and middle-class abandonment that has afflicted so many central city neighborhoods for generations. Nothing is being accomplished in terms of policy and leadership in many schools and communities to make integration work, and too often, useful knowledge remains unknown or unused.

After nearly a quarter century of denial, we need to face the obvious: race matters, inequality and segregation have grown, and many communities are facing racial change with no plan to make it work. Ignoring these issues only deepens the threat to our future. A generation of teachers and administrators who experienced desegregation and retraining in the 1960s and 1970s has been largely replaced by a generation that, lacking these opportunities, is nevertheless facing today's more complex realities with much less institutional knowledge or support. The risks of schools failing to do what only schools can do—reach the great majority of young people in communities and provide them a positive context for learning to live and work successfully in multiracial communities and institutions—have become greater and the needs more urgent. This is a situation that calls for understanding and leadership. This book is a step toward understanding.

Now we need leadership.

In the academic and research worlds we need to explore the issues of increasingly complex school and community settings in far greater depth. We must break the simpleminded assumption that we can succeed by merely ignoring racial and ethnic issues or pretending that all schools and students are identical and will respond to the same policies and approaches. We need to demonstrate powerfully the gains for all students that come with successful integration in the elementary and secondary context, as was done so well in the Supreme Court case about integration in higher education. We need to develop and systematically evaluate techniques for dealing with rarely explored, but increasing common diversity situations, such as the treatment of Latino students in predominantly Asian schools or intra-ethnic issues among Asians, Latinos, and Blacks coming from different nations. People in academia, school systems, and state governments must speak out about the value of integrated schools and the problems of resegregation. Multicultural curricula and serious training of teachers in diverse settings are badly needed. At a federal level it is clearly time to review the strong evidence about the gains produced by the desegregation assistance program in the 1970s and to consider a new one, perhaps offering special support to racially changing suburbs and metropolitan magnet schools and student transfer plans. Federal courts need to seriously reconsider their rush to terminate desegregation plans that are working, judicial actions that push school systems back toward patterns of segregation that produce neither equal opportunity nor preparation for a multiracial society. Such decisions can build in deepening economic and social stratification, and leave the dominant groups unprepared to operate effectively in a transformed society.

This book is a call to reopen a long interrupted conversation. For a generation we have been abandoning successful desegregation experiences and returning, in every part of the country, to schools that are polarizing and resegregating or are already separate and unequal. To do this in the face of demographic transformation and deepening inequality amounts to reckless disregard of the nation's future. We are floating backward toward the shoals of deepening racial stratification. Powerful leadership at many levels is needed if we are to avoid predictable failures and realize the potential gains of our astonishing diversity. It is time to recognize clearly the challenges we face and to make a new beginning toward creating the kinds of schools that can best serve the society we are becoming.

Notes

1. At the time this book went to press, the Supreme Court was reviewing the constitutionality of Seattle's and Louisville's race-conscious student-assignment plans.

Bibliography

Aboud, F. E. (1988). *Children and prejudice.* New York: Basil Blackwell.

Aboud, F. E. (1992). Conflict and group relations. In C. U. Shantz & W. W. Hartup (Eds.), *Conflict in child and adolescent development* (pp. 356–379). Cambridge, UK: Cambridge University Press.

Aboud, F. E. (2003). The formation of in-group favoritism and out-group prejudice in young children: Are they distinct attitudes? *Developmental Psychology, 39,* 48–60.

Aboud, F. E., & Amato, M. (2001). Developmental and socialization influences on intergroup bias. In R. Brown & S. Gaertner (Eds.), *Blackwell handbook of social psychology: Intergroup relations* (pp. 65–85). Oxford: Blackwell Publishers.

Aboud, F. E., & Levy, S. R. (2000). Interventions to reduce prejudice and discrimination in children and adolescents. In S. Oskamp (Ed.), *Reducing prejudice and discrimination* (pp. 269–293). Mahwah, NJ: Erlbaum.

Aboud, F. E., & Mendelson, M. J. (1998). Determinants of friendship selection and quality: Developmental perspectives. In W. M. Bukowski & A. F. Newcomb (Eds.), *Company they keep: Friendship in childhood and adolescence* (pp. 87–112). New York: Cambridge University Press.

Abrams, D., Hogg, M. A., & Marques, J. M. (Eds.). (2005). *Social psychology of inclusion and exclusion.* New York: Psychology Press.

Adarand Constructors, Inc. v. Peña. 515 U.S. 200 (1995).

Adelman, C. (1999). *Answers in the tool box: Academic intensity, attendance patterns and bachelor's degree attainment.* Office of Educational Research, U.S. Department of Education. Washington, DC: Retrieved May 5, 2001, from http://www.ed.gov/pubs/Toolbox.

Agee, J. (1998). Confronting issues of race and power in the culture of schools. In M. Dilworth (Ed.), *Being responsive to cultural differences* (pp. 21–38). Washington, DC: Corwin.

Aguilar, T. E., & Pohan, C. A. (1998). A cultural immersion experience to enhance cross-cultural competence. *Sociotam, 8*(1), 29–49.

Alba, J. W., & Hasher, L. (1983). Is memory schematic? *Psychological Bulletin, 93,* 203–231.

Albrow, M. (1998, May). *Frames and transformations in transnational studies.* Paper presented at the Economic and Social Research Council Transnational Community Programme Seminar, Oxford, UK.

Alesina, A., & Glaeser, E. L. (2004). *Fighting poverty in the U.S. and Europe: A world of difference.* New York: Oxford University Press.

Alexander, P., Entwisle, D. R., & Olson, L. S. (2004). Schools, achievement, and inequality: A seasonal perspective. In G. Borman & M. Boulay (Eds.), *Summer learning: Research, policies, and programs* (pp. 25–52). Mahwah, NJ: Erlbaum.

Alexander, P. A., & Murphy, K. (1998). The research base on APA's learner-centered psychological principles. In N. Lamber & B. Combs (Eds.), *Issues in school reform: A sampler of psychological perspectives on learner-centered schools* (pp. 33–60). Washington, DC: American Psychological Association.

Allport, G. W. (1954). *The nature of prejudice.* Reading, MA: Addison-Wesley.

American Educational Research Association. (2004, Fall). Closing the gap: High achievement for students of color. *Research Points, 2*(3). Retrieved December 28, 2004, from http://www.aera.net/uploadedFiles/Journals and Publications/ Research_Points/RPFall-04.pdf.

Anderson, J. (1988). *The education of blacks in the South, 1860–1935.* Chapel Hill: University of North Carolina Press.

Arias, M. B., & Poyner, L. (2001). A good start: A progressive, transactional approach to diversity in pre-service teacher education. *Bilingual Research Journal, 25*(4), 417–434.

Armaline, W. D. (1995). Reflecting on cultural diversity through early field experiences: Pitfalls, hesitations, and promise. In R. J. Martin (Ed.), *Practicing what we teach: Confronting diversity in teacher education* (pp. 163–180). Albany: SUNY Press.

Armor, D. J. (1995). *Forced justice: School desegregation and the law.* New York: Oxford University Press.

Arnold, C. A. (1993). *Using HLM with NAEP.* Paper presented at the Advanced Studies Seminar on the Use of NAEP Data for Research and Policy Discussion, Washington, DC.

Aronson, E. B., Blaney, N., Stephan, C., Sikes, J., & Snapp, M. (1978). *The Jigsaw Classroom.* Thousand Oaks, CA: Sage.

Aronson, E., & Osherow, N. (1980). Cooperation, prosocial behavior, and academic performance: Experiments in the desegregated classroom. *Applied Social Psychology Annual, 1,* 163–196.

Astone, N. M., & McLanahan, S. S. (1991). Family structure, parental practices and high school completion. *American Sociological Review, 56*(3), 309–320.

Attewell, P. (2001). The winner-take-all high school: Organizational adaptations to educational stratification. *Sociology of Education, 74,* 267–295.

Avery, P. G., & Walker, C. (1993). Prospective teachers' perceptions of ethnic and gender differences in academic achievement. *Journal of Teacher Education, 44*(1), 27–37.

Avila v. Berkeley Unified School District. No. RG03–110397 (Sup. Ct., Alameda County, April 6, 2004).

Banks, J. A. (1995). Multicultural education and the modification of students' racial attitudes. In W. D. Hawley & A. W. Jackson (Eds.), *Toward a common destiny: Improving race and ethnic relations in America* (pp. 315–339). San Francisco: Jossey-Bass.

Banks, J. A., & Banks, C. A. M. (Eds.). (1995). *Handbook of research on multicultural education.* New York: MacMillan.

Banks, J. A., Cookson, P., Gay, G., Hawley, W. D., Irvine, J. J., et al. (2001). *Diversity within unity: Essential principles for teaching and learning in a multicultural society.* Seattle: Center for Multicultural Education, University of Washington.

Banks, J. A., & McGee-Banks, C. A. (Eds.). (2004). *Handbook of research on multicultural education* (2nd ed.). San Francisco: Jossey-Bass.

Bankston, C., & Caldas, C. (2000). White enrollment in nonpublic schools, public school racial composition, and student performance. *Sociological Quarterly, 41*(4), 539–550.

Bankston, C., & Caldas, C. (2002). *A troubled dream: The promise and failure of school desegregation in Louisiana.* Nashville, TN: Vanderbilt University Press.

Bankston, C., & Caldas, S. (1996). Majority African American schools and social injustice: The influence of de facto segregation on academic achievement. *Social Forces, 75,* 535–552.

Barlow, A. L. (2003). *Between fear and hope: Globalization and race in the United States.* Lanham, MD: Rowman & Littlefield.

Baron, A., & Banaji, M. (2005). *The development of implicit attitudes: Evidence of race evaluations from ages 6, 10, and adulthood.* Harvard University. Unpublished Manuscript.

Barry, N. H., & Lechner, J. V. (1995). Preservice teachers' attitudes about and awareness of multicultural teaching and learning. *Teaching and Teacher Education, 11*(2), 149–161.

Bar-Tal, D. (1996). Development of social categories and stereotypes in early childhood: The case of "the Arab" concept formation, stereotype and attitudes by Jewish children in Israel. *International Journal of Intercultural Relations, 20,* 341–370.

Barth, P., & Haycock, K. (2004). A core curriculum for all students. *Harvard Education Letter, 20*(3), 8, 7.

Bartlett, F. C. (1932). *Remembering.* Cambridge, MA: Harvard University Press.

Belk v. Charlotte-Mecklenburg Board of Education. 269 F.3d 305 (4th Cir. 2001).

Ben-Ari, R., & Amir, Y. (1986). Contact between Arab and Jewish youth in Israel: Reality and potential. In M. Hewstone & R. Brown (Eds.), *Contact and conflict in intergroup encounters* (pp. 45–58). Cambridge, MA: Basil Blackwell.

Bennett, C., Cole, D., & Thompson, J. (2000). Preparing teachers of color at a predominantly white university. *Teaching and Teacher Education, 16*(4), 445–64.

Bennett, M., Barrett, M., Lyons, E., & Sani, F. (1998). Children's subjective identification with the group and ingroup favoritism. *Developmental Psychology, 34,* 902–909.

Bernstein, J., Schindler-Zimmerman, T., Werner-Wilson, R. J., & Vosburg, J. (2000). Preschool children's classification skills and a multicultural education intervention to promote acceptance of ethnic diversity. *Journal of Research in Childhood Education, 14,* 181–192.

Betts, J. R., Zau, A. C., & Rice, L. A. (2003, August). *New insights into school and classroom factors affecting student achievement* (Research Brief No. 76). San Francisco: Public Policy Institute of California.

Bigler, R. S. (1995). The role of classification skill in moderating environmental influences on children's gender stereotyping: A study of the functional use of gender in the classroom. *Child Development, 66,* 1072–1087.

Bigler, R. S. (1999). The use of multicultural curricula and materials to counter racism in children. *Journal of Social Issues, 55,* 687–705.

Bigler, R. S., Brown, C. S., & Markell, M. (2001). When groups are not created equal: Effects of group status on the formation of intergroup attitudes in children. *Child Development, 72,* 1151–1162.

Bigler, R. S., Jones, L. S., & Lobliner, D. B. (1997). Social categorization and the formation of intergroup attitudes in children. *Child Development, 68,* 530–540.

Bigler, R. S., & Liben, L. S. (1992). Cognitive mechanisms in children's gender stereotyping: Theoretical and educational implications of a cognitive-based intervention. *Child Development, 63,* 1351–1363.

Bigler, R. S., & Liben, L. S. (1993). A cognitive-developmental approach to racial stereotyping and reconstructive memory in Euro-American children. *Child Development, 64,* 1507–1518.

Black-Gutman, D., & Hickson, F. (1996). The relationship between racial attitudes and social-cognitive development in children: An Australian study. *Developmental Psychology, 32,* 448–456.

Blau, P. M. (1977). *Inequality and heterogeneity.* New York: Free Press.

Blau, P. M., Blum, T., & Schwartz, J. (1982). Heterogeneity and Intermarriage. *American Sociological Review, 47,* 45–62.

Bloom, H. S., Ham, S., Melton, L., & O'Brient, J. (2001). *Evaluating the accelerated schools approach: A look at early implementation and impacts on student achievement in eight elementary schools.* New York: Manpower Demonstration Research Corporation.

Boaler, J., & Staples, M. (2005, April). *Transforming students' lives through an equitable mathematics approach: The case of Railside School.* Paper presented at the meeting of the American Educational Research Association, Montreal, Canada.

Board of Education of Oklahoma City Public Schools v. Dowell. 498 U.S. 237 (1991).

Bobo, L., Kluegel, J. R., & Smith, R. A. (1997). Laissez-faire racism: The crystallization of a kinder, gentler antiblack ideology. In S. A. Tuch & J. K. Martin (Eds.), *Racial attitudes in the 1990s: Continuities and changes* (pp. 15–41). Westport, CT: Praeger.

Boger, J. C., & Orfield, G. (Eds.). (2005). *School resegregation: Must the South turn back?* Chapel Hill: University of North Carolina Press.

Bollinger, L. (2003, May 1). *David Dinkins forum at Columbia University.* Retrieved February 26, 2005, from http://www.columbia.edu/cu/news/vforum/03/leeBollinger.ram.

Bonilla-Silva, E. (2003). *Racism without racists: Color-blind racism and the persistence of racial inequality in the United States.* Lanham, MD: Rowman and Littlefield.

Borman, K. M., Eitle, T. M., Michael, D., Eitle, D. J., Lee, R., et al. (2004, Fall). Accountability in a postdesegregation era: The continuing significance of racial segregation in Florida's schools. *American Education Research Journal, 41*(3), 605–631.

Bowman, P. J., & Howard, C. (1985). Race-related socialization, motivation, and academic achievement: A study of black youths in three-generation families. *Journal of the American Academy of Child Psychiatry, 24,* 134–141.

Boykin, A. W., & Toms, F. D. (1985). Black child socialization: A conceptual framework. In H. P. McAdoo & J. L. McAdoo (Eds.), *Black children: Social, educational, and parental environments* (pp. 33–51). Thousand Oaks, CA: Sage.

Boyle-Baise, L., & Sleeter, C. E. (2000). Community-based service learning for multicultural teacher education. *Educational Foundations, 14*(2), 33–50.

Boyle-Baise, M. (2002). *Multicultural service learning.* New York: Teachers College Press.

Braddock, J. H., II, Crain, R. L., & McPartland, J. (1984). A long-term view of school desegregation: Some recent studies of graduates as adults. *Phi Delta Kappan, 66*(4), 259–264.

Braddock, J. H., II, & Dawkins, M. P. (1993). Ability grouping, aspirations, and attainments: Evidence from the National Educational Longitudinal Study of 1988. *Journal of Negro Education, 62*(3), 324–336.

Braddock, J. H., II, Dawkins, M. P., & Wilson, G. (1995). Intercultural contact and race relations among American youth. In W. D. Hawley & A. Jackson (Eds.), *Toward a common destiny: Improving race relations in America.* San Francisco: Jossey-Bass.

Braddock, J. H., II, & Eitle, T. M. (2004). The effects of school desegregation. In J. A. Banks & C. A. McGee-Banks (Eds.), *Handbook of research on multicultural education* (2nd ed., pp. 828–843). San Francisco: Jossey-Bass.

Braddock, J. H., II, & McPartland, J. (1989). Social psychological processes that perpetuate racial segregation: The relationship between school and employment desegregation. *Journal of Black Studies, 19,* 267–298.

Braddock, J. H., II, McPartland, J., & Dawkins, M. (1986). Applicant race and job placement: A national survey experiment. *Journal of Sociology and Social Policy, 6,* 3–4.

Bradshaw, C. K. (1992). Beauty and the beast: On racial ambiguity. In M. P. P. Root (Ed.), *Racially mixed people in America* (pp. 77–88). Thousand Oaks, CA: Sage.

Brandell, J. R. (1988). Treatment of the biracial child: Theoretical and clinical issues. *Journal of Multicultural Counseling and Development, 16*(4), 176–187.

Bransford, J. D., Brown, A. L., & Cocking, R. R. (Eds.). (2000). *How people learn: Brain, mind, experience, and school.* Washington, DC: National Academy Press.

Bransford, J. D., & Schwartz, D. L. (1999). Rethinking transfer: A simple proposal with multiple implications. *Review of Research in Education, 24,* 61–100.

Brawarsky, S. (1996). *Improving intergroup relations among youth.* New York: Carnegie Corporation of New York.

Brewer, D. J., Rees, D. I., & Argys, L. M. (1995). Detracking America's schools: The reform without cost? *Phi Delta Kappan, 77,* 210–212, 214–215.

Brewer, M. B. (2000). Reducing prejudice through cross-categorization: Effects of multiple social identities. In S. Oskamp (Ed.), *Reducing prejudice and discrimination* (pp. 165–183). Mahwah, NJ: Erlbaum.

Brewer v. West Irondequoit Central School District. 212 F.3d 738 (2d Cir. 2000).

Bridgeland, J. M., DiIulio, J. J., Jr., and Morison, K. B. (2006). *The silent epidemic: Perspectives of high school dropouts.* Washington, DC: Civic Enterprises.

Brittain, C. (2002). *Transnational messages: Experiences of Chinese and Mexican immigrants in American schools.* New York: LFB Scholarly Publishing.

Brookhart, S. M. (1997). A field-based introduction to urban education at the middle school. *Mid-western Educational Researcher, 10*(2), 2–8.

Brown, A. L., et al. (1996). Distributed Expertise in the Classroom. In G. Salomon (Ed.), *Distributed cognitions: Psychological and educational considerations* (pp. 188–228). New York: Cambridge University Press.

Brown, C. S., & Bigler, R. S. (2005). Children's perceptions of discrimination: A developmental model. *Child Development, 76,* 533–553.

Brown, P. M. (1990). Biracial identity and social marginality. *Child and Adolescent Social Work, 7*(4), 319–37.

Brown, S. (1999, August). *High school racial composition: Balancing equity and excellence.* Paper presented at the annual meeting of the American Sociological Association, Chicago, IL.

Brown v. Board of Education of Topeka. 347 U.S. 483 (1954).

Bruer, J. T. (1993). *Schools for thought: A science of learning in the classroom.* Cambridge, MA: MIT Press.

Burant, T. J. (1999). Finding, using, and losing voice: A preservice teacher's experiences in an urban educative practicum. *Journal of Teacher Education, 50*(3), 209–219.

Burris, C. C. (2003). Providing accelerated mathematics to heterogeneously grouped middle-school students: The longitudinal effects on students of differing initial achievement levels. *Dissertations Abstracts International, 64*(5), 1570.

Burris, C. C., Heubert, J., & Levin, H. (2004). Math acceleration for all. *Educational Leadership, 61*(5), 68–71.

Burris, C. C., & Welner, K. G. (2005). Closing the achievement gap by detracking. *Phi Delta Kappan, 86*(8), 594–598.

Burris, C. C., Welner, K. G., Wiley, E., & Murphy, J. (in press). [Special issue.] *Teachers College Record.*

Bush, G. W. (2003, January 15). *President Bush discusses Michigan affirmative action case.* Retrieved February 26, 2005, from The White House Web site: http://www.whitehouse.gov/news/releases/2003/01/20030115-7.html.

Bush, G. W. (2005, November 16). *President discusses freedom and democracy in Kyoto, Japan.* Retrieved November 20, 2005, from The White House Web site: http://www.whitehouse.gov/news/releases/2005/11/20051116-6.html.

Bush, G. W. (2006, February 8). *President signs S.1932, Deficit Reduction Act of 2005.* Retrieved August 10, 2006, from http://www.whitehouse.gov/news/releases/2006/02/20060208-8.html.

Bustop, Inc. v. Board of Education. 439 U.S. 1380 (1978).

Cairns, E. (1989). Social identity and intergroup conflicts in Northern Ireland: A developmental perspective. In J. Harbison (Ed.), *Growing up in Northern Ireland* (pp. 115–130). Belfast: Stranmillis College.

California Tomorrow. (2004). *Ready or not? A California Tomorrow think piece on school readiness and immigrant communities.* Oakland: California Tomorrow.

Cameron, J. A., Alvarez, J. M., & Ruble, D. N. (2001). Children's lay theories about ingroups and outgroups: Reconceptualizing research on prejudice. *Personality and Social Psychology Review, 5,* 118–128.

Campbell, D. T., & Kenny, D. A. (1999). *A primer on regression artifacts.* New York: Guilford.

Campbell, D. T., & Stanley, J. C. (1963). *Experimental and quasi-experimental designs for research.* Chicago: Rand McNally.

Canniff, J. (2001). *Cambodian refugees' pathways to success.* New York: LFB Scholarly Publishing.

Cappachione et al. v. Charlotte-Mecklenburg Schools. 57 F.Supp. 2d 228 (1999).

Capps, R., Fix, M., & Murray, J. (2005). *The new demography of America's schools.* Research Report. Baltimore, MD: Urban Institute.

Carlson, C. I., & Lein, L. (1998). *Intergroup relations among middle school youth: Final report to the Carnegie Corporation.* Austin: Department of Educational Psychology, University of Texas.

Carnevale, A. P., & Deroschers, D. M. (2004). *Standards for what? The economic roots of K–16 reform.* Princeton, NJ: Educational Testing Service.

Carter, D. B., & Patterson, C. J. (1982). Sex roles as social conventions: The development of children's conceptions of sex-role stereotypes. *Developmental Psychology, 18,* 812–824.

Castañeda v. Pickard. 648 F.2d 989 (5th Cir. 1981).

Causey, V. E., Thomas, C. D., & Armento, B. J. (2000). Cultural diversity is basically a foreign term to me: The challenges of diversity for preservice teacher education. *Teaching and Teacher Education, 16*(1), 33–45.

Center for Research on Excellence and Diversity in Education (CREDE). (2002). *The five standards for effective pedagogy.* Retrieved October 15, 2004, from http://www.crede.ucsc.edu/standards/standards.html.

Center on English Learning and Achievement (CELA). (2003, Spring). Tracking and the literacy gap. *English Update,* 1–3.

Century Foundation. (2003, March 31). *Should race count? A policy discussion on the future of affirmative action.* Retrieved March 9, 2005, from http://www.tcf.org/Events/03-31-03/transcript.pdf.

Chemerinsky, E. (2005). The segregation and resegregation of American public education: The courts' role. In J. C. Boger & G. Orfield (Eds.), *School resegregation: Must the South turn back?* (pp. 29–47). Chapel Hill: University of North Carolina Press.

Cheng, S. (2004). *Gaining interactional leverage: School racial compositions and multiracial youths.* Paper presented at the annual meeting of the American Sociological Association, San Francisco, CA.

Cheng, S., & Powell, B. (2002). *Resource allocation to young children from biracial families.* Paper presented at the annual meeting of the American Sociological Association, Chicago, IL.

Cheng, S., & Starks, B. (2002). Racial differences in the effects of significant others on students' educational expectations. *Sociology of Education, 75*(4), 306–327.

Chesler, M., Bryant, B., & Crowfoot, J. (1981). *Making desegregation work: A professional guide to effecting change.* Thousand Oaks, CA: Sage.

Chew, K., Eggebeen, D. J., & Uhlenberg, P. R. (1989). American children in multiracial households. *Sociological Perspectives, 32,* 65–85.

Chiong, J. A. (1998). *Racial categorization of multiracial children in schools.* Critical Studies in Education and Culture Series. Westport, CT: Bergin & Garvey.

Cintrón, J. (2004). Bilingual/multicultural ed. marks ten-year anniversary. *Capital University News,* California State University Sacramento. Retrieved December 19, 2004, from http://www.csus.edu/news/110104bilingualInc.stm.

City of Richmond v. J. A. Croson. 488 U.S. 469 (1989).

Clark, K. (1979). Introduction. In G. Allport, *The nature of prejudice* (pp. ix–xi). Cambridge, MA: Perseus.

Clotfelter, C. T. (2004). *After "Brown": The rise and retreat of school desegregation.* Princeton, NJ: Princeton University Press.

Clotfelter, C. T., Ladd, H. F., & Vigdor, J. (2003). *Who teaches whom? Race and the distribution of novice teachers.* Working paper. Stanford Institute of Public Policy.

Clotfelter, C. T., Ladd, H. F., & Vigdor, J. (2005). Classroom-level segregation and resegregation in North Carolina. In J. C. Boger & G. Orfield (Eds.), *School re-*

segregation: Must the South turn back? (pp. 70–86). Chapel Hill: University of North Carolina Press.

Coalition for Asian American Children and Families. (2004). *Hidden in plain view: An overview of the needs of Asian American students in the public school system*. Retrieved July 7, 2005, from http://www.cacf.org.

Cochran-Smith, M. (1991). Learning to teach against the grain. *Harvard Educational Review, 61*(3), 279–310.

Cogan, L. S., Schmidt, W. H., & Wiley, D. E. (2001). Who takes what math and in which track? Using TIMSS to characterize United States students' eighth-grade mathematics learning opportunities. *Educational Evaluation and Policy Analysis, 23*(4), 323–341.

Cohen, E. G. (1986). *Designing groupwork: Strategies for the heterogeneous classroom*. New York: Teachers College Press.

Cohen, E. G. (1994, Spring). Restructuring the classroom: Conditions for productive small groups. *Review of Educational Research, 64*(1), 1–35.

Cohen, E. G. (2004). Producing equal-status interaction amidst classroom diversity. In W. G. Stephan & W. P. Vogt (Eds.), *Education programs for improving intergroup relations, theory, research, and practice* (pp. 37–54). New York: Teachers College Press.

Cole, C., Arafat, C., Tidhar, C., Zidan, W. T., Fox, N. A., et al. (2003). The educational impact of *Rechov Sumsum/Shara'a Simsim,* a television series for Israeli and Palestinian children. *International Journal of Behavioral Development, 27,* 409–422.

Coleman, J. (1988). Social capital in the creation of human capital. *American Journal of Sociology, 100,* 1448–1478.

Coleman, J. S., Campbell, E. Q., Hobson, C. F., McPartland, J. M., Mood, et al. (1966). *Equality of educational opportunity*. Office of Education, U.S. Department of Health, Education, and Welfare, National Center for Education Statistics. Washington, DC: U.S. Government Printing Office.

Coleman, P. T., & Deutsch, M. (1995). In W. D. Hawley & A. W. Jackson (Eds.), *Toward a common destiny: Improving race and ethnic relations in America* (pp. 371–397). San Francisco: Jossey-Bass.

College Board. (2004). *College bound seniors 2004: A profile of SAT program test takers*. Retrieved May 9, 2005, from http://www.collegeboard.com/about/news_info/cbsenior/yr2004/reports.html.

Collins, J. F. (2000). Biracial Japanese American identity: An evolving process. *Cultural Diversity & Ethnic Minority Psychology, 6*(2), 115–133.

Comas-Diaz, L. (1996). LatiNegra: Mental health issues of African Latinas. In M. P. P. Root (Ed.), *The multiracial experience: Racial borders as the new frontier* (pp. 167–190). Thousand Oaks, CA: Sage.

Comfort v. Lynn School Committee. 100 F.Supp. 2d 57 (D. Mass. 2000).

Comfort v. Lynn School Committee. 159 F.Supp. 2d 285, 288–89 (D. Mass. 2001).

Comfort v. Lynn School Committee. 283 F.Supp 2d 328 (D. Mass. 2003).

Comfort v. Lynn School Committee. No. 03-2415 (1st Cir. October 20, 2004). (2004a).

Comfort Panel Decision, *withdrawn.* 2004 WL 2348505 (1st Cir. November 24, 2004). (2004b).

Comfort v. Lynn School Committee. 418 F.3d 1 (1st Cir. 2005). (2005a).

Comfort v. Lynn School Committee. 126 S. Ct. 798 (No. 05-348 2005). (2005b).

Community Schools v. Seattle District No. 1. 126 S. Ct. 2351 (No. 05-9089) (2001).

Cook, T. (1984). What have black children gained academically from school integration? Examination of the meta-analytic evidence. In T. Cook, D. Armor, R. Crain, N. Miller, W. Stephan, et al. (Eds.), *School desegregation and black achievement* (pp. 6–42). Washington, DC: National Institute of Education.

Cook, T., Armor, D., Crain, R., Miller, N., Stephan, W., et al. (Eds.). (1984). *School desegregation and black achievement.* Washington, DC: National Institute of Education.

Cooney, T. M., & Radina, M. E. (2000). Adjustment problems in adolescence: Are multiracial children at risk? *American Journal of Orthopsychiatry, 70*(4), 433–444.

Cooper, R., & Slavin, R. E. (2004). Cooperative learning: An instructional strategy to improve intergroup relations. In W. G. Stephan, & W. P. Vogt (Eds.), *Education programs for improving intergroup relations, theory, research, and practice* (pp. 55–70). New York: Teachers College Press.

Costello, E. J., Compton, S. N., Keeler, G., & Angold, A. (2003). Relationships between poverty and psychopathology: A natural experiment. *Journal of the American Medical Association, 290,* 2023–2029.

Crain, R. L. (1984). Is nineteen really better than ninety-three? In T. Cook, D. Armor, R. Crain, N. Miller, W. Stephan, et al. (Eds.), *School desegregation and black achievement* (pp. 68–88). Washington, DC: National Institute of Education.

Crain, R. L., & Mahard, R. E. (1978). Desegregation and black achievement: A review of the research. *Law and Contemporary Problems, 42*(3), 17–56.

Crawford v. Board of Education. 17 Cal. 3d. 280 (1976).

Crawford v. Board of Education of the City of Los Angeles. 113 Cal. App. 3d 633 (1980), *aff'd,* 458 U.S. 527 (1982).

Cross, W. E., Jr. (1995). Oppositional identity and African American youth: Issues and prospects. In W. D. Hawley & A. W. Jackson (Eds.), *Toward a common destiny: Improving race relations in America* (pp. 185–204). San Francisco: Jossey-Bass.

Crystal, D. S. (Manuscript under review). *Social reasoning about racial exclusion: The role of context and intergroup experience.* Georgetown University.

Cushner, K. (2004). Conditions in the organizational environment that support positive intergroup relations. In W. G. Stephan, & W. P. Vogt (Eds.), *Education programs for improving intergroup relations, theory, research, and practice* (pp. 211–226). New York: Teachers College Press.

Darling-Hammond, L. (1997). *The right to learn: A blueprint for creating schools that work*. San Francisco: Jossey-Bass.

Darling-Hammond, L. (2000). *Teaching quality and student achievement: A review of state policy evidence*. Seattle: Center for Teaching and Policy, University of Washington.

Davis, K. A. (1995). Multicultural classrooms and cultural communities of teachers. *Teaching and Teacher Education, 11*(6), 553–563.

Dawkins, M. P. (1983). Black students' occupational expectations: A national study of the impact of school desegregation. *Urban Education, 18*, 98–113.

Dee, J. R., & Henkin, A. B. (2002). Assessing dispositions toward cultural diversity among preservice teachers. *Urban Education, 37*(1), 22–40.

Dee, T. S. (2004). Teachers, race, and student achievement in a randomized experiment. *Review of Economics and Statistics, 86*(1), 195–210.

Deever, B. (1994). Living *Plessey* in the context of *Brown:* Cultural politics and the rituals of separation. *Urban Review, 26*(4), 273–288.

Delpit, L. (1995). *Other peoples' children: Cultural conflict in the classroom*. New York: New York Press.

DeNavas-Walt, C., Proctor, B. D., & Lee, C. H. (2005). *Income, poverty, and health insurance coverage in the United States: 2004*. Washington, DC: U.S. Census Bureau, Government Printing Office.

Department of Public Instruction and State Board of Education. (1999). *North Carolina performance report, year 1998–99*. Raleigh: Public Schools of North Carolina.

Derman-Sparks, L. (1989). *Anti-bias curriculum: Tools for empowering young children*. Washington, DC: National Association for the Education of Young Children.

Derman-Sparks, L., & Phillips, C. B. (1997). *Teaching/learning anti-racism: A developmental approach*. New York: Teachers College Press.

Devine, P. G., Monteith, M. J., & Zuwerink, J. R. (1991). Prejudice with and without compunction. *Journal of Personality and Social Psychology, 60*, 817–830.

Devine, P. G., Plant, E. A., & Boswell, B. N. (2000). Breaking the prejudice habit: Progress and obstacles. In S. Oskamp (Ed.), *Reducing prejudice and discrimination* (pp. 185–208). Mahwah, NJ: Erlbaum.

Dovidio, J. F., & Gaertner, S. L. (Eds.). (1986). *Prejudice, discrimination, and racism*. Orlando, FL: Academic Press.

Dovidio, J. F., Gaertner, S. L., Stewart, T. L., Esses, V. M., ten Vergert, M., et al. (2004). From intervention to outcome: Processes in the reduction. In W. G. Stephan, & W. P. Vogt (Eds.), *Education programs for improving intergroup relations, theory, research, and practice* (pp. 243–265). New York: Teachers College Press.

Dovidio, J. F., Kawakami, K., & Beach, K. R. (2001). Implicit and explicit attitudes: Examination of the relationship between measures of intergroup bias. In R. Brown & S. Gaertner (Eds.), *Blackwell handbook in social psychology: Vol. 4. Intergroup processes* (pp. 175–197). Oxford: Blackwell.

Dovidio, J. F., Kawakami, K., & Gaertner, S. L. (2000). Reducing contemporary prejudice: Combating explicit and implicit bias at the individual and intergroup level. In S. Oskamp (Ed.), *Reducing prejudice and discrimination* (pp. 137–163). Mahwah, NJ: Erlbaum.

Doyle, A. B., Beaudet, J., & Aboud, F. (1988). Developmental changes in the flexibility of children's ethnic attitudes. *Journal of Cross-Cultural Psychology, 19*, 3–18.

Dred Scott v. Sanford. 60 U.S. 393 (1857).

Duke, N. (2000). For the rich it's richer: Print experiences and environments offered to children in very low- and very high-socioeconomic status first-grade classrooms. *American Educational Research Journal, 37*(2), 441–478.

Duncan, O. D., & Duncan, B. (1955). A methodological analysis of segregation indexes. *American Sociological Review, 20*(2), 210–217.

Educational Research Service. (2003). *Focus on: Differentiating instruction to help all students meet standards*. Arlington, VA: Educational Research Service.

Educational Testing Service. (2004). *Equity and adequacy: Americans speak on public school funding*. Retrieved November 20 2005, from http://www.ets.org/Media/Education_Topics/pdf/2004report.pdf.

Ehrlich, H. J. (1973). *The social psychology of prejudice: A systematic theoretical review and propositional inventory of the American social psychological study of prejudice*. New York: Wiley.

Eisenberg v. Montgomery County Public Schools. 197 F.3d 123 (4th Cir. 1999), *cert. denied*, 529 U.S. 1019 (2000).

Employment Securities Commission of North Carolina. (2003). *Civil labor force estimates—Area unemployment rate—December 2002*. Raleigh, NC: Employment Securities Commission.

Entwisle, D. R., & Alexander, K. L. (1994). Winter setback: The racial composition of schools and learning to read. *American Sociological Review, 59*(3), 446–460.

Epstein, J. L., & MacIver, D. J. (1992). *Opportunities to learn: Effects on eighth graders of curriculum offerings and instructional approaches (Report No. 34)*. Washington, DC: Office of Educational Research and Improvement.

Exposito, S., & Favela, A. (2003). Reflective voices: Valuing immigrant students and teaching with ideological clarity. *Urban Review, 35*(1), 73–91.

Faltis, C. (1994). Doing the right thing: Developing a program for immigrant and bilingual secondary students. In R. Rodríguez, N. Ramos, & J. A. Ruíz-Escalante (Eds.), *Compendium of reading in bilingual education: Issues and practices* (pp. 39–47). San Antonio: Texas Association of Bilingual Education.

Faltis, C. (1999). Creating a new history. In C. Faltis & P. Wolfe (Eds.), *So much to say: Adolescents, bilingualism, and ESL in the secondary school* (pp. 1–9). New York: Teachers College Press.

Faltis, C. (2005). *Teaching English language learners in elementary school communities: A joinfostering approach*. Columbus, OH: Prentice Hall/Merrill.

Faltis, C. J., & Arias, M. B. (1993). Speakers of languages other than English in the secondary school: Accomplishments and struggles. *Peabody Journal of Education, 69*(1), 6–29.

Faltis, C., & Wolfe, P. (Eds.). (1999). *So much to say: Adolescents, bilingualism, and ESL in the secondary school.* New York: Teachers College Press.

Farkas, S., Johnson, J., Immerwahr, S., & McHugh, J. (1998). *Time to move on: African-Americans and white parents set an agenda for public schools.* New York: Public Agenda.

Feld, S. L., & Carter, W. C. (1998). When desegregation reduces interracial contact: A class size paradox for weak ties. *American Journal of Sociology, 5,* 1165–1186.

Ferguson, R. F. (1998). Can schools narrow the black-white test score gap? In C. Jencks and M. Phillips (Eds.), *The black-white test score gap* (pp. 318–374). Washington, DC: Brookings Institution Press.

Ferguson, R. F., & Mehta, J. (2004). An unfinished journey: The legacy of *Brown* and the narrowing of the achievement gap. *Phi Delta Kappan, 85*(9), 656–669.

Figlio, D., & Page, M. (2000). *School choice and the distributive effects of ability tracking: Does separation increase equality?* Working paper. National Bureau of Economic Research.

Figlio, D. N., & Page, M. E. (2002). School choice and the distributional effects of ability tracking: Does separation increase inequality? *Journal of Urban Economics, 51,* 497–514.

Finder, A. (2005, September 25). As test scores jump, Raleigh credits integration by income. *The New York Times,* p. A1.

Finkel, S. E. (1995). *Causal analysis with panel data.* Thousand Oaks, CA: Sage.

Fisher, C. B., Jackson, J. F., & Villarruel, F. A. (1998). The study of African American and Latin American children and youth. In W. Damon (Ed.) & R. M. Lerner (Vol. Ed.), *Handbook of child psychology: Vol. 1. Theoretical models of human development* (5th ed., pp. 1145–1207). New York: Wiley.

Fiske, S. T. (1998). Stereotyping, prejudice, and discrimination. In D. T. Gilbert, S. T. Fiske, & G. Lindzey (Eds.), *The handbook of social psychology.* (4th ed., Vol. 2, pp. 357–411). New York: McGraw Hill.

Fiske, S. T. (2000). Interdependence and the reduction of prejudice. In S. Oskamp (Ed.), *Reducing prejudice and discrimination* (pp. 115–135). Mahwah, NJ: Erlbaum.

Fiske, S. T., & Taylor, S. E. (1984). *Social cognition.* Menlo Park, CA: Addison-Wesley.

Fletcher, A. C., Rollins, A., & Nickerson, P. (2004). The extension of school-based inter- and intraracial children's friendships: Influences on psychosocial well-being. *American Journal of Orthopsychiatry, 74,* 272–285.

Flinspach, S. L., & Banks, K. E. (2005). Moving beyond race: Socioeconomic diversity as a race-neutral approach to desegregation in Wake County schools. In J. C. Boger & G. Orfield (Eds.), *School resegregation: Must the South turn back?* (pp. 261–280). Chapel Hill: University of North Carolina Press.

Foeman, A. K., & Nance, T. (1999). From miscegenation to multiculturalism: Perceptions and stages of interracial relationship development. *Journal of Black Studies, 29*(4), 540–557.

Foner, E. (1988). *Reconstruction: America's unfinished revolution, 1863–1877* (1st ed.). New York: Harper & Row.

Frankenberg, E., & Lee, C. (2002). *Race in American public schools: Rapidly resegregating school districts.* Cambridge, MA: The Civil Rights Project at Harvard University.

Frankenberg, E., & Lee, C. (2003). *Charter schools and race: A lost opportunity for integrated education.* Cambridge, MA: The Civil Rights Project at Harvard University.

Frankenberg, E., Lee, C., & Orfield, G. (2003). *A multiracial society with segregated schools: Are we losing the dream?* Cambridge, MA: The Civil Rights Project at Harvard University.

Freeman, D. J., Brookhart, S. M., & Loadman, W. E. (1999, March). Realities of teaching in racially/ethnically diverse schools: Feedback from entry-level teachers. *Urban Education, 34,* 89–114.

Freeman, J. (2005). Permission to be gifted: How conceptions of giftedness can change lives. In R. J. Sternberg & J. E. Davidson (Eds.), *Conceptions of giftedness* (2nd ed.). New York: Cambridge University Press.

Freeman, Y., Freeman, D., & Mercuri, S. (2002). *Closing the achievement gap: How to reach limited-formal school and long-term English learners.* Portsmouth, NH: Heinemann.

Frey, M. C., & Detterman, D. K. (2003). Scholastic assessment or g? The relationship between the Scholastic Assessment Test and general cognitive ability. *Psychological Science, 15*(6), 373–378.

Frey, W. H. (2001, June). *Melting pot suburbs: A census 2000 study of suburban diversity.* Census 2000 Series. The Brookings Institution Center on Urban and Metropolitan Policy.

Fry, R. (2005). *The high schools Hispanics attend.* Research Report. Washington, DC: Pew Research Center.

Fu, X., Tora, J., & Kendall, H. (2001). Marital happiness and interracial marriage: A study in a multi-ethnic community in Hawaii. *Journal of Comparative Family Studies, 32*(1), 47–60.

Fuller, M. L. (1992). Teacher education programs and increasing minority school populations: An educational mismatch? In C. A. Grant (Ed.), *Research and multicultural education: From the margins to the mainstream* (pp. 184–200). London: Falmer.

Gaertner, S. L., & Dovidio, J. F. (1986). The aversive form of racism. In J. F. Dovidio & S. L. Gaertner (Eds.), *Prejudice, discrimination, and racism* (pp. 61–89). Orlando, FL: Academic Press.

Gaertner, S. L., & Dovidio, J. F. (2000). *Reducing intergroup bias: The common ingroup identity model.* Philadelphia: Psychology Press.

Gamoran, A., & Mare, R. D. (1989). Secondary school tracking and stratification:

Compensation, reinforcement, or neutrality? *American Journal of Sociology,*
94, 1146–1183.

Gamoran, A., Nystrand, M., Berends, M., & LaPore, P. C. (1995). An organizational analysis of the effects of ability grouping. *American Educational Re-*
search Journal, 32, 667–714.

Gándara, P., Maxwell-Jolly, J., & Driscoll, A. (2005). *Listening to teachers of En-*
glish language learners: A survey of California teachers' challenges, experiences,
and professional development needs. Santa Cruz, CA: The Center for the Future
of Teaching and Learning.

García, E. (2004). *Who are English language learners in the United States?* Paper
presented at the NCREST Conference, Scottsdale, AZ.

Garcia et al. v. St. Paul Independent School District 625. No. Civ-3-76-158 (Minn.
Dist., 3d Div. 1976).

Garmon, M. A. (1998). Using dialogue journals to promote student learning in a
multicultural teacher education course. *Remedial & Special Education, 19*(1),
32–45.

Garrity, D. (2004). Detracking with vigilance. *School Administrator, 61*(7), 24–27.

Gelman, S. A. (2003). *The essential child: Origins of essentialism in everyday*
thought. London: Oxford University Press.

Gelman, S. A., & Heyman, G. D. (1999). Carrot-eaters and creature-believers: The
effects of lexicalization on children's inferences about social categories. *Psycho-*
logical Science, 10, 487–493.

Gelman, S. A., Taylor, M. G., & Nguyen, S. P. (2004). Mother-child conversations
about gender. *Monographs of the Society for Research in Child Development,*
69, vii–127.

Genesee, F., Hamayan, E., & Cloud, N. (2000). *Dual language instruction: A hand-*
book for enriched education. Boston: Heinle & Heinle.

Genzuk, M. (2003). *Latino and language minority teacher projects.* Center for
Multilingual and Multicultural Research, University of Southern California.
Retrieved December 19, 2004, from http://www-ref.usc.edu/~cmmr.LTP.html.

George, P. (1992). *How to untrack your school.* Alexandria, VA: Association for
Supervision and Curriculum Development.

Gibbs, J. T. (1987). Identity and marginality: Issues in the treatment of biracial
adolescents. *American Journal of Orthopsychiatry, 57*, 265–278.

Gibbs, J. T. (1989). Biracial adolescents. In J. T. Gibbs & L. N. Huang (Eds.), *Chil-*
dren of color: Psychological intervention with minority youth (pp. 322–50). San
Francisco: Jossey-Bass.

Gibbs, J. T., & Hines, A. M. (1992). Negotiating ethnic identity: Issues for black-
white biracial adolescents. In M. P. P. Root (Ed.), *Racially mixed people in*
America (pp. 223–238). Thousand Oaks, CA: Sage.

Gibson, M. (1995). Additive acculturation as a strategy for school improvement.
In R. Rumbaut & W. Cornelius (Eds.), *California immigrant children: Theory*
research and implications for educational policy (pp. 77–106). San Diego: University of California Press.

Giroux, H. A. (2005). *Schooling and the struggle for public life: Democracy's promise and education's challenge*. Boulder, CO: Paradigm.

Gomez, M. L. (1993). Prospective teachers' perspectives on teaching diverse children: A review with implications for teacher education and practice. *Journal of Negro Education, 62*(4), 459–474.

Good, C., Aronson, J., & Inzlicht, M. (2003, December). Improving adolescents' standardized test performance: An intervention to reduce the effects of stereotype threat. *Journal of Applied Developmental Psychology, 24,* 645–662.

Good, T. L. (1987, July–August). Two decades of research on teacher expectations: Findings and future directions. *Journal of Teacher Education, 38*(4), 32–47.

Goodheart, A. (2004, May–June). Change of Heart. *AARP: The Magazine, 93,* 45–47.

Goodman, J., & Fish, D. R. (1997). Against-the-grain teacher education: A study of coursework, field experience, and perspectives. *Journal of Teacher Education, 48*(2), 96–108.

Goodwin, A. L. (1994). Making the transition from self to other: What do preservice teachers really think about multicultural education? *Journal of Teacher Education, 45*(2), 119–131.

Gordon, E. W., & Bridglall, B. L. (2005). Nurturing talent in gifted students of color. In R. J. Sternberg & J. E. Davidson (Eds.), *Conceptions of giftedness* (2nd ed.). New York: Cambridge University Press.

Goyette, K., & Xie, Y. (1999). Educational expectations of Asian American youths: Determinants and ethnic differences. *Sociology of Education, 72,* 22–36.

Gradstein, M., Justman, M., & Meier, W. (2005). *The political economy of education: Implications for growth and inequality*. Cambridge, MA: MIT Press.

Gratz v. Bollinger. 539 S. Ct. 244 (2003).

Green v. County School Board of New Kent County. 391 U.S. 430 (1968).

Grissmer, D., Flanagan, A., & Willamson, S. (1998). Why did the black-white score gap narrow in the 1970s and 1980s? In C. Jencks and M. Phillips (Eds.), *The black-white test score gap* (pp. 182–228). Washington, DC: Brookings Institution Press.

Grissmer, D., Kirby, S. N., Berends, M., & Willamson, S. (1994). *Student achievement and the changing American family*. Santa Monica, CA: Rand.

Grutter v. Bollinger. 539 U.S. 306, 123 S. Ct. 2325 (2003).

Guillaume, A., Zuniga, C., & Lee, I. (1995). Prospective teachers' use of diversity issues in a case study analysis. *Journal of Research and Development in Education, 28*(2), 69–78.

Guinier, L. (2003, November). Admission rituals as political acts: Guardians at the gates of our democratic ideals. *Harvard Law Review, 117(1),* 114–224.

Guinier, L. (2004, June). From racial liberalism to racial literacy: *Brown v. Board of Education* and the interest-divergence dilemma. *Journal of American History, 91*(1), 92–118.

Gurin, P. (1999, January). The compelling need for diversity in higher education. Expert reports prepared for *Gratz et al. v. Bollinger et al.,* No. 97-75231 (E.D.

Mich.); and *Grutter et al. v. Bollinger et al.*, No. 97-75928 (E.D. Mich.), Retrieved May 9, 2005, from at http://www.umich.edu/~urel/admissions/research/.

Gurin, P., Dey, E., Hurtado, S., & Gurin, G. (2002). Diversity and higher education: Theory and impact on educational outcomes. *Harvard Educational Review, 72*(3), 330–366.

Haberman, M. (1995). *Star teachers of children in poverty*. West Lafayette, IN: Kappa Delta Pi.

Haberman, M. (1996). Selecting and preparing culturally competent teachers for urban schools. In J. Sikula, T. J. Buttery, & E. Guyton (Eds.), *Handbook of research on teacher education* (2nd ed., pp. 747–760). New York: MacMillan.

Haberman, M., & Post, L. (1992). Does direct experience change education students' perceptions of low-income minority students? *Midwest Educational Researcher, 5*(2), 29–31.

Hallinan, M. (1994). Tracking: From theory to practice. *Sociology of Education, 67*(2), 79–91.

Hallinan, M. T., & Smith, S. S. (1985). The effects of classroom racial composition on students' interracial friendliness. *Social Psychology Quarterly, 48*(1), 3–16.

Hallinan, M. T., & Teixeira, R. A. (1987). Opportunities and constraints: Black-white differences in the formation of interracial friendships. *Child Development, 58,* 1358.

Hamilton, D. L., & Sherman, J. W. (1994). Stereotypes. In R. S. Wyer Jr. & T. K. Srull (Eds.), *Handbook of social cognition* (2nd ed., pp. 1–68). Hillsdale, NJ: Lawrence, Erlbaum & Associates.

Hanushek, E. A., Kain, J. F., & Rivkin, S. G. (1998). *Teachers, schools, and academic achievement*. Working paper 6691. National Bureau of Economic Research.

Hanushek, E. A., Kain, J. F., & Rivkin, S. G. (2004a). *New evidence about "Brown v. Board of Education": The complex effects of school racial composition on achievement*. Paper presented at the 2001 Brookings Conference on Empirics of Social Intentions. Washington, DC Revised December 2004.

Hanushek, E. A., Kain, J. F., & Rivkin, S. G. (2004b). Why public schools lose teachers. *Journal of Human Resources, 39*(2): 326–354.

Hanushek, E. A., & Wobmann, L. (2005). *Does educational tracking affect performance and inequality? Differences-in-differences evidence across countries.* Working paper 11124. National Bureau of Economic Research.

Hardesty, M. (2001). Biracial lived experience: From encapsulated to constructive self. *Studies in Symbolic Interaction, 24,* 113–143.

Harris, D. R., & Sim, J. J. (2002). Who is multiracial? Assessing the complexity. *American Sociological Review, 67*(4), 614–627.

Hatano, G., & Miyake, N. (1991). Commentaries: What does a cultural approach offer to research on learning? *Learning and Instruction, 1,* 237–281.

Hawley, W. D. (1992). School desegregation. In M. C. Alfin (Ed.), *Encyclopedia of educational research* (6th ed., pp. 1132–1139). New York: Macmillan.

Hawley, W. D. (2003, September). *Diversity and educational quality: The post-*

desegregation pursuit of diverse learning opportunities. Paper presented at the Color Lines Conference, Harvard University.

Hawley, W. D., Banks, J. A., Padilla, A. M., Pope-Davis, D. B., & Schofield, J. W. (1995). Strategies for reducing racial prejudice: Essential principals for program design. In W. D. Hawley & A. W. Jackson (Eds.), *Toward a common destiny: Improving race and ethnic relations in America* (pp. 423–434). San Francisco: Jossey-Bass.

Hawley, W. D., Crain, R. L., Rossell, C. H., Schofield, J. W., & Fernandez, R. (1983). *Strategies for effective desegregation: Lessons from research*. Lexington, MA: Lexington Publishers/D. C. Heath.

Heck, R. H., Price, C. L., & Thomas, S. L. (2004, August). Tracks as emergent structures: A network analysis of student differentiation in a high school. *American Journal of Education, 110*(4), 321–353.

Hedges, L. V., & Nowell, A. (1998). Black-white test score convergence since 1965. In C. Jencks & M. Phillips (Eds.), *The black-white test score gap* (pp. 149–181). Washington, DC: Brookings Institution Press.

Hedges, L. V., & Nowell, A. (1999). Changes in the black-white gap in achievement test scores. *Sociology of Education, 72,* 111–135.

Helms, J. E. (1990). *Black and white racial identity: Theory, research, and practice*. Westport, CT: Praeger.

Henze, R. (2000, January). Leading for diversity: How school leaders achieve racial and ethnic harmony. *Research Brief #6*. Santa Cruz, CA: Center for Research on Education, Diversity, and Excellence.

Henze, R., Katz, A., Norte, E., Sather, S., & Walker E. (2002). *Leading for diversity: How school leaders promote positive interethnic relations*. Thousand Oaks, CA: Corwin.

Herring, R. D. (1992). Biracial children: An increasing concern for elementary and middle school counselors. *Elementary School Guidance and Counseling, 27,* 123–30.

Herrnstein, R. J., & Murray, C. (1994). *The bell curve: Intelligence and class structure in American life*. New York: Free Press.

Heubert, J. (2005). High-Stakes testing, nationally and in the South: Disparate impact, opportunity to learn, and current legal protections. In J. C. Boger & G. Orfield (Eds.), *School resegregation: Must the South turn back?* (pp. 212–235). Chapel Hill: University of North Carolina Press.

Heubert, J. P., & Hauser, R. M. (Eds.). (1999). *High stakes: Testing for tracking, promotion, and graduation*. Washington, DC: National Academy Press.

Hewstone, M., Macrae, C. N., Griffiths, R., & Milne, A. B. (1994). Cognitive models of stereotype change: Measurement, development, and consequences of subtyping. *Journal of Experimental Social Psychology, 30,* 505–526.

Hirschfeld, L. A. (1993). Discovering social difference: The role of appearance in the development of racial awareness. *Cognitive Psychology, 25,* 317–350.

Hirschfeld, L. A. (1995). The inheritability of identity: Children's understanding of the cultural biology of race. *Child Development, 66,* 1418–1437.

Hirschfeld, L. A., & Gelman, S. A. (1997). What young children think about the relationship between language variation and social difference. *Cognitive Development, 12,* 213–238.

Holmes, R. M. (1995). *How young children perceive race.* Thousand Oaks, CA: Sage.

Hopwood v. Texas. 78 F.3d 932 (5th Cir. 1996).

Hoxby, C. M. (2000, August). *Peer effects in the classroom: Learning from gender and race variation.* Working paper 7867. National Bureau of Economic Research.

Hughes, D. (2003). Correlates of African American and Latino parents' messages to children about ethnicity and race: A comparative study of racial socialization. *American Journal of Community Psychology, 31,* 15–33.

Hughes, J. M., & Bigler, R. S., & Levy, S. R. (under review). Darkness cannot drive out darkness: African American children's responses to learning about historical racism.

Hunter, M. (2005). *Hunter instructional model.* Retrieved January 15, 2005, http://www.humboldt.edu/~tha1/hunter-eei.html.

Hunter v. Regents of University of California. 190 F.3d 1061 (9th Cir. 1999).

Immerwahr, J. W., & Foleno, T. (2000). *Great expectations: How the public and parents—white, African American and Hispanic—view higher education.* The National Center for Public Policy and Higher Education. Retrieved November 13, 2005, from http://www.publicagenda.org/research/research_reports_details.cfm?list=29.

Ingersoll, R. (2003). The teacher shortage: Myth or reality? *Educational Horizons, 81*(3), 146–152.

Inhelder, B., & Piaget, J. (1964). *The early growth of logic in the child: Classification and seriation.* New York: Harper & Row.

Institute for Policy Studies and Cities for Progress. (2005). *Fact sheet on national poverty.* Retrieved November 29, 2005, from www.citiesforprogress.org.

Janis, I. L., & Mann, L. (1977). *Decision making: A psychological analysis of conflict, choice, and commitment.* New York: Free Press.

Jencks, C., & Phillips, M. (Eds.). (1998). *The black-white test score gap.* Washington, DC: Brookings Institution Press.

Jennings, L. B., & Smith, C. P. (2002). Examining the role of critical inquiry for transformative practices. *Teachers College Record, 104*(3), 456–481.

Jessor, R. (1992). Risk behavior in adolescence: A psychological framework for understanding and action. In D. E. Rogers & E. Ginzburg (Eds.), *Adolescents at risk: Medical and social perspectives* (pp. 19–34). Boulder, CO: Westview.

Jessor, R. (1993). Successful adolescent development among youth in high-risk settings. *American Psychologist, 48,* 117–126.

Johnson, D. W., & Johnson, R. T. (2000). The three Cs of reducing prejudice and discrimination. In S. Oskamp (Ed.), *Reducing prejudice and discrimination* (pp. 239–268). Mahwah, NJ: Erlbaum.

Johnson, J., & Kean, E. (1992). Improving science teaching in multicultural settings: A qualitative study. *Journal of Science Education and Technology, 1*(4), 275–287.

Johnson, J. H. (2001, October 3). *Immigration driven demographic change: Implications and challenges for North Carolina public schools.* Issues session presentation to the State Board of Education.

Johnson, M. K., Crosnoe, R., & Elder, J. (2001). Students' attachment and academic engagement: The role of race and ethnicity. *Sociology of Education, 74*(4), 318–340.

Johnson v. California. 125 S. Ct. 1141 (2005).

Jolla, A. V. (2005, March 11). *Closing the achievement gap by increasing access to the AIG (Academically and Intellectually Gifted) Program: A case study of Southwest Elementary School.* Submitted for MPA at UNC.

Jones, N. A., & Smith, A. S. (2001, November). *The two or more races population: 2000.* Census 2000 Brief.

Jussim, L., Coleman, L. M., & Lerch, L. (1987). The nature of stereotypes: A comparison and integration of three theories. *Journal of Personality and Social Psychology, 52*(3), 536–546.

Kahlenberg, R. D. (2001). *All together now: Creating middle-class schools through public school choice.* Washington, DC: Brookings Institution Press.

Kain, J. F., & O'Brien, D. M. (2002). *Black suburbanization in Texas metropolitan areas and its impact on student achievement.* Dallas: University of Texas Press.

Kalmijn, M. (1993). Trends in black/white intermarriage. *Social Forces, 72*(1), 119–146.

Kandel, D. B. (1978, September). Homophily, selection, and socialization in adolescent friendships. *American Journal of Sociology, 84*(2), 427–436.

Kane, T. J. (2002). *Racial subgroup rules in school accountability systems.* Paper presented at the Taking Account of Accountability: Assessing Politics and Policy Conference, Kennedy School of Government, Cambridge, MA.

Kao, G. (1999). Racial identity and academic performance: An examination of biracial Asian and African American youth. *Journal of Asian American Studies, 2*(3), 223–249.

Kao, G. (2004). Social capital and its relevance to minority and immigrant populations. *Sociology of Education, 77*(2), 172–175.

Kao, G., & Tienda, M. (1998). Educational aspirations of minority youth. *American Journal of Education, 106,* 349–384.

Katz, P. A. (1973). Stimulus differentiation and modification of children's racial attitudes. *Child Development, 44,* 232–237.

Katz, P. A. (1988). Children and social issues. *Journal of Social Issues, 44,* 193–209.

Katz, P. A. (2003). Racists or tolerant multiculturalists? How do they begin? *American Psychologist, 58,* 897–909.

Kaufman, P., Alt, M. N., & Chapman, C. D. (2004). *Dropout rates in the United States: 2000.* NCES 2002–114. Washington, DC: National Center for Education Statistics.

Kerckhoff, A. C. (1986). Effects of ability grouping in British secondary schools. *American Sociological Review, 51*(6), 842–858.

Kifer, E. (1993). Opportunities, talents and participation. In L. Burstein (Ed.), *The IEA study of mathematics III: Student growth and classroom processes* (pp. 279–308). Oxford: Pergamon.

Killen, M. (1991). Social and moral development in early childhood. In W. M. Kurtines & J. L. Gewirtz (Eds.), *Handbook of moral behavior and development* (Vol. 2, pp. 115–138). Hillsdale, NJ: Lawrence, Erlbaum & Associates.

Killen, M., Crystal, D. S., & Ruck, M. (2006, May). Social and moral evaluations of interracial peer interactions. In M. Killen (Organizer), *Developmental perspectives on intergroup attitudes and relationships*. Association for Psychological Science, New York City.

Killen, M., & Hart, D. (Eds.). (1995). *Morality in everyday life: Developmental perspectives*. Cambridge, UK: Cambridge University Press.

Killen, M., Henning, A., Kelly, M. C., Crystal, D. S., & Ruck, M. (in press). Evaluations of interracial peer encounters by majority and minority U.S. children and adolescents. *International Journal of Behavioral Development*.

Killen, M., Lee-Kim, J., McGlothlin, H., & Stangor, C. (2002). How children and adolescents evaluate gender and racial exclusion. *Monographs for the Society for Research in Child Development, 67*(4).

Killen, M., Margie, N. G., & Sinno, S. (2006). Morality in the context of intergroup relationships. In M. Killen & J. Smetana (Eds.), *Handbook of moral development* (pp. 155–183). Mahwah, NJ: Lawrence, Erlbaum & Associates.

Killen, M., McGlothlin, H., & Lee-Kim, J. (2002). Between individuals and culture: Individuals' evaluations of exclusion from social groups. In H. Keller, Y. Poortinga, & A. Schoelmerich (Eds.), *Between biology and culture: Perspectives on ontogenetic development* (pp.159–190). Cambridge, UK: Cambridge University Press.

Killen, M., & Nucci, L. (1995). Morality, autonomy, and social conflict. In M. Killen & D. Hart (Eds.), *Morality in everyday life: Developmental perspectives* (pp. 52–86). Cambridge, UK: Cambridge University Press.

Killen, M., & Stangor, C. (2001). Children's social reasoning about inclusion and exclusion in gender and race peer group contexts. *Child Development, 72,* 174–186.

Kim, J., & Sunderman, G. L. (2004a, February). *Does NCLB provide good choices for students in low-performing schools?* Cambridge, MA: The Civil Rights Project at Harvard University.

Kim, J., & Sunderman, G. L. (2004b, February). *Large mandates and limited resources: State response to the No Child Left Behind Act and implications for accountability*. Cambridge, MA: The Civil Rights Project at Harvard University.

Kim, R., & Ness, C. (2001, March 31). Mixed-race Americans are happy finally to make the count. *San Francisco Chronicle,* pp. A1–14.

King, M. L., Jr. (1963). Letter from a Birmingham jail. In *Why we can't wait* (pp. 76–95). New York: Signet Books.

King, M. L., Jr. (1991). The ethical demands for integration. In J. B. Washington (Ed.), *A testament of hope: The essential writing and speeches of Martin Luther King Jr.* (pp. 117–125). San Francisco: HarperSan Francisco.

Kjolseth, R. (1982). Bilingual education programs in the United States: For assimilation or pluralism? In P. Turner (Ed.), *Bilingualism in the Southwest* (2nd ed., pp. 3–28). Tucson: University of Arizona Press.

Knapp, M., McCaffrey, L., & Swanson, J. (2003). *District support for professional learning: What research says and has yet to establish.* Seattle, WA: Center for the Study of Teaching & Policy, University of Washington.

Knight, M. G. (2004). Sensing the urgency: Envisioning a black humanist vision of care of teacher education. *Race Ethnicity and Education, 7*(3), 211–228.

Kohl, H. (1995). *Should we burn Babar? Essay on children's literature and the power of stories.* New York: New York Press.

Koslin, S., Koslin, B., & Pargament, J. W. (1972). Classroom racial balance and students' interracial attitudes. *Sociology of Education, 45*(4), 386–407.

Kozol, J. (1991). *Savage inequalities: Children in America's schools.* New York: Crown Publishing.

Kozol, J. (2005). *The shame of the nation: The restoration of apartheid schooling in America.* New York: Crown Publishing.

Krugman, P. (2005, March 8). The debt-peonage society. *The New York Times,* p. A23.

Kuhn, D., Nash, S. C., & Brucken, L. (1978). Sex role concepts of two- and three-year olds. *Child Development, 49,* 445–451.

Kulik, J. A. (1992). *An analysis of the research on ability grouping: Historical and contemporary perspectives.* Storrs, CT: National Center on the Gifted and Talented, University of Connecticut.

Kunen, J. S. (1996, April 29). The end of integration. *Time, 39,* 44.

Kurlaender, M., & Yun, J. (2001). Diversity and legal education: Student experiences in leading law schools. In G. Orfield (Ed.), *Diversity challenged: Evidence on the impact of affirmative action* (pp. 111–141). Cambridge, MA: Harvard Education Publishing Group.

Kurlaender, M., & Yun, J. (2002). *The impact of racial and ethnic diversity on educational outcomes: Lynn, MA, School District.* Cambridge, MA: The Civil Rights Project at Harvard University.

Labaton, S. (2005, March 8). Senate rejects 2 proposals to raise minimum wage. *The New York Times,* p. C2.

Laczko-Kerr, I., & Berliner, D. C. (2002). The effectiveness of "Teach for America" and other under-certified teachers on student academic achievement: A case of harmful public policy. *Education Policy Analysis Archives, 10*(37). Retrieved January 12, 2005, from http://epaa.asu.edu/epaa/v10n37/.

Ladson-Billings, G. (1995). Toward a theory of culturally relevant pedagogy. *American Educational Research Journal, 32*(3), 465–491.

Lane, R. E. (2000). *The Loss of Happiness in Market Democracies.* New Haven: Yale University Press.

Laosa, L. M. (2001). The new segregation. *ETS Policy Notes, 10*(1), 1–11.

Laosa, L. M. (2002). *Implications of school segregation for Hispanic/Latino children*. Paper presented at the annual meeting of the American Educational Research Association, New Orleans.

Lau v. Nichols. 414 U.S. 563 (1974).

Lawrence, Charles R., III (2005). Forbidden conversations: On race, privacy, and community (a continuing conversation with John Ely on racism and democracy). *Yale Law Journal, 114,* 1353.

Lee, C. (2004). *Racial segregation and educational outcomes in metropolitan Boston.* Cambridge, MA: The Civil Rights Project at Harvard University.

Lee, J. (1998). State policy correlates of the achievement gap among racial and social groups. *Studies in Educational Evaluation, 24*(2), 137–152.

Lee, J. (2002). Racial and ethnic achievement gap trends: Reversing the progress toward equity? *Educational Researcher, 31,* 3–12.

Lee, J. (2004). Multiple facets of inequity in racial and ethnic achievement gaps. *Peabody Journal of Education, 79*(2), 51–73.

Lee, J., & Bean, F. D. (2004, August). America's changing color lines: Immigration, race/ethnicity, and multiracial identification. *Annual Review of Sociology, 30,* 221–242.

Lee, J., & Wong, K. K. (2004). The impact of accountability on racial and socioeconomic equity: Considering both school resources and achievement outcomes. *American Educational Research Journal, 41*(4), 797–832.

Lee, V. E., & Bryk, A. S. (1988). Curriculum tracking as mediating the social distribution of high school achievement. *Sociology of Education, 61*(2), 78–94.

Leithwood, K., Jantzi, D., & Steinbach, R. (1998). Leadership and other conditions which foster organizational learning in schools. In K. Leithwood & K. Seashore Lewis (Eds.), *Organizational learning in schools* (pp. 67–93). Lisse, Netherlands: Swets & Zeitlinger Publishers.

Leonhardt, D. (2005, May 24). The college dropout boom. *The New York Times,* p. A24.

Lerner, M. J., & Simmons, C. H. (1966). Observer's reaction to the "innocent victim": Compassion or rejection? *Journal of Personality and Social Psychology, 4,* 203–210.

Levin, H. M. (1997). Raising school productivity: An x-efficiency approach. *Economics of Education Review, 16*(3), 303–312.

Levy, S. R. (1999). Reducing prejudice: Lessons from social-cognitive factors underlying perceiver differences in prejudice. *Journal of Social Issues, 55,* 745–766.

Lewis, A. E. (2003). *Race in the schoolyard: Negotiating the color line in classrooms and communities.* New Brunswick, NJ: Rutgers University Press.

Leyens, J. P., Yzerbyt, V. Y., & Schadron, G. H. (1994). *Stereotypes and social cognition.* London: Sage.

Liben, L. S., & Bigler, R. S. (2002). *The developmental course of gender differentiation: Conceptualizing, measuring, and evaluating constructs and pathways.* Boston, MA: Blackwell Publishing.

Liben, L. S., & Signorella, M. L. (1993). Gender-schematic processing in children: The role of initial interpretations of stimuli. *Developmental Psychology, 29,* 141–149.

Lindley, H. A., & Keithley, M. E. (1991). Gender expectations and student achievement. *Roeper Review, 13*(4), 213–215.

Lindsey, R. B., Robins, K. N., & Terrell, R. D. (2003). *Cultural proficiency: A manual for school leaders* (2nd ed.). Thousand Oaks, CA: Corwin.

Lippman, L., Burns, S., & McArthur, E. (1996). *Urban schools: The challenge of location and poverty.* Office of Educational Research and Improvement, U.S. Department of Education. Washington, DC: National Center for Education Statistics.

Liska, A. E., & Reed, M. D. (1985). Ties to conventional institutions and delinquency: Estimating reciprocal effects. *American Sociological Review, 50*(4), 547–560.

Logan, J. R., Oakley, D., Smith, P., Stowell, J., & Stults, B. (2001). *Separating the children.* Albany: SUNY Press.

Longshore, D. (1982). Race composition and white hostility: A research note on the problem of control in desegregated schools. *Social Forces, 61*(1), 73–78.

Longshore, D., & Prager, J. (1985). The impact of school desegregation: A situational analysis. *Annual Review of Sociology, 11,* 75–91.

Loveless, T. (1998). The tracking and ability grouping debate. *Thomas B. Fordham Foundation, 2*(8). Retrieved July 12, 2000, from http://www.edexcellence.net/library/track.html.

Loveless, T. (1999). *The tracking wars: State reform meets school policy.* Washington, DC: Brookings Institution Press.

Loving v. Virginia. 388 U.S. 11 (1967).

Lucas, S. (1999). *Tracking inequality: Stratification and mobility in American high schools.* New York: Teachers College Press.

Lucas, S. R., & Gamoran, A. (1993). *Race and track assignment: A reconsideration with course-based indicators of track location.* Washington, DC: Office of Educational Research and Improvement.

Lucas, T. (1998). *Into, through, and beyond secondary school: Critical transitions for immigrant youths.* McHenry, IL: Delta Systems.

Lucas, T., Henze, R., & Donato, R. (1990). Promoting the success of Latino language minority students: An exploratory study of six high schools. *Harvard Educational Review, 60*(3), 315–340.

Ludwig, J., Ladd, H. F., & Duncan, G. J. (2001). Urban poverty and educational outcomes. In W. G. Gale & J. Rothenberg Pack (Eds.), *Brookings-Wharton papers on urban affairs 2001* (pp. 147–201). Washington, DC: Brookings Institution Press.

Mace-Matluck, B., Alexander-Kasparik, R., & Queen, R. (1998). *Through the golden door: Educational approaches for immigrant adolescents with limited schooling.* McHenry, IL: Delta Systems/Center for Applied Linguistics.

Macias, R., & Kelly, C. (1996). *Summary report of the survey of the states' limited*

English proficiency students and available educational programs and services,
1994–1995. Santa Barbara, CA: University of California Language Minority Research Institute.

Mackie, D. M., Hamilton, D. L., Susskind, J., & Rosselli, F. (1996). Social psy-
chological foundations of stereotype formation. In C. Macrae, C. Stangor,
& M. Hewstone (Eds.), *Stereotypes and stereotyping* (pp. 41–77). New York:
Guilford.

Macrae, C. N., Stangor, C., & Hewstone, M. (Eds.). (1996). *Stereotypes and stereotyping.* New York: Guilford.

Mahan, J. (1982). Native Americans as teacher trainers: Anatomy and outcomes
of a cultural immersion project. *Journal of Educational Equity and Leadership,*
2(2), 100–110.

Mahard, R. E., & Crain, R. L. (1983). Research on minority achievement in desegregated schools. In C. H. Rossell & W. D. Hawley (Eds.), *The consequences of
school desegregation* (pp. 103–125). Philadelphia: Temple University Press.

Majete, C. A. (1997). *Black and white interracial parents' perceptions of their biracial children's identity and adjustment.* Paper presented at the annual meeting
of the Society for the Study of Social Problems.

Mandela, N. (1993). *Nobel Lecture.* Retrieved 20 November 2005, from http://
nobelprize.org/peace/laureates/1993/mandela-lecture.html.

Mansfield, E., & Kehoe, J. (1993). A critical examination of anti-racist education.
Canadian Journal of Education, 19, 418–430.

Marcus, R. F., & Sanders-Reio, J. (2001). The influence of attachment on school
completion. *School Psychology Quarterly, 16(4),* 427–444.

Margie, N. G., Killen, M., Sinno, S., & McGlothlin, H. (2005). Minority children's
intergroup attitudes about peer relationships. *British Journal of Developmental
Psychology, 23,* 251–259.

Margo, R. A. (1990). *Race and schooling in the South, 1880–1950: An economic
history.* Chicago: University of Chicago Press.

Marshall, S. (1995). Ethnic socialization of African American children: Implications for parenting, identity development, and academic achievement. *Journal
of Youth & Adolescence, 24,* 377–396.

Martin, C. L., & Halverson, C. F. (1981). A schematic processing model of sex-
typing and stereotyping in children. *Child Development, 52,* 119–134.

Mason, D. A., Schroeter, D. D., Combs, R. K., & Washington, K. (1992). Assigning
average-achieving eighth graders to advanced mathematics classes in an urban
junior high. *Elementary School Journal, 92(5),* 587–599.

Massey, D., & Denton, N. (1993). *American apartheid.* Cambridge, MA: Harvard
University Press.

McAfee, W. M. (1998). *Religion, race, and Reconstruction: The public school in
the politics of the 1870s.* Albany: SUNY Press.

McArthur, E. (1993). *Language and schooling in the United States: A changing picture, 1979 and 1989.* Office of Educational Research and Improvement, Department of Education. Washington, DC: National Center for Education Statistics.

McDiarmid, G. W. (1992). What to do about differences? A study of multicultural education for teacher trainees in the Los Angeles Unified School District. *Journal of Teacher Education, 43*(2), 83–93.

McDonnell, L., & Hill, P. (1993). *Newcomers in American schools: Meeting the educational needs of immigrant youth.* Santa Monica, CA: Rand.

McDonough, S. (2005, April 24). U.S. prison population soars in 2003, 2004. *The Associated Press.*

McFarland v. Jefferson County Public Schools. 330 F.Supp. 2d 834 (W.D. Ky. 2004).

McFarland v. Jefferson County Public Schools. 416 F.3d 513, 2005 WL 1693700 (6th Cir. Ky. July 21, 2005).

McGlothlin, H., & Killen, M. (2006). Intergroup attitudes of European American children attending ethnically homogeneous schools. *Child Development, 77,* 1375–1386.

McGlothlin, H., Killen, M., & Edmonds, C. (2005). European-American children's intergroup attitudes about peer relationships. *British Journal of Developmental Psychology, 23,* 227–249.

McGregor, J. (1993). Effectiveness of role playing and antiracist teaching in reducing student prejudice. *Journal of Educational Research, 86,* 215–226.

McIntyre, A. (1997). Constructing an image of a white teacher. *Teachers College Record, 98*(4), 653–681.

McKenzie, K. B., & Scheurich, J. J. (2003). *Equity traps: A useful construct for preparing principals to lead schools that are successful with racially diverse students.* Paper presented at the AERA, Chicago, IL.

McLaurin v. Oklahoma State Regents for Higher Education. 339 U.S. 637 (1950).

McRoy, R. G., & Freeman, E. (1986). Racial-identity issues among mixed-race children. *Social Work in Education, 8,* 164–174.

McRoy, R. G., & Zurcher, L. A. (1983). *Transracial and interracial adoptees: The adolescent years.* Springfield, IL: Charles C Thomas.

Mehan, H., & Hubbard, L. (1999). *Tracking "untracking": Evaluating the effectiveness of an educational innovation.* San Diego: University of California.

Meier, K. J., Stewart, J. J., & England, R. E. (1989). *Race, class, and education: The politics of second-generation discrimination.* Madison: University of Wisconsin Press.

Menard, S. (1995). *Applied logistic regression analysis.* Thousand Oaks, CA: Sage.

Meredith v. Jefferson County Board of Education. 126 S. Ct. 2351 (No. 05-915). (June 5, 2006).

Mickelson, R. (2001). Subverting Swann: First and second generation segregation in Charlotte-Mecklenberg schools. *American Educational Research Journal, 38*(2), 215–252.

Mickelson, R. A. (2005). The incomplete desegregation of the Charlotte-Mecklenburg schools and its consequences, 1971–2004. In J. C. Boger & G. Orfield (Eds.), *School resegregation: Must the South turn back?* (pp. 87–110). Chapel Hill: University of North Carolina Press.

Mikow-Porto, V. A. (1999). *Bilingual education: Current state of knowledge*. Raleigh, NC: Office of the State Superintendent.

Miller, S. M., Miller, K. L., & Schroth, G. (1997). Teacher perceptions of multicultural training in preservice programs. *Journal of Instructional Psychology, 24*(4), 222–232.

Milliken v. Bradley. 418 U.S. 717 (1974).

Milner, H. R. (2003). Teacher reflection and race in cultural contexts: History, meanings, and methods in teaching. *Theory into Practice, 42*(3), 173–180.

Minicucci, C., & Olsen, L. (1992). *Programs for secondary limited English proficient students: A California study*. Washington, DC: National Clearinghouse for Bilingual Education.

Moll, L. C., Amanti, C., Neff, D., & González, N. (1994). Funds of knowledge for teaching: Using a qualitative approach to connect homes and classrooms. *Theory into Practice, 31*(2), 132–141.

Monteith, M. J. (1993). Self-regulation of prejudiced responses: Implications for progress in prejudice-reduction efforts. *Journal of Personality & Social Psychology, 65*, 469–485.

Monteith, M. J., & Walters, G. L. (1998). Egalitarianism, moral obligation, and prejudice-related personal standards. *Personality and Social Psychology Bulletin, 24*, 186–199.

Moody, J. (2001). Race, school integration and friendship segregation in America. *American Journal of Sociology, 107*(3), 679–716.

Morgan v. Hennigan. 379 F.Supp. 410 (D. Mass. 1974).

Morgan v. Nucci. 831 F.2d 313 (1st Cir. 1987).

Morris, R. C. (1981). *Reading, 'riting, and Reconstruction: The education of freedmen in the South, 1861–1870*. Chicago: University of Chicago Press.

Mosteller, F., Light, R., & Sachs, J. (1996). Sustained inquiry in education: Lessons from skill grouping and class size. *Harvard Educational Review, 66*(4), 797–843.

Mouton, S. G., & Hawkins, J. (1996). School attachment: Perspectives of low-attached high school students. *Educational Psychology, 16*(3), 297–304.

Munck, R. (2005). *Globalization and social exclusion: A transformationalist perspective*. Bloomfield, CT: Kumarian Press.

Murtadha-Watts, K. (1998). Teacher education in urban school-based, multiagency collaboratives. *Urban Education, 32*(5), 616–628.

NAACP Legal Defense and Educational Fund. (2004). *Court upholds Berkeley School District's integration plan in face of Proposition 209 challenge*. Retrieved April 7, 2004, from http://www.naacpldf.org/content.aspx?article=284.

NAACP Legal Defense and Educational Fund, the Civil Rights Project, & the Center for the Study of Race and Law at the University of Virginia School of Law. (2005). *Looking to the future: Voluntary K–12 school integration*. Retrieved October 23, 2005, from http://www.civilrightsproject.harvard.edu/resources/manual/manual.pdf.

Narode, R., Rennie-Hill, L., & Peterson, K. (1994). Urban community study by preservice teachers. *Urban Education, 29*(1), 5–19.

National Academy of Education. (1999). *Recommendations regarding research priorities.* Educational Research Policy and Priorities Board. Washington, DC: Office of Education Research and Improvements.

National Center for Education Statistics. (2002). *Selected characteristics of students, teachers, parent participation, and programs and services in traditional public and public charter elementary and secondary schools: 1999–2002.* Retrieved September 16, 2004, from http://nces.ed.gov/.

National Center for Education Statistics. (2003). *The condition of education 2003.* Washington, DC: U.S. Department of Education.

National Center for Education Statistics. (2004). *The condition of education 2004.* Washington, DC: U.S. Department of Education.

National Commission on Teaching and America's Future. (2004). *Fifty years after "Brown v. Board of Education": A two-tiered education system.* Washington, DC: Author.

National Governors Association. (1989). *Charlottesville summit.* Retrieved August 30, 2006, from http://www.nga.org/portal/site/nga/menuitem.

National Governors Association. (1993). *Ability grouping and tracking: Current issues and concerns.* Washington, DC: National Governors Association.

National Governors Association. (2000). *America 2000 program.* Retrieved August 30, 2006, from http://govinfo.library.unt.ed/negp/reports/negp30.pdf.

National Research Council. (1999). *Improving student learning: A strategic plan for education research and its utilization.* Washington, DC: National Academy Press.

National Research Council. (2004). *Engaging schools: Fostering high school students' motivation to learn.* Washington, DC: National Academies Press.

National Research Council of the National Academies. (2004). *Measuring racial discrimination.* Washington, DC: National Academy of Science.

Neisser, U. (Ed.). (1998). *The rising curve: Long-term gains in IQ and related measures.* Washington, DC: American Psychological Association.

Newmann, F. M., & Wehlage, G. G. (1995). *Successful school restructuring: A report to the public and educators.* Center on Organization and Restructuring Schools, University of Wisconsin at Madison. Washington, DC: U. S. Department of Education.

Nieto, S. (2001). School reformed student learning: A multicultural perspective. In J. A. Banks & C. A. M. Banks (Eds.), *Multicultural education: Issues and perspectives* (pp.401–416). Boston: Allyn & Bacon.

Noordhoff, K., & Kleinfeld, J. (1993). Preparing teachers for multicultural classrooms. *Teaching and Teacher Education, 9*(1), 27–39.

Oakes, J. (1982). The reproduction of inequity: The content of secondary school tracking. *Urban Review, 14*(2), 107–120.

Oakes, J. (1986). Keeping track, part 1: The policy and practice of curriculum inequality. *Phi Delta Kappan, 68,* 12–18.

Oakes, J. (1990). *Multiplying inequalities: The effects of race, social class, and tracking on opportunities to learn math and science.* Santa Monica, CA: Rand.

Oakes, J. (1992). Can tracking research inform practice? Technical, normative, and political considerations. *Educational Researcher, 21*(4), 12–22.

Oakes, J. (2005). *Keeping track: How schools structure inequality* (2nd ed.). New Haven, CT: Yale University Press.

Oakes, J., Gamoran, A., & Page, R. (1992). Curriculum differentiation: Opportunities, outcomes, and meanings. In P. Jackson (Ed.), *Handbook of research on curriculum* (pp. 570–608). New York: Macmillan.

Oakes, J., Rogers, J., Lipton, M., & Morrell, E. (2000). *The social construction of college access: Confronting the technical, cultural, and political barriers to low-income students of color.* Los Angeles: Institute for Democracy, Education, and Access.

Oakes, J., & Wells, A. S. (1996). *Beyond the technicalities of school reform: Policy lessons from detracking schools.* Los Angeles: UCLA Graduate School of Education and Information Studies.

Oakes, J., & Wells, A. S. (1998). Detracking for high student achievement. *Educational Leadership, 55*(6), 38–41.

Oakes, J., & Wells, A. S. (1999). *The comprehensive high school, detracking, and the persistence of social stratification.* Paper prepared for the New York University Seminar on the Future of the Comprehensive High School. Retrieved April 20, 2001, from http://pages.nyu.edu/~fmh1/oakeswells.htm.

Oakes, J., Wells, A. S., Jones, M., & Datnow, S. (1997). Tracking: The social construction of ability, cultural politics and resistance to reform. *Teachers College Record, 98,* 482–510.

Ogbu, J. (2003). *Black American students in an affluent suburb.* Mahwah, NJ: Lawrence, Erlbaum & Associates.

Ogbu, J. U. (1978). *Minority education and caste.* New York: Academic Press.

Oliver, M. L., & Shapiro, T. M. (1995). *Black wealth/white wealth: A new perspective on racial inequality.* New York: Routledge.

Olmedo, I. M. (1997). Challenging old assumptions: Preparing teachers for inner-city schools. *Teaching and Teacher Education, 13*(3), 245–258.

Olsen, L. (1995). School restructuring and the needs of immigrant students. In R. Rumbaut & W. Cornelius (Eds.), *California's immigrant children: Theory, research, and implications for educational policy* (pp. 103–150). San Diego: Center for U.S.–Mexican Studies, University of California.

Olsen, L. (1997). *Made in America: Immigrant students in our public schools.* New York: New Press.

Olsen, L., & Jaramillo, A. (1999). *Turning the tides of exclusion: A guide for educators and advocates for immigrant students.* Oakland: California Tomorrow.

Omi, M., & Winant, H. (1994). *Racial formation in the United States from the 1960s to the 1990s* (2nd ed.). New York: Routledge.

Opotow, S. (1990). Moral exclusion and injustice: An introduction. *Journal of Social Issues, 46,* 1–20.

Orfield, G. (1978). *Must we bus? Segregated schools and national policy.* Washington, DC: Brookings Institution Press.

Orfield, G. (1996). The growth of segregation: African Americans, Latinos, and unequal education. In G. Orfield, S. E. Eaton, & the Harvard Project on School Desegregation (Eds.), *Dismantling desegregation: The quiet reversal of "Brown v. Board of Education"* (pp. 53–72). New York: New Press.

Orfield, G. (Ed.). (2001). *Diversity challenged: Evidence on the impact of affirmative action.* Cambridge, MA: Harvard Education Publishing Group.

Orfield, G. (2004). *Dropouts in America: Confronting the graduation rate crisis.* Cambridge MA: Harvard University Press.

Orfield, G. (2005). Introduction. The southern dilemma: Losing *Brown,* fearing *Plessy.* In J. C. Boger and G. Orfield (Eds.), *School resegregation: Must the South turn back?* (pp. 1–28). Chapel Hill: University of North Carolina Press.

Orfield, G., & Eaton, S. E. (1996). *Dismantling desegregation: The quiet reversal of "Brown v. Board of Education."* New York: New Press.

Orfield, G., & Lee, C. (2004). *Brown at 50: King's Dream or Plessy's Nightmare?* Cambridge, MA: The Civil Rights Project at Harvard University.

Orfield, G., & Lee, C. (2005). *Why segregation matters: Poverty and educational inequality.* Cambridge, MA: The Civil Rights Project at Harvard University.

Orfield, G., & Lee, C. (2006). *Racial transformation and the changing nature of segregation.* Cambridge, MA: The Civil Rights Project at Harvard University.

Orfield, G., Losen, D., Wald, J., & Swanson, C. (2004). *Losing our future: How minority youth are being left behind by the graduation rate crisis.* Cambridge, MA: The Civil Rights Project at Harvard University.

Orfield, G., & Yun, J. T. (1999). *Resegregation in American schools.* Cambridge, MA: The Civil Rights Project at Harvard University.

Orfield, M., & Luce, T. (2005, May). *Minority suburbanization and racial change: Stable integration, neighborhood transition, and the need for regional approaches.* Presented May 6–7, 2005, at Race and Regionalism Conference, Minneapolis. Institute on Race and Poverty.

Oskamp, S. (Ed.). (2000). *Reducing prejudice and discrimination.* Mahwah, NJ: Erlbaum.

Ovando, C., Collier, V., & Combs, M. C. (2003). *Bilingual and ESL classrooms: Teaching in multicultural contexts* (3rd ed.). Boston: Allyn & Bacon.

Panetta, L., and Gall, P. (1971). *Bring us together: The Nixon Team and the Civil Rights Retreat.* Philadelphia: Lippincott.

Parents Involved in Community Schools v. Seattle School District No. 1. 137 F.Supp. 2d 1224 (D. Wash. 2001).

Parents Involved in Community Schools v. Seattle School District No. 1. 426 F.3d 1162 (9th Cir. Wash. October 20, 2005).

Park, R. (1931). Mentality of racial hybrids. *American Journal of Sociology, 36*(4), 534–551.

Parker, L., & Hood, S. (1995). Minority students versus majority faculty and administrators in teacher education: Perspectives on the clash of cultures. *Urban Review, 27*(2), 159–174.

Patchen, M. (1982). *Black-white contact in schools: Its social and academic effects.* West Lafayette, IN: Purdue University Press.

Pattillo-McCoy, M. (1999). *Black picket fences: Privilege and peril among the black middle class.* Chicago: University of Chicago Press.

Pearce, D. (1980). *Breaking down the barriers: New evidence on the impact of metropolitan school desegregation on housing patterns.* Washington, DC: National Institute of Education.

Perie, M., Grigg, W., & Dion, G. (2005). *The nation's report card: Mathematics 2005 (NCES 2006–453).* Washington, DC: U.S. Department of Education, National Center for Education Statistics.

Perie, M., Grigg, W., & Donahue, P. (2005). *The nation's report card: Reading 2005 (NCES 2006–451).* Washington, DC: U.S. Department of Education, National Center for Education Statistics.

Peters, M. F. (1985). Racial socialization of young black children. In H. P. McAdoo, J. L. McAdoo (Eds.), *Black children: Social, educational, and parental environments* (pp. 159–173). Thousand Oaks, CA: Sage.

Peterson, J. M. (1989). Remediation is no remedy. *Educational Leadership, 46*(6), 24–25.

Pettigrew, T. (1998). Intergroup contact theory. *American Review of Psychology, 49,* 65–85.

Pettigrew, T. F. (2004). Intergroup contact: Theory, research, and new perspectives. In J. A. Banks, & C. A. McGee-Banks (Eds.), *Handbook of research on multicultural education* (2nd ed., pp. 770–781). San Francisco: Jossey-Bass.

Pettigrew, T. F., & Tropp, L. R. (2000). Does intergroup contact reduce prejudice? Recent meta-analytic findings. In S. Oskamp (Ed.), *Reducing prejudice and discrimination* (pp. 93–114). Mahwah, NJ: Erlbaum.

Pew Hispanic Center/Kaiser Family Foundation. (2004). *National survey of Latinos: Education.*

Pewewardy, C. (2005). Shared journaling: A methodology for engaging white preservice students into multicultural education discourse. *Teacher Education Quarterly, 32*(1), 1–20.

Phelan, P., Davidson, A. L., & Cao, H. T. (1991). Students' multiple worlds: Negotiating the boundaries of family, peer and school cultures. *Anthropology and Education Quarterly, 22*(3), 224–250.

Phelan, P., Davidson, A. L., & Yu, H. C. (1998). *Adolescents' worlds: Negotiating family, peers, and school.* New York: Teachers College Press.

Phinney, J. S. (1990). Ethnic identity in adolescents and adults: Review of research. *Psychological Bulletin, 108,* 499–514.

Phinney, J. S. (1996). Understanding ethnic diversity: The role of ethnic identity. *American Behavioral Psychologist, 40,* 143–152.

Phinney, J. S., Cantu, C. L., & Kurtz, D. A. (1997). Ethnic and American identity as predictors of self-esteem among African American, Latino, and White adolescents. *Journal of Youth & Adolescence, 26*, 165–185.

Phinney, J. S., Ferguson, D., & Tate, J. D. (1997). Intergroup attitudes among ethnic minority adolescents: A causal model. *Child Development, 68*, 955–969.

Piaget, J. (1965). *The moral judgement of the child.* New York: Free Press.

Plessy v. Ferguson. 163 U.S. 537 (1896).

Pollock, M. (2004). *Colormute: Race talk dilemmas in an American school.* Princeton, NJ: Princeton University Press.

Portes, A. (1995). Segmented assimilation among new immigrant youth: A conceptual framework. In R. Rumbaut & W. Cornelius (Eds.), *California immigrant children: Theory research and implications for educational policy* (pp. 71–76). San Diego: University of California Press.

Portes, A. (1998). Social capital: Its origins and applications in modern sociology. *Annual Review of Sociology, 24*, 1–25.

Portes, A. (1999). Towards a new world: The origins and effects of transnational activities. *Ethnic and Racial Studies, 22*(2), 463–477.

Portes, A., Guarnizo, L., & Landolt, P. (1999). The study of transnationalism: Pitfalls and promise of an emergent research field. *Ethnic and Racial Studies, 22*(2), 217–237.

Poussaint, A. F. (1984). Study of interracial children presents positive picture. *Interracial Books for Children Bulletin, 15*(6), 9–10.

Powell, J. A. (2004). Symposium: The needs of members in a legitimate democratic state. *Santa Clara Law Review, 44*, 969.

Powlishta, K. K. (1995). Gender bias in children's perceptions of personality traits. *Sex Roles, 32*, 17–28.

Proposition 54: Classification by race, ethnicity, color, or national origin, 2003. Sacramento, CA.

Public Agenda. (2002). *Knowing it by heart.* Retrieved November 13, 2005, from http://www.publicagenda.org/press/press_release_detail.cfm?list=48.

Qian, A. (1997). Breaking the racial barriers: Variations in interracial marriage between 1980 and 1990. *Demography, 34*(2), 263–276.

Quintana, S. M. (1994). A model of ethnic perspective-taking ability applied to Mexican-American children and youth. *International Journal of Intercultural Relations, 18*, 419–448.

Quintana, S. M., & Vera, E. M. (1999). Mexican American children's ethnic identity, understanding of prejudice, and parental ethnic socialization. *Hispanic Journal of Behavioral Sciences, 21*, 387–404.

Radina, M. E., & Cooney, T. M. (2000). Relationship quality between multiracial adolescents and their biological parents. *American Journal of Orthopsychiatry, 70*(4), 445–454.

Raudenbush, S. W., & Bryk, A. S. (2002). *Hierarchical linear models: Applications and data analysis methods.* Thousand Oaks, CA: Sage.

Raudenbush, S. W., Bryk, A. S., Cheong, Y. F., & Congdon, R. (2002). *HLM 5:*

Hierarchical linear and non-linear modeling. Chicago: Scientific Software International.

Rawls, J. (1971). *A theory of justice.* Cambridge, MA: Belknap Press of Harvard University Press.

Reardon, S. F., & Yun, J. T. (2002). *Private school racial enrollments and segregation.* Cambridge, MA: The Civil Rights Project at Harvard University.

Reardon, S. F., & Yun, J. T. (2005). Integrating neighborhoods, segregating schools: The retreat from school desegregation in the South, 1990–2000. In J.C. Boger & G. Orfield (Eds.), *School resegregation: Must the South turn back?* (pp. 51–69). Chapel Hill: University of North Carolina Press.

Reed, D., & Cheng, J. (2003). *Racial and ethnic wage gaps in the California labor market.* San Francisco: Public Policy Institute of California.

Reeder, J., Douzenis, C., & Bergin, J. (1997). The effects of small group counseling on the racial attitudes of second grade students. *Professional School Psychology, 1,* 15–18.

Reid, K. S. (2004). Survey probes views on race. *Education Week, 23*(36), 1.

Reis, N. M. (2001). *A case study on the impact of professional development grounded in multicultural education on improving the quality of teachers of Latino students.* Unpublished doctoral dissertation, LaVerne University, LaVerne, CA.

Resnick, L. B., Levine, J. M., & Teasley, S. D. (1991). *Perspectives on socially shared cognition.* Washington, DC: American Psychological Association.

Rice, J. K. (2003). *Teacher quality: Understanding the effectiveness of teacher attributes.* Washington, DC: Economic Policy Institute.

Riojas Clark, E., & Bustos Flores, B. (1997). Instructional snapshots (IS) in Mexico: Pre-service bilingual teachers take pictures of classroom practices. *Bilingual Research Journal, 21*(2,3), 273–282.

Rios, F., & Montecinos, C. (1999). Advocating social justice and cultural affirmation. *Equity & Excellence in Education, 32*(3), 66–77.

Ritchey, P. N., & Fishbein, H. D. (2001). The lack of an association between adolescent friends' prejudices and stereotypes. *Merrill-Palmer Quarterly, 47,* 188–206.

Rolstad, K., Mahoney, K., & Glass, G. (2005). The big picture: A meta-analysis of program effectiveness research on English language learners. *Educational Policy, 19*(4), 572–594.

Romero, A. J., & Roberts, R. F. (1998). Perception of discrimination and ethnocultural variables in a diverse group of adolescents. *Journal of Adolescence, 21,* 641–656.

Romo, H. (1998). *LATINA high school leaving: Some practical solutions.* Charleston, WV: ERIC Clearinghouse on Rural Education and Small Schools. ERIC Document Reproduction Service No. ED 423 096.

Root, M. P. P. (Ed.). (1992). *Racially mixed people in America.* Thousand Oaks, CA: Sage.

Rosato, J. L. (1997). "A color of their own": Multiracial children and the family. *Brandeis Journal of Family Law, 36*(1), 41–51.

Ross, D. D., & Smith, W. (1992). Understanding preservice teachers' perspectives on diversity. *Journal of Teacher Education, 43*(2), 94–103.

Rossell, C. H. (1990). *The carrot or the stick for school desegregation policy: Magnet schools or forced busing?* Philadelphia: Temple University Press.

Rothstein, R. (2004). *Class and schools: Using social, economic, and educational reform to close the black-white achievement gap.* Washington, DC: Economic Policy Institute.

Rubin, B. C., & Noguera, P. A. (2004). Tracking detracking: Sorting through the dilemmas and possibilities of detracking in practice. *Equity & Excellence in Education, 37,* 92–101.

Ruble, D., & Martin, C. (1998). Gender development. In W. Damon (Ed.) & N. Eisenberg (Vol. Ed.), *Handbook of child psychology: Vol. 3. Socialization* (pp. 933–1016). New York: Wiley.

Ruck, M. D., Abramovitch, R., & Keating, D. (1998). Children's and adolescents' understanding of rights: Balancing nurturance and self-determination. *Child Development, 64,* 404–417.

Rueda, R., & Monzó, L. D. (2002). Apprenticeship for teaching: Professional development issues surrounding the collaborative relationship between teachers and paraeducators. *Teaching and Teacher Education, 18*(5), 503–521.

Rumbaut, R., & Cornelius, W. (Eds.). (1995). *California immigrant children: Theory research and implications for educational policy.* San Diego: University of California Press.

Rumbaut, R., & Ima, K. (1988). *The adaptation of Southeast Asian refugee youth: A comparative study.* Washington, DC: Office of Refugee Resettlement.

Rumberger, R. W., & Palardy, G. J. (2005). Does resegregation matter? The impact of social composition on academic achievement in southern high schools. In J. C. Boger & G. Orfield (Eds.), *School resegregation: Must the South turn back?* (pp. 127–147). Chapel Hill: University of North Carolina Press.

Rushton, S. P. (2001). Cultural assimilation: A narrative case study of student-teaching in an inner-city school. *Teaching and Teacher Education, 17*(2), 147–160.

Rutland, A. (2004). The development and self-regulation of intergroup attitudes in children. In M. Bennett & F. Sani (Eds.), *The development of the social self* (pp. 247–265). East Sussex, UK: Psychology Press.

Salzer, M. S. (1998). Narrative approach to assessing interactions between society, community, and person. *Journal of Community Psychology, 26*(6), 569–580.

San Antonio v. Rodriguez. 411 U.S. 1 (1973).

Sanders, W. L., & Horn, S. P. (1998). Research findings from the Tennessee Value-Added Assessment System (TVAAS) data base: Implications for educational evaluation and research. *Journal of Personnel Evaluation in Education, 12*(3), 247–256.

Sardo-Brown, D., & Hershey, M. (1995). A study of teachers' and students' multi-cultural attitudes before and after the use of an integrated multi-cultural lesson plan. *Journal of Instructional Psychology, 22,* 259–276.

Schiff, J., Firestone, W., & Young, J. (1999, April). *Organizational context for student achievement: The case of student racial composition.* Paper presented at the annual meeting of the American Educational Research Association, Montreal, Canada.

Schmidt, W. H. (1993). The distribution of instructional time to mathematical content: One aspect of opportunity to learn. In L. Burstein (Ed.), *The IEA study of mathematics III: Student growth and classroom processes* (pp. 279–308). Oxford: Pergamon.

Schmidt, W. H., Houang, R., & Cogan, L. (2002). A coherent curriculum: The case of mathematics. *American Educator.* Retrieved October 15, 2003, from http://www.aft.org/american_educator/summer2002/curriculum.pdf.

Schmidt, W. H., McKnight, C. C., Cogan, L. S., Jakwerth, P. M., & Houang, R. T. (1999). *Facing the consequences: Using TIMSS for a closer look at U.S. mathematics and science education.* Drodrecht, Netherlands: Kluwer Academic.

Schneider, B., & Coleman, J. S. (1993). *Parents, their children, and schools.* Boulder, CO: Westview.

Schofield, J. W. (1982). *Black and white in school: Trust, tension, or tolerance?* New York: Praeger.

Schofield, J. W. (1986). Causes and consequences of the color-blind perspective. In J. F. Dovidio & S. L. Gaertner (Eds.), *Prejudice, discrimination, racism* (pp. 231–253). San Diego: Academic Press.

Schofield, J. W. (1989). *Black and white in school: Trust, tension, or tolerance?* New York: Teachers College Press.

Schofield, J. W. (1991). School desegregation and intergroup relations: A review of the literature. *Review of Research in Education, 17,* 335–409.

Schofield, J. W. (1995). Review of research on school desegregation's impact on elementary and secondary school students. In J. A. Banks and C. A. McGee Banks (Eds.), *Handbook of research on multicultural education* (pp. 597–617). New York: Macmillan.

Schofield, J. W. (1997). School desegregation forty years after *Brown v. Board of Education:* Looking forward and looking backward. In D. Johnson (Ed.), *Minorities and girls in school: Effects on achievement and performance* (pp. 1–36). Pittsburgh: Learning Research & Development Center.

Schofield, J. W. (2001). Is diversity a compelling educational interest? Evidence from Louisville. In G. Orfield (Ed.), *Diversity challenged: Evidence on the impact of affirmative action* (pp. 99–109). Cambridge, MA: Harvard Education Publishing Group.

Schofield, J. W. (2004). Fostering positive intergroup relations in schools. In J. A. Banks, & C. A. McGee Banks (Eds.), *Handbook of Research on Multicultural Education* (2nd ed., pp. 799–812). San Francisco: Jossey-Bass.

Schofield, J. W., & Sagar, H. A. (1977). Peer interaction patterns in an integrated middle school. *Sociometry, 40*(21), 130–139.

Schultz, E. L., Neyhart, K., & Reck, U. M. (1996). Swimming against the tide: A study of prospective teachers' attitudes regarding cultural diversity and urban teaching. *Western Journal of Black Studies, 20*(1), 1–7.

Sconzert, K., Iazzetto, D., & Purkey, S. (2000). Small-town college to big-city school: Preparing urban teachers from liberal arts colleges. *Teaching and Teacher Education, 16*(4), 465–490.

Scott, J., & Leonhardt, D. (2005, May 15). Class in America: Shadowy lines that still divide. *The New York Times,* p. A1.

Sebring, D. L. (1985). Considerations in counseling interracial children. *Journal of Non-White Concerns in Personnel and Guidance, 13*(1), 3–9.

Sefa Dei, G. J. (1996). Critical perspectives in racism: An introduction. *Canadian Review of Sociology & Anthropology, 33,* 247–267.

Sen, A. (2000). Merit and justice. In K. Arrow, S. Bowles, & S. Durlaf (Eds.), *Meritocracy and economic inequality* (pp. 1–16). Princeton: Princeton University Press.

Shade, B. J., Boe, B. L., Garner, O., & New, C. A. (1998). The road to certification: A different way. *Teaching and Change, 5*(3–4), 261–275.

Shapiro, T. (2004). *The hidden cost of being African American: How wealth perpetuates inequality.* New York: Oxford University Press.

Shen, J. (1998). *Alternative certification minority teachers and urban education. Education and Urban Society, 31*(1), 30–41.

Shen, J., Wegenke, G. L., & Cooley, V. E. (2003). Has the public teaching force become more diversified? *Educational Horizons, 81*(3), 112–118.

Shepard, L. A., & Smith, M. L. (Eds.). (1989). *Flunking grades: Research and policies on retention.* New York: Falmer.

Singham, M. (2003). The achievement gap: Myths and reality. *Phi Delta Kappan, 84*(8), 586–591.

Slavin, R. (1979). Effects on biracial learning teams on cross-racial friendships. *Journal of Educational Psychology, 3,* 381.

Slavin, R. (1985). *Using student team learning* (3rd. ed.). Baltimore: Johns Hopkins University Press.

Slavin, R. E. (1990). Achievement effects of ability grouping in secondary schools: A best-evidence synthesis. *Review of Educational Research, 60*(3), 471–500.

Slavin, R. E. (1995a). *Cooperative learning: Theory, research, and practice* (2nd. ed.). Boston: Allyn & Bacon.

Slavin, R. E. (1995b). Detracking and its detractors: Flawed evidence, flawed values. *Phi Delta Kappan, 77,* 220–223.

Slavin, R., & Braddock, J., II. (1993). Ability grouping: On the wrong track. *College Board Review, 168,* 11–17.

Slavin, R. E., & Chueng, A. (2004). How English language learners learn to read. *Educational Leadership, 61*(6), 52–57.

Slavin, R. E., & Cooper, R. (1999). Improving intergroup relations: Lessons learned from cooperative learning programs. *Journal of Social Issues, 55,* 647–663.

Slavin, R. E., & Madden, N. A. (1979). School practices that improve race relations. *American Educational Research Journal, 16,* 169–180.

Sleeter, C. E. (1996). *Multicultural education as social activism.* Albany: SUNY Press.

Sleeter, C. E. (2001). *Culture, difference, and power.* New York: Teachers College Press.

Sleeter, C. E., Hughes, B., Meador, E., Whang, P., Rogers, L., et al. (2005). Working an academically rigorous, multicultural program. *Equity & Excellence in Education, 38*(4), 290–299.

Smetana, J. G. (1995). Morality in context: Abstractions, ambiguities, and applications. In R. Vasta (Ed.), *Annals of child development* (pp. 83–130). London: Jessica Kinglsey.

Smith, R. W. (2000). The influence of teacher background on the inclusion of multicultural education: A case study of two contrasts. *Urban Review, 32*(2), 155–176.

Smylie, M. A., & Hart, A. W. (1999). School leadership for teaching, learning, and change: A human and social capital development perspective. In J. Murphy & K. S. Louis (Eds.), *Handbook of Research on Educational Administration* (pp. 421–442). San Francisco: Jossey-Bass.

Snow, C. E., Burns, S., & Griffin, P. (Eds.). (1998). *Preventing reading difficulties in young children.* Washington, DC: National Academy Press.

Sørensen, A. B., & Hallinan, M. T. (1985). Student diversity and instructional grouping. In A. Kerckhoff (Ed.), *Research in sociology of education and socialization* (Vol. 5, pp. 59–81). Greenwich, CN: JAI Press.

Spencer, M. B. (1985). Black children's race awareness, racial attitudes, and self-concept: A reinterpretation. *Annual Progress in Child Psychiatry & Child Development,* 616–630.

Stachowski, L. L., & Mahan, J. M. (1998). Cross-cultural field placements: Student teachers learning from schools and communities. *Theory into Practice, 37*(2), 155–163.

Stangor, C., & Ruble, D. N. (1989). Differential influences of gender schemata and gender constancy on children's information processing behavior. *Social Cognition, 7,* 353–372.

Stangor, C., & Schaller, M. (1996). Stereotypes as individual and collective representations. In C. N. Macrae, C. Stangor, & M. Hewstone (Eds.), *Stereotypes and stereotyping* (pp. 3–37). New York: Guilford.

Stanton-Salazar, R. D. (1997). A social capital framework for understanding the socialization of racial minority children and youths. *Harvard Educational Review, 67*(1), 1–40.

Steele, C., & Aronson, J. (1995). Stereotype threat and the intellectual test performance of African Americans. *Journal of Personality & Social Psychology, 69,* 797–811.

Steele, C. M., & Aronson, J. (1998). Stereotype threat and the test performance of academically successful African Americans. In C. Jencks and M. Phillips (Eds.), *The black-white test score gap* (pp. 401–430). Washington, DC: Brookings Institution Press.

Steele, C. M., Spencer, S., & Aronson, J. (2002). Contending with group images: The psychology of stereotype and social identity threat. In M. P. Zanna (Ed.),

Advances in experimental and social psychology (pp. 379–440). San Diego: Academic Press.

Steelman, L. C., & Powell, B. (1993). Doing the right thing: Race and parental locus of responsibility for funding college. *Sociology of Education, 66*(4), 223–244.

Steelman, L. C., Powell, B., Werum, R., & Carter, S. (2002). Reconsidering the effects of sibling configuration: Recent advances and challenges. *Annual Review of Sociology, 28,* 243–269.

Stein, G. M. (1973). Children's reactions to innocent victims. *Child Development, 44,* 805–810.

Stephan, C. W. (1992). Mixed-heritage individuals: Ethnic identity and trait characteristics. In M. P. P. Root (Ed.), *Racially mixed people in America* (pp. 50–63). Thousand Oaks, CA: Sage.

Stephan, C. W., Renfro, L., & Stephan, W. (2004). The evaluation of multicultural education programs: Techniques and a meta-analysis. In W. G. Stephan, & W. P. Vogt (Eds.), *Education programs for improving intergroup relations, theory, research, and practice* (pp. 227–242). New York: Teachers College Press.

Stephan, W. G. (2002). Improving intergroup relations in the schools. In C. H. Rossell, D. J. Armor, & H. J. Walberg (Eds.), *School desegregation in the twenty-first century* (pp. 267–290). Washington, DC: Brookings Institution Press.

Stephan, W. G., & Finlay, K. (1999). The role of empathy in improving intergroup relations. *Journal of Social Issues, 55,* 729–743.

Stephan, W. G., & Stephan, C. W. (2001). *Improving intergroup relations.* Thousand Oaks, CA: Sage.

Stephan, W. G., & Stephan, C. W. (2004). Intergroup relations in multicultural education programs. In J. A. Banks, & C. A. McGee-Banks (Eds.), *Handbook of research on multicultural education* (2nd ed., pp. 782–798). San Francisco: Jossey-Bass.

Stevenson, H. C. (1995). Relationship of adolescent perceptions of racial socialization to racial identity. *Journal of Black Psychology, 21,* 49–70.

St. John, N. (1975). *School desegregation: Outcomes for children.* New York: Wiley.

Stoddart, T., & Turiel, E. (1985). Children's concepts of cross-gender activities. *Child Development, 56,* 1241–1252.

Su, Z. (1997). Teaching as a profession and as a career: Minority candidates' perspectives. *Teaching and Teacher Education, 13*(3), 325–340.

Suárez-Orozco, C., & Todorova, I. (2003, Winter). The social worlds of immigrant youth. *New Directions for Youth Development, 15–25.*

Suárez-Orozco, M. (Ed.). (1998). *Crossings: Mexican immigration in interdisciplinary studies.* Cambridge, MA: Harvard Fellows.

Suárez-Orozco, M. (2000). Everything you wanted to know about assimilation but were afraid to ask. *Daedalus, 129*(4), 1–30.

Suárez-Orozco, M., & Suárez-Orozco, C. (1995). *Transformations: Immigration, family life, and achievement motivation among Latino adolescents.* Stanford: Stanford University Press.

Sunderman, G. L., Kim, J., & Orfield, G. (2005). *NCLB meets school realities: Lessons from the field.* Thousand Oaks, CA: Corwin.

Sunderman, G. L., Tracey, C. A., Kim, J., & Orfield, G. (2004, September). *Listening to teachers: Classroom realities and no child left behind.* Cambridge, MA: The Civil Rights Project at Harvard University.

Swann v. Charlotte-Mecklenburg Board of Education. 402 U.S. 1 (1971).

Swanson, C. B. (2004). *Who graduates? Who doesn't? A statistical portrait of public high school graduation, class of 2001.* Washington, DC: Urban Institute.

Sweatt v. Painter. 339 U.S. 629 (1950).

Sykes, R. E., Larntz, K., & Fox, J. (1976). Proximity and similarity effects on frequency of interaction in a class of naval recruits. *Sociometry, 39*(3), 263–269.

Tate, W. F., Ladson-Billings, G., & Grant, C. A. (1996). The *Brown* decision revisited: Mathematizing a social problem. In M. J. Shujaa (Ed.), *Beyond segregation: The politics of quality in African American schooling.* Thousand Oaks, CA: Corwin.

Tatum, B. D. (1992). Talking about race, learning about racism: The application of racial identity development in the classroom. *Harvard Educational Review, 62,* 1–24.

Tatum, B. D. (1997). *Why are all the black kids sitting together in the cafeteria?* New York: Basic Books.

Taylor, S. E., & Crocker, J. (1981). Schematic bases of social information processing. In E. T. Higgins, C. P. Herman, & M. P. Zanna (Eds.), *Social cognition: The Ontario symposium* (Vol. 1, pp. 89–134). Hillsdale, NJ: Erlbaum.

Teixeira, R. (2000). Critical support: The public view of public education. In R. D. Kahlenberg (Ed.), *A notion at risk: Preserving public education as an engine for social mobility.* New York: Century Foundation Press.

Testimony of Malcolm Chancey Jr. (2003). *McFarland v. Jefferson County Board of Education.* C.V. No. 3:02CV-620-H, Trial Transcript, Vol. 1, p. 135.

Thernstrom, A., & Thernstrom, S. (2003). *No excuses: Closing the racial gap in learning.* New York: Simon & Schuster.

Thomas, A. J., & Speight, S. L. (1999). Racial identity and racial socialization attitudes of African American parents. *Journal of Black Psychology, 25,* 152–170.

Tisak, M. (1995). Domains of social reasoning and beyond. In R. Vasta (Ed.), *Annals of child development* (Vol. 11, pp. 95–130). London: Jessica Kingsley Publishers.

Tomlinson, C. (2003). *Fulfilling the promise of the differential classroom: Strategies and tools for responsive teaching.* Alexandria, VA: Association for Supervision and Curriculum Development.

Torok, C. E., & Aguilar, T. E. (2000). Changes in preservice teachers' knowledge and beliefs about language issues. *Equity & Excellence in Education, 33*(2), 24–31.

Trueba, E. (1998). The education of Mexican immigrant children. In M. Suárez-Orozco (Ed.), *Crossings: Mexican immigration in interdisciplinary studies* (pp. 251–275). Cambridge, MA: Harvard Fellows.

Tse, L. (2001). *"Why they don't learn English?" Separating fact from fallacy in the U.S. language debate.* New York: Teachers College Press.

Turiel, E. (1983). *The development of social knowledge: Morality and convention.* Cambridge, UK: Cambridge University Press.

Turiel, E. (1998). The development of morality. In W. Damon (Ed.) & N. Eisenberg (Vol. Ed.), *Handbook of child psychology: Vol. 3. Socialization* (pp. 863–932). New York: Wiley.

Turiel, E., Hildebrandt, C., Wainryb, C. (1985). Judging social issues: Difficulties, inconsistencies, and consistencies. *Monographs of the Society for Research in Child Development, 56*(224).

Turiel, E., Killen, M., & Helwig, C. C. (1987). Morality: Its structure, functions, and vagaries. In J. Kagan & S. Lamb (Eds.), *The emergence of morality in young children* (pp. 155–244). Chicago: University of Chicago Press.

Tuttle v. Arlington County School Board. 195 F.3d 698 (4th Cir. 1999), *cert. dismissed,* 529 U.S. 1050 (2000).

Twenge, J. M., & Baumeister, R. F. (2005). Social exclusion increases aggression and self-defeating behavior while reducing intelligent thought and prosocial behavior. In D. Abrams, M. A. Hogg, & J. M. Marques (Eds.), *Social psychology of inclusion and exclusion* (pp. 27–46). New York: Psychology Press.

United Nations. (2001). *World conference against racism, racial discrimination, xenophobia and related intolerance executive summary.*

United Nations Educational, Scientific, and Cultural Organization (UNESCO). (2005). *Guidelines for inclusion: Ensuring access to education for all.* Paris: UNESCO.

United States Census Bureau. (2001a). *Census 2000 redistricting data (P.L. 94–171): Summary files for states.* Washington, DC: Government Printing Office.

United States Census Bureau. (2001b). *Census 2000.* Summary files 1 and 3. Retrieved August 7, 2006, from http://factfinder.census.gov/servlet/.

United States Census Bureau. (2001c). *Census 2000.* Summary file 4. Retrieved August 8, 2006, from http://factfinder.census.gov/servlet/.

United States Census Bureau. (2005). *Poverty status, by age, race and Hispanic origin.* Table 3. Housing and Household Economic Statistics Division, DC: U.S. Department of Commerce, Washington. DC (last revised December 14, 2005).

United States Department of Education, Office for Civil Rights (OCR). (2000). *Elementary and secondary school survey (E&S).* Washington, DC: U.S. Department of Education.

United States National Commission on Excellence in Education. (1983). *A nation at risk: The imperative for educational reform: A report to the nation and the Secretary of Education, United States Department of Education.* Washington, DC: The Commission.

United States Senate, Select Committee on Equal Educational Opportunity. (1972). *Toward equal educational opportunity*, 92d Cong., 2nd Sess. Washington, DC: Government Printing Office.

United States v. Paradise. 480 U.S. 149 (1987).

United States v. Virginia. 518 U.S. 515 (1996)

Updegrave, W. (1989, December 1). Race and money. *Money*, 152–172.

Vail, K. (2004, November). High school. *American School Board Journal, 191*(11), 14–19.

Valdés, G. (2001). *Learning and not learning English: Latino students in American schools*. New York: Teachers College Press.

Valenzuela, A. (1999). *Subtractive schooling: U.S.–Mexican youth and the politics of caring*. Albany: SUNY Press.

Valli, L. (1995). The dilemma of race: Learning to be color blind and color conscious. *Journal of Teacher Education, 46*(2), 120–130.

Valli, L., & Hawley, W. (2002). Designing and implementing school-based professional development. In W. D. Hawley & D. L. Rollie (Eds.), *The keys to effective schools: Educational reform as continuous improvement* (pp. 86–96). Thousand Oaks, CA: Corwin.

VanGunten, D. M., & Martin, R. J. (2001). Complexities and contradictions: A study of teacher education courses that address multicultural issues. *Journal of Intergroup Relations, 28*(1), 31–42.

Vigil, J. D. (2002). *A rainbow of gangs: Street cultures in the mega-city*. Austin: University of Texas Press.

Wadlington, W. (1966). The *Loving* Case: Virginia's anti-miscegenation statute in historical perspective. *Virginia Law Review, 52*(7), 1189–1223.

Wadsworth, H. (2004). *Teaching interrupted: Do discipline policies in today's public schools foster the common good?* New York: Public Agenda.

Waggoner, D. (1999). Who are secondary newcomer and linguistically different youth? In C. Faltis & P. Wolfe (Eds.), *So much to say: Adolescents, bilingualism, and ESL in the secondary school* (pp. 13–41). New York: Teachers College Press.

Walqui, A. (2000). *Access and engagement: Program design and instructional approaches for immigrant students in secondary school*. McHenry, IL: Delta Systems.

Washington v. Seattle School District No. 1. 458 U.S. 457 (1982).

Washington, W. (2004, May 16). Bush plans talk about race on desegregation case's anniversary, mistrust lingers. *The Boston Globe*.

Waters, M. (1995). *Globalization*. London: Routledge.

Waters, M. C., & Eschbach, K. (1995). Immigration and ethnic and racial inequality in the United States. *Annual Review of Sociology, 21*, 419–446.

Waxman, S., & Booth, A. (2003). The origins and evolution of links between word learning and conceptual organization: New evidence from eleven-month-olds. *Developmental Science, 6*, 128–135.

Waxman, S., & Gelman, R. (1986). Preschoolers' use of superordinate relations in classification and language. *Cognitive Development, 1*, 139–150.

Waxman, S. R., & Markow, D. B. (1998). Object properties and object kind: Twenty-one-month-old infants' extension of novel adjectives. *Child Development, 69,* 1313–1329.

Weiler, J. (1998). Recent changes in school desegregation. *ERIC Digest.* Retrieved May 26, 2004, from http://www.ericdigests.org.

Weinberg, M. (Ed.). (1970). *Desegregation research: An appraisal* (2nd ed.). Bloomington, IN: Phi Delta Kappa.

Weinberg, M. (1977). The relationship between school desegregation and academic achievement: A review of the research. In B. Levin & W. D. Hawley (Eds.), *The courts, social science, and school desegregation* (pp. 241–270). New Brunswick, NJ: Transaction Books.

Weiner, M. J., & Wright, F. E. (1973). Effects of undergoing arbitrary discrimination upon subsequent attitudes toward a minority group. *Journal of Applied Social Psychology, 3,* 94–102.

Weissglass, J. (2003). Reasons for hope: You can challenge educational inequities. *Principal Leadership, 3*(8), 24–29.

Wellisch, J. B., Marcus, A. H., MacQueen, R. A., & Duck, G. A. (1978). School management and organization in successful schools. *Sociology of Education, 51,* 211–221.

Wells, A. S. (2001). The "consequences" of school desegregation: The mismatch between the research and the rationale. *Hastings Constitutional Law Quarterly, 28,* 771.

Wells, A. S., & Crain, R. L. (1994). Perpetuation theory and the long-term effects of school desegregation. *Review of Educational Research, 6,* 531–555.

Wells, A. S., & Holme, J. J. (2005). No accountability for diversity: Standardized tests and the demise of racially mixed schools. In J. C. Boger & G. Orfield (Eds.), *School resegregation: Must the South turn back?* (pp. 187–211). Chapel Hill: University of North Carolina Press.

Wells, A. S., Holme, J. J., Revilla, A. T., & Atanda, A. K. (in press). How desegregation changed us. Cambridge, MA: Harvard University Press.

Wells, A. S., & Serna, I. (1996). The politics of culture: Understanding local political resistance to detracking in racially mixed schools. *Harvard Educational Review, 66*(1), 93–118.

Welner, K. G. (2001). *Legal rights, local wrongs: When community control collides with educational equity.* Albany: SUNY Press.

Welner, K. G., & Burris, C. C. (in press). Alternative approaches to the politics of detracking. *Theory into Practice.*

Welner, K. G., & Oakes, J. (2000). *Navigating the politics of detracking.* Arlington Heights, IL: Skylight Publications.

Wenglinsky, H. (2004). Closing the racial achievement gap: The role of reforming instructional practices. *Education Policy Analysis Archives, 12* (64), 1–22.

Wessmann v. Gittens. 160 F.3d 790 (1st Cir. 1998).

West, J., & Bose, J. (2002). *Parental reports of children's race and ethnicity in a na-*

tional longitudinal cohort study. Paper presented at the Joint Statistical Meeting, New York.

Western, B., Schiraldi, V., & Ziedenberg, J. (2003). *Education and incarceration.* Washington, DC: Justice Policy Institute.

What Works Clearinghouse. (2006). Retrieved September 4, 2006, from http://whatworks.ed.gov/.

Wheelock, A. (1992). The case for untracking. *Educational Leadership, 50,* 6–10.

White, P., Gamoran, A., Porter, A. C., & Smithson, J. (1996). Upgrading the high school math curriculum: Math course-taking patterns in seven high schools in California and New York. *Educational Evaluation and Policy Analysis, 18,* 285–307.

Williams, D. (2004a, September). Talk to kids about . . . difficult racial history. *Teaching Tolerance.* Retrieved from January 27, 2005, http://www.tolerance.org/parents/kidsarticle.jsp?p=0&ar=26.

Williams, D. (2004b, April). Talk to kids about . . . the n-word. *Teaching Tolerance.* Retrieved from January 27, 2005, http://www.tolerance.org/parents/kidsarticle.jsp?p=0&ar=24.

Williams, J. E., Best, D. L., Boswell, D. A., Mattson, L. A., & Graves, D. J. (1975). *Preschool racial attitude measure II. Educational and psychological measurement, 35,* 3–18.

Williams, K. M. (2005). Multiracialism and the civil rights future. *Daedalus, 134*(1), 53–60.

Wilson, W. J. (1987). *The truly disadvantaged: The inner city, the underclass, and public policy.* Chicago: University of Chicago Press.

Wilson, W. J. (1998). The role of the environment in the black-white test score gap. In C. Jencks and M. Phillips (Eds.), *The black-white test score gap* (pp. 501–510). Washington, DC: Brookings Institution Press.

Winant, H. (1998). Racism today: Continuity and change in a post-civil rights era. *Ethnic and Racial Studies, 21*(4), 755–766.

Wolff, E. N. (2002). *Top heavy: The increasing inequality of wealth in America and what can be done about it.* New York: New Press.

Wolff, E. N. (2004). Recent trends in living standards in the United States. In E. N. Wolff (Ed.), *What has happened to the quality of life in the advanced industrialized nations?* New York: Levy Economics Institute.

Wong, K. K., & Lee, J. (1998). Interstate variation in the achievement gap among racial and social groups: Considering the effects of school resources and classroom practices. In K. K. Wong (Ed.), *Advances in educational policy* (pp. 119–142). Greenwich, CT: JAI.

Wood, P. B., & Sonleitner, N. (1996). The effect of childhood interracial contact on adult anti-black prejudice. *International Journal of Intercultural Relations, 20*(1), 1–17.

Woodrow Wilson National Fellowship Foundation. (2005). *Diversity and the Ph.D.: A review of efforts to broaden race and ethnicity in U.S. doctoral education.*

Princeton: The Woodrow Wilson National Fellowship Foundation. Retrieved May 24, 2005, from http://www.woodrow.org/newsroom/News_Releases/WW_Diversity_PhD_web.pdf.

Wygant v. Jackson Board of Education. 476 U.S. 267 (1986).

Xie, Y., & Goyette, K. (1997). The racial identification of biracial children with one Asian parent: Evidence from the 1990 Census. *Social Forces, 76*(2), 547–570.

Yonezawa, S., Wells, A. S., & Serna, I. (2002). Choosing tracks: "Freedom of choice" in detracking schools. *American Educational Research Journal, 39*(1), 37–67.

Young, M. D. (1961). *The rise of the meritocracy, 1870–2033: An essay on education and equality.* Baltimore, MD: Penguin.

Yun, J. T., & Kurlaender, M. (2004). School racial composition and student educational aspirations: A question of equity in multiracial society. *Journal of Education for Students Placed at Risk, 9,* 143–168.

Zill, N. (2003, May). *School readiness skills of biracial children: Findings from the ECLS-K.* Paper presented at the annual meeting of the Population Association of America, Minneapolis, MN.

Contributors

M. Beatriz Arias is Associate Professor of Curriculum and Instruction at the College of Education at Arizona State University, and currently serves as the faculty director for the Vice President's Office for University–School Partnerships. In this capacity she coordinates programs to address the needs of underperforming students in K–12 schools in inner-city Phoenix. Dr. Arias is nationally recognized for her expertise in issues of equity and access for English Language Learners. Along with Professor Christian Faltis, also of Arizona State University, she is developing and conducting research on teacher preparation programs that address the needs of inner-city immigrant students. Among her most recent publications is "The Impact of *Brown* on Latinos: A Study of Transformation of Policy Intentions" (*Teachers College Record*, 2005). Her most recent work on desegregation, *Latino Apartheid and School Desegregation in the Southwest*, is forthcoming.

Rebecca S. Bigler received her Ph.D. from Pennsylvania State University in 1991. Currently she is Professor of Psychology and Women's and Gender Studies at the University of Texas at Austin. Her work has concerned the development of racial and gender stereotyping and prejudice, including how contextual factors serve to exaggerate or diminish their growth. She has also been active in developing and evaluating interventions designed to discourage the establishment and maintenance of racial and gender stereotypes among children.

Carol Corbett Burris has served as the principal of South Side High School in the Rockville Centre School District in New York since 2000. She received her doctorate from Teachers College, Columbia University, and her dissertation, which studied her district's detracking reform in math, received the 2003 National Association of Secondary Schools'

Principals Middle Level Dissertation of the Year Award. Dr. Burris has taught a course in school reform to doctoral students at Teachers College and to aspiring school leaders in a Teachers College Leadership Academy. She regularly gives presentations on the positive effects of detracking at both local and national conferences. Articles she coauthored with Jay Heubert and Hank Levin of Teachers College, based on her dissertation findings, appeared in the February 2004 issue of *Educational Leadership* and the Spring 2005 edition of the *American Educational Research Journal*.

Simon Cheng is Assistant Professor in the Department of Sociology at the University of Connecticut. His substantive research is in race and ethnicity, family–school relationships, quantitative methods, and political-economic development. He has recently published articles in the *American Journal of Sociology, Sociological Methods & Research*, the *Journal of Marriage and Family, Sociology of Education, Social Forces,* and the *Handbook of Data Analysis*. Professor Cheng is currently working on a series of projects concerning the educational experiences of multiracial populations.

James Cohen is a doctoral student at Arizona State University in the College of Education. His most recent publications focus on high school English Language Learners and literacy education. He has also published on teacher education programs and the needs of Hispanic students. Cohen is the lead editor of the *Proceedings of the Fourth International Symposium on Bilingualism* (April 2005).

Richard W. Cole is former Assistant Attorney General and Senior Counsel for Civil Rights & Civil Liberties for the Massachusetts Office of Attorney General. He is National Chair of the Civil Rights Task Force of the National Association of Attorneys General. Mr. Cole is a graduate of the Boston University School of Law. He has successfully litigated precedent-setting civil rights, discrimination, and public interest law cases in state and federal court, including a civil rights case in the U.S. Supreme Court. He serves as the lead trial and appellate attorney for the state and Lynn defendants in the *Comfort v. Lynn School Committee* case. He co-chaired a national initiative that culminated in a U.S. Department of Education publication in 1999 entitled *Protecting Students from Harassment and Hate Crime: A Guide for Schools*.

David S. Crystal (Ph.D., University of Michigan, 1993) is Associate Professor of Psychology at Georgetown University. He is the associate editor of the *International Journal of Behavioral Development*. He was an invited speaker on cross-cultural differences in education at the National Research Council, and on U.S./Japanese negotiations at the Woodrow Wilson Center. He has wide-ranging interests in developmental, clinical, and cross-cultural psychology. Dr. Crystal is presently conducting research into the psychobiological correlates of prejudice, predictors of social and political problem solving, and social reasoning about race-based exclusion among children and adolescents.

Christian Faltis is Professor of Multicultural Education at the College of Education at Arizona State University. He currently serves as the review editor for *Anthropology and Education Quarterly* and has served as editor for *TESOL Quarterly, TESOL Journal,* and *Educational Researcher.* He has written and lectured extensively on bilingual teaching and curricula development. Along with Dr. M. Beatriz Arias, also of Arizona State University, he is currently developing and conducting research on teacher preparation programs that address the needs of inner-city immigrant students. His most recent work, *Teaching Adolescent Immigrants and English Learners in Secondary School Settings* (with Cathy Coulter), will be published by Merrill in 2007.

Erica Frankenberg is a doctoral candidate in Education Policy at the Harvard University Graduate School of Education and a research assistant at the Civil Rights Project. She received her M.Ed. at Harvard with a concentration in Administration, Planning, and Social Policy, and she earned an A.B. in Education Policy from Dartmouth College. Ms. Frankenberg's research interest in school desegregation stems from her experience as a student in desegregated public schools. Recent publications include "The Impact of School Segregation on Residential Housing Patterns: Mobile, Alabama, and Charlotte, North Carolina," in *School Resegregation: Must the South Turn Back?*; "Reviving *Brown v. Board of Education:* How Courts and Enforcement Agencies Can Produce More Integrated Schools" (with Gary Orfield), in *"Brown" at Fifty: The Unfinished Legacy: A Collection of Essays;* and "Charter Schools and Race: A Lost Opportunity for Integrated Education" (with Chungmei Lee), in *Education Policy Analysis Archives.*

Willis D. Hawley is Professor Emeritus of Education and Public Policy at the University of Maryland, where he served as Dean of the College of Education from 1993 to 1998. He is currently Scholar in Residence at the American Association of School Administrators and the director of the

KEYS Institute of the National Education Association. From 1998 to 2000 he was the executive director of the National Partnership for Excellence and Accountability in Teaching. He taught at Yale, Duke, and Vanderbilt Universities before going to Maryland. Professor Hawley has published numerous books, articles, and book chapters dealing with teacher education, school reform, urban politics, political learning, organizational change, school desegregation, and educational policy. His most recent research deals with the preparation and professional development of teachers and school administrators, school restructuring and effectiveness, and race relations. He also organized and directed the Common Destiny Alliance, a coalition of national organizations and scholars interested in using research to improve intergroup relations.

Rebecca High has researched the impacts of race and poverty and effective responses, especially in the educational context, at the Institute on Race and Poverty at the University of Minnesota Law School and the University of North Carolina Center for Civil Rights. She holds a B.A. from Harvard University and a J.D. from UNC at Chapel Hill.

Julie Milligan Hughes is a doctoral student in developmental psychology at the University of Texas at Austin. Her research interests include children's affective and attitudinal reactions to antiracism interventions, as well as the development of stereotype knowledge among children and adolescents. She has also been working on the development of a new racial attitude measure for use with children and adolescents.

Melanie Killen (Ph.D., Developmental Psychology, University of California at Berkeley, 1985) is Professor of Human Development and the associate director for the Center for Children, Relationships, and Culture at the University of Maryland. She is also the associate editor for the journal *Human Development,* and is currently the director of the NIH Graduate Training Program in Social Development at the University of Maryland. Dr. Killen has coedited four books, is the editor of the *Handbook on Moral Development,* and has published over seventy journal articles and book chapters. Her research interests are social development, moral development, cultural influences on development, and, specifically, how children, adolescents, and adults evaluate exclusion on the basis of group membership, such as gender, race, culture, and ethnicity.

Jaekyung Lee is Associate Professor of Education at SUNY Buffalo. He received his Ph.D. from the University of Chicago and was a 1999 National Academy of Education Spencer Postdoctoral Fellow. He specializes in educational policy research and evaluation. His current research focuses on the issues of educational accountability and equity, particularly closing the achievement gaps among different racial and socioeconomic groups of students. Exemplary publications include "Racial and Ethnic Achievement Gap Trends: Reversing the Progress toward Equity?" in *Educational Researcher* (2002), and "The Impact of Accountability on Racial and Socioeconomic Equity: Considering Both School Resources and Achievement Outcomes" (with K. K. Wong), in *American Educational Research Journal* (2004).

Gary Orfield is Professor of Education and Social Policy at the Harvard University Graduate School of Education. He is interested in the study of civil rights, education policy, urban policy, and minority opportunity. He is the cofounder and director of The Civil Rights Project at Harvard University, an initiative that is developing and publishing a new generation of research on multiracial civil rights issues. In addition to his scholarly work, Professor Orfield has been involved with development of governmental policy and has served as an expert witness in court cases related to his research. He has participated as an expert witness or as a court-appointed expert in several dozen civil rights cases, including the University of Michigan Supreme Court case that upheld the policy of affirmative action in 2003, and he has been called to give testimony in civil rights suits by the U.S. Department of Justice and many civil rights, legal services, and educational organizations.

María Teresa Unger Palmer is a native of Peru and a naturalized U.S. citizen. She first came to the United States as an exchange student in 1978. She graduated from Jacksonville State University in Alabama with a B.S. in Education. After graduation she worked with migrant farm workers. She attended seminary in Louisville, Kentucky, and also received an M.Ed. from the University of Louisville. After working in student development and teaching high school Spanish, Dr. Palmer moved to Chapel Hill, North Carolina, to pursue a doctorate in educational leadership. While completing her Ed.D. at UNC, she was ordained and founded a Hispanic congregation of the United Church of Christ—Iglesia Unida de Cristo—and Mi Escuelita Spanish Immersion Preschool. In 1999 Governor Jim Hunt appointed Dr. Palmer to the North Carolina State Board of Education, where she served until 2005. From 2004 to 2006 Dr. Palmer was the principal of David D. Jones Elementary School in Guilford County, North Carolina. She is currently the director of the Multicultural Student Center at North Carolina A&T State University.

john a. powell is Executive Director of the Kirwan Institute for Race and Ethnicity and Gregory H. Williams Professor of Civil Rights and Civil Liberties at the Moritz School of Law at Ohio State University. The founder, in 1993, of the Institute on Race and Poverty at the University of Minnesota Law School, Professor powell is also a former national legal director of the American Civil Liberties Union. He holds a B.A. from Stanford University and a J.D. from the University of California at Berkeley.

Martin Ruck (Ph.D., University of Toronto, 1994) is Associate Professor of Developmental Psychology at the Graduate Center, City University of New York. He serves on the editorial board of *Child Development,* and for five years he was the senior researcher with the Commission on Systemic Racism in the Ontario Criminal Justice System. Dr. Ruck's research interests include social development, ethnic minority students' perceptions of high school disciplinary practices, and children's political socialization at the intersection of race, ethnicity, and gender.

Christine E. Sleeter is Professor Emerita in the College of Professional Studies at California State University, Monterey Bay. Her research focuses on antiracist multicultural education and multicultural teacher education. She also lectures nationally and internationally. Dr. Sleeter has received several awards for her work, including the California State University Monterey Bay President's Medal, the National Association for Multicultural Education Research Award, and the AERA Committee on the Role and Status of Minorities in Education Distinguished Scholar Award. Her most recent books include *Un-Standardizing Curriculum; Culture, Difference, and Power; Turning on Learning* (with Carl Grant); and *Doing Multicultural Education for Achievement and Equity* (with Carl Grant).

Kevin G. Welner is Associate Professor of Education at the University of Colorado at Boulder. He is codirector of the Education in the Public Interest Center (EPIC). Dr. Welner's research examines the intersection between education rights litigation and educational opportunity scholarship. Specifically his research has studied the issues of tracking, of disproportionate placement of students of color in special education, and of the change process associated with equity-minded reform aimed at benefiting those who hold less powerful school and community positions (primarily Latinos, African Americans, and the poor). A former attorney, he has also worked with plaintiffs in several educational equity lawsuits. Dr. Welner was the 2006 recipient of the American Educational Research Association's Early Career Award in recognition of extensive scholarly research.

Index

ability grouping, 43–45, 52, 209. *See also* tracking
academic achievement: and integration, 34–36; and socioeconomic status (SES), 35. *See also* "achievement gap"
accelerated curriculum, 22, 221, 225
accountability, 89, 119n1
"achievement gap," 4, 17, 51, 74, 76, 79, 81, 207, 226, 274, 284, 287; Black-White, 86; correlation with segregation, 85; definition, 78; and desegregation, 74–75, 81–86; Hispanic-White, 86; and poverty, 274; and tracking, 210
additive acculturation, 115. *See also* cultural pluralism
Advanced Placement (AP), 76, 122, 220
affirmative action, 278
Allport, Gordon, 2, 17, 19, 47, 59, 62, 72
A Nation at Risk, 4–5
antiracism curricula, 34
antiracism education, 196
antiracism lessons, 199–202; for African American children, 201–2; for European American children, 199–200
assimilation, 107, 109, 112
AVID program, 47

Berkeley (California), 279, 281
bilingual education, 4, 45, 101, 102, 247
Bilingual Education Act of 1968, 4
bilingual teachers, 19
biracial families, educational practices of, 158–62

biracial students, 166n1. *See also* interracial status
Black-White gap, 4; *See also* "achievement gap"
B/MED program, 177
Boston Latin School, 234
Brown v. Board of Education, 1, 8, 11, 13, 17, 25, 58, 74, 145, 190, 207, 235, 256, 265–68, 278, 289
Bush, George H. W., 5
Bush, George W., 15, 24, 269

Calexico High School (California), 114
California, 112, 114, 166n3
California State University (Monterey Bay), 184
Carter administration, 4
Castañeda v. Pickard, 102
Census of 1990, 121, 157, 166n6
Census of 2000, 8, 24, 120, 149, 167n14
Center on English Learning and Achievement (CELA), 42–43
Charlotte-Mecklenburg schools, 77, 276
Charlottesville Educational Summit, 5
charter schools, 6
children: and moral knowledge, 64–66; and stereotypes, 61–63
City of Richmond v. J. R. Croson, 232
Civil Rights Act of 1964, 18, 25
civil rights movement, 7
Civil Rights Project at Harvard University, vii, 11, 61
classroom-based coach, 187, 188

Clinton, Bill, 5
Coleman Report, 14
collaborative activities, 33, 46
color-blind ideology, 11, 12, 13, 26, 51, 194, 198
Columbus High School (North Carolina), 122
Comfort v. Lynn School Committee, 10, 228, 230, 244, 248, 250–55
Common Core of Data (CCD), 88
Common Destiny Alliance, 49
community-based learning, 180, 182
compelling interests, 10. *See also* strict scrutiny
complex instruction, 46, 52, 56n4
concentrated poverty, 88, 89, 291. *See also* high-poverty schools; socioeconomic segregation
Connecticut, school segregation in, 82
cooperative learning, 46, 47, 52, 55n4, 89, 198, 242, 247
counselors, 128, 130
critical mass, 39, 243, 247, 250
critical thinking, 35, 58
cross-cultural community-based learning, 178–82
cross-cultural competence, 39; of preservice teachers, 175
cross-cultural knowledge, 172
cross-race friendships, 40, 47, 61, 62, 72, 247; in early grades, 41
cultural assimilation, 103, 107–8
cultural broker, 187
cultural pluralism, 19, 102, 103, 106–7
culture shock, of novice teachers, 187
curricula, 3, 4, 35, 181, 215, 244; cooperative learning, 47, 198, 242, 247; multicultural, 47, 183, 198; and school integration, 46

Delpit, Lisa, 132
demographic transition, 6, 8–9, 120, 147, 172, 292, 294, 295
desegregation, school, 59, 163; and achievement, 35, 36, 75–76, 77; adolescent attitudes toward, 61; assistance law, 3, 4; court orders, 1, 9, 35, 75, 76; early days of, 2; in northern cities, 1; orders, 4; plans, 1, 7, 9, 22, 101, 295; psychological effects of, 59–61;

research, benefits of, 10, 13–16, 32–37, 59, 74, 243; "root and branch," 3; "unitary" school systems and, 3; White students and benefits of, 15
detracking, 22, 27n10, 89, 114; and "achievement gap," 220; essential components of, 221–24; politics of, 208–9; and Rockville Center School District, 211–24
differentiated instruction, 45, 46, 52, 55n4, 112
discrimination, racial, 2, 24, 31, 51, 53, 54, 132; perceptions of, 57
dissimilarity, 80, 96n6. *See also* segregation, school
dissimilarity index, 78, 89. *See also* segregation, school
diverse teaching force, 21, 117
diverse workforce, 59
diversity, optimal, 39–40
Diversity Assessment Questionnaire (DAQ), 67, 238
Dred Scott v. Sanford, 266
dropouts, high school, 24, 277; Black male, 24; Latinas, 121
dual-language programs, 107, 118
Durham (North Carolina), 284

Early Childhood Longitudinal Study: Kindergarten Class of 1998–99 (ECLS-K), 159, 161, 167n8
economic inequality, 268–71
economic segregation. *See* socioeconomic segregation
educational aspirations, 72
Elementary and Secondary Education Act, 5
Elementary Certification for Ethnic Colleagues for the Elementary School (EC3), 177
Emergency School Aid Act, 3
English as a Second Language (ESL), 120, 121, 122
English-language learners (ELLs), 45, 101, 103, 114, 122; adolescent, 108
English-only initiatives, 19
equal-status contact, 2, 107, 117, 242, 245. *See also* intergroup contact
ethnographic research, 181
"excellence" movement, 5

exclusion: in children, 65–66; and adolescents, 68, 71. *See also* racial exclusion

extracurricular activities, and school integration, 45–46, 246, 283, 286

feeling tone, 226n5

First Circuit Court of Appeals, 234–35, 248, 254, 259n12, 260n28

Florida schools, 77

foreign-born students, 101. *See also* immigrant students

"freedom of choice," 3

gang violence, and immigrant students, 104, 106

Garrity, Delia, 213, 222

Gates Foundation, 144

Goals 2000: Educate America Act, 5

Gratz v. Bollinger, 233, 254

Green v. County School Board of New Kent County, 3

Grutter v. Bollinger, 10, 11, 23, 25, 26, 31, 229, 232, 233, 248–50, 251, 254, 255, 258n6, 265, 267, 278, 285, 289

guided reflection, 185

harassment, 134

heterogeneous schools, 57, 62; positive effects of, 34. *See also* desegregation, school; integration, school

heterogeneously grouped classes, 22, 43, 116, 221. *See also* detracking

high-poverty schools, 27, 270, 271. *See also* concentrated poverty; poverty, child

high school graduation, 277

high-stakes testing, 88, 97n16, 101, 107

higher education, access to, 277–78

higher-level curricula, 275, 281. *See also* accelerated curriculum; curricula

homogeneous schools, 33. *See also* segregation, school

Hopwood v. Texas, 232

housing segregation. *See* residential segregation

Hurricane Katrina, 13

identity, 134, 136. *See also* racial identity

immersion experiences, preservice teachers, 179–81

immigrant students: adolescent, 102, 237; children, 120; successful schools for, 113–18; variation among, 108–12

immigration, Latino, 101, 120; in North Carolina, 120–21

Immigration Act of 1965, 18

Immigration and Naturalization Service (INS), 123

immigration studies, 110

Improving America's Schools Act, 5

income, household, by race, 24

Indiana University, 177

induction programs, 188. *See also* professional development, of teachers; teacher preparation

inner-city schools, 89

inservice teachers, multicultural training of, 183–84; classroom support for, 184–89. *See also* professional development, of teachers; teacher preparation

instructional strategies, 35, 36, 38, 43

integration, school, 2, 10; and academic achievement, 34–36; in classrooms and schools, 16, 37–52; critical mass for, 250; learning environments and, 242; litigation strategy for, 234–38; plan, 23; psychological effects of, positive vs. negative, 155–56; value of, 32–37; voluntary, 228. *See also* desegregation, school

intercultural competence, 32, 33, 34, 48, 52, 54

intergroup conflict, 47, 52, 107, 137. *See also* racial tension (conflict) in schools

intergroup contact, 17, 36, 57, 61, 62, 68, 69–71, 102, 106, 116–18, 242, 260n22; benefits of, 57; theory of, 59, 241–42, 243–44. *See also* Allport, Gordon

intergroup relations, 9, 36, 45, 105–6, 241

International Baccalaureate (IB) curriculum, 215, 221, 224

International High School (New York), 115

interracial contact, 241–42. *See also* intergroup contact

interracial couples, 158, 159. *See also* interracial marriage

interracial groups, 46

interracial marriage, 19, 147, 149

interracial status, 145; advantages, 148; disadvantages, 149–51; growth of, 147; psychological and school outcomes, 156–58; and school attachment, 150–56

interracial violence, 238. *See also* racial tension (conflict) in schools

Jim Crow, 27n3, 266

Johnson administration, 6n1

Johnson, William H., 211, 222

Kentucky, 23

King, Rev. Martin Luther, Jr., 25, 267, 288

language-minority children, 4, 101. *See also* English-language learners

Latino and Language Minority Teacher Projects, 177

Latino population growth, 101

Lau v. Nichols, 4, 102

Louisiana, school segregation in, 82

Louisville (Kentucky), 23, 258n7, 279–80

Loving v. Virginia, 19, 147, 162

Lynn (Massachusetts), 228–61, 275, 279; demographic history of, 230

Lynn Plan, 229, 230–31, 233–34, 236–37, 249, 251, 254, 258nn9–11

magnet schools, 3, 7, 9, 10; in Lynn (Mass.), 243–44

Mandela, Nelson, 273, 288

Massachusetts Board of Education, 230

MCAS (Massachusetts Comprehensive Assessment System), 239

McFarland v. Jefferson County Public Schools, 4, 10, 257n4, 279

McLaurin v. Oklahoma State Regents for Higher Education, 10

Milliken v. Bradley, 1

minority suburbanization, 8, 9

Mondale, Walter, 3, 6n2

moral reasoning, in children and adolescents, 69

Morgan v. Nucci, 231

multicultural teaching, 172. *See also* curricula: multicultural

multiple (bicultural) identities, 50, 62

multiracial children, 147

multiracial movement, 156

multiracial schools, 40, 291

multiracial status, in U.S. Census, 20, 166n1. *See also* interracial status

narrow tailoring, 229, 233

National Academy of Sciences, 210

National Assessment of Educational Progress (NAEP), 18, 75, 77–78, 88, 90, 95n1, 96n7

National Center on School Restructuring, 49

National Educational Longitudinal Study of 1988, 77

National Governors Association, 5

National Institute of Child Health and Human Development (NICHD), 66

National Institute of Education, 4

National Longitudinal Study of Adolescent Health of 1994–95, 151, 155, 167n12, 168n17

National Research Council, 210

National Underground Railroad Freedom Center, 191

needs-based grouping. *See* ability grouping

New High Schools Project (North Carolina), 144

New York, 115

New York State Regents diploma, 215, 217, 224

Nixon, Richard, 2, 3

No Child Left Behind Act (NCLB), vii, 5, 17–18, 24, 75, 102, 107, 207, 276

North Carolina, 96n9, 120

O'Connor, Sandra Day, 11, 31

paraprofessionals, 178, 186

Parents Involved in Community Schools v. Seattle School District No. 1, 10, 257n4

peer group, effects of, 82

peer groupings, 106, 155

peer tutoring, 46, 52, 55n4, 89. *See also* instructional strategies

"perspective taking," 286. *See also* instructional strategies

Plessy v. Ferguson, 266

positive intergroup contact, 112, 116

poverty, child, 269; in high-poverty schools, 271

prejudice, 2, 31, 33, 64; racial and social class, 223; and reducing, 59, 62. *See also* racial prejudice: in children; racism

Preliminary Scholastic Aptitude Test (PSAT), 217, 218

preservice teachers, 172; diversity of, 171

principals, school, 50–52

prisons, funding and population, 268

professional development, of teachers, 50

Project TEAM (Transformative Educational Achievement Model), 177

Proposition 54 (California), 190

Proposition 209 (California), 281

pullout programs, 45

Punjabi Sikh students, 115

race, 12, 55n1, 145, 190, 217; politics of, 272

race-conscious integration plans, 10. *See also* student assignment plans

race-neutral alternatives, 252–53. *See also* narrow tailoring

race relations, 4, 5, 51

racial attitudes, 47, 57, 60, 62

racial composition, 238; of schools, 154, 155

racial exclusion, 65, 68, 71

racial identity, 149, 157. *See also* identity

Racial Imbalance Act (RIA), of Commonwealth of Massachusetts, 229, 230, 231, 257n5, 258n10

racial income gap, 269. *See also* income, household, by race; wealth gap

racial isolation, 31, 231, 240, 241, 252; and Asian students, 103; and Latino students, 103–4. *See also* segregation, school

racial labeling, effects on children: negative, 193; positive, 194–95

racial prejudice, 21, 48, 161, 162; in children, 192

racial segregation, 54, 75, 78, 267. *See also* segregation, school

racial stereotypes, 250, 254. *See also* stereotypes; stereotypical thinking

racial tension (conflict) in schools, 40, 117; Black-Latino/Hispanic, 137–38. *See also* intergroup conflict

racial transformation, 294. *See also* demographic transition; minority suburbanization

racism, 12, 191; discussion in schools, 195–98; negative effects of, 196; positive effects of, 197

Raleigh (North Carolina), 282

Reagan administration, 3, 4

reciprocal teaching, 46, 52, 55n4. *See also* instructional strategies

Regents diploma. *See* New York State Regents diploma

resegregation, school, 1, 9, 41, 74, 295; within schools, 40, 41, 208, 291

residentially integrated communities, 6

residential segregation, 7, 13, 26, 27n12, 104, 253, 270

Robinson, Jackie, 205

Rockville Center (Long Island, New York), 208, 211, 221–24, 279

Rothstein, Richard, 274

Sacramento State University, 177

"safe schools," for immigrant students, 105

San Antonio v. Rodriguez, 281

school culture, 221, 223

school leadership, 221; principals and, 50–52

schools, high-poverty. *See* high-poverty schools

Seattle (Washington), 258n7, 279–80

secondary school, 106, 113, 114; successful models for immigrants, 113–18

segregation, residential, 26, 270

segregation, school, 7, 16, 75, 232; achievement, 75, 77; between schools, 80–81; Black-White, 81; in Connecticut, 82; Hispanic-White, 76, 81, 83; impact of, 241–42, 275–76; increasing, 9, 80, 83, 270, 291; Latino, 103; long-term effects of, 80, 87, 277; in Louisiana, 82; short-term effects of, 80; and standardized testing, 275–76; within schools, 13–14, 18, 80–81. *See also* socioeconomic segregation

Sen, Amartya, 278

Senate Select Committee on Equal Educational Opportunity, 6n2

September 11, 123

shared journaling, 183

social cognition, 33–34
social psychology, 61–63
socioeconomic segregation, 9, 97n15, 282
socioeconomic status (SES), 35, 40, 42, 97n14, 217
Southeast Asian immigrant students, 116
Southern Poverty Law Center, vii, 11
"southern strategy," 2
South Side High School (New York), 211, 216
special needs, 41
staff development, 144
standardized testing, 275–76
standards-based reform, 5
standards movement, 5
stereotypes, 33, 57, 61–62, 63, 136, 182, 276, 284, 287, 291; in children, 63–64, 191–92, 228, 241; in preservice teachers, 172, 175, 181
stereotypical thinking, 63
strict scrutiny, 232. See also compelling interests; narrow tailoring
student assignment plans, 39, 237
Supreme Court, 19, 25, 26, 27n2, 31, 147, 229, 230, 232, 233, 254–55, 257n4, 258n7, 265–67, 270, 278, 280–81, 291; decisions, 83
Swann v. Charlotte-Mecklenburg Board of Education, 3
Sweatt v. Painter, 13

teacher expectations, 207
teacher preparation: curriculum for diversity, 182–83; for cross-cultural schools, 171; programs, 21; recruiting for diversity, 177
teachers, 21; of color, 172; and demographic gap with students, 172; leaving the profession, 174
Teach for America (TFA), 184–85

Third International Mathematics and Science Study (TIMSS), 210
Title I, 5. See also No Child Left Behind Act (NCLB)
tracking, 14, 22, 41–45, 62, 76, 77, 79, 208; and "achievement gap," 210–11; negative consequences of, 42. See also ability grouping; detracking; resegregation, school
transnational spaces, 111

"unitary status," 3
University of Michigan, 15, 31
University of Michigan Law School, 11, 229, 232, 251, 255. See also University of Michigan
University of Southern California, 177
urban education program, 171, 172
U.S. Constitution, 229, 271, 280

Virginia, 147
voluntary desegregation. See voluntary integration
voluntary integration, 228, 280; and Lynn Plan, 229. See also integration, school
voluntary integration plan, 23, 281. See also integration, school; Lynn plan; student assignment plans

Warren, Earl, 11
Washington State's Civil Rights Act, 280
wealth gap, 269. See also economic inequality
Wessmann v. Gittens, 232, 243–55
White student achievement, 14
White flight, 4, 27n1, 236, 238. See also demographic transition
Wisconsin, 177
World Conference against Racism, Racial Discrimination, Xenophobia, and Related Intolerance (2001), 191

Race, Ethnicity, and Politics

Louis DeSipio, *Counting on the Latino Vote: Latinos as a New Electorate*

Sheila L. Croucher, *Imagining Miami: Ethnic Politics in a Postmodern World*

Bernard Grofman, editor, *Legacies of the 1964 Civil Rights Act*

Gary M. Segura and Shaun Bowler, editors, *Diversity in Democracy: Minority Representation in the United States*

Taeku Lee, S. Karthick Ramakrishnan, and Ricardo Ramírez, editors, *Transforming Politics, Transforming America: The Political and Civic Incorporation of Immigrants in the United States*

Erica Frankenberg and Gary Orfield, editors, *Lessons in Integration: Realizing the Promise of Racial Diversity in American Schools*